INTERPRETING MEDIEVAL EFFIGIES

INTERPRETING MEDIEVAL EFFIGIES

THE EVIDENCE FROM YORKSHIRE TO 1400

BRIAN AND MOIRA GITTOS

OXBOW | books
Oxford & Philadelphia

Published in the United Kingdom in 2019 by
OXBOW BOOKS
The Old Music Hall, 106–108 Cowley Road, Oxford, OX4 1JE

and in the United States by
OXBOW BOOKS
1950 Lawrence Road, Havertown, PA 19083

Hardback Edition: ISBN 978-1-78925-128-9
Digital Edition: ISBN 978-1-78925-129-6 (epub)

A CIP record for this book is available from the British Library

Library of Congress Control Number: 2018966635

Typeset in India by Versatile PreMedia Services. www.versatilepremedia.com

For a complete list of Oxbow titles, please contact:

UNITED KINGDOM
Oxbow Books
Telephone (01865) 241249
Email: oxbow@oxbowbooks.com
www.oxbowbooks.com

UNITED STATES OF AMERICA
Oxbow Books
Telephone (800) 791-9354, Fax (610) 853-9146
Email: queries@casemateacademic.com
www.casemateacademic.com/oxbow

Oxbow Books is part of the Casemate Group

Front cover: The effigy under the arch at Goldsborough, (West Riding). Sir Richard de Goldesburgh, early fourteenth century.
Back cover: Top: William de la Mare's south aisle, Welwick (East Riding). Mid-fourteenth century. Bottom right: Alabaster angel beside the head of Elizabeth Marmion, West Tanfield (North Riding). End of the fourteenth century.

For Helen and Alan, who have lived with this all their lives

Contents

List of figures

List of colour plates

Acknowledgements

Acknowledging the help of all who have assisted us is impossible, not least because we are indebted to generations of incumbents, churchwardens and key holders without whom this work could not have been done. Many provided assistance far beyond their remit. We are indebted too to the private property owners who allowed access, particularly at Coverham Abbey and Watton Priory. Some items are in store and we must first express out appreciation of the unfailing professionalism of the English Heritage team at Helmsley, led by Susan Harrison. Elsewhere, Jane Whittaker at the Bowes Museum, Jennifer Dunne of Scarborough Museums Trust and staff of the York Museums Trust, the York Archaeological Trust, Kirkleatham Old Hall Museum and its predecessor the Langbaurgh Museum, all facilitated access to material in their care. John Buglass alerted us to the Easby head. Our extensive use of libraries warrants thanks to the staff of the Society of Antiquaries of London, the Bodleian Library, York University Library, and the local authority services in the East Riding and Somerset. Most photographs are our own but Martin Stutchfield kindly allowed us to use his image of Crathorne, while Susan Harrison and Eleanor Matthews of English Heritage photographed the Barton-Upon-Humber glass for us.

Friends have helped in many ways. Some, such as Rita Wood and Barbara English have discussed particular monuments. Jerome Bertram provided a far better translation of the Scarcliffe inscription than our own, while David Carrington made available his unpublished research on the Sprotbrough effigies with details of his practice's work there and at Bilton (in Ainsty). Tony and Jane Dodsworth arranged access to the vault beneath Doncaster, St George and joined us in search of the missing effigy. Richard Goldsbrough provided a likely living link with some of our subjects and a copy of the family history. Anne Norman helped us access the late Nick Norman's notes. Tim Palmer has given freely of his geological expertise while Sue and Laurance Kelland have discussed conservation. Some have had particularly far reaching influence, offering new avenues for investigation and fresh ways of evaluating evidence. Jerry Sampson, Philip Lankester and John Allan come into this category. Without their knowledge and insights, this would have been a different book.

We are indebted to the University of York, Centre for Medieval Studies, for our Research Associateships that have done so much to smooth the way and alleviate the difficulty of being based in Somerset. Julie Gardiner and the team at Oxbow Books have been a pleasure to work with, tolerant of our editorial foibles, understanding of timetable revisions and ever ready with a response to queries: our debt to them is enormous. The Francis Coales Charitable Foundation provided important grant aid for the publication. Four intrepid people (Tobias Capwell, Helen Gittos, Philip Lankester and David Palliser) undertook to read some or all of the text. We are deeply indebted to them for their wise advice and helpful comments but especially to Helen in her quest for clarity. We have taken heed but, needless to say, all remaining errors, opacities and deficiencies are our own.

Finally, we would like to thank our companions in discovery. Our children and their grandmother, Muriel Gittos, displayed true forbearance in visiting yet more churches (one of the eldest's earliest words was a version of 'effigy'), providing entertainment and diversions along the way. One other person deserves special mention. Sally Badham has travelled the whole journey with us, a constant sounding board and companion in developing new ideas, sharing her own research as it has developed. We hope that Sally and all the other people with whom we have debated Yorkshire effigies will think it was worth the wait.

Conventions

1 The effigies

The effigies are catalogued in Appendix 1 and a summary list follows the Index. Their locations are plotted on the Endpaper Map, where the numbers relate to the places in the List.

2 Place names and counties

The spelling of place names is drawn from O.S. 1987. Counties are only specified in the text if the place has no effigy in the List. The abbreviations 'E.R.', 'N.R.', 'W.R.' signify the pre-1974 Yorkshire Ridings (East, North and West).

3 Cross-references

Cross-references are provided throughout the book to where effigies or particular aspects are covered in greater detail. Consequently, the text is arranged in numbered sections, those prefixed with 'A' refer to Appendices. When they occur in the narrative, the references adopt the format 'Section 4c.v' or 'Appendix A6b', otherwise they are italicised within brackets, as (*5c.iii*) or (*A2d*).

4 Series

Frequent references will be found to effigies belonging to a 'Series'. Details of these are set out in Section 4c.

5 Left and right in descriptions

In descriptions, positions relative to an effigy follow the heraldic convention of being described from the viewpoint of the figure rather than the observer.

6 Arms and armour terminology

Whilst a specialist area, definitions of most arms and armour terms are readily available. We have largely followed the usage of Capwell (2015, esp. pp. 306–307) and Blair (1958). Spur terminology is based on Blanche Ellis (1995) while buckles, strap ends and mounts are from Egan & Pritchard (1991). However, in two areas accepted nomenclature has proved inadequate: sword belts and the non-defensive outermost layer worn over armour. In both cases we have coined our own terms.

Sword belts of the thirteenth and through most of the fourteenth centuries were made in two sections. The longer part, termed the **rear belt**, passes around the back of the figure, one end attached to the scabbard and the other passing through the buckle. The shorter section, termed the **front belt**, is also attached at one end to the scabbard but the other holds the buckle.

The fabric outer garments worn over armour varied through time and have been called by a variety of names. In the absence of a current consensus, we have opted to use the following terms. **Coat-armour** has been reserved for the short, fitted garment seen on armoured effigies from *c.* 1340s, even though it should, properly, only be used for heraldic garments. It is the garment often referred to as a 'jupon'. **Short-fronted surcoat** denotes the mid-fourteenth-century garments that are shorter at the front than the back. Sometimes described as the 'cyclas', this name fell out of favour in the later twentieth century when specialists argued it was not a medieval term. We have coined the term 'short-fronted surcoat' as a convenient way of describing them. **Surcoat** has been used in preference to 'gown' and 'coat armour' to denote the full-length, loose-fitting outer garment used up until the mid-fourteenth century.

Finally, a piece of equipment that has not previously been recognised required a term and we have used '**mail-clad skull-cap**' for the bascinet-like head covering seen on the Series D knights.

7 Illustrations: Permissions and copyright

All the illustrations are copyright Brian and Moira Gittos, except for the following. Plate 65 is copyright Martin

Stutchfield; Fig. 30 and Plate 52, copyright English Heritage Trust; Figs 173 (YM5581), 174 (YM5306), 176 (YM5412) and 181 (YM5307), copyright Crown Copyright, Historic England Archive; Fig 120, copyright of the Board of Trustees of The Royal Armouries; Figs 78, 79, 83, 91, 97 and 138 are published by kind permission of The Bodleian Library, University of Oxford; and Fig. 96 is published by permission of the National Portrait Gallery under Creative Commons licence CC BY-NC-ND 3.0, for image NPG D27179.

Section 1

Introduction

The prehistory of a study

'To begin at the beginning' involves a weekend break in London in December 1973 (a last gasp of freedom before the imminent birth of our first child), where our first venue was the Temple Church. We were impressed by the outstanding group of early military effigies and back in the East Riding a week or so later, a chance visit to the church of St Helen, Welton, revealed a battered and neglected figure of a knight, which was clearly related to what we had just seen in London. Through the help of Philip Brown, Beverley's Deputy Borough Librarian, we had become aware of W. M. I'Anson's survey of the county's military effigies in *The Yorkshire Archaeological Journal*, which we regarded as something of a bible. To our surprise, he described the Welton effigy as a product of a Durham workshop, copying the style of the earlier effigies in the south of England (1926, p. 368). With recent memories of the Temple Church collection, we were unconvinced by the argument and found ourselves questioning for the first time the veracity of I'Anson's pronouncements. It was to be the first step in a process that has culminated in the writing of this book. Our earliest written record of a Yorkshire effigy was made on 22nd March 1974. Notes made at Welton speculated on the possibility that it might actually be Purbeck marble – it is (Fig. 1).

If Welton were a pivotal point, the sight of the better preserved knight at Stillingfleet was certainly another, where the richness of detail these monuments might offer became apparent, launching a life-time's involvement with Yorkshire effigies. 1978 brought the Monumental Effigy Symposium at the Tower of London, a watershed event thronged with people who shared our interest. Out of it came the International Society for the Study of Church Monuments (now the Church Monuments Society) and we have been active members throughout its life. Many new contacts were formed at the Effigy Symposium, including Harry Tummers, then finalising his work on English thirteenth-century secular effigies (1980). He encouraged us to go ahead with the article we were drafting on Welton, which was published in 1981. Our scepticism about some of I'Anson's assessments had already prompted a close scrutiny of his groupings and we began to evolve something more robust that took account of a range of additional factors, crucially including non-military figures. The study of Yorkshire effigies has continued to develop in the intervening years, punctuated by lectures and published articles on aspects of commemoration, ranging across the British Isles and further afield. This, then, is the backdrop of our involvement with these monuments over more than forty years. We are conscious that previous publications have covered only limited parts of a large subject and there is a need for something much more comprehensive. What follows, therefore, is a thorough treatment of all the Yorkshire effigies of which we are aware down to 1400.

Objectives

This book provides the opportunity to fulfil a number of objectives. First and foremost, it can bring Yorkshire's amazing and exciting medieval effigies to a wider audience, comprising not only the few who already share our passion but also the church-visiting public; those who are responsible for the churches and scholars of sculpture, medieval monuments, clothing and armour. We hope that greater awareness of the monuments' importance will increase the respect shown to them, thereby improving their protection and preservation. The intention is also to use

Fig. 1 Welton. Purbeck marble knight.

the richness and depth of the Yorkshire evidence to make worthwhile contributions to the understanding of medieval effigies as a whole. This can both enhance interpretation of what survives and provide a basis for future research. Finally, in particular instances, some long-standing problems and popular misconceptions can be addressed. However, after such a long gestation, we felt the need to underpin the book with a fresh survey. Carried out to consistent standards, it was undertaken between 2010 and 2017. It is the resulting detailed records that provide the authority for the statements made here. The approach has been essentially archaeological, giving primacy to the on-site observations of the monuments and their settings, but background research has been carried out concurrently, including some limited examination of antiquarian sources. The survey's methodology and fieldwork are described in Appendices A2 and A3 while the parameters for both it and the book follow.

Yorkshire is the largest county in England and its churches still host a profusion of intrinsically interesting medieval funerary monuments. Their state of preservation varies from complete monuments in good condition to small fragments. Amongst them are considerably more carved effigies than any other English county. Appendix A1 lists the corpus of 231 figures, which were covered in the survey and the places are plotted on the Endpaper Map. Whilst the numbers are a reflection of the county's size, they are a significant proportion of those remaining countrywide, allowing meaningful conclusions to be drawn. The study's scale provides opportunities for a better understanding of monuments and commemoration more widely, so while this book is based on Yorkshire's monuments, it is also about medieval effigies in general. Unlike previous accounts, the current work gives weight to the non-military majority, as important opportunities are lost when the evidence afforded by the lady who lies beside her spouse is ignored and the couple are not considered together. Particularly relevant is the evidence of female clothing, which can be helpful for dating purposes, as can a monument's location. Where effigies still remain in situ, there is much to be gained from studying both their immediate setting (canopies, tomb chest etc.) and the development of the building or site.

The survey has treated the monuments as artefacts, extracting the maximum information from what survives. For example, subtle or worn detail can often be enhanced (or even discovered) by the use of favourable lighting. Although painstaking recording has provided the evidence, the interpretation is multi-disciplinary. A knowledge of medieval clothing construction and styling greatly assists in understanding what a carver has depicted and, as many Yorkshire military effigies have heraldry, this has required special attention. Petrology is important both in tracking effigies to their source and demonstrating relationships.

Understanding the carving process can explain otherwise puzzling features, just as appreciating the historical context surrounding the creation of an effigy can help explain why it was made and the significance of its location. Despite the obvious difficulty of moving heavy stone effigies, some figures have been relocated many times and a little of this history can be teased out from earlier accounts. Where relevant, comparisons and analogies have been made outside the area, since many of the issues presented by Yorkshire's effigies are found elsewhere. Many avenues have been followed to provide this account of Yorkshire's medieval effigies, which we hope will help interpret them more fully.

Date range

The chronological span is 1200 to 1400.

The pre-Conquest material is already covered by *Corpus of Anglo-Saxon Stone Sculpture* (CASSS III, VI, VIII) and the post-Conquest tradition was of non-figurative commemoration, with the overwhelming majority of eleventh-, twelfth- and thirteenth-century stone monuments either bearing a cross or plain. Figurative exceptions stand out for their rarity, most notably the highly decorated slab at Conisbrough, dated *c.* 1160 by Rita Wood, who regards it as iconographic rather than representational (2001). This makes a starting date of 1200 tenable, as there are only two minor effigies that may predate the pivotal, mid-thirteenth-century monument to Archbishop Walter de Gray in York Minster. The apparent lack of early effigies in Yorkshire must be significant, as in southern England they are found before the mid-twelfth century and became well established from the start of the thirteenth. There is no Yorkshire equivalent to the imported twelfth-century Tournai marble effigies at Westminster Abbey and Salisbury Cathedral or the early Purbeck marble figures at Sherborne Abbey, Tolpuddle (both Dorset), Exeter and Salisbury Cathedrals, although the reason for this is unclear.

The later limit has been set arbitrarily at 1400. There are no stylistic, material or iconographic divisions at this point to provide a natural break and alternative upper limits were considered. The line might have been drawn at the Black Death or the end of the reign of Edward III, which would have given a neat historical limit but excluded a number of particularly interesting monuments, such as the alabaster pairs at Hull (Holy Trinity) and Pickering. Ultimately, *c.* 1400 emerged as the compromise, recognising that to have included the fifteenth century would have magnified the task to a point where it would have been unachievable. However, since the dating of monuments is an imprecise art, we have tried to err on the side of inclusivity, rather than applying a guillotine. Effigies such as those to Joan de Lellay at Goxhill (Fig. 2); the small male civilian at Nafferton and the two alabaster figures at Darfield can all be dated from internal evidence to the years around 1400 and have been included.

What constitutes an effigy

The study is limited to three-dimensional carvings intended as personal memorials where all or part of a figure (including the head) is depicted.

A lacuna exists in the published literature for Yorkshire as far as this type of monument is concerned. The county's two dimensional monuments are already well served, initially by Mill Stephenson but followed by Sally Badham on the monumental brasses and by Frank Greenhill on incised slabs (Stephenson 1926; Badham 1989; Greenhill 1976). Work by Aleks McClain and Peter Ryder is in progress on cross slabs, which were the commonest form of monument during most of the period (see Cross Slabs in Northern England digital database). An understanding of the characteristics and development of cross slabs is important for dating purposes since there are many instances of effigies being combined with this type of commemoration. A half effigy of a female is contained within a cross base at Howden (Fig. 3) and the bust of a man in armour occupies most of a cross head at Gilling East (Fig. 34). The two slabs at Melsonby have only the head of the deceased occupying the centre of the cross (Fig. 33). This raises the question of what constitutes an effigy, and for the purposes of this study we have chosen to include all examples that display a head. This means that all the semi-effigial slabs are part of the corpus, *i.e.* those where the figure is incomplete (*2a.vii*). Monuments with just a hand and arm occur at Guisborough Priory (in the custody of English Heritage) and another at Sproatley (E.R.) commemorating Walter, the priest of Keyingham. It consists of an incised cross and inscription but also bears in relief an arm emerging from the side of the slab, holding a host over a paten with a chalice below. The design is analogous to slabs, for example, at Dorchester Abbey (Oxfordshire) and Romsey Abbey (Hampshire), where an arm or hand comes from the side of the slab and holds a crosier. These commemorate abbots and abbesses, the hands holding the crosiers symbolic of office rather than representing the individual. The Sproatley slab must signify Walter's status as an ordained priest capable of celebrating mass and giving communion and was judged not to constitute an effigy.

Geographical limits

The geographical limits have been defined as the pre-1974 Ridings of Yorkshire. Effigies from elsewhere are included if we believe they have a Yorkshire origin.

These boundaries are more closely related to the medieval divisions than those of the modern administrative units and often relate to natural rather than artificially drawn divisions. They carry the additional benefit of coinciding with much of the published literature and were also the boundaries current at the inception of the work. The Temple Church effigy was

Fig. 2 Goxhill. Joan de Lellay.

Fig. 3 Howden. Female effigy in cross base.

Fig. 4 Ormesby. Feet of a knight.

transported to London in the seventeenth century, but others, *e.g.* Burton Stather and Winteringham, seem to have been exported when new.

Fragments

The study includes figural fragments if there are grounds to believe them effigial.

Very few of the monuments covered by this study are undamaged. Indeed, given the almost total loss of the more ephemeral adjuncts, such as painting, glass, metalwork and textiles, it is true to say that none have survived intact. The mechanisms behind such loss are covered in Appendix A6 and the illustrations show the extent of this damage. Very few figures have complete faces and a significant proportion betray the handiwork of iconoclasts. Undercut sections are frequently broken off and some monuments have been deliberately smashed. These processes leave debris for the archaeologist to interpret, in some instances the only evidence that a monument has ever existed. Examples where very little remains include the four pieces from two monuments at Goodmanham; the poorly preserved torso of an armoured man at Felkirk; the armoured feet at Ormesby (Fig. 4) and a small portion of a shoulder at Etton. These are in parish churches but monastic houses were devastated following the Dissolution. Many monuments were destroyed completely and the group of mail-carved scraps from Rievaulx Abbey present a problem in even determining how many figures

Fig. 5 Watton Priory. Excavated fragments built into a wall.

they represent. Tomb chests and canopies suffered too, although some finely carved, small scale fragments, probably belonged to tombs, for example from Kirkham and Guisborough Priories. St John Hope (1900a) recorded the discovery of pieces from a canopied arch and effigy at Watton Priory and what are probably all that remains now form a jumbled pattern built into a garden wall on the site (Fig. 5). They may be all that survive from the monument of Gilbert de Aton, d. 1350, who willed to be buried in the canons' choir there (*Test. Ebor.* I, p. 62). Watton also once had a tomb chest panel that probably came from a different monument. Amotherby has a dissociated chest panel that may belong to the effigy but no context is known for the panels from Fountains Abbey, even whether they come from a monument, an altar, a reredos or some other decorative feature. We have included fragments, however small, that can reasonably be identified as coming from effigies.

Series

Through close acquaintance with the effigies certain similarities become apparent, a sharing of layout, of forms and ways of carving common details, such as mail links or eyes, that is akin to a handwriting style. Groups of effigies with a common nexus have been identified, which have been termed 'Series' and their designations are referred to throughout the book. All five Series are described in Section 4c.

Lost effigies

Only extant material is included in the corpus but lost effigies have been considered where evidence for them has been found.

The lost effigies of which we are aware are listed in Section 2c.i. It has been beyond the scope of this archaeologically-based study to conduct an exhaustive search for lost effigies through potentially fruitful antiquarian records. Consequently, the listing will be far from complete but does demonstrate something of what no longer exists.

Conclusions

The work involved in the survey demonstrated why such an approach has not previously been attempted on this scale, not simply cataloguing obvious features but seeking to understand how and why the monuments are as we see them. The magnitude is also its strength, yielding many discoveries. In what follows, the monuments are examined from many perspectives and the most important discoveries are highlighted. Such close examination has revealed surprising details about their original appearance and traces of surviving colour reveal how sumptuous they once looked. Amongst them are some wonderfully preserved figures, which the historical context helps bring to life. We review the evidence before shifting focus, first to the masons who carved the effigies and then to the people who commissioned them and are commemorated.

Section 2

The effigies

2a Description of the corpus

2a.i Introduction

So what of the effigies themselves? This section provides an overview of the whole population, with consideration of their material, carving, repair etc. covered in Section 4 and the symbolism employed being reserved to Section 5c. Here, attention focuses on the types of people depicted, how they are shown and possible identifications. Semi-effigial monuments and cases of two effigies carved from the same slab are reviewed in their own right. Base slabs and gablettes are included here, since they are carved integrally with the figures. Aspects of costume, armour and equipment are examined, revealing some surprising features that are of value more widely. The concluding parts chart the fate of particular figures since they were set up and describe what is known about some of those that have been lost.

The Yorkshire total is 231, with all but seven located in the county (Endpaper Map). Those outside are recognisable either by being a member of a group (*4c*) or by being carved from a Yorkshire stone. They are in the neighbouring counties of Durham and Lincolnshire together with another now in London but known to have been taken there from Yorkshire. The total number of medieval effigies is unknown as there is no country-wide listing. However, as explained below, a means has been devised to estimate the overall total, so the significance of the Yorkshire population can be appreciated. The only country-wide survey is Downing's county listings of military figures, which can be used as a starting point. They suggest the largest populations are in Yorkshire, Gloucestershire, Lincolnshire and Somerset. The approximate totals of all types in these counties for the thirteenth and fourteenth centuries (derived from published sources and our own records) are: Gloucestershire 101, Lincolnshire 143 and Somerset 141. So, Yorkshire's 231 leads the field, something that can be explained by its size, as it is larger than its nearest rivals (Lincolnshire and Devon) added together. However, in terms of density, Somerset boasts nine effigies per hundred square miles, while Yorkshire can only muster four, presumably because large areas are sparsely populated upland, creating effigy-free zones. Turning from totals to types (discounting those too damaged to categorise), the overall gender divide is heavily male biased at 68% (150). Although a few of the seventy-one females wear coronets, perhaps suggesting some enhanced status, as a whole they form a coherent group. The men, however, can be further broken down into three broad categories: ninety-one in armour, twenty-one ecclesiastics and thirty-eight civilians, so the military figures constitute 39% of the overall total. This is typical of what is found elsewhere. In the five other counties where the information is reasonably complete, Somerset stands at 28% military, Devon 37%, Durham 42%, Gloucestershire 44% and Dorset 55%. A preliminary estimate for Lincolnshire suggests something very similar to Yorkshire at about 43%. The average percentage of armoured figures in these counties is 41%, which can be extrapolated to estimate a total of all types. If the starting figure of 41% is valid countrywide, the total number of surviving effigies for our period would be a little in excess of 1800. Whilst only an estimate, this is currently the best figure available. Two other values are of particular interest. Yorkshire's proportion of ecclesiastical figures is low at only 9%, whereas it has the second highest percentage of male civilians (16%). Somerset is the most populous county for both types and each constitute 23% of its total. These variations are difficult to explain in regional terms but the number of civilians may reflect Yorkshire's relatively wealthy economy (*5a*).

Fig. 6 Acklam. East lady with shields on her cushions.

The overall figure of 231 out of the estimated population of 1800 countrywide, means Yorkshire's total represents more than 10% of all the effigies remaining in England, making it a valid and worthwhile sample.

Before considering the categories of effigy, it is worth covering some aspects common to all types. For example, the figure's posture alters with time and involves technical aspects of carving, such as undercutting. As such, it seems to have been at the discretion of the mason and is dealt with in Section 4b.vi. Most effigies have supports for their heads, usually following the custom of the day. The great majority rest their heads on either one or two cushions (usually with the upper set diagonally). Only the knight at Nunnington has three cushions, something rarely seen elsewhere during the medieval period (Fig. 271). An example is the effigy of Richard de Stapledon (d. *c.* 1332) in Exeter Cathedral. Most economically, the couple at Lowthorpe probably share a bolster but it is largely hidden by drapery. Cushions of later date usually have corner tassels, which can be quite prominent, as at Acklam where the later lady's cushions also have seven carved shields (Fig. 6). There are exceptions to the use of cushions, some with nothing visible, like the priests at Beeford and Winestead (whose heads are closely framed by their gablettes) and the Wycliffe male civilian. The unusual arrangement of the Ampleforth couple (one figure behind the other) precludes the need for head supports and the same is true at Hutton Rudby, where the priest's head is set within a cross. The Welwick ecclesiastic has both a small cushion and blind tracery beneath him. Twelve knights from the last three decades of the fourteenth century, rest their heads on great helms. Some retain their crests, such as the plumes of feathers at Swine and West Tanfield, a ram's head at Catterick, a bull's head at Ripley and, seemingly, a kettle hat surmounting the Darfield helm. However, the most impressive was that carved across the two Markenfield effigies in Ripon Minster. The antlers of a stag, mounted on the helm rather like a Viking cartoon, were so large that they extended right across the end of the slab of his wife's effigy. This area is badly damaged, with the lady's head lost, but one of the antlers survives showing the wife's figure was deliberately set slightly lower, to accommodate the antlers and avoid her being impaled by them. It would have been necessary to position the two separate effigies very precisely to ensure the antlers joined up. This change to portraying military effigies resting their heads on their helms occurs in Yorkshire when it is seen elsewhere in England, except in the south west where the fashion began as early as the 1320s, as demonstrated by two knights in Exeter Cathedral. It was also adopted by the Ham Hill stone carvers shortly after its appearance at Exeter (Gittos 2012a). As well as having support for their heads, most effigies also have something beneath their feet. The symbolism of foot supports is discussed in Section 5c, together with angel supporters and additional figures. Here, it is sufficient to notice that of the surviving and recognisable foot supports, about half are lions, occasionally coupled with dragons (69). Dogs are the next most popular (37) followed by brackets and pedestals (19). Although hounds can be found beneath the feet of both male and females, they are a popular choice for the women and in one case (Pickering) two dogs face each other with their muzzles affectionately together. Other design aspects (base slabs and gablettes) are considered in Section 2b.

2a.ii Male civilian effigies

Of the thirty-eight male civilian figures (*i.e.* those neither armoured nor in ecclesiastical clothing), the great majority belong to the first half of the fourteenth century, when effigial commemoration was at its height. The semi-effigial figure at Goodmanham is an exception, as his gablette has leafy crocketting, which could be late thirteenth century. The small jaunty youth at Nafferton with one hand in his pocket (Fig. 7) has a late fourteenth/early fifteenth-century hair style. The men at Ampleforth, Stonegrave (later) and Yarm are also from the late fourteenth century, all double monuments sharing the same slab as their wives (*2a.viii*). The only other civilian from this time lies in Batley churchyard. Tucked under his left arm, Batley has what looks like a broad bladed sword (Fig. 8). However, a strong case can be made that this is not a weapon but a weaving sword – a wooden tool used in cloth making and no other example on a medieval effigy is currently known to the authors. The West Riding saw rapid growth in its textile industry during the later fourteenth century (Kermode 2000, p. 677). By that date such implements were outmoded, since loom technology had moved on, so its depiction may simply be emblematic. True swords are shown on the civilians at Ampleforth, Hedon, Loversall, Skerne, Wadworth and probably Hornsea. The semi-effigial figure at Hickleton has a sword in relief to the left of the cross shaft and the head slab (which is of uncertain type) at Hauxwell has a sword

Fig. 7 Nafferton. Small male civilian.

incised in a similar position. Just the pommel of a sword is present on the truncated monument at Wycliffe (Fig. 9). There are daggers at Stonegrave (later) and Batley, where there is also a purse. The swords at Skerne and Wadworth are accompanied by bucklers and there is a full shield at Loversall. Although the great majority are bare headed, two are shown with their hoods raised (Hornsea and Loversall) and five wear a coif (Garton-on-the-Wolds, Goodmanham, Lowthorpe, Methley and the earlier Stonegrave).

Very few of the male civilians can confidently be identified. Five have inscriptions but only at Hickleton is a full name given, Robert Haringel (Fig. 39). Little is known about him but he was joint holder of Hickleton manor in 1316 (*Feudal Aids* VI, p. 199) and seems to have been last mentioned in 1340 (CCR 1339–1341, p. 489; typescript held by the South Yorkshire Archaeology Service, *The Haringel Family*). The inscription at Yarm is not original since it records the appropriation of the double effigy in 1638. Only fragmentary inscriptions remain at Ampleforth, Methley and Wycliffe, insufficient to provide identification. However, it is said that 'WILELMVS DE' could once be read at Ampleforth (Gill 1852, p. 279) and the Pedigree of Thornton (Jackson 1873) mentions a late fourteenth-century William Kirkby of Ampleforth, who married Joan Thornton. Comparison with the contemporary double effigy at Stonegrave, only five miles east, makes it highly likely that Ampleforth commemorates William and Joan. Stonegrave's identification is heraldic, a chevron between three hawthorn leaves, which the *Little Guide* suggests is the canting arms of Thornton (Morris 1931, p. 367) although the coat does not appear in any of the medieval rolls. However, the published version of *Dugdale's*

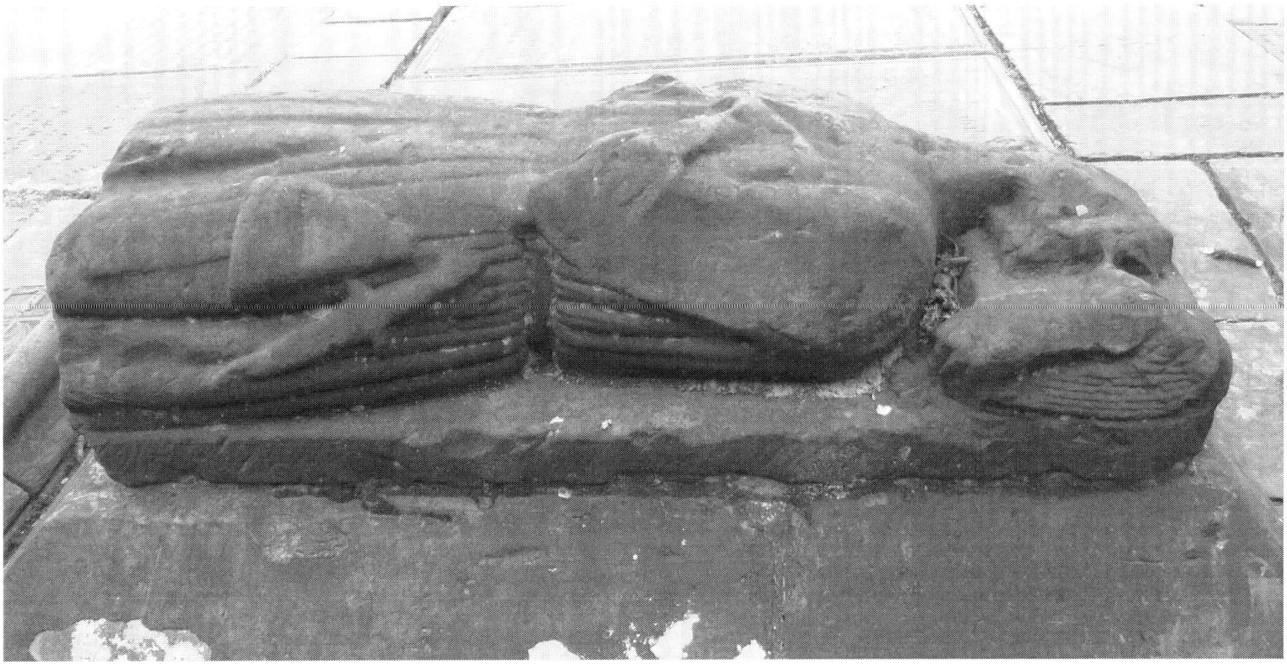

Fig. 8 Batley. Male civilian.

Fig. 9 Wycliffe. Male civilian.

Visitation of Yorkshire (Clay 1900, p. 16), quotes the arms of Thornton of East Newton (in the parish of Stonegrave) as 'Argent, a chevron Sable between three hawthorn trees proper' and mentions many burials of that family in the church of Stonegrave from 1545 onwards. A notice in the church suggests that the effigy commemorates Robert Thornton, who in 1397/8 obtained permission for Mass in his private Chapel of St Peter at East Newton. Robert Thornton was the brother of Joan who married William Kirkby and hence brother and sister would appear on the two monuments, which show such similarities that they were probably carved by the same local mason *c.* 1400. I'Anson believed the earlier Stonegrave effigy (Fig. 10) represented Sir John Stonegrave who died in 1295 (I'Anson 1927, p. 28

Fig. 10 Stonegrave. Male civilian.

fn. 1), which would have made it the earliest to be assigned a name. However, it is more likely to represent one of the holders of East Newton manor in Stonegrave parish (*5b.i*). There is heraldry at Loversall but unfortunately the arms (on a canton, a cross patonce) have not been identified. Historical evidence and assessment of probable dating provides attributions for five more male civilians: Birkin, Hull (Holy Trinity), Lowthorpe, Wadworth and York Minster. A good case can be made for identifying the monument in the south choir aisle of Holy Trinity, Hull (Plate 1) as Robert de Selby and his wife Emma (Badham 2015a). Traditionally attributed to members of the wealthy de la Pole family who are known to have been buried elsewhere, de Selby was a mayor of Hull and is last mentioned in 1386 (CPR 1385–1389, p. 184), consistent with the clothing depicted. The monument was described as his by Leland (I, p. 50) but given the size and wealth of the Hull merchant community, there may be other possibilities. It seems highly likely Lowthorpe represents Sir John de Heslerton (and his wife) who founded a college of chaplains there in 1333 and was dead by 1348 (Collier 1923; Saltmarshe 1914, pp. 49–51). The little civilian in York Minster commemorates Prince William of Hatfield. He died within a few weeks of his birth in December 1336 (Ormrod 2011, p. 174, n. 113; French 1991) but the effigy is later and its setting later still (*3c*).

The attributions for Birkin (Fig. 11) and Wadworth are more speculative. Richard Knowles (1985, p. 92) tentatively concluded of the former, 'It seems a distinct possibility that the fine effigy may commemorate John de Everingham who, it seems, died *c.* 1328' (but see Appendix 1), and on the basis of his legal costume Sally Badham has suggested the semi-effigial male at Wadworth may be a justice of the common pleas, John of Doncaster (*2a.vii*). The other male civilians are quite anonymous with little prospect that further research will uncover their identities.

2a.iii Ecclesiastical effigies

The impressive Purbeck marble figure of Archbishop Walter de Gray (d. 1255) might have heralded a wealth of

Fig. 11 Birkin. Male civilian.

Fig. 12 Hutton Rudby. Priest.

ecclesiastical monuments but it failed to create a precedent, as did the cast bronze effigy of Dean Langton (d. 1279, formerly in York Minster) which also went unheeded. The heads of the religious houses, despite often possessing considerable wealth, continued to prefer cross slab grave covers, as can still be seen in the chapter house floors at Rievaulx and Jervaulx abbeys. The same must hold good for parish clergy, to judge from surviving cross slabs inscribed with chalices (*e.g.* Ampleforth, Hornby, Lastingham and Tickhill). Medieval ecclesiastics are difficult to date, as vestments developed little and other evidence must be employed when available. Like the male civilians, few Yorkshire ecclesiastics can confidently be assigned to the thirteenth century. In addition to de Gray, Bedale and Hutton Rudby also predate 1300. The Series A priest at Bedale (Fig. 243) now rests on parts of two unrelated tomb chests under a later canopy arch, so it is completely out of context. Nevertheless, the carver has provided much additional detail, which links it to other effigies and suggests a late thirteenth century date – for instance, the use of naturalistic foliage. Unusually he holds a tablet displaying a crucifix, using both hands from beneath. The only other Yorkshire effigy holding an object in this way was Dean Langton (also late thirteenth century), interpreted as a book (Badham 1980, p. 62) but it is so like Bedale that it too may have been an image. The Hutton Rudby chalice-holding priest is a complete bas-relief effigy with his head at the centre of a cross constructed from sprigs of foliage (Fig. 12). These are typical thirteenth-century stiff leaf but each arm also contains two naturalistic oak leaves, with acorns forming the terminals. This juxtaposition of two successive foliate forms is a transitional arrangement of the later thirteenth century. However, the arch above the effigy has a gentle ogee form belonging to the next century. The effigy fits the arch well but is carved from a different variety of sandstone. Perhaps the effigy was carved first and the arch constructed to house it, a couple of decades or so later. (For details of other priests with chalices see Section 5c.ii.) As befits his status, Archbishop de Gray holds his crosier in his left hand and he alone is blessing with his right, although two angels at Welwick (*6a*) and a kneeling ecclesiastic beside Thornhill's feet (Fig. 270) also give blessing. The semi-effigial priest at Cantley is holding what is probably a heart or heart casket but it cannot easily be inspected because of its situation, high on the exterior of the chancel east wall. Heart-holding is more common with the secular effigies.

Fig. 13 Ingleby Greenhow. 'Wilks de Wrelton' inscription on priest's vestments.

The majority of the ecclesiastics (thirteen) simply have their hands at prayer, although in a few cases it is difficult to be sure due to their condition.

Only two have inscriptions. The Methley priest, like the male civilian effigy opposite, has an inscription incised on the chamfer of his base slab but it is too fragmentary to interpret. However, that incised vertically down the orphrey on the Ingleby Greenhow priest identifies him as William de Wrelton (Fig. 13). He was clerk to Archbishop Romeyn and in 1291 became involved in a power struggle between the Archbishop and Antony Bek, bishop of Durham (part of a long-running precedence dispute between the two Sees). Wrelton was one of two clerks despatched from York with a mandate to compel Bek to obey the Archbishop. Bek's response was to imprison both clerks in Durham Castle (Brown 1913/16, II, pp. xxv–xxviii). When Bek refused to release them, the Archbishop began proceedings to excommunicate him and matters were brought before the King. The case dragged on until 1293 when Romeyn was obliged to pay a fine of four thousand marks to avoid his own imprisonment, having lost his case, which established the important principle of Bek's dual responsibilities to the Archbishop and the King. What happened to the unfortunate clerks is not recorded but they may already have been released because on 21st September 1292 William de Wrelton, subdeacon, was instituted to the church of Hawksworth in Nottinghamshire (Brown 1913/16, I, p. 306). Unfortunately, there seems to be no record connecting him with Ingleby Greenhow. However, as his name suggests, William did hail from North Yorkshire and was also known as William de Pickering, Wrelton being very close to Pickering. Nonetheless this unassuming effigy apparently commemorates someone who was caught up in a major power struggle between the Sees of York and Durham.

In one case – Beverley Minster – heraldry assists an ecclesiastic's identification. The priest on an altar tomb in the north transept is probably unsurpassed amongst English medieval effigies in the number of heraldic shields carved on the figure itself (Fig. 14). His amice, maniple

Fig. 14 Beverley Minster. Huggate effigy from Gough's illustration (Gough 1786–96, II.3, p. 312).

and the apparel of his alb carry nineteen shields. One is defaced and another mostly hidden by his stole but all the remainder show different arms, although without tinctures. Rather than the deceased's heraldry, they can be interpreted as representing the people of note (including royalty) with whom he had associated during his career, like the side figures that populate the mid-fourteenth-century brass to Sir Hugh Hastings at Elsing (Norfolk). Amongst the attempts to identify him using the heraldry, the most convincing is McDermid's, who makes the case for Nicholas Huggate, Provost, who died in 1338 (McDermid 1980, I, p. 365–97). What is known about his life certainly justifies this heraldic display. Huggate's effigy is also notable for depicting an almuce raised up to frame his head, which is uncommon. Of the other ecclesiastics, Bedale may be a relative of Brian FitzAlan, whose effigy also lies in the church and the priest at Thwing may be a member of the Thwing family (*5b.i*) but there is little to suggest attributions for the remainder. However, the priest at Great Langton may be datable by his setting (Fig. 15). It fits well in an arched recess on the north side of the chancel, where it probably belongs. The reticulated east window of the mid-fourteenth century suggests money being spent on the chancel contemporaneously with the installation of the tomb. That being so, Robert Worship, Rector in 1343, would be a candidate (Jowitt 2012).

The twenty-one ecclesiastics comprise less than 10% of the corpus, so it would seem that effigial commemoration was not popular with the religious community in Yorkshire. Some, such as Archbishop Greenfield (d. 1315), adopted monumental brasses, but the parish clergy seem to have remained faithful to the traditional cross slab.

2a.iv Female effigies

The full date range and a wide spectrum of form and detail are provided by seventy-one female effigies. The great majority span the fourteenth century and lie straight, with their hands at prayer. The head slab at Stanwick, probably of the first half of the thirteenth century, is the earliest. She wears a goffered pill-box style headdress above a barbette, something not seen on any other Yorkshire effigy. Two females at Hornby have their hands in the relaxed style typically seen on effigies of the thirteenth century. Their left hands finger their cloak cord and their right lie on their stomachs, although this is less clear on that in the churchyard (Plate 5) because it is so decayed. The Bedale lady of *c.* 1290, holds a long scroll (*5c.iii*), while the Selby Abbey lady holds two shields by her sides, in a highly unusual stance. It has been suggested she is also late thirteenth century, since her gablette resembles work of that date in the choir (Hodges 1893, pp. 387–88; but see Section 4a.vi). Others probably dating from before 1300 include Bilton (in Ainsty) and one from Nunkeeling (now at Hornsea) holding her rosary. Many figures gather up their cloaks under each elbow as they might when walking but there is little evidence of the swayed posture seen elsewhere, with the notable exception of Bedale, who lies with her knees together, slightly to her right, making a willowy curve. Howden is unique amongst Yorkshire ladies as she has crossed legs under her very full gown (Fig. 16). Although this attitude is normal for military effigies of the late thirteenth and first half of the fourteenth, women are rarely shown in this way. However, there is another in the south aisle at Aldworth (Berkshire) and further afield (all in the Irish Republic): three late thirteenth-century ladies at Cashel are cross legged, as is the lady of a recently discovered double effigy at St Mary's, Kilkenny (Fig. 17). The Cashel figures are reset dramatically upright in a churchyard wall, which creates the impression that they are walking (for Cashel see Hunt 1974, pls. 26–28; for Kilkenny see Gittos forthcoming). These rare and far flung comparisons underscore the originality of the way the Howden lady is presented.

Fig. 15 Great Langton. Priest in his chancel.

Seven of the female effigies are carved in very low relief – half of all the figures in the area that use this type of presentation. The Patrington lady's effigy is carved entirely in bas-relief, framed by her gablette and its side shafts (see Section 5c.viii for the cross lying over her). However, such low relief carving shows considerable variation, exemplified by the lady from Denton (Co. Durham) made from a Yorkshire limestone (Egglestone marble). Her head, cushion and shoulders are only just proud of the surface and below her elbows the relief dies away completely with just two edging lines delineating the figure. Detail is missing from the head and hands, so it is possible that the lower part was originally incised but has been lost to wear. Something similar occurs at Bitton (Gloucestershire), where the upper half of a knight is in very low relief and the lower part incised, although his cushion is also incised. An analogy can be found amongst monumental brasses and incised slabs, where the incised technique is used across a mixture of materials on a single slab. Yorkshire examples include Hemingbrough (E.R.) where one figure and the inscription were inlaid in brass, one figure was partly brass and partly incised on the stone while a third figure was wholly incised; the slab at Patrington where most detail was inlaid in brass but the lower part of the figure was

Fig. 16 Howden Minster. Metham pair, trimmed down.

Fig. 17 Kilkenny, St Mary (Republic of Ireland). Double effigy, discovered by excavation 2016.

incised; and Pocklington and Welwick where the figures had inlaid heads, hands, marginal inscriptions and parts of the canopy, the remainder being simply incised on the stone (Gittos 1989). Such mixed methods were probably utilised to reduce the cost of manufacture. The Kirkleatham lady is a variant, whose top half is in medium relief, tapering to low relief for the remainder. Other figures, *e.g.* Danby Wiske (Fig. 18) and Wistow (Fig. 50), are in low relief throughout. The former is significant because she is closely related to other Series E figures that are fully carved, such as Appleton-le-Street and Wilton (in Cleveland). A deliberate choice was made to produce Danby Wiske in much lower relief than her counterparts rather than it being the carver's style. The reason might have been pragmatism, such as being constrained by the depth of the available block, or it could simply reflect a lower budget. Tailoring monuments for less wealthy patrons is a likely explanation of the popularity of the semi-effigial figures in the county and there are nine females of this category, plus the half effigy at Howden. The female and male semi-effigials are considered together below, as are double effigies (carved on the same slab). Both types are symptomatic of a diversity of form, which seems to reach its zenith in the first half of the fourteenth century.

The headdress of the lady at Hornby lying next to the knight appears idiosyncratic, the wimple held out beside the temples and caught up high at the sides. The top of the head is relatively flat and the front of the veil comes down over the forehead, in a line that resembles the peak of a cap (Fig. 19). This creates very sharp triangular gaps at either side that provide glimpses of ribbons binding up the hair. The arrangement cannot be paralleled within the corpus, the dipping line of the veil across the forehead running quite contrary to English fashions. But comparisons are found with Tuscan and Umbrian work, where the vogue for a dipped line over the forehead seems to span *c.* 1260 to *c.* 1390 (Fig. 20) and is well represented amongst the work of the Pisano family. The forehead line is sometimes so low as to touch the eyebrows, as in Orsanmichele, Florence, commissioned 1349×1352 (Kreytenberg 1994, pls. 13, 66). In many cases, the line is the edge of the veil (probably an elongated oval shape) but a similar feature also appears on unveiled women, apparently made by a looped ribbon or fillet binding the hair, for example on Giovanni Pisano's Pistoia and Pisa Duomo pulpits (Ayrton & Moore 1969, pls. 132, 168, 172, 173). In some other examples, the front of the veil is arranged to be smooth, with a straight lower edge across the forehead (Ayrton & Moore 1969, pl. 163)

Fig. 18 Danby Wiske. FitzAlan lady.

but even these variations seem to be manifestations of the same basic fashion. The dipped line at Hornby is comparable to Giovanni Pisano's effigy of Margaret of Luxembourg in Genoa (*c*. 1311), although her wimple is held close to the head (Ayrton & Moore 1969, pl. 181). The Italian examples lack the width at the temples and the triangular spaces since Hornby's underlying hair must be arranged more in an English fashion, but the style is far more Italian than English. Maybe this lady came from Italy and brought the custom of her native land to Yorkshire.

Given the male dominated social context, it is surprising that only about a third of the females are accompanied by their spouses. Some companion effigies may have been lost but most women who had memorials were commemorated alone, often making them difficult to name. The occurrence of couples together aids identification and, as a result, names can be suggested with some confidence for all five in prestigious alabaster (Darfield, Hull, Pickering, Swine and West Tanfield). Inscriptions are rarely found and, in fact, there are only four including the fragment at Ampleforth on William and Joan Kirkby's slab, mentioned above. The other three inscriptions are complete (Denton, Goxhill and the Wistow bas-relief). Disappointingly the Denton inscription omits her Christian name, simply asserting that she was the consort of Aubrey de Conyers who has not been identified. Goxhill names her as Joanna, the wife of Robert de Lellay, but evidence about her is lacking. Wistow is the converse of Denton, identifying the figure both as 'Margeri' and 'Dame Margeri' but omitting the family name – presumably because at the time everyone knew who she was.

However, many Yorkshire women (at least twenty-one) once had heraldic identification. Much carved heraldry does survive, for instance at Acklam, where shields on the cushions (Fig. 6) identify the later lady as the wife of Sir Thomas Boynton (d.1402) who was born a Conyers. More significant for identifying the Selby lady than the shields she holds (see above), are those on her surcoat: a bend between six hammers, for Hammerton. These are the arms that the Selby knight displays on his shield and so the two monuments are related. However, since his sword belt must date from the fourteenth century (*2b.iii*), it casts doubt on the Hodges' case for the lady belonging to the late thirteenth (see above). The lady at Aldbrough has the griffons of de Meaux carved on her cote (Fig. 21), helping to identify her as Maud, the wife of Sir John de Meaux (d.1377), whose effigy lies nearby with the same arms on his coat-armour. The alabaster pair at West Tanfield both have heraldry – Sir John de Marmion displaying his arms (vair with a fesse) on his coat-armour, while his wife Elizabeth St Quintin wears Marmion impaling St Quintin. Thornton Dale has six shields, three lying on the slab either side of her (Fig. 22). They form a pattern of just two arms, suggestive of an alliance, such as a marriage. One is again St Quintin and the other may be Conyers with a label (VCH:NR:II, p. 497) as at Acklam, but no connection has been found between Thornton Dale and either of these families. Alternatively, the maunche with a label might be Hastings, a branch of whom had their seat in the adjoining parish of Allerston from the early thirteenth century. By the sixteenth century, they also held the advowson of Thornton Dale (VCH:NR:II, pp. 421–24, pp. 492–97). Consequently, a marriage between the St Quintins and Hastings of Allerston seems most likely, but this does demonstrate that even such an ostentatious display of heraldry is not always sufficient to provide identification. More helpful are the two small cloak mount shields at Danby Wiske, which display the barry of eight coat of FitzAlan of Bedale. Brian FitzAlan's second wife Maud survived him by more than thirty years until the 1340s, which is the period the effigy dates from because of its association with other closely dated members of the Series E group (Gittos 2002b). The Birdsall lady has a large shield at the head end

Fig. 19 Hornby. Lady with veil worn low on her forehead.

Fig. 20 Pisa, San Matteo National Museum. Virgin with similar veil line to Hornby.

carved with the arms of Brideshale – *argent 2 bars azure, in chief 3 mullets gules* (Brault 1997, 2, p. 54) (Plate 7). The colour is modern but conforms to the arms of Sir Gilbert de Briddeshale in the Galloway roll of *c.* 1300 (Brault 1997, I, p. 461) and of whom this lady must have been a close relation. In some cases only the blank shields remain, as on the gablette at Howden, the margins of the base slabs at Hornsea and Wilton (in Cleveland), plus the tomb chests at Hull and Darfield. Most, if not all of these, would have had painted heraldry and, if the paint had survived, it is likely that many more of the females would be seen to have worn heraldic clothing. Heraldry was a signifier of status and identity, both desirable attributes on a tomb. Although the majority of female effigies remain unidentifiable, names can be assigned to many more of them than is possible with either the ecclesiastics or the male civilians.

2a.v Military effigies

The ninety-one military effigies exceed the total number of effigies for most English counties and are challenging to describe as a whole. Moreover, the earliest figures are difficult to date, making the origins of the military effigy in Yorkshire unclear and a consensus on their genesis is lacking. Harry Tummers includes only six out of 143 thirteenth-century military effigies across England but fails to indicate any sequence, describing them all as 'late thirteenth century' (Tummers 1980, pp. 135–43). I'Anson has seven before 1300 (I'Anson 1926), including West Tanfield and Foston-on-the-Wolds, both absent from Tummers, but omits Treeton of which he seems ignorant. However, he provided a chronology, beginning *c.* 1270 with Bulmer (Fig. 23) and the larger Coverham, followed by Jervaulx, West Tanfield and Foston-on-the-Wolds, all at *c.* 1280 and concluding with Welton *c.* 1290 and Pickhill *c.* 1295–1300. Downing has five figures at *c.* 1300 but only Welton from the thirteenth century, which he dates *c.* 1280–1300 (Downing 2014; 2015). All three, therefore, agree on Welton and we once thought it definitely thirteenth century (Gittos 1981) but it is now seen as belonging to the final phase of Purbeck marble effigy production (Blair, Goodall & Lankester 2000), which continued as late as *c.* 1330 (Gittos 1998) and is, therefore, quite likely to date from the early fourteenth century. To bring the Yorkshire figures into better focus it is worth considering one of Harry Tummers' key dating tools: attitude. For example, he saw sword-handling as a thirteenth-century trait, replaced thereafter by hands at prayer. This is largely true, with the notable exception of the south west, where the Exeter and Ham Hill stone carvers and the Purbeck marblers of

Fig. 21 Aldbrough. Lady with heraldic cote.

Fig. 22 Thornton Dale. Lady with shields beside her.

Dorset continued producing sword-handling effigies into the fourteenth century. A few anachronistic military effigies were made in County Durham (largely of Frosterley marble) but, with the exception of Romaldkirk, it does not seem to have been so in Yorkshire.

Sword-handling effigies are therefore a good place to begin and Yorkshire has eight: the smaller wooden figure at Allerton Mauleverer; the torso at Coverham Abbey (although not recognised as such by I'Anson); Foston-on-the-Wolds; Jervaulx Abbey; Romaldkirk; Treeton; Welton; and the torso held by the York Archaeological Trust. At first sight Romaldkirk appears a prime candidate for the earliest figure (Fig. 24). He has a single cushion, a long shield and the mail is of simple alternating rows of shallow crescents. His sword belt has bar mounts, like some thirteenth-century figures – for instance at the Temple church – and is probably unique in England in showing a surcoat split right down the side. His straight legged stance appears to confirm his early credentials. However, the cranked terminals of his spurs are slotted to accept the straps, a feature which would suggest a late thirteenth or even fourteenth century date. Similarly, the surcoat's graduated hem, which is several inches longer at the back than the front, is unexpected in a thirteenth-century context, being more likely to date from the period when the garments were shaped to give enhanced freedom (Capwell 2015, p. 20). The *c.* 1331–1338 brass of Sir William FitzRalph at Pebmarsh (Essex) is a good comparison, with a similarly graduated hem and spurs with cranked, slotted, terminals. These features conflict with the side slit, giving the impression that he is not wearing coherent armour of a single period. Perhaps the effigy was retrospective and deliberately archaic. There can be no doubt that it represents a FitzHugh since the arms, fretty with a chief, are faintly incised on both the shield and surcoat. A very good candidate is Hugh FitzHenry who held the manor of Romaldkirk and the advowson of its church. He died in March 1305 and according to one account was buried at Romaldkirk with the Prior of Guisborough officiating (Brown 1889/91, 2, p. xlii n. 2). This Romaldkirk burial was unusual as from the thirteenth century into the fifteenth, the family were normally buried at Jervaulx Abbey, (Burton 1758, p. 373; CP, V, pp. 416–25). The establishment of a monument long after Hugh died, perhaps by his son and heir Sir Henry FitzHugh (d. 1356), could explain the confused attempt to create the appearance of an old knight.

Fig. 23 Bulmer. Knight.

Amid the ruins of Jervaulx Abbey we have an excellent candidate for Yorkshire's earliest military effigy. An incomplete, broken and badly weathered figure of a knight carries a long shield also bearing traces of the arms of FitzHugh (Plate 3). I'Anson identifies the figure as Ranulf FitzHenry who died *c.* 1280, brother of Hugh FitzHenry (I'Anson 1926, pp. 365–66). This contention is supported by the *Complete Peerage* (CP, V, p. 416), which says that Randolf FitzHenry was son and heir of Sir Henry FitzRanulph and was buried at Jervaulx. Randolf died without issue and was succeeded by his brother Hugh but the date of Randolf's death is not given, so *c.* 1280 may just be an assumption by I'Anson. If the Jervaulx knight does commemorate a head of the family, Randolf seems the only possibility. He is sword-handling with violent intent, his right leg thrown out to the side and bent at the knee, while his left shoulder is so raised that his whole body is twisted and contorted in the urgency of unsheathing his weapon. From the thirteenth century, only the knight at Dorchester (Oxfordshire) can compete with this drama and to a lesser extent the retrospective wooden effigy to Robert Curthose, son of the Conqueror, in Gloucester Cathedral. Arguably, Jervaulx is the most active of the three, which are probably contemporary. Philip Lankester's analysis of the Dorchester knight considers a range of possible dates but favours the late thirteenth century, with the possibility that it commemorates William Valence the younger, who was killed in action in 1282 (Lankester 1987, p. 172). There is nothing to suggest that Dorchester and Jervaulx came from

Fig. 24 Romaldkirk. Knight of the FitzHugh family.

the same source but they may well have been carved under some common influence in the 1280s.

The three Series A effigies at Coverham Abbey and Routh complete the thirteenth-century military contingent, although none are sword-handling. At first sight the two Coverham men, dramatically posed upright against a wall (Plate 6), appear very different, leading commentators to date them widely apart. I'Anson separates them by more than sixty years, giving the larger figure *c.* 1270 and the other *c.* 1330–1335. Tummers accepts only the larger figure as thirteenth-century and Downing sees both figures as fourteenth-century – the larger he assigns to his group three (1315–1330) and the smaller to his group five (1330–1340) (*A7*). Yet the reality is that, despite their differences, some aspects are so similar (the knees, corner of the surcoat over the lower leg and the mail creases under the chin) that they must be by the same hand and contemporary. The date range for Series A spans *c.* 1290 – *c.* 1300 with the Coverham effigies falling comfortably within the 1290s, since the later (smaller) figure has both naturalistic foliage and a simple gablette with pellet in a hollow moulding like that on Kirkham Priory gateway of the 1290s (*A8*). Unfortunately, there is no heraldry to assist with identification but they may be members of the Neville family who were patrons until 1331 (Stöber 2007, Appendix). Around 1300, three closely related effigies (Escrick, Fountains Abbey and Scarborough) mark the transition from Series A to Series B. The bulk of the military effigies (about 70%) belong to the first half of the fourteenth century, including the Series B, C, D and E, each of which will be described later (*4c*).

Within this majority occur all nine heart or heart casket holding military effigies, suggesting a fashion popular in the second quarter of the fourteenth century (*5c.iv*). In fact, if the non-military heart-holding effigies are included, the only possible earlier example is the male civilian at Goodmanham (for which the only indication of date is the gablette) and after 1350 there is just the heart-holding lady at Holy Trinity, Hull. Her heart is between her finger tips, very like the brass of Sir John de St Quintin (d. 1397) at Brandesburton (E.R.). William de Aldeburgh (d. 1388) at Aldborough is another heart-holding brass, so this imagery continued in Yorkshire to the end of the century.

In Yorkshire, the effect of the Black Death on military effigies appears profound. The large numbers of pre-Black Death military effigies make it all the more obvious as a watershed. Of the fifteen military effigies post-1349, none can confidently be dated before 1370. Sir John Sutton at Sutton-on-Hull is a possibility. He died in 1356 and was buried in the chancel (Fig. 128) but the effigy is likely to have been installed as part of the work to make the church collegiate in 1347 (*3g.iii*) and there is nothing about this figure to suggest a later date. Another candidate for the immediate post-Black Death period is Sir Ralph Bulmer at Wilton (in Cleveland), last mentioned in 1349 and dead by

Fig. 25 Pickering. Battered remains of alabaster de Roucliffe knight.

1356, but he may have provisioned his monument in his lifetime, as the range for Series E spans the 1340s (Gittos 2002b; also Section 5a.v). Following the Black Death, over twenty years elapsed before the next military figures appear, the tombs of Mowbray at Kirklington (Plate 8), Ingleby at Ripley (Fig. 106) and Hilton at Swine (Fig. 26). The apparent cluster of figures *c.* 1400 is probably more marked because of our wish to include all effigies around that date but two military figures from the later fourteenth century appear to have been misunderstood. One is the alabaster fragment at Pickering (Fig. 25), which has been described variously as a Bruce, a Lascelles and even John of Gaunt (*2c.ii*). Pauline Routh gave a good summary of these fantasies but failed to note any surviving heraldry. Downing is more definite, stating 'Heraldry: none' (2015, p. 35). However, his jupon did carry carved heraldry both front and back with part of a chevron visible on the back just above the waist and small traces of another at the front. Most detail has worn off his chest but vestiges remain on his right, probably of animal fur. They are interpretable when compared with the other alabaster knight. He displays (lacking the tinctures) the arms of Roucliffe, 'argent, on a chevron between 3 lion's heads erased gules a chess rook or' (DBA 2, p. 471). So, both knights were members of the Roucliffe family, which is confirmed by the decoration on their bascinets. The vervelle cover has a pattern of alternating S's and chess rooks, clearly another allusion to the family arms. That on the mutilated figure retains appropriate gilding. The second misrepresented effigy is at Catterick (*5b.i*), which has been considered unusual in not having a sword and compared with the Kirklington knight for that reason (I'Anson 1927, p. 64 fn. 5). Having described the sword belt, Downing claims 'There are no signs that a sword or dagger was represented' (2015, p. 12). In fact, he almost certainly did have a sword that was a separate piece of wood or metal (*4b.v*).

Fig. 26 Swine. Hilton family member, with arming chains.

Fig. 27 Treeton. Knight wearing a coronet.

The usual weapons depicted are swords and shields, daggers only appearing in the later fourteenth century. Sir John de Meaux (d. 1377) at Aldbrough is one of the earliest to show a dagger but, as is often the case, it has broken off, leaving just a slight scar, together with a remnant of the cord securing it to his hip belt. The same is true of the Hilton knight at Swine (*c.* 1370) who is unique in Yorkshire in having arming chains (Fig. 26). These are two long chains fastened to a ring at the centre of his breast plate, one attached to the sword and the other to his dagger. They are slack, with spare chain lying on the base slab near where the hilts of both weapons would have been. Swine is one of only eleven effigies in England with arming chains (for an account of all of them see Downing 1995). They are widely scattered as far apart as Kent and Worcestershire and span about fifty years, with Swine seemingly the last. They enabled the knight to recover his weapon if it fell or was knocked from his hand. A statue of St George in York Minster nave triforium (south side), has a single arming chain without an obvious purpose. Downing has suggested that his missing right hand may have held his helm, the chain being linked to it (1995, p. 8) but his sword is another possibility.

Some unusual features of the armour depicted on Yorkshire effigies, including mail-clad skull-caps and double ring mail are dealt with in Section 2b.iii while the few wearing the short-fronted surcoat are described below, but what the knight at Treeton wears on his head is unique in the county (Fig. 27). This effigy is in poor condition (*2c.ii*), having suffered considerable abuse, and probably for that reason it has largely been ignored. However, it was originally of good quality, as attested by the survival of small areas of well-carved mail within the arm hole of his surcoat and on the top right of his head. This is part of his coif, which is secured not with a fillet but a coronet and we are unaware that this has previously been recognised, although there is a hint of it on Johnston's drawing (C 14, fo. 229r), Fig. 91. It is extremely difficult to account for. Some female effigies have coronets, such as at West Tanfield (most westerly) and Bilton (in Ainsty), but the only Yorkshire male is Prince William of Hatfield in York Minster, for whom it is clearly appropriate. A brief survey of medieval effigies wearing coronets suggests they were restricted to people who held ducal or comital rank. However, some of that rank were depicted without, such as Ralph Neville, Earl of Westmorland (d. 1365) at Staindrop (Co. Durham) who has just an orle on his bascinet, even though his two wives beside him wear coronets. Lady Margaret Holland's tomb in Canterbury Cathedral is an interesting case because the two husbands (lying beside her) were of different rank.

Her second husband was Thomas, Duke of Clarence (d. 1421), second son of Henry IV, and he wears a coronet. Her first husband John Beaufort Earl of Somerset (d. 1410) has an orle, so the coronet is being used as a signifier of rank. Our conclusion is that a coronet would not be shown on a military effigy of this period without good cause and, despite its abused, mutilated and neglected state, the Treeton effigy was probably made for someone amongst the nobility. As nobody of such rank is known to have had close association with Treeton, it is likely the effigy has been brought from elsewhere, probably following the Dissolution of the Monasteries. The nearest abbey to Treeton is Roche and amongst its benefactors were the Earls of Warenne who had their seat at Conisbrough. Perhaps a context of this kind would account for such an effigy being found in a modest parish church. The local tradition of calling him 'Earl Gilbert' could hold the clue to unpicking the puzzle, if we only knew what to make of it, as there seem to have been no Gilbert de Warennes. In the context of noble headgear, the lion at the Sprotbrough knight's feet is curious. He wears a coronet or crown, which may be a heraldic or fealty reference but is unlike any other in Yorkshire and, possibly, country-wide.

Six of the military effigies wear what we term the 'short-fronted surcoat' but is widely and incorrectly known in the literature as the 'cyclas' (Blair 2003). It was once thought to be a brief fashion of the 1320s until the reassessment of some key brasses, including Westley Waterless (Cambridgeshire) and Stoke d'Abernon (Surrey), moved it to the 1340s (Binski 1987, p. 132). This is significant as the Yorkshire examples all date from this decade and therefore reflect up-to-date fashion. Two of them are the 'double mail' figures at Bedale and Pickering and two more are members of Series E: Sir Robert Capon from Upleatham (Fig. 219) and Sir William de Crathorne at Crathorne (Plate 65), who both died in 1346. The set is completed by Sir Thomas Cressacre at Barnburgh and Sir John de Sutton at Sutton-on-Hull. Some Yorkshire effigies appear to show a variation. For instance, Burton Stather, Kildwick, Sheriff Hutton (Fig. 28), and Sprotbrough all wear full surcoats but the front openings are cut on a slope. Probably a transitional form, they are increasingly being recognised. The Yorkshire evidence suggests they may have been depicted earlier than short-fronted surcoats and by the middle of the century the two forms were concurrent.

Fig. 28 Sheriff Hutton. Edmund de Thwing of Cornbrough, d. 1344.

Whereas this fashion was only briefly popular, ailettes had a much longer life, their date range in Europe as a whole was *c.* 1275 to *c.* 1350 (Blair 1958, pp. 45–46), which spans the eight Yorkshire examples. Although once thought to be a neck defence, Claude Blair was convinced their main function was heraldic display because they were usually too flimsy to provide protection. Traces of heraldry remain on the ailettes at Ingleby Arncliffe, in line with documentary references to elaborate heraldic decoration (Richardson 2016, p. 192 fn. 4). Richardson has recently suggested ailettes were 'probably of stiffened textile' (2016, p. 233) and leather examples are mentioned as early as 1278 in a tournament context (Lysons 1814). The two complete Coverham effigies probably have the earliest ailettes in the county, curving over the cushions and confirming their flexibility (Plate 32). Less certain is the shape shown flat on the slab behind the right shoulder at Routh. Fountains has his behind him on the cushion like Coverham, whereas at Treeton there is the stump of a broken of ailette upright on his left shoulder and possibly something behind his right shoulder. The sequence is completed by the two figures at Ingleby Arncliffe and the related knight at Wilton (in Cleveland). Ailettes were once thought to be extremely rare on effigies and I'Anson (1927) only knew of eight examples. Downing's survey has increased the total to twenty-seven (2010, p. 58) and Routh would be a further addition, giving Yorkshire between a quarter and a third of the total.

2a.vi Uncertain types

In ten cases it is very difficult to determine the type and they break down into two categories – those with insufficient evidence and those where it is inconclusive. The five in the first category include the possible semi-effigial at Easby Abbey (which is almost worn out), the extremely weathered semi-effigial at Loversall (Fig. 29) and the nearly effaced stone in the boundary wall where St George, Fishergate, once stood in York. The fourth is the piece from Egglestone Abbey showing part of an animal foot rest but nothing remaining from the effigy (Fig. 30). The intriguing figure in the churchyard at Middleton on-the-Wolds (Plate 2) is one of Yorkshire's earliest effigies (*3d*) but, disappointingly, is too eroded to be certain of its type, although the features either side of the head might have assisted had they been clearer.

In the second category, the Hauxwell slab has a small sunk relief head within a circular opening and an incised sword. The face is badly worn but there is just a hint of a male hair outline. A painted cross may originally have completed the design, which would resemble the cross slabs bearing symbols of the deceased commonly found in the area. A sword is usually taken to indicate a male burial, not

Fig. 29 Loversall. Semi-effigial of uncertain type.

Fig. 30 Egglestone Abbey. Foot support beast. Copyright English Heritage Trust.

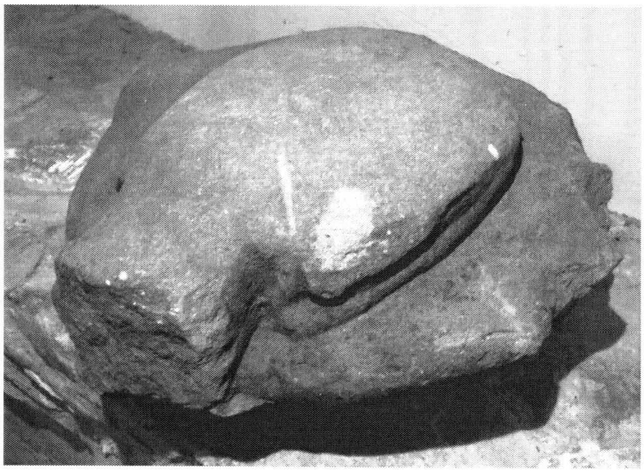

Fig. 31 Easby church. Head worn smooth.

necessarily a soldier. However, it is a large and prominent feature of the monument, stressing its significance. The Easby head is worn smooth (Fig. 31) but the little detail remaining around the edge, hints at a short female veil. Filey is simply dressed (Fig. 99) and could be a male civilian or perhaps a canon. The lower legs and feet at Etton belong to a figure in a full-length gown, which could have been either male or female. The final member of this motley band is built into the porch at Moor Monkton (Fig. 32). It was probably of good quality and wears a voluminous garment belted at the waist. Damage to both ends of this diminutive effigy makes interpretation difficult – the arms and head having disappeared. The feet rested on an animal and the legs may have been crossed. The very full skirt flared out at both sides would suit a female but as the lower legs appear to be visible, this can be ruled out. Male civilian effigies, such as Birkin and Garton-on-the-Wolds, wear their cotes loose and unbelted but the drapery pattern below the belt resembles that of a long, wide surcoat. This would be consistent with the impression of crossed legs, so Moor Monkton could be a military figure. However, in the absence of either sword or shield, Moor Monkton remains an enigma.

2a.vii Semi-effigial monuments

Yorkshire has a good selection of semi-effigial monuments. The term is usually taken to denote monuments where parts of a figure, typically the head, hands and feet, are shown in sunken compartments. Here, it encompasses any effigial representation that is intentionally incomplete. They

Fig. 32 Moor Monkton. Small effigy of uncertain type.

are one of the least studied categories of medieval effigy, despite the fact that in the mid-nineteenth century the Rev. Charles Boutell devoted the whole of Section II of *Christian Monuments* to the subject (1854). Particular examples and some groups have been dealt with subsequently but no attempt has been made at a country-wide survey and many individual figures remain unpublished. A recent overview by Jerome Bertram (2015) and an examination of semi-effigial effigies in Lincolnshire (Badham forthcoming) are welcome additions to this poor coverage but it is against this incomplete picture that the Yorkshire monuments must be considered. As far as can be judged, Boutell's view of the subject (set out in a footnote on p. 119) is still broadly true:

> The greater portion of the monuments of this class which are known to be in existence, are in the churches of Yorkshire, Lincolnshire, Derbyshire, Nottinghamshire, and Rutland, and also in some parts of Wales. They appear, however, to have been in occasional use throughout the kingdom during the latter part of the thirteenth and throughout the fourteenth century; and in some instances, examples of a later date have been observed.

All that seems to be missing is a recognition of those slabs, particularly in south west England and south Wales, which have just the head carved in relief (one of which, at Bitton, Gloucestershire, is illustrated in Boutell 1847, facing p. 158), and the probability that the overall occurrence of semi-effigials is more numerous than Boutell might have thought (for south Wales see Badham 1999 and Biebrach 2017). What is particularly perceptive are his opinions regarding dating, which ran contrary to a widely-held belief that semi-effigials were part of a developmental process in which figures in low relief gradually became more deeply carved until they were almost completely released from the slab. This view persisted long after Boutell's work was published but he expressed his opinion very well in the same footnote:

> It has been considered that these partial effigies are of earlier date than complete figures; and, in fact, that from them complete figures were derived. A careful observation of the monuments themselves shews this opinion to be altogether erroneous.

Without a comprehensive country-wide survey, the total number of semi-effigials remains elusive. Boutell illustrated or mentioned forty-five, of which nine were in Lincolnshire, but that county is now known to have more than thirty (Badham forthcoming). Boutell gives two in Yorkshire, whereas we have logged twenty-four, including two pairs carved together. On this basis it might be anticipated that the total for England and Wales could approach, or even exceed, 200. The Yorkshire group represents just over 10% of the projected total and is sufficient to demonstrate the range and versatility of the genre.

The great majority (eighteen) display parts of figures as if seen through apertures in the stone. They are sometimes linked together by a stem as if they were the head and base of a cross. The shape of the openings varies, with a quatrefoil mostly used to frame the head and hands, plus a flat-based trefoil for the feet. However, at Amotherby, Cantley, Throapham and York St Olave, the lower parts are lost and, with them, any feet, while Easby Abbey is too damaged to know the original arrangement. So, only Aldborough and Hauxwell definitely omit the feet. The latter is a special case, with just a sunk-relief head within a small circle and it is also the only one carved in a polishable crinoidal limestone. The female head at Stanwick is simply cut in bas-relief without any aperture and the two slabs (male and female) at Melsonby are different again. They are closely related, with heads set within leafy crosses (Fig. 33). Below the male head is some worn carving, which could be a mound of foliage but might also have included his hands (McClain 2005, II, p. 222).

Fig. 33 Melsonby. Female head slab.

Fig. 34 Gilling East. Semi-effigial knight.

Like very many cross slabs, symbols occur and three semi-effigials have swords. The meaning is unclear at Hauxwell and one accompanies a male civilian at Hickleton (see below) but the military message of Gilling East is unambiguous (Fig. 34). The knight's bust wearing a coif and bascinet replaces the cross head (*5c.viii*) while his sword lies beside the shaft, in its scabbard and on its belt, partially covered by an armorial shield. Opposite is what might be a horse's head crest but might even represent his steed. The Skerne lady has a foliate cross shaft, like Melsonby and Gilling East, but this low relief detail is barely visible because of the slab's poor condition. Like the other figures at Skerne (*2c.ii*), she has been heavily restored and seemingly only two pieces of the original survive within the reconstituted slab. Similarly, only the head and feet in their apertures survive from two semi-effigials at Goodmanham. Now built into an inside wall, they represent male and female. Unfortunately, their heads and feet are transposed but are shown correctly in Fig. 35. The lady is so mutilated, only her right foot and part of the left side of her head remain. A drainage hole beside her head shows that this was once a churchyard monument (*3h*). The man lacks the drainage holes but his apertures are complete and show little sign of weathering, so the monuments have experienced different histories. The male civilian at Moor Monkton is complete and in good condition, built into the east wall of the porch in a modern frame (Plate 18). He has bare curling hair, tightly buttoned sleeves and his hood loosely draped around his neck, so that it gapes at the sides. This is where his drainage holes have been positioned, with room for them provisioned by the open way the hood lies. This is a clear case of the carver anticipating the requirements of a monument to be set up in the churchyard. The result of failing to add drainage holes is obvious at Loversall (Fig. 29). This is a very thick slab with an integral plinth only 39″ (1 m) long, with recesses for the head and feet. With the water unable to escape, all detail has been lost within the apertures and the head has weathered to a shapeless lump.

High in the east gable at Cantley, a flat-bottomed trefoil opening contains the bust of what is probably a priest wearing an amice (Fig. 36). His head rests on a cushion and something is clasped between his praying hands. This is likely to be a heart casket but has a small circular feature at its base, which is difficult to interpret from the ground. It also is impossible to confirm he is tonsured. Directly above, at the apex of the gable, is a second man, also praying. He is integrally carved with the socket stone used for the modern

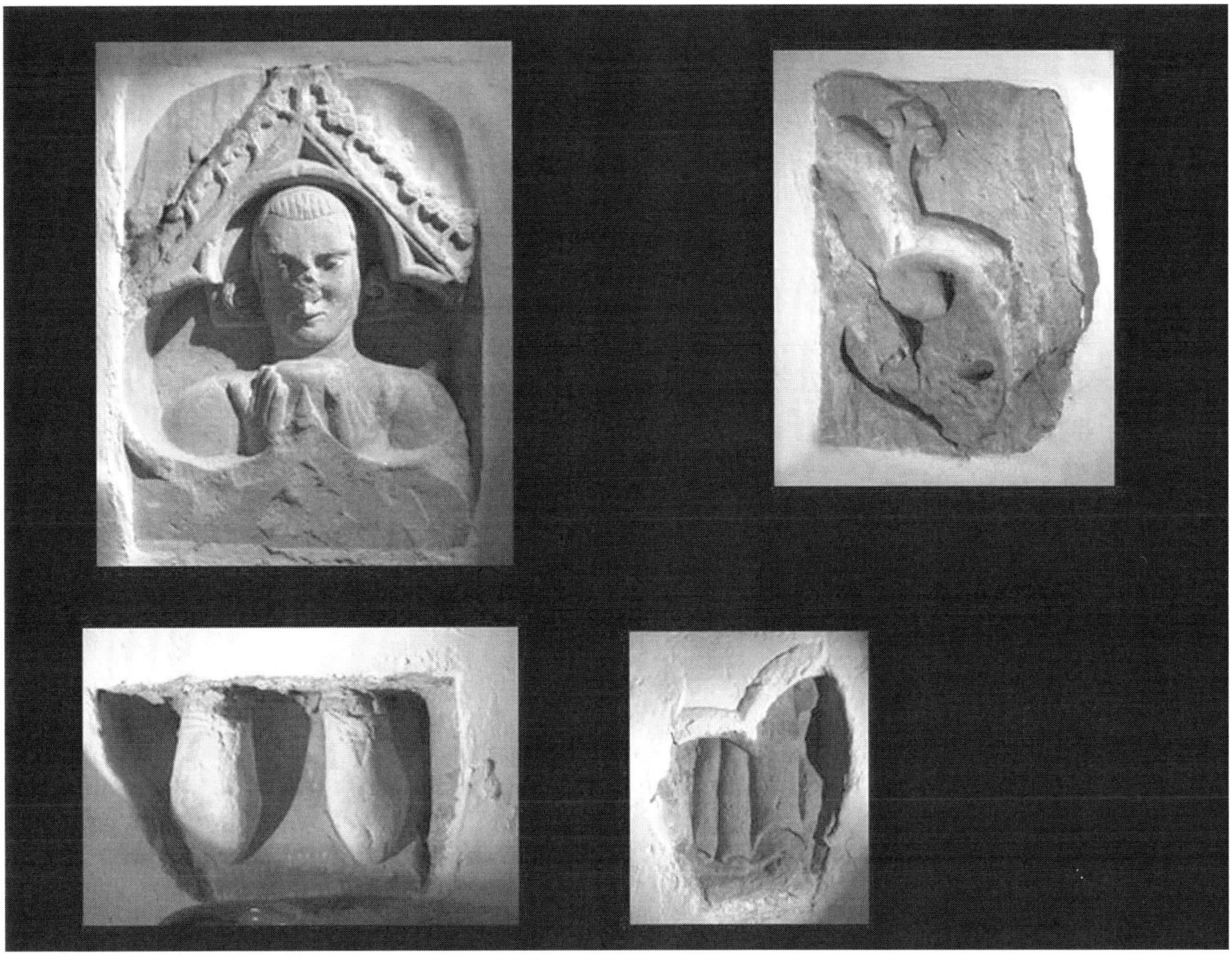

Fig. 35 Goodmanham. Semi-effigial male and female fragments, correctly re-arranged.

Fig. 36 Cantley. Semi-effigial priest.

gable cross. The lower part is hedged around by pebble-dash rendering, which may obscure some detail. There is nothing to relate him to the semi-effigial below or to indicate when he was carved and, although a donor figure might have been intended (Gittos 2014a), we see no reason to regard him as a pre-1400 effigy.

The Stanwick semi-effigial is puzzling but important as it is potentially the earliest Yorkshire effigy (Fig. 37). The broken slab has a deeply cut female head with a fierce fish-like beast above and a pair of shears below. Beside her, a stalk bears a stylised leaf or flower recalling the Romanesque motif described as being 'like that of a pie with its four edges folded inward' and associated with the Sarum Master (King 1990, p. 73). This is best seen on the tympanum of the north doorway at Lullington (Somerset), probably of the 1130s. Stanwick's face is stylised, like a child's drawing, with circular eyes and a straight nose. It is framed by a barbette topped with a tall, straight-sided, circlet resembling a 'pill-box' shape. Circlets worn with barbettes were fashionable through most of the thirteenth century but they seem to

Fig. 37 Stanwick. Female head slab.

have become progressively narrower. Stanwick is relatively tall and worn low on the forehead with a frilled or goffered edge to the barbette. Good comparisons can be seen on the Purbeck marble lady in Worcester Cathedral, probably of the 1240s, and worn by ladies on the west front of Wells Cathedral, of a similar date. However, unlike them (and other depictions) Stanwick shows the barbette outside the circlet. Normally the only item worn over the circlet is a light veil (as, for instance, on the west front) so this may be a misunderstanding on the part of the carver. Peter Ryder's Stanwick study (2002) of the large number of cross slabs and grave makers describes it as 'perhaps of twelfth century date' and compares the leaf-like feature to details on a slab at Berwick-Upon-Tweed. This was found by excavation in situ and is archaeologically datable to the late eleventh/early twelfth century. However, this is too early for the lady's headdress, which probably gives the most useful dating evidence. Peter Ryder considered the slab was originally larger but had been cut down for reuse, possibly as an impost based on the chamfered edges, presumably because the beast, leaf stalk and shears are all clipped by the chamfers. However, the chamfers (which are present on three sides, the fourth being a broken edge) would also make sense if this were a small rectangular monument, perhaps for a heart burial. If little is lost from the broken edge, the head would be fairly central, which would be less likely if the slab had been randomly cut for reuse. A square memorial of similar size, with a chamfered edge and incised figure, is in the Museum of London. It marked the heart burial of Joan de St Edmunds, who is likely to have died in the late thirteenth century (Badham and Norris 1999, pp. 126–27). Even if Stanwick were as late as the 1240s, it would still compete with Middleton on-the-Wolds for the accolade of Yorkshire's earliest effigy.

The small female half-length effigy at Howden Minster represents another different form, where the praying figure is framed by a niche representing the cross base (Fig. 3). The slab stands upright against the east wall of the ruined chancel and is severely weathered. The original carving was in quite high relief and the general outline can still be discerned, but unfortunately the lower part of the slab is more badly affected. Cutts (1849, pl. LXXII) published an immaculate drawing, which seems to be an 'improved' version of the Howden slab, despite it being labelled 'Hendon, Yorkshire'.

Semi-effigials required much less work than fully carved figures and could be produced more rapidly, at lower cost. This made them affordable by a larger clientele of more modest means – the emerging classes of lower gentry and professional people that developed in the later thirteenth and fourteenth centuries. It is, therefore, not surprising that most of the semi-effigial monuments are anonymous with little to indicate whom they might represent. However, in a few cases, such as at Lowthorpe, it is possible to suggest who is commemorated (*e.g.* Sir John de Heslarton and his wife Marjorie). Lowthorpe is by far the most elaborate of Yorkshire's semi-effigial monuments, standing apart from its fellows. It is a massive double effigy, seeming to show a couple in bed with a tree springing from them and the heads of their children on its branches. It is somewhat analogous to double effigies in Lincolnshire, at Careby and Stoke Rochford, both of which show couples with covers over them. However, Stoke Rochford is more akin to a typical semi-effigial, displaying the couple's feet as well as their praying busts, and the Careby cover is turned down like a counterpane, hiding their feet. Unlike Lowthorpe, which is in low relief, both of these monuments also resemble semi-effigials by enclosing the figures in sunken panels. Lowthorpe has attracted much comment in the literature (*e.g.* Oosterwijk 2005) but there is still more to be gleaned from a detailed examination and some aspects of its history have gone entirely unnoticed. For a fresh assessment and details of the identification see Section 5c.ix.

Fig. 38 Wadworth. Semi-effigial male in legal dress.

A semi-effigial that invites speculation is the male civilian at Wadworth (Fig. 38). Both apertures have sweeping ogees, typical of the second quarter of the fourteenth century and the slab is rectangular rather than coffin-shaped, so a date late in that period seems likely, when his strongly fashioned hair curls would still be appropriate. In 1869, this slab, described as 'apparently of a priest' was set in the south chapel floor (Glynne 2007, p. 418) and was still there forty years later (Morris 1911, p. 517). The south chapel was probably rebuilt in the 1330s, its piscina and sedilia with ogee heads matching the openings on the monument. In fact, the upper opening is treated like an architectural niche with cusped canopy arch, foliate crocketing and side pinnacles, all with finials. It seems very likely that the person commemorated was responsible for the south chapel and set up his memorial there, in a position of honour as its founder, only to be displaced by later monuments. Far from being dressed as a priest, he wears legal clothing (Badham 2010a), including a collobium with two tongues at the neck, his hood shown folded down over the edge of his collobium. The lack of a coif (worn by Sergeants at Law and judges) may be explained by the relatively fluid nature of legal clothing at this date (Baker 2013). It has been suggested that it might possibly commemorate a specific judge of the period, John de Doncaster (Badham 2010a), though this can only be conjecture. He was still active in the early months of 1336 (CPR 1334–1338, p. 263) but no association with Wadworth has been found.

The only Yorkshire semi-effigial whose name is known with certainty is that at Hickleton. In 1983, Robert Haringel's monument was discovered in situ by excavation, covering a burial beneath the floor of the south aisle (*ex inf.* South Yorkshire Archaeological Service). His bust (Fig. 39) is placed where the cross head would have been with a sword in the same position as Hauxwell and Gilling East. However, Robert seems not to have been knighted and is dressed as a civilian. He holds a small object, probably his heart, and his face is full of character with moustache, bushy beard and small pouting lips. The stiff presentation is not great art but is well executed and gives a strong impression that the carver was attempting to portray a real person. Robert Haringel's last mention in 1340 (*2a.ii*) is an appropriate date for the elegant and sweeping ogee curve at the base of the cross. The slab is now set in the pavement near where it was found and, because it was quickly buried, it is exceptionally well preserved, with the delicate flourishes on the lettering still evident and only a little damage. It gives a good impression of how some of the more damaged examples may once have appeared.

Several complete Yorkshire effigies have been wrongly claimed as semi-effigial, including priests at Hutton Rudby and Thrybergh (2) and the two monuments at Nafferton (Badham 2009, pp. 21–22). The Nafferton couple (Fig. 40) are least understood, with many sources seeing them as comparable to Lowthorpe (which happens to be the next parish). Recent commentaries include: 'A broadly similar composition [to Lowthorpe] is to be found at Nafferton ... It is worn and, although what may be branches of a tree cover the slab, there is no trace of heads of children' (Badham 2009, p. 22) and '... a very worn monument depicts the busts of a man and woman in prayer, the bodies

Fig. 39 Hickleton. Robert Haringel.

covered by a fluted pall with raised cusped decoration' (Barker 2017, p. 120). These confused assessments may in part relate to the fact that two separate effigies have been roughly cemented together, making them superficially appear as one. They certainly form a pair but are essentially conventional figures of the mid-fourteenth century, with hands at prayer, heads on cushions and gablettes. Until the last century (when they were placed in the north aisle) they were in the churchyard (Morris 1906, p. 258) where they probably originated, which would be consistent with their heavy weathering. What makes them special is that both figures have architectural tracery laid over them, as if their bodies were being viewed through a window. Carved in high relief, the tracery forms symmetrical patterns with pierced cusping and that on the lady is more elaborate. Both figures have hanging sleeves which have been cleverly carved to blend with the tracery. The 'fluted pall with cusped decoration' is the drapery of their full-length clothing seen through the tracery without any tree branches. The only slight comparison with Lowthorpe is that the figures have something laid over them. They are different in every other respect. Why they should be shown thus is open for debate. Perhaps they were donors of a window (or windows) and buried in the churchyard close by, with the monuments reflecting their benefaction. Maybe the man was a stone carver or architect who just wished to be remembered in this way. Whatever the reason, they are extraordinary and

Fig. 40 Nafferton. Separate male and female effigies with tracery carved over them.

Fig. 41 Eastrington. Remains of knight and lady double effigy.

idiosyncratic effigies, which deserve better appreciation than they have received to date.

2a.viii Double effigies

The Lowthorpe tomb described above is not only semi-effigial but one of a small group of Yorkshire effigies that have two figures carved on the same stone. Double effigies do occur elsewhere but they are an uncommon form and seem never to have been studied in their own right. There are eight double effigies in Yorkshire and they seem to span most of the fourteenth. They are very disparate, each being an individual piece unrelated to the others. It seems a double slab was only produced by special order and was not part of a carver's regular output.

The fragment at Eastrington (Fig. 41) is one of two military examples and the most damaged of the eight (*2c.ii*; *A6*). What remains is the lower central section of two effigies, lacking their heads and feet and trimmed on both sides. Only the lowest level of the carving survives but it shows an armoured man with (presumably) his wife and, uniquely in Yorkshire, the knight is depicted lying on his shield. A buckled strap attached inside the shield passes under his left arm and, if this is the guige, then the second strap must be an enarm looping over his upper arm, where a little carved mail is preserved. The enarm is rivetted to (or through) a feature, itself fixed to the inside of the shield, that may be a reinforcing plate or the lower part of the padded lining. Very little can be seen of the lady except the edge of her cloak (or surcoat) with just a glimpse of a waist belt underneath. The male was probably straight legged but it is difficult to be certain. Knights lying on their shields are extremely rare. At Minster in Sheppey (Kent) the effigy of Sir Robert Shurland reclines on his left side with his shield beneath him and his head resting on his helm, while at Great Haseley (Oxfordshire) the shield lies crossways under the knight's neck, helping the stretched-out saddle to support the cushion under his head. The knight at Chew Magna (Somerset) props himself on his left arm, while his right rests on the shield beneath him. These are quite exceptional effigies, suggesting the Eastrington pair must be similarly regarded. To be shown lying on your shield and effectively hiding it negates the obvious messages both of its role as a defensive weapon and it usefulness for heraldic display. However, the arrangement is very deliberate and must have had a purpose for which there is now no clue.

The severely weathered double semi-effigial monument at Wadworth is probably the earliest double effigy (Fig. 42). It is in poor condition and all detail has weathered away except for a central groove forming a division line between them. This gives the monument the appearance of two tapered slabs joined together, a conceit also seen on slabs at Tintern Abbey (Monmouthshire) and, in miniature, at Pittington (Co. Durham). With male and female heads, they almost certainly represent a couple, like all but one of the Yorkshire examples. The exception to this norm is South Anston (Fig. 43), where a male civilian is accompanied by a small figure, presumably his daughter (Oosterwijk 2010). There is a subtle indication of the protective relationship between them in the way the tippet from the father's left elbow wraps over the child's head, similar to how the slightly earlier lady at Bodenham (Herefordshire) rests her arm over her child. Two angels stretch out in their efforts to guide her on the journey to heaven. It is a very moving and accomplished piece of mid-fourteenth-century sculpture.

The other four double effigies all date from later in the century. The praying couple at Yarm (Fig. 44) have two large symbols of the Evangelists above their heads (St John and St Matthew) with the composition looking decidedly unbalanced. However, the bottom edge of the slab is broken across and made up with cement, so the emblems of St Mark and St Luke are probably lost. In the seventeenth century this monument was appropriated by the addition of an inscription with the date 1638 still clear. The second armoured example lies in the churchyard at Kirby (in Cleveland) where he held hands with his wife beside him. The monument is extremely weathered and has probably always been outside (Plate 4). The damage means dating is difficult but it is likely to be around 1400. The knight has lost his legs and his lady her head, while his rests on his helm, but what makes it special is their attitude. His right and her left arms are both broken off just below the elbow but they lie together on the slab, converging in a manner that suggests they held hands, an attitude discussed by both Nigel Saul and Peter Coss (2009, pp. 302–307; 1998, pp. 86–104). Countrywide, a dozen or so stone effigies did this but Kirby is the only Yorkshire example. It differs from the rest, which all have their right hands clasped, usually with the lady reaching across her husband, as at Wimborne Minster (Dorset) and Lowick (Northants). The right and left gesture is seen, however, on a double effigy in Ireland that commemorates William Goer and his wife Margaret at St Mary's, Kilkenny

Fig. 42 Wadworth. Semi-effigial double effigy.

Fig. 43 South Anston. Probably a father and daughter.

(Hunt 1974, pl. 114; Gittos forthcoming). At Kirby, the right hand-left hand variation may be because the sculptor wished to avoid undercutting on a churchyard monument.

The couple at Ampleforth are another fourteenth-century curiosity (Fig. 45). The wife is set behind her praying husband and slightly above him. She inclines to the left and he to the right, which enables a little more of her to be seen. Whilst suggesting a degree of intimacy between the pair, this also results in a considerable economy of effort by the carver, but the composition was presumably acceptable to the patron. The monument has often been misinterpreted. Walbran considered, 'It represents a warrior wearing a sleeved surcoat over chain armour which appears at his wrist and neck: his sword suspended from a belt passing over his right shoulder: and his hands elevated in prayer' (1864, p. 224). I'Anson also thought the figure was in armour (1927, p. 35) but Downing does not include it in his Yorkshire catalogue (2015). I'Anson suggested a date of *c.* 1330 for the monument, which has been endorsed by others (*e.g.* Badham 2011, p. 58). However, Downing is correct in omitting Ampleforth from his list of military

Fig. 44 Yarm. Civilian and wife double effigy.

Fig. 45 Ampleforth. Unusually portrayed double effigy.

Fig. 46 Stonegrave. Double effigy, members of the Thornton family.

effigies because, although he carries a sword, he is dressed as a civilian. What has been seen as worn rows of mail are, in reality, just the way his tunic is quilted at the neck and wrists, as is clearly shown by the rows of buttons on the latter. Additionally, a date of *c.* 1330 is much too early for the monument. The same high neck and quilting at the wrists can be seen on the late fourteenth-century civilian at Hull (Holy Trinity) who is also bearded and the high neck line at Ampleforth suggests a date even closer to 1400. Ampleforth's identification and association with Stonegrave are considered above. Although the two double effigies are very similar in style and date, Stonegrave shows no intimacy, with a gap left between the figures and separate cushions. They wear almost identical costume, except that the lady sports gloves and is the only Yorkshire example to do so (Fig. 46). The similarity of their attire prompted an early nineteenth-century writer to describe them as two females (Eastmead 1824, p. 191), so he must not have noticed the man's dagger and beard. Although their heads are at the same level the lady is deliberately shorter, enabling her side of the slab to fit into the arched recess (which is too narrow for her husband). The result is to give him much more prominence. He is bare headed, with a central parting and full beard, like Ampleforth. The dagger hangs by a strap from his waist belt and, like the civilians at Loversall and Skerne, he has a shield. In this case it is very small and oddly suspended by a hook from a fold in his sleeve. It seems to have been incorporated solely for the purpose of displaying his arms. This is yet another detail on a Yorkshire effigy that seems unparalleled.

The block of stone needed for double effigies would have been awkward to carve, heavy and costly to transport. So it is perhaps significant that only two of the double monuments are of Magnesian Limestone. South Anston is a quarrying centre, while Eastrington is only about three miles from river transport along the Humber. The others all seem to be of local stone. However, the bulk and weight would have been seen as an advantage for monuments set up in the churchyard (*3h*) as seems to have been the case with many of the Yorkshire examples. This is a class of effigy that would benefit from further study.

Yorkshire's monumental effigies range across many spectra. They represent people from the high-born and powerful to the lower gentry and the parish priest. Sources range from the royal masons to the very locally made, while the materials can be prestigious stone imported from hundreds of miles away or what was convenient and close at hand. Some of the effigies were made with mechanical simplicity while others are superbly crafted, individually detailed and thoughtful masterpieces. It is this diversity that makes Yorkshire's effigies a microcosm of the whole subject. The interpretive challenges can be considerable but the rewards for understanding them are commensurate.

2b Aspects of design

2b.i Base slabs

Most monumental effigies, unlike statues, are not carved in the round but depicted as lying on an integral surface or base slab, which varies in shape and proportion. Most of the earliest examples are coffin-shaped (broader at the head than the foot). During the first half of the fourteenth century, this changed to a rectangle. The same evolution in plan applies equally to double effigies, whose slabs have to be

Fig. 47 Goldsborough. Series B effigy with pointed end to base slab.

Fig. 48 South Anston. Rough dressing of base slab edge.

sufficiently wide to accommodate both figures. Examples are the earlier and mid-fourteenth-century monuments at Wadworth and South Anston, which are coffin-shaped, while the mid and late fourteenth-century examples at Lowthorpe and Kirby (in Cleveland) are rectangular. As ever, there were exceptions. For example, the lady at Bilton (in Ainsty), has a coffin-shaped slab but the corners have been chamfered off, as (on a more modest scale) have those of the Amotherby knight. Some, such as the two de Metham figures at Howden (*c.* 1310), are slightly pointed at both ends, forming an irregular hexagon. Apart from the change to a rectangle, the variations appear not to have any particular significance and were probably down to the carver's discretion, perhaps in collaboration with the commissioner. They can even be out of register with the rest of the monument. The de Goldesburgh effigy also has a pointed head end (Fig. 47) but rests under an arch with straight sides. At Bedale the FitzAlan knight's base slab is pointed at both ends, which extends the centre line by some four to six inches (10–15 cm), even though he is known to have rested on a rectangular tomb chest. A similar mismatch occurred at Howden.

The surface of the slab is normally either level or coped up to the figure, which was probably the result of the sculptor's or workshop's preference. For instance, the closely related Series B effigies are roughly evenly split while the C Series are mostly flat, with only two, Sheriff Hutton and Kildwick, being very slightly coped. A surface coped to the figure would give more support to extravagant skirt drapery, but perhaps be a less dramatic presentation. A related consideration is the amount of exposed surface around the figure. This can differ quite markedly from a figure that virtually fills the space available, even spilling over the edges, such as FitzAlan at Bedale, whereas Church Fenton's is more akin to a display background. At the highest quality, these extremes can be seen as relating to the sculptor's vision of the finished product and other aspects of style, such as the degree of undercutting to be used, their handling of drapery and incorporation of ancillary features. The effects are of opulence on the one hand (Goldsborough Series B) and of stark, modernist, elegance at the other (Church Fenton). However, at the lower end of the scale of competence, a figure filling the slab, as at Stainton, Beeford and Ampleforth, may be no more than a desire to minimise the amount of work (and thus cost) involved. On occasion, the slab can be used to present the effigy in a particular scenario. At both Welwick and Hutton Rudby, priests are cut recessed within the slab presenting them as if seen inside their coffins. So, whilst base slabs might seem a minor aspect, they have much to contribute.

The edges of a slab often provide vital clues about the original configuration of a monument, sometimes allowing one to relate an effigy to a setting that has been lost. The unfinished vertical edges of slabs, such as the Bruce effigy at Pickering, the lady at Kirby Sigston or the civilian at Wycliffe, were not intended to be seen. They might have been hidden by the panels of a tomb chest, inside a recess or even set flush with the pavement, as the lawyer at Wadworth once was. An unmoulded edge that was meant to be seen is at Sutton-on-Hull, which is carefully finished since it was to lie atop a chest. At a number of places part of the carving spills over, including Womersley and Thornhill, where the lowest part of the shields is cut into the vertical edge of the slab. If the effigy were to be set within a recess or against a wall, sometimes only the visible sides were finished, the concealed edges being left rough. At South Anston, the two ends and the edge on the figure's left are fully finished with a small straight chamfer, whereas the long edge on the right side has been left straight, with diagonal axe dressing clearly visible (Fig. 48). The axe dressing is uniform, showing it was done when the monument was made, rather than a later trimming, and probably remains from the initial squaring of the block, before carving began. As this edge was hidden, the figure was almost certainly set up against a south wall, given that burials were always laid out with the feet to the east. It may not be a coincidence that the south wall of the south aisle in this largely Decorated church has a shallow tomb recess that would fit the monument. Hunter (1828, I, p. 306) also associated the effigy with this recess, although it was then in the churchyard. Paying attention to a slab's edges can reveal much about its original setting.

On many base slabs, the arris where the upper surface meets the vertical edge is chamfered off. This is often quite modest but ranges in size from only *c.* 1″ (*c.* 2.5 cm) at Selby Abbey to the broad, sweeping, almost architectural moulding at Harpham. Chamfers might be used to carry an inscription (*e.g.* both effigies at Methley) or decoration, such as the four-petal flowers seen on many of the Series E effigies (*4c.v*) and those which are now plain may originally have had painted decoration. Unless the detail was cut in the stone, there is no way of telling how a seemingly plain chamfer was used. Alternatively, the edge may be entirely moulded, implying it was meant to be seen, such as on the Beverley civilian and the pair at Ripley. The most extravagantly worked slab edge is the visible side at Welwick, which has been carved with wave tracery joining the symbols of the Evangelists.

Effigies intended to lie on tomb chests were occasionally larger than the support, as is the case with the pair at Stonegrave and the earliest lady at West Tanfield. Indeed, at Bainton, the slab with its under chamfer is integral with the plinth below. Consequently, when an under chamfer is seen on an effigy without a chest, it is reasonable to deduce that there must originally have been one, as is the case with the Wadworth forester, and the deduction is corroborated by Bloxham's 1849 record (p. 7) describing it as on 'a low raised tomb'. The edges of these slabs were sometimes fashioned into symmetrical compositions, with the under chamfer the same width as an upper chamfer and a similar vertical separation between them. This concept is well illustrated by the knight on the chest at Goldsborough and again at Spofforth. Spofforth lies under an arch that appears to be contemporary, so any chest is likely to have been quite low but almost certainly once existed.

Occasionally, the effigy is not presented as lying level but angled either so that the head is higher than the feet, or one side is higher than the other. An example of this is at Birkin, which is sited in a deep recess. At the inner edge, the slab is thicker and the differential works with the stance of the effigy to make it more visible to the onlooker, turning it to face out of the recess. It may also have served to visually engage the figure with a nearby devotional image, light or altar. Birkin is a useful demonstration of many of these principles, since in addition to its canted surface, it has a broad chamfer on the three visible edges while that against the back of the recess has a much narrower chamfer and the outer edge also has an under chamfer to take account of the slab being wider than its plinth. The Series B effigy at Goldsborough is an instance of the head being higher than the feet but due to the plinth course having a wedge-shaped section (Plate 26). This example and its benefits are discussed in Section 3g.i.

Very occasionally, a figure may have been made detached, with no slab, with the intention of it being placed on a surface of a different character. Examples of this technique are often of extremely high quality and in high status materials. For instance, the white marble effigy of Queen Philippa (d. 1369) in Westminster Abbey lies directly on top of a tomb chest made from highly polished black Tournai marble. Structurally, this arrangement is more vulnerable and other separate elements, including part of her surrounding canopy work, have been lost even though they had originally been fixed down. Yorkshire has a few effigies that appear to be carved without slabs (Pickhill, Upleatham, Whorlton, Barnburgh and the smaller figure at Allerton Mauleverer). The two stone figures are both badly mutilated and no evidence survives at Pickhill but Upleatham's right side has slight vestiges of what could have been a base slab that elsewhere has been totally lost. The other three are all of wood. Barnburgh has areas of flat surface (for instance, below the legs around the feet and under the neck), which could be left after trimming, possibly when he was incorporated into the late fifteenth-century setting. Allerton Mauleverer shows a little such evidence and as he is in rather poor condition, the base may have decayed away. However, that would mean both legs must have been fully undercut, including the heel of the lower leg that is almost invariably in contact with the slab. Whorlton is more equivocal. The bottom of the composition, around the beast and under the lower legs, has a base slab, which is slightly coped to the centre, but this only stretches as far as the surcoat hem. The remainder (most of the effigy) is shown without a slab, although a surprisingly coherent rectangular plan is still achieved that looks suspiciously like the proportions of the original block. The condition or situation of all five figures is such that their base slabs may have been lost, but that begs the question of how they have disappeared so thoroughly. To have been entirely removed but produce this regular effect is particularly puzzling in respect of the stone figures, a question that might only be resolved if it were possible to fully examine the undersides.

Base slabs appear at first sight to be a routine and uncontroversial aspect of an effigy. They can, however, be surprisingly revealing and a valuable source of information, helping to chart a monument's history. In common with other strands of evidence they can also pose further questions.

2b.ii Gablettes

As described above, the majority of effigies are carved on a base slab. In contrast, only a limited number are made with a canopy over their heads, termed gablettes. Country-wide, they are fairly common but Yorkshire only has twenty-six. In some cases, an effigy is presented as if it were a statue in a canopied recess. Archbishop Walter de Gray in York Minster has a steep, straight-sided gable, enclosing a trefoil arch, which frames the prelate's head (Fig. 49). It rests on side shafts with moulded capitals of the mid-thirteenth century. The impression of a statue in a niche is even stronger at Wistow (Fig. 50), where the lady has a solid, flower-decorated foot support like the base of a niche and the side shafts are carved with blind architectural details. The same is true of the Goxhill lady with her elaborate triple canopy, side shafts and a solid base, reminiscent of some monumental brasses (Fig. 2). The ladies at Aldbrough (Fig. 21), Garton-on-the-Wolds (Fig. 132) and Patrington (Fig. 273) are the only other effigies with side shafts to support their gablettes. The latter is minimalistic, without any crocketing or capitals and the arch is an ogee trefoil rather than cusped. The plain side shafts function merely as edging to the composition. Patrington's gablette is pinched between the side shafts, which is a recognisable architectural form and shared with other Wolds figures at Beeford and Winestead (*4c.vi*). They lack the pinnacled side shafts but do have leafy crocketing. Aldbrough has more detail with moulded capitals and bases and the curve of the arch is very like those on the sedilia at Beverley Minster. All the other gablettes act like a shelter above the effigy's head and are unsupported. They show considerable variety even when from the same grouping, particularly so with ten of the Series A/B figures, the earliest having highly individual compositions. The smaller knight at Coverham Abbey has a large straight-sided gable with multiple cusping and a small figure for the surviving corbel (Fig. 51). The crocketing is on only one side and, in its weathered state, resembles a row of balls. The other side is covered by naturalistic foliage representing a wood, the hoped-for refuge of the fleeing stag beside his shield. Similar globular crocketing, although with a little more detail remaining, occurs on the mutilated gablette of the Bedale ecclesiastic. It is thoroughly integrated into the monument's design and includes a panel of the seated Christ facing west (Fig. 168). The Series A/B figures from Fountains Abbey (Fig. 182) and Scarborough have similar gablettes with a broad central arch flanked by small side arches. Fountains shows these as miniature gablettes: straight-sided over a slightly ogee trefoil arch between side pinnacles. Both Fountains and Scarborough have flat tops roughly finished, as though not intended to be seen (Fig. 52). They also have moulded cornices, decorated with flowers at Fountains. The Series B figures at Bedale (Plate 54), Goldsborough, Howden and Norton have freely carved gablettes with their arches becoming more of a sinuous wave (at Goldsborough with a groined interior, Fig. 187). The carver uses them as vehicles for a range of features, including shields hanging from pegs and crouching, bearded men as corbels. As on the side arches of Fountains, he is experimenting with the ogee curve, which appears as a minor upward turn at the apex of the arch in all four places. Bedale alone has ballflower around the arch, something not seen elsewhere in the county, which again shows this exceptional carver experimenting with the very latest style motifs. The exterior ribs on the tops of some of these gablettes even hint at vaulting. The Thornhill knight, although very much a one-off figure, has the same form of gablette as Fountains Abbey and Scarborough, flat topped, with a cornice and side arches but crocketing of extremely simple, angular stylised leaves not seen elsewhere. Just one more effigy has a gablette with side arches, the Thornton Dale lady (Fig. 53). They mirror the form of the main arch (cinquefoil within a straight-sided gable) but only half of these arches is shown, the remainder seemingly buried in the base slab. This gablette is also unusual in having a second (trefoil) arch behind. Perhaps designed to provide some depth to the carving, it may indicate a rear opening or just a back panel. Two of the Hornby effigies

Fig. 49 York Minster. Archbishop Walter de Gray.

Fig. 50 Wistow. 'Dame Margery'.

Fig. 51 Coverham Abbey. Smaller knight's gablette.

Fig. 52 Fountains Abbey. Rough dressing of the flat gablette top.

Fig. 53 Thornton Dale. Lady's gablette.

have gablettes. The single lady inside the church dates from the late thirteenth century and is an early case, predated only by Archbishop de Gray. Unfortunately, it is badly mutilated and difficult to make out. The knight's gablette seems quite simple but its appearance is misleading because both sides have been trimmed back and its full shape can no longer be seen. Unusually the lady at his side, which is otherwise closely related, has no gablette.

The overall picture suggests gablettes were not considered an important aspect of effigial representation. They were favoured by the Series A/B carver and also amongst the Wolds Series, which together account for just over half the relatively small total. Other than that, they are just seen on a few one-off effigies. The clients were clearly not requesting them but they seem to have formed part of the repertoire of particular carvers, who indulged themselves.

2b.iii Clothing and armour

Yorkshire's effigies present an under-exploited wealth of information on clothing and armour, a rich resource for their better understanding. The three-dimensional nature of effigies can help explain how things were made or worn, although the evidence is tempered by wide variations in quality. Some, such as the lady at Church Fenton (Fig. 54), give the impression that the sculptor was in full command of his subject, understanding the materials he was depicting, the way the clothing was constructed and the underlying anatomy. Others, such as the figure at Loversall (Fig. 55), seem quite well carved but show no such insight – witness the rigid folds of the skirt, and instead of depicting the belts and fittings of the waist area, everything is hidden behind the shield and arm. A third, and even less competent craftsman, carved the civilian at Stainton (Fig. 248), which is little more than a hunched shape. Consequently, the quality of an effigy must be a primary factor in assessing its reliability, but the value of the best is beyond price.

Fig. 54 Church Fenton. Unknown lady.

Fig. 55 Loversall. Male civilian with shield.

Fig. 56 Sprotbrough. FitzWilliam knight's curious poleyn.

A factor to be considered is whether innate conservatism may have influenced the design, leading, for example, to a generic 'knight', which was not a reflection of current appearance. This might stem from a sense of propriety; because someone was comfortable with the styles of their active years; a desire to represent the person in their actual armour; or even as an idealised figure. Claude Blair (1992, p. 14) noted a discrepancy between developed plate armour entering common use by the end of the thirteenth century and its first depiction on effigies in the 1330s, posing problems of interpretation. Other authors have made similar observations. Philip Lankester (2011) in discussing the chalice held by the effigy of a priest at Barton-Upon-Humber (Lincolnshire), found it did not fit within the published classification. He concluded that chalice shapes on monuments were liable to be of archaic form. They should perhaps be seen as pictograms, shorthand for the person's status. On the other hand, Tobias Capwell (2015) accepted that the armour on fifteenth-century effigies relates to their period of production, as did Margaret Scott (1986) for civilian clothing. The overall message is cautionary. Care needs to be exercised in assessing any effigy and judgements must be broadly based, not dependant on single factors. Nevertheless, the thorough study of a large corpus such as the effigies of Yorkshire, presents opportunities to advance understanding that are not present when dealing with individual or small numbers of figures. One example is the discussion of sword belts (below), which uses the Yorkshire evidence to suggest a situation more complex than the established view acknowledges.

Some effigies have an archaic appearance that can be challenging to interpret. For example, the Sprotbrough knight (*3g.ii*) combines several anachronistic features, even though the same highly competent sculptors turned out a particularly memorable effigy as his female companion (Fig. 241; Plate 34). The relatively advanced, almost horizontal sword belt is coupled with a simple primitive-looking scabbard attachment and the length of the mail coif, covering the shoulders, would be more appropriate for an aventail fitted to a bascinet. The poleyns are most strange (Fig. 56) apparently rivetted directly on to the mail chausses, with the lower edges serrated, possibly just left uncarved when the adjacent mail links were cut. This may be a confused attempt to create the appearance of old-fashioned armour. The Romaldkirk knight, discussed in Section 2a.v, does seem to be a deliberate attempt at archaism and suggests that such an approach was, on occasion, considered appropriate.

Any such deviations from what might be considered normal would have needed to satisfy the patrons. A design would not have been approved and payment sanctioned unless the effigy met the patrons' expectations. This raises the question of what a patron's expectations might have been in the thirteenth and fourteenth centuries. While some testators would be content with (for example) 'an image of an armed man', others sought a more personalised approach. For instance, when Philip Darcy asked to be buried at Guisborough Priory in 1399, he directed, 'super sepulchram meum lapidem marmoreum operatum cum duabus ymaginibus de laton, ad similitudinem mei et Elizabetae uxoris meae' [over my burial, a marble stone worked with two images of latton in the likeness of myself and Elizabeth my wife] (*Test. Ebor*. I, p. 255). The convincing portrayal of clothing and attempts at portraiture (*4b.vi*) amongst the Yorkshire corpus suggests a desire for verisimilitude could be a factor in the thirteenth and fourteenth centuries just as much as amongst Capwell's fifteenth-century effigies depicted in actual armours (Capwell 2015, pp. 36–38).

Realism was key for some Yorkshire sculptors, who were sufficiently talented to faithfully reproduce what they observed. Their carvings record not only the form of the costume and armour but also show constructional details. One example of such attention to detail appears on the alabaster figures at Hull where the sculptor shows a knowledge of needlework, each of the figures displaying two different buttonhole techniques, appropriate to the garments and their fabrics. The lady's tight-fitting cote sleeve has rouleau loops (Fig. 57) while her loose surcoat has buttonholes cut through the fabric and worked with thread (Fig. 58). Her husband's rather heavier garments are handled differently, his supertunic has bound buttonholes (Fig. 59) while his hooded cloak's buttonholes are on a facing (Fig. 60). Although worn, the four sets of buttons are also different.

Hair arrangements can be instructive. The hairnet worn by Swine's Magnesian Limestone lady, clearly shows its structure, based on a tight head band, with clusters of beads or pearls at the intersections and on the band. She must wear a bourrelet underneath, as the net follows its contours. At Church Fenton, Ryther and Kirby Sigston, the ladies' hair is dressed into plaits that are brought forwards, up and over rounded cauls or nets of hair, towards the top of the head. The plaits naturalistically diminish in thickness, at Church Fenton crossing on the crown, outlined under the veil. Ribbons take their place at Ryther. Bands or ribbons run across the foreheads, under the veils, probably to help keep the cauls in place and they all have narrow fillets overall, to secure their veils. In a different arrangement, the Felixkirk lady wears two veils with frilled edges and a third, folded on top of her head (Fig. 61). Hull had multiple veils, supported high above her forehead, as at Harpham, presumably on a frame. The topmost layer at Hull seems narrow, running only over the top of the head, and is secured at the front with at least one round-headed pin, possibly because there was a risk this narrow strip would fly up or slide backwards. The Hornsea lady has her hair in a net, dressed to each side in sharp points so that, taken with the tightly stretched wimple, the overall shape is triangular. Her veils are pinned through into the corners of the hair and, notably, the wimple covers her mouth (Fig. 62). This adaption is extremely rare on effigies but occasionally encountered in sculpture and painting, instances including heads on the Southwell Minster pulpitum and a particularly similar label stop in the north nave aisle of York Minster. Might it be an arrangement for travelling, in the way that desert dwellers often cover their mouths to protect against dust?

The knightly figures too exhibit much important detail and can contribute to understanding the construction and development of armour. Until *c.* 1350 they are all mail clad with varying degrees of additional defences but in two cases the mail itself attracts attention. They are Sir William Bruce (d. 1345) at Pickering (Plate 9) and the closely related figure at Bedale (Fig. 63), attributed to Thomas Sheffield (d. 1346) but displaying unidentified arms (DBA 2, p. 344). In both cases the mail is shown with each link carved twice but slightly out of register like a photographic double image. It has been described as 'double interlinked chain mail' (I'Anson 1927, pp. 61–62). Elsewhere in England this peculiar form is almost unknown but Stothard's drawing of the de l'Isle figure at Rampton (Cambridgeshire) has just one row of links carved in this manner (Stothard 1832, pl. 21). The way it is carved gives the appearance of a double ring being used for each link. It may perhaps be a variant form in the same way the neckband of a mail collar in the British Museum collection (1856.07–01.2244) differs by each link passing through six others instead of the usual four (Richardson 2016, pp. 30–31). Meyrick's reconstruction of Sir Robert de Mauley's effigy (Meyrick 1845, p. 248), formerly in York Minster, shows it was also clad in double ring mail except for the top of the head (Fig. 64). Meyrick thought that the coif changed from double to single mail at the point where it would have been covered by the helm but this seems unlikely. Only one small piece of the head remained (top centre) together with the left shoulder, including the lower edge of the coif.

What Meyrick illustrates, but fails to recognise, is that de Mauley is wearing a mail-clad skull-cap or *secret* over his coif and it is this rigid plate defence which carries the single mail. The drawing has a sharp division between the two, rather

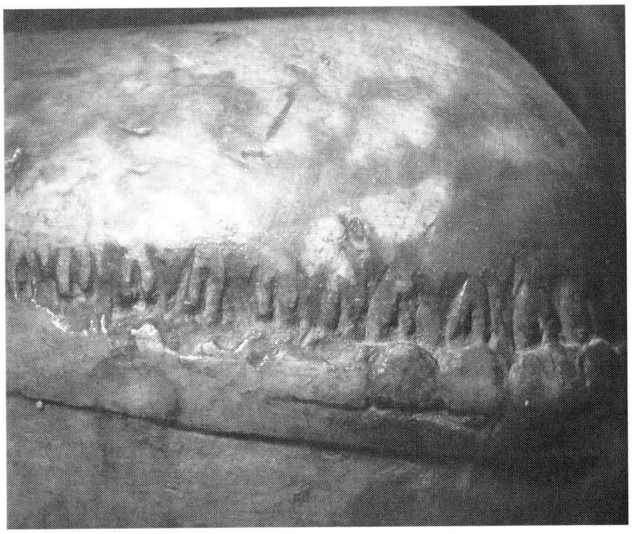

Fig. 57 Needlework features at Holy Trinity, Hull. Lady's rouleau loop buttonholes.

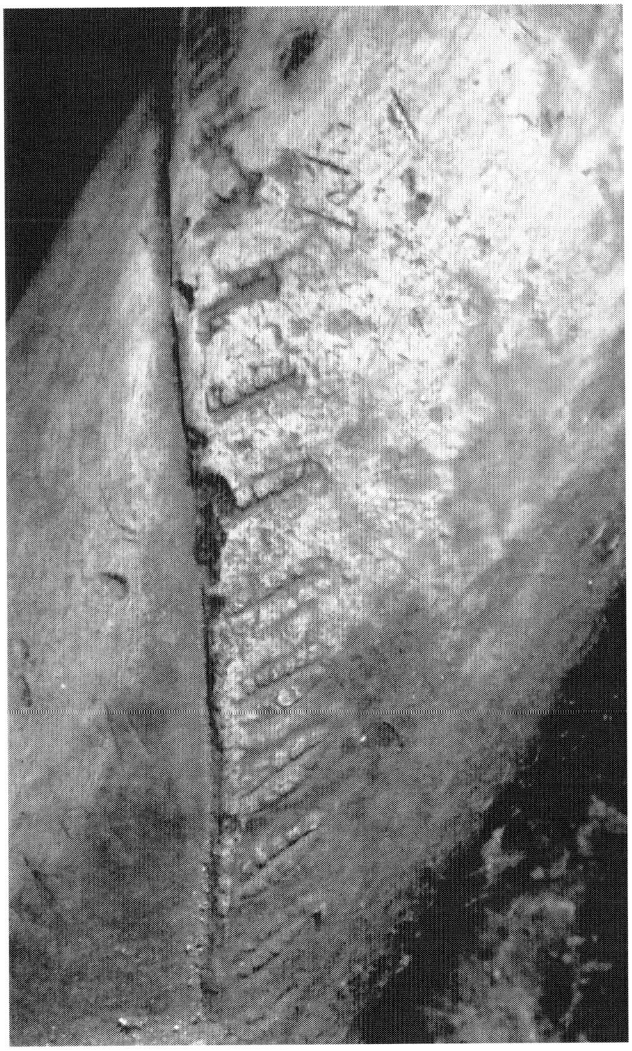

Fig. 58 Needlework features at Holy Trinity, Hull. Lady's thread-finished buttonholes.

Fig. 59 Needlework features at Holy Trinity, Hull. Man's lined buttonholes.

Fig. 60 Needlework features at Holy Trinity, Hull. Man's buttonholes on a facing.

Fig. 61 Felixkirk. Johanna de Walkingham's stacked veils.

Fig. 62 Hornsea (ex Nunkeeling). Lady's wimple covering her mouth.

Fig. 63 Bedale. 'Sheffield' knight with double ring mail.

Fig. 64 York Minster. Lost de Mauley effigy, Meyrick's drawing.

Fig. 65 Whorlton. Knight with bascinet modelled beneath his coif.

than the more usual fillet or browband holding the mail coif in place. The only evidence for the upper part of the coif itself being of single mail is a tiny area above the left eye where the links are not well shown. Meyrick is not alone in failing to recognise the mail-clad skull-cap as it does not seem to have appeared in print, although Claude Blair suspected such head gear existed (Blair, pers. comm. late 1990s). Something of this nature appears on four Yorkshire knights: the Series D figures at Felixkirk, Ilkley, Stillingfleet and Winteringham. The first three are well shaped, fitting tight to the brow and curving down at the sides over the ears, while Winteringham is simpler, lacking the shaped sides (Plates 10–13). Three layers can be seen: the mail coif under what in life was presumably the skull-cap's lower edge and finally, the outer covering of mail. The theoretical construction of the skull-cap in hardened leather rather than iron might explain why both an inner layer (the coif inside) and an outer cladding of mail was thought necessary. Leather was much less expensive than a comparatively large single piece of iron at a time when almost all iron bloomeries were small and capable of producing only 1–2 kg blooms of workable iron at most, and often less, but it was much more vulnerable to puncture and laceration than iron. An additional mail facing would certainly have been an easy way of enhancing a piece of leather armour. In each case the mail facing of the skull-cap follows a very different alignment to that of the coif, making it explicit that they are separate pieces of equipment. Mark Beabey found his experimentally fabricated hardened leather headpiece surprisingly satisfactory (Beabey & Richardson 1997). Made using a combination of water and locally-applied heat, it was hard, strong and durable. An outer layer of mail would enhance its viability.

It is possible other Yorkshire effigies were intended to show this feature because, although both Acaster Malbis and Slingsby have the appearance of wearing coifs with fillets, they do have changes in orientation in the mail, either side of the 'fillet'. The knight at Harrington in Lincolnshire also appears to wear a coif constrained by a fillet but, above and below it, the orientation of the mail changes through a right angle. This form of defence is likely to have been widely adopted and can be seen on brasses at Buslingthorpe (Lincolnshire) and Pebmarsh (Essex). In both cases the bottom edge is low on the brow and curves down at the sides just like a plate bascinet but the brass makers have not shown any change in direction of the mail, which is in any case very stylised. Another variant head covering is seen at Whorlton, which has no carved mail. It would have been originally represented by gesso and/or paint, but it is evident from the modelling of the sides of the head that the mail coif was being worn over a shaped bascinet (Fig. 65). This arrangement was discussed by Claude Blair with reference to the wooden knight at Abergavenny (1994, pp. 37–80).

Fig. 66 Sutton-on-Hull. Knight's sabatons with leather scales.

The Series D knights have very similar poleyns, all moulded with the same design. Winteringham's also have a row of stitching along the bottom margin that seems to fix the moulded layer to an inner element, just visible below the edge of the outer face (Plate 15). The use of stitching indicates that the poleyns were made of leather. Very little fourteenth-century leather armour has survived but there are documentary references from the late thirteenth century and inventories of armour from the Tower of London show leather pieces were more numerous than metal in the mid-fourteenth century (Richardson 2017, pp. 50–51). They include at least 115 pairs of leather poleyns in the 1353–1360 account. Studies of important excavated deposits from the Netherlands, have concluded that much about leather armour is still not understood and that since the material was found in high status contexts, leather 'was not a poor man's solution for metal plate armour' (Rijkelijkhuizen & Volken 2017, p. 75). Indeed, the Tower accounts reinforce the latter point since they detail leather pieces carrying the royal arms. Sir Robert de Mauley, the subject of Meyrick's drawing, was Steward of the future Edward III's household and was able to afford burial in York Minster, so he certainly could not be considered 'a poor man'.

Other pieces of armour are also instructive. The Sutton knight has distinctive sabatons (Fig. 66), the vamp composed of scales. They are similar in appearance to the surviving armoured leather gauntlet in the Tradescant Collection of the Ashmolean Museum (Waterer 1981, p. 85). Waterer compared it with the scale gauntlets on the monumental brass at Buslingthorpe (Lincolnshire), which he thought would also have been of leather. Sutton's sabatons may also have been leather. Many Series B (*4c.ii*) shields, such as Goldsborough and East Harlsey, depict the inside padding in great detail. The upper part of the shield is covered by a substantial material, probably intended for thick leather. This covers padding that is thicker at the top, by the shoulder, tapering down towards the lower edge. The lining is attached to the shield with dome-headed fixings that resemble upholstery nails. Such attention to detail provides a valuable insight into what people were actually wearing and using during this period in Yorkshire, creating opportunities for better understanding what is seen elsewhere.

Clarity is not an inevitable outcome of more information. This is certainly true of the complex subject of sword belts and the methods used to attach scabbards, which were evolving during the first half of the fourteenth century. Yorkshire's effigies show a considerable variety, some of which have attracted comment in the literature (*A8*) when they have been used to date the effigies. Sword belts in general have received little recent attention, so it is worthwhile examining the subject in some detail. The primary, and still generally accepted, account was set out by Albert Hartshorne in 1891 in a paper for the Royal Archaeological Institute. Derived primarily from effigies but also from other contemporary depictions, his dating was based on that accepted at the time for his source material. Nothing systematic seems to have appeared since to refine, update or challenge Hartshorne's narrative, although Claude Blair argued (1959) that ring lockets were introduced from the first decade of the fourteenth century and were widely adopted by *c.* 1325. Hartshorne used only two examples from Yorkshire: the effigy of William of Hatfield (to illustrate the emergence of horizontal hip belts) and the figure now in the Temple Church, London. The Temple Church figure puzzled Hartshorne, because he was relying on Hewitt's dating of *c.* 1285 but it combined a surcoat design he understood as being of *c.* 1300 with a ring-locket attachment method he regarded as fully developed and likely to date from the 1320s. Sadly, he did not cover the many attachment variations of the Yorkshire corpus, such as hinges (*e.g.* at Ingleby Arncliffe, Fig. 67) and the hybrid methods like the partly hinged and partly wrapped arrangement on the Saltmarshe figure at Howden. He did, however, acknowledge two very important points. The first is that new methods did not overtake old in a smooth transition:

> But fashions in sword belts, as in all other things, overlap and run both ways into each other. Some men, as we have seen, preferred the old, while those more travelled, or more fashionably-minded, brought in the new style. (Hartshorne 1891, pp. 330–31)

However, he may not have anticipated the extent to which this is shown in Yorkshire, if not elsewhere. The second underlying principal that should be borne in mind is that:

> Throughout the whole story of the sword belt it may be taken for granted that its fashion was influenced, as was that of the armour, by the military events of the time. So great a tactician as Henry V, for instance, the greatest soldier of his age, is not likely to have ignored these particulars. (Hartshorne 1891, p. 337)

To the modern military historian this process of learning lessons from training and combat is very familiar. However, it is only in recent years that these principles have been rigorously applied to medieval armour. Tobias Capwell's 2015 ground-breaking study of English armour in the first half of the fifteenth century looks at its development in the light of contemporary English tactics and fighting practices but the fourteenth century lies outside its remit except as background. A comparable study of sword belts has not yet been carried out.

The following analysis is drawn from the Yorkshire examples. The belts vary from the relatively narrow (*c.* 1″–1½″, 2.5–4 cm) at Treeton, Bulmer, Jervaulx and the most easterly knight at West Tanfield to 3″ (7.6 cm) or more at East Harlsey, Norton and on the de Goldesburgh under the arch. The horizontal hip girdles of the later fourteenth century are at the wider end of the scale, with the exception of the complete alabaster effigy at Pickering, which is composed of large-scale, open, chain links (Fig. 68). Horizontal hip girdles aside, there seems little correlation between width and date but belts do become shorter with time. In the first decades of the fourteenth century they can be very long indeed, with a variety of methods employed to manage the free end. At Romaldkirk, the end of the belt below the buckle hangs down to the knee, the end rests on the knee at Darrington, while at Bainton and Kirkby Fleetham, it reaches the calf. In all these cases, the end is uncontrolled, hanging directly from the buckle. The two complete effigies at Coverham show the end looped up and under the fastened section with the end lying loosely down outside the belt, from the point where it is restrained. Escrick, Fountains, Hauxwell, Temple Church and Scarborough are similar, while the eastern knight at West Tanfield shows the end looping outside and then being tucked through the fastened section. By far the most frequent arrangement is for the free end to be looped behind the sword hilt and left to hang on the left side, as at Burton Stather, Ilkley (Fig. 211), Goldsborough (on chest), Hornsea, Nunnington, Whorlton, Womersley and many others. A few with this pattern (Series B only) have the end lapped over the scabbard, the underside exposed, or the very tip on the edge of the shield. Some are far more practical than others, but the variations seem to be a matter of the sculptor's choice. The shortest buckled belts date from the middle of the fourteenth century as they are all worn over short-fronted surcoats with side splits and the men carry relatively small shields (Barnburgh, Bedale, Pickering and Sutton). They are worn rather differently, adjusted to fit much more closely and without long trailing ends. This is consistent with the sleeker outline of the fitted surcoats and the process that culminated in horizontal hip girdles.

Fig. 67 Ingleby Arncliffe. South side knight's hinged scabbard attachment.

Fig. 68 Pickering. de Roucliffe knight's chain-style sword belt.

Belts both with and without mounts span the corpus, from the thirteenth century until the point when horizontal hip belts with large mounts set edge to edge become the norm. The mounts themselves can be shaped bars, with or without central holes, discs, flowers or geometric shapes. There are also three instances of lion masks, the dating of which has proved controversial (*A8*). Some of the types occur only on a small number of related effigies. For instance, the discs (some retaining the central pimples they all seem likely to have had originally) appear on Series C effigies at Darrington, Leeds, Spofforth and Goldsborough (Figs 69, 70). These effigies are so close they must have been carved within a short period and emanate from a common source. The only other discs are at Hauxwell (where they are chunkier and lack the central pimple) and at Hornsea but these are domed and more like miniature bosses. Flowers are well represented as mounts, all slightly different except those on the two figures at Ingleby Arncliffe which, as in so many other aspects, are a pair. Here, the four-petal flowers seem to have a central trumpet and look suspiciously like four-petalled daffodils (wild daffodils famously still flourish in the vicinity).

Fig. 69 Goldsborough. Series C knight's sword belt with disc mounts.

Fig. 70 Leeds. Series C knight's sword belt.

Fig. 71 West Tanfield. Knight in recess, showing shield insets on sword belt.

The most exotic belt belongs to the figure under the arch at West Tanfield, which had small inset shields (Fig. 71), now lost, which may represent something real (*4b.v*). It is very reminiscent of the embroidered English belt of *c.* 1254 found in the tomb of Infante Ferdinando de la Cerda of Castile (d. 1275) in Las Huelgas de Burgos (Spain) (Wild 2011; Collin 1955). Although not a sword belt (Blair 1993, n. 14; Wild 2011), the small shields filling the width are close in proportion to those at West Tanfield except that there, the shields are oriented along its length whereas most of those in Spain lie across it. However, the shields on the prominent strap end of the Spanish example run the same way as those at West Tanfield and are interspersed with groups of three jewels just as the shields at West Tanfield are separated by groups of three insets, rather like the triple stops of a Lombardic letter inscription. This highly unusual belt with its expensive inserts seems unlikely to have been an invention of the carver and more probably a request of the patron, perhaps to represent an actual artefact of significance. The likelihood is supported by the theme being carried onto the visible (right) chamfer of the slab, where another set of more than thirteen shields were inset (*4b.v*). The Burgos belt probably dates from the mid-thirteenth century. Might the West Tanfield belt be of similar date and represent a treasured heirloom?

The purpose of these belts was to support the sword in its scabbard and different means of attachment were employed. The first method described by Hartshorne involved both parts of the belt fixed to the scabbard at the same point, later changing so the suspension points were separated to allow the sword to hang at an angle, the two points connected by a system of thongs (usually termed 'diagonal thong'). This he saw as giving way to the ring lockets, the two parts of the belt attached to the scabbard by metal fittings, again at first using a single position before lowering the rear section. He saw the progression as continuing by adding a dagger to the opposite hip, suspended from the sword belt, before settling for many years as a very heavy horizontal hip belt, densely set with plaques. Hartshorne was well aware that transitions of style resulted in periods of overlap but within a clear progression. The Yorkshire evidence suggests differing methods persisted as alternatives, for decades.

The simplest form of attachment, for ease of reference, we have termed 'wrapped' (Downing uses 'band'). Commentators have tended to describe the method as the belt attached to a band around the scabbard. In at least one surviving example this is indeed the case but the depictions on effigies that we have examined seem more to represent the belt wrapped around the scabbard (forming the band) and secured, perhaps to itself. The earliest wrapped form occurs as both a single position and two, one above the other but close together. Hartshorne's chronology saw the single position earlier than the double and yet in Yorkshire, single point wraps occur in the 1340s at Sprotbrough (*3g.ii*), perhaps *c.* 1330 at Bainton and on Saltmarshe at Howden, in conjunction with a hinge, such as are seen in the 1340s on Series E effigies. (This comparison casts doubt on our previous *c.* 1322 date for the Saltmarshe effigy, see Badham, Gittos & Gittos 1996.) In contrast, the sword handling torso at Coverham, likely to date from the thirteenth century, appears to have a double wrap. Whilst some of these wrapped attachments were an easy option for a less competent carver, that cannot be true of all.

The system of tied thongs was addressed by Claude Blair (1993), who provided a detailed account and a more up to date view of its period of currency. On English effigies he saw it as being introduced after *c.* 1300 and a roughly contemporary development of the ring attachment method. It is well represented in Yorkshire during the second quarter of the fourteenth century and many of the attachments are complicated affairs. The Kirkby Fleetham belt (Fig. 164) is split into three thongs all of which are woven straight through slits in the scabbard (with no diagonal element) and that at Nunnington must be modelled on it. Woven thongs (four) are shown on the related Series C trio of Leeds, Spofforth and Goldsborough – three of the group as have the pimpled disc belt mounts. On these, the top two thongs wrap around the scabbard while the lower two drop diagonally before weaving through slits in the rear belt where it crosses the scabbard. In other cases, such as Winteringham (Fig. 72) and Kildwick, a small thong from the top of the belt threads through slits just below the lip of the scabbard rather like a drawstring. At Winteringham and Nunnington, amongst other places, the lowest two thongs are used to stitch, or whip, the end of the rear belt into position around the scabbard. The permutations are many and ingenious.

The ring locket attachments shown on Yorkshire effigies have attracted some comment in the literature (*e.g.* Blair 1995) but the purpose here is simply to record what is depicted. Some nineteen figures certainly show this feature while another (Routh) may have done but is so eroded as to leave doubt about what was intended. Some examples (Bedale, East Harlsey, Escrick, Fountains, two at Hazelwood, Metham at Howden, Norton and Temple church) either show or imply that both front and back suspension points are opposite one another, mounted on a band around the scabbard close to its top. Amotherby also has mounts on a band but one sited an inch or so above the other. At Barnburgh, Butterwick, Pickering, Ryther, Slingsby, Sutton-on-Hull and Whorlton, the positions are staggered with several inches between suspension points while at Slingsby the front belt is attached via a single point but the rear belt has two (Fig. 73). The suspension loops at Barnburgh, Pickering, Ryther and Sutton-on-Hull are part of broad bands. All except Barnburgh have carved decoration. At Butterwick, the loops seem to be part of quite delicate clasps mounted on slender bands. The arrangement at Selby is very odd (Fig. 74). One side of the scabbard seemingly

Fig. 72 Winteringham. Thong scabbard attachment.

Fig. 73 Slingsby. Complex scabbard attachment.

Fig. 74 Selby Abbey. Scabbard attachment.

Fig. 75 Pickering. de Bruce effigy's belt with twisted wire ring.

has two rings but on the other side, the belt must be directly attached. Slingsby has another variation in which a ring on the rear belt meets two suspension points on the scabbard several inches apart through small intermediate spacers with loops at either end, looking rather like the double ended sections of a child's wooden railway track. It is most like the arrangement shown on the effigy of a de Berkeley in Bristol Cathedral and that on the sword recovered from the burial of Cangrande della Scala, ruler of Verona, who died in 1329 (Oakeshott 1964, pl. 46A). However, the Slingsby depiction is far heavier than the other two, with large rings partially concealed within the loop fittings, themselves closely butted, which would have limited the arrangement's flexibility.

The Yorkshire scabbard suspension loops are all linked to looped fittings on the ends of the belt. Some (Barnburgh, Butterwick, Pickering, Ryther, Selby, Slingsby, Sutton-on-Hull and Whorlton) have intervening rings, an arrangement that would allow both belt and scabbard to lie flat. These rings are, for the most part, quite unobtrusive but those at Sutton-on-Hull and Pickering are a decorative, twisted wire design (Fig. 75). The majority of belts (Amotherby, Bedale, East Harlsey, Escrick, Fountains, Goldsborough, two at Hazelwood, Howden, Norton and Temple Church, all Series B), however, lack the intermediate ring so that the belt and scabbard fittings link directly to each other (Fig. 76). This seems an awkward arrangement that, since all the loops are quite small, would have restricted movement. The final method saw the scabbard attached directly to the belt but the mechanism is not visible. Its emergence seems to coincide with the appearance of the horizontal hip belt.

The arrangements depicted on Yorkshire effigies would make the swords hang in radically different ways: some vertically, some at a slight angle and some at a very sharp angle. This is likely to have implications for ease of use.

Fig. 76 East Harlsey. Variation of a locket scabbard attachment.

Similarly, the fit of the belts varies markedly, some snug while others are so slack they seem as if they would fall off if the effigy stood up. The tightest belts are the horizontal hip girdles of the end of the period, found in combination with closely fitted coat-armours and, except at Kirklington, without a shield. They have no obvious means of adjustment and no free belt end. The close-coupled scabbards hang vertically against the left leg, a position that has almost always forced the carver to undercut both hilt and blade, a vulnerability that has led to their almost total loss. Aldbrough, Darfield, Ripon and West Tanfield (alabaster) are all good examples. A few (Kirklington, Ripley and the Swine alabaster) are less rigidly straight, allowing either

Fig. 77 Swine. Alabaster knight's horizontal hip sword belt.

a little more room or are perhaps not so tightly adjusted. The Swine example is particularly interesting since not only is it looser but its mounts are spaced apart rather than being densely packed, suggesting that the girdle is only just arriving at its settled form (Fig. 77).

The short belts worn by the men in short-fronted surcoats have conventional buckles on short leathers and scabbards attached by the fully developed ring locket system, *i.e.* with an intermediate ring. The scabbard is depicted at a slight angle but given the suspension points are several inches apart, the angle would probably have been much more acute were the person upright. The sword is carried high, which may be, in part at least, by virtue of the belt adjustment. The belt follows the waist around the back of the figure but at the front, it curves down over the abdomen in an asymmetrical shape, that suggests it is being pulled by the weight of the sword. But this is a far less exaggerated line than that of most of the long belts. With these, the point at which the scabbard is attached is usually the lowest point, frequently as low as the groin, for instance at Amotherby, Felixkirk, Kildwick and Kirkby Fleetham. Howden (Saltmarshe) and Whorlton are even lower – over the left thigh. Not all wear their swords low, with notable exceptions at Hornsea, Leeds, Romaldkirk, Routh and Slingsby.

The picture emerging from the Yorkshire evidence is one of great variety, with only the broadest of trends perceptible. There seems little significance in belt width but a noticeable shortening in the middle of the fourteenth century. Decorative mounts were depicted throughout the period but sparingly and mostly on better-carved figures. Whilst new methods of scabbard attachment were devised early in the fourteenth century, in Yorkshire they were concurrent alternatives rather forming a sequence. This means that until the establishment of the horizontal hip girdle in the middle of the fourteenth century, scabbard attachments are unhelpful as a close dating tool. The evidence does, however, suggest that the subject warrants a thorough country-wide study, coupled with reconstructions of the different arrangements, to prove how they functioned. The Yorkshire corpus demonstrates the value of some effigies for understanding the clothing, arms and armour of the period. The better quality figures, in particular, depict detail that can add significantly to knowledge of the subject, the mail-covered skull-caps being an important example. The ability of some sculptors to distinguish the qualities of differing materials can also be very informative. More yet can be gleaned from the Yorkshire evidence but these examples serve to demonstrate the potential of this under-studied resource, not only in the county but countrywide.

2c Fate and fortune

2c.i Lost effigies

Although limited, the written evidence for what has been lost is a valuable adjunct to the surviving effigies. Whilst it has only been possible to trawl a small sample of the manuscripts, we have made extensive use of published material. Some sources are difficult to interpret, so for the sake of completeness, everything likely to be medieval has been included, without imposing the *c.* 1400 cut-off date. The accompanying list records what has been assembled. Certain effigies are well documented and even illustrated, whilst others are barely mentioned. In some instances, *e.g.* Sir Stephen Glynne's reference to several effigies in the churchyard at Batley (2007, p. 85), the number of figures is unclear. So the overall total is uncertain but we know of about forty. Descriptions, even when given, can be all too brief, such as the 1627 mention of the lost female effigy at Bulmer, 'Under an arch, a woman in full proportion' (Dodsworth, p. 178). However, antiquarian drawings of fourteen figures have been noted, allowing them to be better understood. Henry Johnston drew ten in 1669–70 and, judging by his many sketches of surviving effigies, they must be reasonably accurate. So, the male civilian on the churchyard wall of what is now St John the Evangelist, Micklegate (York), may have been a Series B product (Fig. 78). Three of Johnston's illustrations have been published: the lady at Gawthorpe Hall (Routh 1982), the Howden priest (Badham, Gittos & Gittos 1996) and the South Cave knight (Lankester 1993), as have two from Sir William Dugdale's *Yorkshire Arms*: Dean Langton from York Minster and the huge knight formerly in the churchyard at Leake (Badham 1980; 1981 respectively). One of the most interesting of Henry Johnston's unpublished drawings is the lady at Bolton Priory (C 13, fo. 84r). She was then (1669) upright against the chancel wall, reasonably complete and wearing a coronet (Fig. 79). Johnston believed she represented Cecilia de Romilly, co-founder of the Priory in 1120, and quoted the associated legend but, if so, it must have been retrospective. Later published sources contribute

Fig. 78 York, St. John the Evangelist, Micklegate. Johnston's drawing of lost civilian effigy (C 14, fo. 104r).

Fig. 79 Bolton Priory. Johnston's drawing of lost lady (C 13, fo. 84r).

Fig. 80 Doncaster, St. George. Jackson's illustration of lost semi-effigial male civilian.

two semi-effigial monuments, from the Carmelite Friary in York and Doncaster, St George. The latter was only a fragment and is known from the illustration by James Bell published in 1855 by John Jackson (Fig. 80). Some of the accompanying cross slab pieces still exist in the crypt vault, confirming that his drawings are reasonably accurate. It shows the bust of a man wearing a cote with hanging sleeves, coif and hood. The edges of the recess were elaborately cusped and this was evidently a monument of good quality.

Three effigies lost from York Minster were all of note. The extremely rare cast bronze for Dean Langton (d. 1279) was presumably a casualty of the Civil War, having been recorded by Dugdale (*c.* 1641) but lost by 1690. The other two survived until the great fire of 1829 and published drawings include Drake (1736, p. 491 – both) and Britton (1819, pl. XXXVI – military only). The knight was identifiable by his heraldry as Sir Robert de Mauley (dead by March 1331). It was smashed in 1829, some pieces being used in a rockery before Sir Samuel Meyrick rescued them and took them to his chapel at Goodrich Court (Herefordshire). They were subsequently lost but Meyrick had used them to produce a detailed reconstruction drawing (Fig. 64) for his article on the effigy (Meyrick 1845). The male civilian must also have perished in 1829 but is known from Henry Johnston's *c.* 1670 sketch as well as that published by Drake, the two being largely in agreement. Drake portrays the figure as significantly bigger than de Mauley and, if so, it must have been well over life size (Fig. 81). This bearded man in a long robe has not attracted much attention, perhaps being regarded as just an oddity. However, Drake provided a clue for interpreting it. He admitted it puzzled him (Drake

1736, p. 490) but said he had 'read in a manuscript that Bishop Moreton gave it to the church as the image of Constantine the Great'. This was probably Thomas Morton, who was Bishop of Durham from 1632 to 1641. He was born in York and briefly retreated there when the Scots occupied Durham in 1640. He died in 1659 and, amongst his bequests, left a chalice to the parish of his birth (Oxford Dictionary of National Biography). His strong links with York would justify such a gift to the Minster.

There were once many effigies in Morton's cathedral churchyard at Durham, two of which were moved to Chester-le-Street in 1595 by John, Lord Lumley, under license from an earlier bishop (Liddy & Steer 2010, p. 212). This provides an interesting precedent for Morton doing the same thing at York under his own authority. The figures still at Chester-le-Street, like the three that remain in the churchyard, are carved in Frosterley marble and so the lost York civilian may well have been in this stone. An intriguing comparison can be made with a headless Frosterley marble effigy (Fig. 82) at the abbey of Arbroath (Scotland). They wear broadly similar long robes, with their feet on lions and have very similar waist belts, both with extremely long ends hanging down the front, almost to hem level. Both also have a large number of closely-spaced bar mounts like those commonly seen on sword belts. Taken together, it would be surprising if these features were just coincidental. The Arbroath effigy has been attributed to the founder of the abbey, William the Lion, King of Scotland, and a strong case made for its being set up by Robert the Bruce as a replacement for an earlier memorial (Gimson 1995). Gimson convincingly compares the Arbroath figure with surviving Frosterley marble effigies in County Durham, firmly establishing it in that context at the beginning of the fourteenth century. So, the York Minster civilian, is likely to have been a Frosterley marble monument, possibly commemorating a wealthy Durham citizen. The fact that he was considered an appropriate representation of Constantine the Great, who was proclaimed Emperor in York in 306, is a quirk of seventeenth-century antiquarianism. (The City's continuing fascination with this emperor is encapsulated in the bronze statue, commissioned by York Civic Trust and unveiled in the Minster precincts in 1998.)

Of the lost effigies, armoured figures are predominant (53%) followed by ladies (22%), with equal proportions for male civilians and ecclesiastics at 11% each and the unspecified types at Batley completing the picture. This means that the proportion of military effigies is greater than amongst the survivors, perhaps understandably, since the heraldry on military effigies attracted the antiquaries and those noted in the Scrope-Grosvenor roll were, by definition, heraldic (*A6b*). The lost effigies known to the authors are as follows.

- Adlingfleet (W.R.)
  Military (top half), sketch by Henry Johnston (C 14, fo. 158r).
- Batley (W.R.)
  'In the churchyard some ancient sepulchral effigies' (Glynne 2007, p. 85).
- Beverley Minster (E.R.)
  '… 3 tumbes … [one] … of white alabaster Idonea Lady Percy' (Leland & Toulmin Smith 1964, I, p. 46).
- Bolton Priory (W.R.)
  Lady, 1669 sketch by Henry Johnston (C 13, fo. 84r), Fig. 79.
- Bolton Percy (W.R.)
  'A knight lying very old…', recorded by Glover in 1584 (Foster 1875, p. 439).
- Bulmer (N.R.)
  '… a woman in full proportion', recorded by Dodsworth in 1627 (Dodsworth, p. 178).
- Carlton (in Balne) (W.R.)
  Military (head only), sketch by Henry Johnston (C 14, fo.153r).
- Coverham Abbey (N.R.)
  Military, representing Geoffrey Scrope – Scrope & Grosvenor Roll (Nicolas 1832, II, p. 277).
- Doncaster, St George (W.R.)
  Fragment of male civilian semi-effigial (Jackson 1855, pl. V, no. 35), Fig. 80.
- Easby Abbey (N.R.)
  Several military (including Henry & William Scrope) – Scrope and Grosvenor Roll (Nicolas 1832, II, p. 275).
- Escrick (E.R.)
  Alabaster knight and lady (Lankester 1993). They were recorded by Francis Thynne in 1589 (B. L. Sloane MS 3836), see also Gent (1733b, p. 59).
- Folkton (E.R.)
  '… an old monument a knight praying head on helm, feet on animal', see Torre 1692, fo. 914. (We are grateful to Sally Badham for this reference.)
- Gawthorpe Hall Chapel (W.R.)
  Lady – 1669 sketch by Henry Johnston (C 13, fo. 181r), see also Routh 1982.
- Guisborough Priory (N.R.)
  Remains of two military effigies, one in mail and the other found during work to clear away debris at the priory in 1867 (Bruce 1868), see also Oosterwijk 1998. One small fragment of mail displayed on the site in 2017 may be from this collection. William 4th Lord Latimer who died in 1381 was commemorated by an alabaster tomb that probably had an effigy (*A6*).
- Harpham (E.R.)
  'The portraiture of a knight cross leggd' noted by Nathaniel Johnston (C 27, fo. 219r).

Fig. 81 York Minster. Drake's illustration of the lost male civilian.

- Hemsworth (W.R.)
  'In the quyer the portraiture of a man crosslegd, on his shield 3 crescents, his wife lying by him. – Wandervile' recorded in 1618 (Dodsworth, p. 34). Dodsworth's editor suggests this was Sir Nicholas Wortley (d. 1360) and his wife Elizabeth Wannervile (d. 1382) who both willed to be buried at Hemsworth.

Fig. 82 Arbroath Abbey. Frosterley marble effigy attributed to William the Lion.

- Howden (E.R.)
Priest, identified by inscription as John de Metham, Rector of Patrington, many references and sketches, see Badham, Gittos & Gittos 1996.
- Leake (N.R.)
Huge military effigy, reputedly 9′ 6″ (2.9 m) in length, was in the churchyard, holding a naked sword upright in his right hand. Sketch of *c.* 1641 (Dugdale's *Yorkshire Arms*, College of Arms MS/RR14/c fo. 146v). See also Badham 1981 and Johnston 1669/71 (C 31, fo. 159r).
- Ledston Hall (W.R.)
'...and a Beautiful little chapel where a priest has been lying near the altar since Magna Carta' (Mee 1969, p. 164).
- Settrington (E.R.)
'A man in armor and his wife, in ful proportion', recorded in 1620 (Dodsworth, p. 167).
- South Cave (E.R.)
'A knight carved all in alabaster, lying as big as the life', recorded by Glover 1584/5 (Foster 1875, p. 439) and sketched by Henry Johnston in 1670 (C 14, fo. 254v), see also Routh 1987 and Lankester 1993.
- York: Carmelite Friary
Semi-effigial bust of an ecclesiastic set within the head of a foliate cross. It was found on the site of the friary in 1799 and had an inscription identifying him as Simon de Wyntringham. Illustrated by Cutts (1849, pl. xvi) and also in Gough Maps 34 (17,531) see Bertram (2004, p. 31) where it is judged to be an incised slab.
- York: Minster
Male civilian probably brought from Durham and destroyed in the fire of 1829, sketched by Henry Johnston (C 14, fo. 63r) and illustrated in *Eboracum* (Drake 1736, p. 491), Fig. 81.
- York: Minster
Cast bronze effigy of Dean Langton (d. 1279), probably destroyed in the English Civil War, drawing of *c.* 1641 (Dugdale's *Yorkshire Arms*, College of Arms MS/RR14/c fo. 111v) and copied in *Eboracum* (Drake 1736, p. 494), see Badham 1980.
- York: Minster
Military effigy of Robert de Mauley (d. 1331), broken in the fire of 1829. Sketched by Henry Johnston (C 14, fo. 24r), also illustrated in *Eboracum* (Drake 1736, p. 491) and Britton (1819, pl. xxxvi). A detailed reconstruction drawing appears in Meyrick 1845, p. 248, Fig. 64.
- York: St George Fishergate
Male civilian sketched by Henry Johnston in 1670 (C 14, fo. 110r). There is a gablette and an incomplete marginal inscription. Almost certainly an effigy because the praying hands are shown broken off, so must have been undercut.

Fig. 83 York, St. John the Evangelist, Micklegate. Johnston's drawing of lost lady (C 14, fo. 104r).

- York: St John the Evangelist, Micklegate
Male civilian and lady, sketched by Henry Johnston (C 14, fo. 104r), then on top of the churchyard wall. They were 'without that [south] door' when Sir Stephen Glynne visited in 1825 (Glynne 2007, p. 464), Figs 78, 83.
- York: St Martin Micklegate
Military – mention of tomb of one of the Scropes, their arms at his head and feet, in Scrope & Grosvenor Roll (Nicolas 1832, II, p. 279).

2c.ii Afterlife

Introduction

In the centuries since their creation, monuments have experienced many and varied types of afterlife. None have come through unscathed and many have been completely destroyed. Others have experienced abuse, neglect, reuse, appropriation and repairs of varying quality. This complex history means it is often challenging to interpret what remains but some appreciation of what has happened in particular cases is a useful beginning. The most universal problem is neglect. In order to maintain painted sculpture in pristine condition, constant maintenance is necessary, improbable over such a long period. Disrepair of the buildings can have devastating effects on monuments. Damp, whether caused by leaking gutters, a build-up of soil on the outside of a wall or a hole in the roof can very effectively destroy stone. Efflorescence causes limestone to crumble away and a high level of moisture will dissolve alabaster (*e.g.* the bottom of the lady at Hull). Buildings that fall into disrepair end up either becoming ruinous or being demolished. In this situation, monuments within the building will either be smashed or buried, sometimes to be recovered later, sometimes lost forever. Both happened at Bulmer, where most of the male effigy survives but the female does not (*2c.i*). However, many other issues have left their mark, including: iconoclasm, reuse, appropriation, disregard, unsatisfactory repairs and even linkage with folklore. Evidence for all of these processes can be found in Yorkshire and what follows uses particular examples as illustrations but the principles apply universally.

This section may present a rather gloomy picture but the future could be brighter because conservation schemes can radically improve a monument's prospects. Yorkshire examples include the rescue of a crumbling Purbeck marble effigy at Welton and conservation of the important monuments at Goldsborough. The ongoing project at Escrick will see the effigy raised off the floor and carefully re-sited. Advice for churches concerned about their monuments is available from the Conservation Section of the Church Buildings Council.

Iconoclasm

The reforming zeal of the sixteenth century resulted not only in the loss of some monuments but in damage, sometimes severe, to a high proportion of those that did survive. Losses from the religious houses dissolved in the 1530s are covered in Appendix A6 but an example is the damaged face of the Fountains Abbey effigy, viciously attacked by both sharp and blunt instruments (Fig. 228). Whilst early Reformation legislation was based on asset stripping, the mood changed after the death of Henry VIII (1547), when the hard-line reformers ruling in the name of Edward VI had in their sights all religious imagery (Aston 1988, pp. 254–69). The onus was placed on the clergymen to carry out the stipulations, expressly forbidding action by lay folk. The 1550 Injunction ordered that all images from churches had to be destroyed, even if they were now in private hands (p. 267). Although the movement against imagery was at first intended to apply to images being treated in a 'superstitious' manner, and tombs were specifically exempted, the strictures and penalties were such that it must have seemed prudent to many to be safe rather than sorry. This is likely to have been when devotional images found on tomb chest and canopies, such as saints and crucifixions, were damaged. Notably, the Howden chest panels are undamaged, probably because it was recognised that the figures represented family members rather than saints. Putting out the faces of all effigies may have been viewed as prudent, despite the legislation exempting depictions of commemorated people that were not objects of veneration. A temporary *volte face* under Mary saw some reparations to monuments. Aston cites the example of Rolvenden in Kent where 'the tomb stone of the old vicar' was ordered to be put back (Aston 1988, p. 286). But the problem remained and Elizabeth overturned the reforms of Queen Mary, taking pains to deal with the situation. In 1560, Elizabeth issued a proclamation forbidding further such action, 'A proclamation against breakinge or defacing of monumentes of antiquitie, beyng set up in churches or other publique places for memory and not for superstición' (Elizabeth I 1560). It insisted that damage already effected should be made good as far as was possible and set out penalties for non-compliance, which included responsibility for the reparations:

> ... to enioyne them vnder payne of excommunication, to repayre the same by a conuenient day, or otherwyse as the cause shall further require, ...

If the malefactor was not to be found or could not pay, responsibility was to devolve to the heirs (if they were dead) or to the church. Aston (1988, p. 318) questions the effectiveness of the provisions but it may be that many of the attempts to recreate missing elements and to disguise damage, stem from this period.

Monuments also suffered from the hazards of war, particularly during the Civil War. For instance, in Exeter Cathedral (*Mercurius Rusticus*, p. 259) the soldiery were said to have attacked heads, noses, hands and arms, particularly of bishops, since the Puritans did not acknowledge the traditional hierarchy. Faces are a constant target for religious fanatics and Spraggon (2003, p. 149) quotes a record of how, probably in 1641, a Captain Hunt had 'committed sacrilege in his own parish church ... lopping off the hands and pulling out the eyes from the Tombes and Monuments'. This is exactly the kind of damage so frequently encountered, with, for instance, axe cuts across the noses and eyes.

The process of putting out idolatrous images can be followed at Beverley Minster. Phillip Lindley covers iconoclasm in the Minster as part of his very thorough analysis of the Percy Tomb. He concludes that it was 'relatively unsystematic' and that it was 'inconsistent and incomplete, generally – though not always – concentrated on areas which were most readily accessible' (Lindley 2007, p. 169). This may have been the case with the architectural sculpture but there seems to have been a more considered approach when dealing with the monuments. The so called 'Sisters' Tomb' canopy at Beverley is generally in good condition, except that most of the delicate cusping round the arch is roughly broken off, presumably to remove religious imagery (probably angels). Two secular details have been spared, a male head and a bagpipe player. Also undamaged are the two spandrel figures on the inside of the canopy, depicting mythical creatures, one a mermaid and the other a long-haired, naked, human figure with the feet of a beast. The four intricately carved foliate springers for the arch are undamaged, even though they are more accessible, as are the four corbels still further below them, which are much larger than the cusp figures and most accessible of all. However, these four are again secular, being the busts of two men and two women. Given their proximity to the lost tomb chest, which was originally immediately below them, they are most likely members of the family of the person for whom the tomb was made. As such they were not a target for the iconoclasts and even their prominent noses remain intact. In contrast to the damage to the Sisters' Tomb, the much more elaborate Percy Tomb is remarkably well preserved, with every head of the canopy figures still present, including a wealth of religious imagery, mostly of angels. It seems to have largely escaped the ravages of time as well as the iconoclasts, but this is not the full picture because there is significant damage to the very lowest level of carving. Beneath the canopy, on the north and south walls there were four brackets, very similarly placed to the bust corbels on the Sisters' Tomb. They were positioned immediately above the original tomb chest (which was unfortunately removed in 1824) and probably supported four freestanding religious images keeping watch over the tomb itself. On the west side one of the brackets is missing and the other badly damaged, while the pair to the east have fared better. The more northerly one is undamaged and displays a violent conflict between a lion and a dragon. Its companion has a Biblical scene of the men casting dice for Christ's garments (Dawton 2000, p. 142). There is some damage to the heads of two of the men but all that remains of Christ is his feet and part of his robe. As Lindley suggests, the damage to these brackets could indicate a disorganised approach to the destructive process but another possibility is it commenced where the sculpture was most accessible but then stopped abruptly, perhaps by an authoritative intervention, and the canopy was spared.

However, damage does seem to have been done to both the medieval effigies remaining in the Minster. That of Provost Nicholas Huggate displays a panoply of heraldic and other decorative detail on his vestments but the two angels holding his pillow are badly mutilated, as is his face, which subsequently underwent an extremely crude remake, with two gouges for the eyes and a single cut for the mouth (Fig. 84). When this re-cutting was done is uncertain but it might have been in response to the proclamation of 1560 (see above), insisting that damage already done should be made good as far as was possible. This could also provide an explanation for what has happened to the fourteenth-century male civilian effigy. Crude repairs have been made to his hands and face, with new pieces of stone attached by over-large iron pins set in lead plugs, three for his hands and one for his nose (Fig. 85). The replacement hands and forearms remain but the nose has gone. The hands are carved from a stone of a lighter hue than that of the effigy and are seated on a prepared flat surface, where whatever remained of the original hands had been flushed off. Unfortunately, the smoothed area is too large, extending as a shallow slot through the middle of the hood draped round his neck, making it resemble a falling band of the late sixteenth century. This may even betray the date of the repairs, which is also suggested by the re-cutting of his shoes. His toes have been remodelled as square-cut, presumably as part of the tidying up process after they had been broken off. A second slot was cut in the middle of his face, so that the new nose could be attached and a channel created to run in the lead to retain the iron attachment pin. Part of the pin is still present in the midst of a lead puddle. The slot goes up into his forehead and was surprisingly large for just his nose, unless this was of such generous proportions that it is all the better for being lost. The heads of both the angels holding his lower cushion are lost but were repaired with new pieces of stone in a similar way. However, that on his right may have been constructed in this way from new because reddening of the stone implies hot mastic was used at some stage, which is inconsistent with the later repairs (*4b.ii*). Beverley's medieval monuments thus provide a fascinating insight into the process of iconoclasm in a major Yorkshire church, from the deliberate selective destruction of those images judged to be unacceptable, to an intervention or interruption preventing further harm and finally some rough and ready efforts to put right at least to some of the damage.

Fig. 84 Beverley Minster. Nicholas Huggate's recut face.

Two further examples illustrate these processes. The knight at Thornhill has a well carved new face, which has been carefully inserted to replace the original, presumably because of damage (Fig. 86). A good drawing of 1794 (Bertram 2004, frontispiece from MS Gough Drawings, a.2 fol. 123) shows it as it is now, so the face must have been replaced before then. Many more of Yorkshire's effigies exhibit signs of iconoclasm

Fig. 85 Beverley Minster. Male civilian, heavily repaired.

Fig. 86 Thornhill. Knight's new face.

but the lady at Birdsall is a noteworthy case. Six attendant figures kneel beside her, two angels bear up the tiny figure of her soul to heaven and her feet rest on a stag. This arrangement seems to have been a particular target for those bent on destroying images. All six attendants have lost their heads, as has one angel and even the stag. Her face has been damaged and subject to complete, crude, re-cutting (Fig. 87). The eyes are just circles and there is a short, stubby nose above a small, puckered mouth. To achieve this unhappy visage the whole surface must have been cut back, modifying her headdress beyond recognition. Even the tiny face of the soul figure has been put out but in the course of this orgy of destruction something was overlooked. The head and face of the left side angel remains intact. It is much less prominent than the other figures and maybe that is why it escaped notice during what was otherwise a very determined assault. All this evidence shows that the traumas of the Reformation and Civil War, with their concomitant iconoclasm, are encapsulated in a multitude of damaged details and crude reparations, the significance of which can so easily be missed.

Building changes

Building works can have a great influence on the monuments within a church. The evolution of the eastern chapels

Fig. 87 Birdsall. Lady with recut face.

of Howden Minster's south transept not only caused considerable rearrangement of the effigies there, but also resulted in the loss of a priest's effigy and serious damage to both the Metham figures. Stone was gouged from the knight's gablette to fit against a pillar and a partition inserted between them, resulting in a slice being cut from adjacent sides of both figures. After this brutal treatment the chapels suffered a long period of dereliction creating more damage due to weathering. They are now safely under cover and for details of this unhappy history see Badham, Gittos & Gittos 1996. The changing use of areas within a church could also have important implications for monuments, as with Sir John de Meaux's tomb at Aldbrough. In the late eighteenth century, the chapel housing his effigy became a school and, as a consequence, the effigy was 'much defaced by the boys' (Gough 1786–96, I.2, p. 180). The effigy clearly shows the results, with detail worn away, local damage and graffiti. The Roucliffe effigies at Pickering suffered a similar fate when their chapel served for a time as the school house. The knight now lies between his lady and the south wall but during the school era they must have been the other way about because he has the greater damage (Fig. 88). They are shown in this arrangement in an 1813 etching in the

Fig. 88 Pickering. Alabaster pair showing differential wear patterns.

collection of York Art Gallery (YORAG: R4745). Countless small, idle hands, feet and probably posteriors, have worn away the detail and achieved a high polish all down his left side. Some very good carving survives on his right but it is difficult to see as it now faces the wall. His wife is also worn on her left side but less badly. The remaining detail demonstrates that the figures were originally finished to a very high standard. In contrast to Aldbrough, there is very little graffiti, which might relate to how the boys at Pickering were managed. The very heavy wear exhibited by the Thorpe Basset priest (*A6f*) is of a different character. He probably spent time in the churchyard, partly buried in the ground and tilted a little to his left. The wear pattern suggests it was the passage of feet over many years that wore away several inches of stone from the upper surface. His left side, presumably buried somewhat deeper, retains some carved detail, including part of an angel and a short length of his stole with lightly incised decoration, providing a hint of how the figure might once have appeared. An extreme case of wear has been the lot of an effigy at Easby (Fig. 31). Found recently at the base of the churchyard wall during repair work, it is now inside the church. It has been reduced to a head, worn perfectly smooth, with only a little detail remaining at the sides. It may have been female but is too worn to be sure. The severity and evenness of the wear could be explained by its being walked over for a very long period.

Some damage has been caused when effigies have been unnaturally mounted upright. Although now back in his recumbent posture, the priest at Thwing spent time 'ridiculously placed erect' on the north side of the chancel (Allen 1829/31, IV, p. 92). To hold him safely in place it was evidently necessary to provide a clamp at the head end, for which a slot has been cut so deeply that it encroaches into his tonsure. At Weaverthorpe, the male civilian in the churchyard lay for many years in the grass but has recently been elevated onto a modern plinth. In the mid-nineteenth century he was mounted 'over the porch door', externally and held in place 'by iron braces' (Sheahan & Whellan 1856, II, p. 667). This unfortunate procedure has left a rebate cut around his waist where the iron band holding him in place was fixed, giving the false impression that he wears a tight belt (Fig. 89). More serious damage was done when the effigies at Wilton (in Cleveland) were propped against the north wall outside the chancel. I'Anson saw them there *c.* 1895 and noted that the area around the knight's shield was in the shelter of a buttress but the rest was badly eroded (I'Anson 1920, p. 198 fn. 1). The effigies are now protected in the porch but the weathering damage to both is severe, with most detail lost except for the left side of the knight, as noted by I'Anson. The knight at Treeton is set upright in a rectangular opening, seemingly constructed for him in the west wall of the nave internally (Fig. 90). He was already there by *c.* 1670, when Henry Johnston sketched (Fig. 91) and described him (C 14, fo. 229r). Prior to that, his legs had been broken off below the knees and he had also lost most of his right arm. However, his special location did not prevent further indignity. Wooden panelling was installed as a dado round the west end of the nave and the protruding surfaces of the lower part of the already truncated effigy were hacked off so that it would fit flush. A substantial part of the shield was similarly destroyed, even though it was above the woodwork. The panelling has now been removed, fully exposing the extent of the effigy and the damage. What little survives of the carving is gobbed by glutinous layers of plaster and paint, which include yellow ochre bulked out with grit. It is ironic that what has been the object of so much abuse and scant regard may well be one of the few effigies in Yorkshire commemorating a person of noble rank (*2a.v*). Damage caused by building changes is still happening. The installation of heating systems in churches has sometimes been bad for effigies, as thermal cycling draws moisture through walls and causes salting of limestone, which can completely destroy the carved surface. A most worrying example is the localised surface powdering and flaking of the Felixkirk knight (Fig. 92), which is otherwise one of

Fig. 89 Weaverthorpe. Male civilian recessed for a metal band.

Fig. 90 Treeton. Mutilated knight reset in a wall.

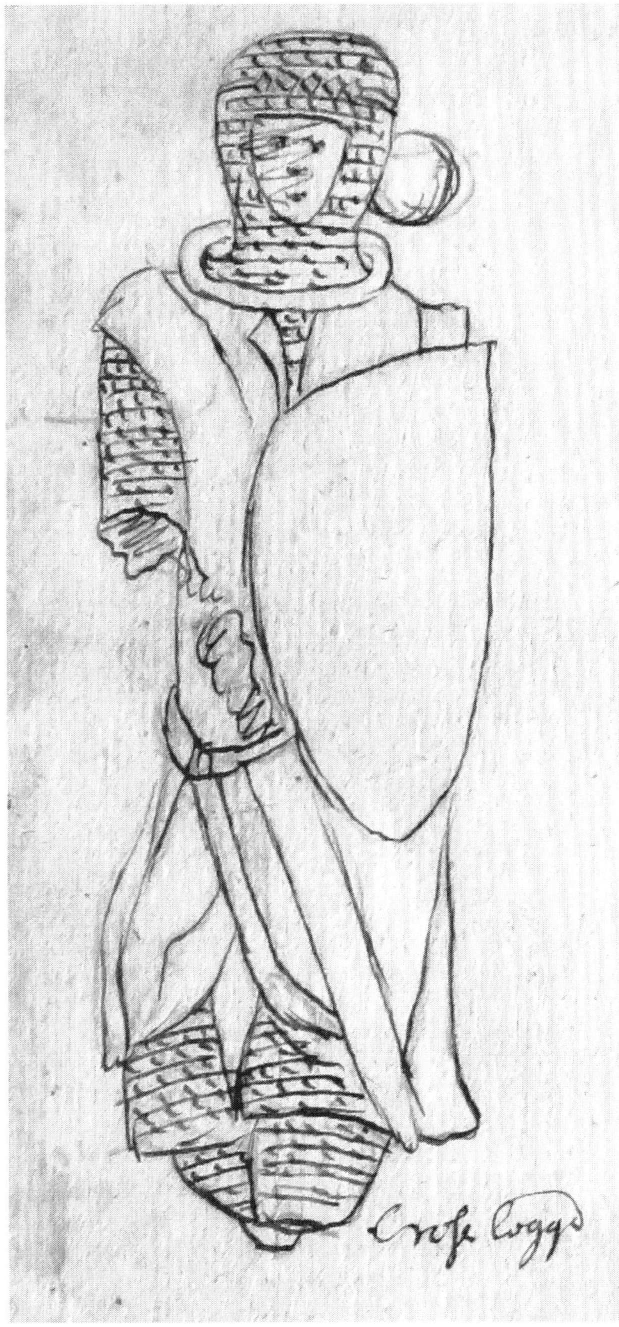

Fig. 91 Treeton. Johnston's drawing (C 14, fo. 229r).

Yorkshire's best-preserved effigies. Elsewhere problems of damp have meant that the two female effigies against the north wall at West Tanfield are now so decayed that they are beyond repair and the finely carved knight at Ryther is green with algae, as was the small male civilian (Plate 16) built into the tomb chest of Judge Portington at Eastrington, when we last saw him. Disrespect for objects that were once major commemorative foci is an unfortunate recurring theme, but the need to understand the different ways monuments have suffered is a crucial facet of their interpretation.

Reuse

Effigies were sometimes discarded altogether but their remains might find secondary use in building work, as rubble or even ashlar. A graphic reminder is part of a double effigy, trimmed down to a masonry block and incorporated into the porch wall at Eastrington (*2a.viii*), which may have been discovered when the chancel fell. This was in 1632, as recorded on a stone tablet:

THIS · CHANCILL · FEL IN · ANNO DOMINI 1632 +
AND · THIS · IS · BVLEDED · THE SAME · YEARE

· BY SIR · MICHAEL · WARTON · OF · BEVERLEI ·
HIGH · LODGE +

More of this intriguing monument probably still survives elsewhere in the church fabric. The same church has another curious case of reuse. The diminutive figure of a male civilian of the early fourteenth century is built into the east end of the strange and puzzling tomb chest supporting the defaced mid-fifteenth-century effigies of Judge Portington and his wife (Gittos 1979b). The civilian's credentials as an effigy are confirmed by the cushion beneath his head and his praying posture (Plate 16). He is incomplete, with his feet and legs lost from just above the knees, and has been set in the Portington chest rather like a gap filler. Perhaps he also was discovered when the chancel fell and was used to repair the Portington tomb, which seems likely to have suffered in the disaster.

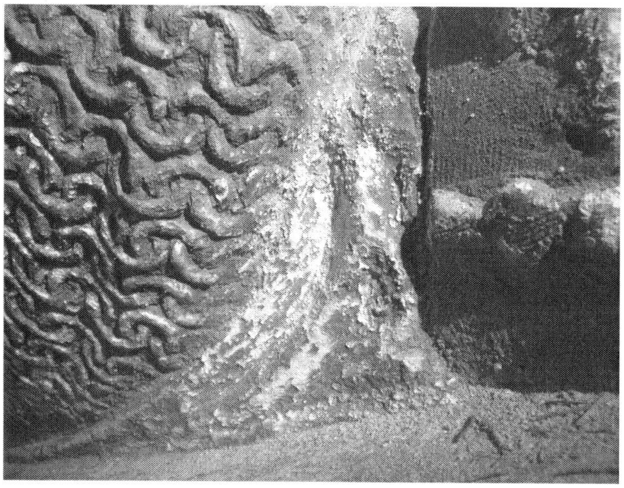

Fig. 92 Felixkirk. Knight, decaying through damp.

An unusual use for discarded effigies has been as way or boundary markers, and at least three knights have performed such duty in and around York, one of which remains in position. This is an early fourteenth-century effigy still bearing the de Ros arms on his shield. He stands upright with the lower part buried in the ground beside the foot path, which leads on to a common known as Hob Moor. He has weathered to little more than a headless hulk but is such a permanent feature of the landscape that he has acquired an Ordnance Survey Benchmark (Plate 17). A rhyming inscription was added in the eighteenth century (Gent 1733b, p. 3) which is now illegible but read:

This Image long Hob's Name has bore,
Who was a Knight in Time of Yore,
And gave this Common to the Poor.
This was erected Anno 1717, W. Tesh, L. Darcy, J. Yates,
J. Luen, Pasture-Masters.

There are cut-outs in the stone that indicate it may also have served other purposes. The second knight is now just a badly weathered torso, which has been in the collections of the Yorkshire Museum since 1851 but was previously 'at the end of the village of Clifton, near York, by the side of the turnpike road leading to Easingwold' (Wellbeloved 1891, p. 90). It was popularly known as 'Mother Shipton's stone' from the tradition that a witch of that name was tied to it and burnt to death. The most impressive of the three served as a boundary marker for the parish of St Margaret Walmgate, 'being half buried in the ground against a wall on the east side of Newtgate [*sic.*]' (Wellbeloved 1891, p. 89).

Fig. 93 York Museums Trust. Knight perhaps of the de Vescy family.

Fig. 94 Etton. Sole remaining fragment of lady.

It was removed when the road was widened and also joined the Yorkshire Museum collection (YORYM: 2010.1218). It is complete but extremely weathered except for parts that must have been buried (Fig. 93). These protected areas, including the lion foot support and part of the shield, show it was of high quality. It probably commemorated Sir William de Vescy of Kildare, who was slain at Bannockburn (Lawrance 1946, p. 47). Presumably these figures were culled from the suppressed religious houses of the city.

Providing it was not hollowed out behind, an effigy could be turned over to serve as a floor slab, as at Church Fenton (*A6g*). The figure was discovered when work was being carried out on the church in 1844 'with its face turned downwards and the upper part used as a flag-stone' (Boyne 1855, p. 31). When and why this happened is unclear but some care must have been taken in doing so because, with the exception of having had the left arm and hands replaced, it is in a remarkably good state of preservation (Fig. 162). If the only consideration was a convenient floor slab, significant damage might have been expected because hacking off some of the carving would have reduced the weight, rendering it less bulky and awkward to level in the floor. Rough handling might also have taken its toll, so the effigy was probably deliberately hidden. An intriguing aspect is the inscription lightly incised on her forehead, which Boyne described as 'unintelligible'. Examination with raking light suggests that it includes the words 'day of May', indicating that a date was intended. Perhaps the person who hid the effigy wanted to remember the day the obit was celebrated or even record the concealment for posterity. Whatever the reason, it must have some significance for the monument, which is otherwise free of graffiti, as it is deliberately placed in a prominent position but done lightly so it is not disfiguring and easy to miss.

Another female effigy was discovered under the floor during work on Etton church (*A6g*) in 1867–68 (Barker 1982, p. 30; White 1997). The broken figure was heart-holding, with two small dogs at her feet and three shields at her side (Mee 1964, p. 126). She spent time in the sanctuary but by the early 1970s was described as 'in a cubbyhole, treated at the time of writing with total disrespect' (Pev:ER 1972, p. 225). Soon afterwards she was cast out into the churchyard, where she was seen briefly by the authors. The *coup de grâce* was administered when she was wheelbarrowed away to provide hard core for a garage base in the village (Gittos 1979a). One small fragment with two shields was rescued from the wheelbarrow (Fig. 94). However, another piece in the church showing legs and feet resting on a dog, which was once thought to belong to the lady (Gittos 1990 and 1991b), is now known to have come from another smaller figure. This modern tale of woe is a reminder that the destruction of monuments is not solely a problem of less enlightened times.

Appropriation

Occasionally effigies have experienced a double life when re-employed to commemorate another person. For the late fourteenth-century double effigy at Yarm it was only necessary to add an inscription and the date 1638 but the Scarborough knight of *c.* 1300 underwent serious remodelling to improve its suitability for a seventeenth-century client (Fig. 95). The face was recut and provided with a wide moustache and a goatee beard, both popular at the time. His mail coif was converted into a curious cap, touselled seventeenth-century hair and a falling collar. No inscription was added but the change of ownership was indicated by re-carving the shield to display a lion rampant within a bordure, respecting the missing top corner. These arms still await identification and failure to recognise their non-originality has compounded the problem. A possible theory is that, during the siege of Scarborough Castle in 1645, the effigy was displaced and then appropriated for the Parliamentary commander mortally wounded in the conflict. This was Sir John Meldrum, a professional soldier knighted in 1622, who had a significant role in the Civil War. It is not known what arms he adopted but those dealing with his demise may have only been aware of his Scottish ancestry and so chose an approximation to the royal arms of Scotland. Sir John's portrait (Fig. 96) does show him with similar straggly hair and the same style of moustache and beard but, although there is no way of proving this hypothesis, it does provide one explanation for Scarborough's bizarre mutilation.

Abuse

For a complex afterlife, the military effigy from Fountains Abbey (Fig. 182) deserves top prize. It seems originally to have been set up about 1300 as the lid of a surviving stone coffin on the north side of the choir, to commemorate Lord Mowbray who died in 1297 (*4c.ii & 5bi*). Following

Fig. 95 Scarborough. Series A knight, recut in the seventeenth century.

Fig. 96 1647 engraving of Parliamentarian commander killed at Scarborough.

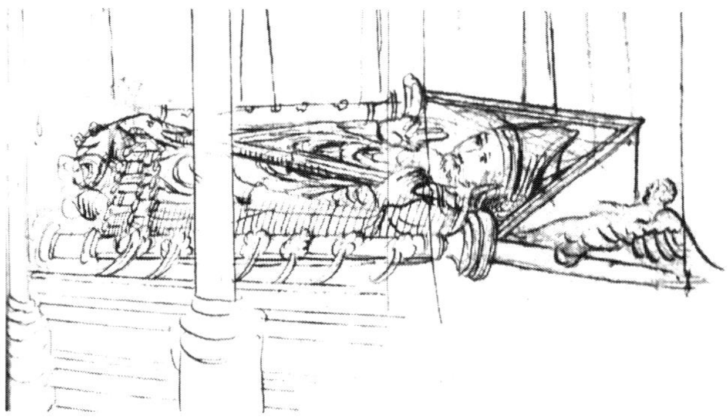

Fig. 97 York Minster. Johnston's drawing of de Gray effigy (C14, fo. 30r).

Fig. 98 York Minster. De Gray's repaired crosier head.

the Dissolution, the coffin was opened and its contents dispersed. The effigy was stood up against the adjacent north wall and remained there until about 1800 when 'while standing in its old position against the wall' it was 'wantonly thrown down and broken one Sunday afternoon … by a party of drunken militiamen from Ripon' (Walbran 1854, p. 58). It was afterwards placed in the cloisters and then spent time under an arch in a chapel off the north transept before being moved to the abbey museum above the great kitchen on 16th August 1858 (Walbran 1875, p. 109). It remained there into the twentieth century, until it was cast out again to the mercy of the weather and put in the central chapel on the east side of the south transept where it was seen by the authors in 1982, gathering moss, behind metal railings. By 1988 its fortune changed for the better when it was selected for a major exhibition in the Yorkshire Museum (York), entitled 'Abbeys: Yorkshire's Monastic Heritage', being thoroughly cleaned for this event. A detailed two view sketch was produced for the catalogue (Coppack 1988, p. 6) but the detached lower portion was shown wrongly positioned, an unfortunate error as this image has been reproduced many times since. Fresh from its triumph at the exhibition, the knight was displayed in the site museum but by 1999 it had left the abbey for the English Heritage store at Helmsley. At the time of writing it is still there, where he acts as a spectacular focus for visitors.

Repairs

Many effigies have been subject to repairs that vary greatly in quality and validity, a process that can alter how they are perceived. Those made during carving are normally done by the original mason (*4b.ii*) but later repairs often fail to achieve that standard. They are more easily noticed but still have the capacity to mislead. The crosier head on the effigy of Archbishop Walter de Gray in York Minster is an example. It is absent from Henry Johnston's sketch of *c.* 1669 (Fig. 97), although Gent describes the tomb as 'beautiful and entire' (Gent 1730, p. 26) and Drake has a sketch of the whole monument showing a crosier head in place (Drake 1736, p. 427). This bears some relation to the current form but the tip curls inwards while the head faces the opposite way. The drawing is inaccurate in many other respects too, but taken with Gent's comment, it is possible that the staff head had been replaced by then. The only acknowledgement of a repair we have found is in Ramm's detailed description of the tomb (Ramm 1971) where he comments that the 'carved crook' has 'three clusters of foliage ornament which are mostly restoration in stucco'. However, the open, outward curling, shepherd's crook form of the head is inappropriate in the thirteenth century, being found neither on contemporary effigies nor surviving crosiers. The painted image of the Archbishop on the coffin lid beneath the effigy shows him holding an archepiscopal cross and the crosier found inside the tomb in 1968 has a typical later medieval spiral shape, with a pierced foliate design, bordered by a metal band set with thirteen stones (Ramm 1971). The conclusion is that the whole head, not just the foliage, is an imaginative replacement and very expertly blended in with the rest of the carving (Fig. 98). The joint between the original Purbeck marble and the replacement piece can be traced down to the knop, overlying original detail on the angel and, probably, the gable. Unfortunately, there is nothing to indicate the form of the original, which would have been very different. A crosier of 1688 (YORDC.2013.104) may have provided inspiration for the replacement design. The closed form of the head is different but the ornamental foliage is used in a similar way to that of the replacement piece and it would have been in the Minster when the repair seems to have been effected. De Gray also has a new nose, fashioned less cleverly than the crosier head but still good enough for it not to have been noted by Ramm.

A particularly bad 'nose job' can be seen at Filey (Fig. 99). This overly large organ is part of a particularly ugly and disfiguring reworking of his whole head, with basin cut hair and hollows for eyes. The figure is otherwise well carved and his new features greatly detract, giving a false impression of its quality. Similar comments can be levelled at the restoration of the Skerne civilian who has undergone considerable reconstruction to his shins, hands, shield and head (*A2*). Again, it is the latter that creates an unfortunate and misleading appearance. His plaster chin and partly open mouth create the impression of someone in pain and the treatment of his hair looks as though he has just had it rinsed and set at a local salon (Fig. 100). However, it serves to indicate when his restoration is likely to have been done (and that of the semi-effigial female close by) since the style recalls that of fashionable male wigs of the late eighteenth century. The Skerne estate is said to have been purchased by the Arkwright family in 1792 and they were subsequently responsible for much rebuilding in the village. This may have included work on the church with the effigies being incorporated into the blocking of the demolished north aisle, where they may have originated (Ternent 1983). Pevsner mentions only that the church was restored in the 1840s (Pev:ER 1995, p. 684). The amateurish work at Skerne contrasts with the expertly-made repairs to the Yorkshire-made de Ros effigy in the Temple Church, London, when it and the other knights there were restored by Richardson in 1842. This provides a rare, documented account of a Yorkshire effigy's nineteenth-century restoration. Richardson (1843, p. 29) says:

> The defects in this effigy were not great, but troublesome to repair from the hardness of the stone. The nose, the right lock of hair, a small part of the shield, the lower part of the scabbard and a small portion of the plinth were gone; and the upper surface of the mail which covered the hands and legs was nearly rubbed away in the exposed parts.

For the most part, this accords well with the visible evidence. The addition to the top corner of the shield is in a darker coloured stone, the right hair curl can be seen to be modelled on the left while the new, rather long and angular nose lacks conviction. However, Richardson does not mention the lion masks on the sword belt. This is surprising as the pre-restoration drawing by Stothard (1832, pl. 37) depicts the belt mounts as just domed discs (Fig. 236), which he describes as 'broad studs'. In other respects, Stothard's drawing accurately records the defects listed by Richardson and the inescapable conclusion is that, for whatever reason, Richardson worked up the plain mounts into lion masks. Their indifferent quality contrasts with the skilful workmanship of the figure as a whole and compares unfavourably with the lion masks at Bedale and Goldsborough, both carved by the same man as the Temple effigy. Some repair seems pre-Richardson, as the lion's head was drawn by Stothard in 1811 (Lindley 2012) but appears to be a replacement. It is separately attached, set at a very awkward angle and with a face unlike that on any related effigy (Fig. 101).

Fig. 99 Filey. Male effigy with badly refashioned face.

Fig. 100 Skerne. Male civilian with rebuilt head and hands.

The repair was perhaps done as an improvement, when the figure was brought to London, as the head resembles those on royal arms of the period.

An even more imaginative repair has been inflicted on the civilian effigy at Holy Trinity, Hull. This alabaster civilian was complete save for his hands and new ones have been supplied, seemingly moulded in rough plaster or cement and with a book clasped between them (Fig. 102). The thinking behind this adjunct is difficult to understand. It is uncommon for medieval effigies of any type to hold books, exceptions include three displaying open books, Queen Eleanor of Aquitaine at Fontevraud in France; an ecclesiastic at Rippingale (Lincolnshire) and a male civilian at Gresford (Denbighshire), plus a deacon with a closed book at Furness Abbey (Lancashire). Books only become common in the aftermath of the Reformation. A case comparable with Hull is Bishop Stapledon (d. 1326) in Exeter Cathedral, whose book and hands are also replacements, the tomes themselves being remarkably similar. Stapledon was probably given his book in the eighteenth century, it was certainly done before 1820 when Buckler made a sketch now in the British Library. It is very unlikely that a former denizen of Hull originally held a book, which must betray the post-Reformation mindset of the restorer. So, the monument viewer should beware false messages, always looking hard at any anomalous features and suspicious joints.

Folklore

Folklore and legend are other factors that can influence the shaping of a monument's history. Monuments have occasionally acquired fanciful identities and even become the stuff of legend, for instance, the Batley tradition of the effigy commemorating a schoolmaster killed by his own scholars (*A6f*). The examples mentioned above of 'Hob' (associated with the devil) and 'Mother Shipton's Stone' (relating to a witch) have quite long pedigrees but this is not always so. At Pickering, a strong local tradition identifies the broken alabaster torso as representing no less a person than John of Gaunt, son of Edward III and father of Henry

Fig. 101 London, Temple Church. Replacement head of de Ros knight's lion.

Fig. 102 Holy Trinity, Hull. Male civilian with replacement hands holding book.

IV, but he was buried in St Paul's cathedral and drawings survive of the tomb. This impossible attribution only seems to go back to the early twentieth century and was included in a free leaflet, which was once available in the church. This explained that John of Gaunt's first wife Blanche was 'heiress of Pickering', ignoring the fact that she was actually joint heiress to the vast estates of the Duchy of Lancaster, of which the Honour of Pickering was only a minor part. Although later church guides no longer include the tale, visitors may discover the association still lingers in local memory. Some acquired names are difficult to account for. Poulson says Sir John de Meaux's effigy at Aldbrough was once 'commonly call'd Giant Morrell' (Poulson 1841, II, p. 20) and where he lay has been known as Morrell's aisle (VCH:ER:VII, p. 24). Morrell is a surname not uncommon in Yorkshire but why it should be used in this way is unclear. Perhaps it was applied to him by the schoolboys (see above) to signify a sort of bogeyman or fairytale giant.

Folklore of some antiquity clings to the mid-fourteenth-century armoured effigy at Barnburgh. It was already the subject of a long-established tradition by Hunter's time (Hunter 1828, I, p. 373), which held that it commemorated a member of the Cressacre family who was set upon by a wild cat. There was a running fight that culminated with the death of both combatants in the church porch. A comparable legend of combat with a monster is attached to the slightly earlier knight at Sockburn (Co. Durham). That effigy is said to represent the knight who fought and slew a monster (the Sockburn worm). The legend was attached to Sockburn by the seventeenth century and recorded by Dugdale in 1666 (Hunter Blair 1925, pp. 58–59). In this case, the story may stem from the use of a dragon as one of the foot supports. It is conceivable that the Barnburgh tradition derived from the Cressacre crest, as noted in 1620 by Dodsworth (p. 121) from what was probably late medieval glass in the church, 'a catt-a-mount sejant, her tayle betwixt her leggs and over her back, argent'. However, the family legend may equally have given rise to the crest. Dodsworth also recorded the Cressacre arms, 'or, three lyons salyent purpure', on the effigy's shield. They may not have been original to the effigy but their presence means he must have been understood to be a Cressacre by the seventeenth century. Since at least 1620 (Dodsworth, p. 120) the effigy has rested on a highly idiosyncratic canopied chest tomb (Fig. 103), commemorating Sir Percival Cressacre who made his will in January 1476–77 (*Test. Ebor*. II, p. 38). The authors know of nothing comparable. The figure is significantly earlier than the tomb and has been trimmed at both ends in order to make it an exact fit. The many inscriptions on the tomb are so arranged to leave clear

Fig. 103 Barnburgh. Wooden knight in later tomb.

the centre of the chest top where the effigy rests and there must be a possibility that the tomb was always intended to incorporate it, perhaps because the figure was already understood to depict a famous and honoured ancestor. If so, the local respect engendered by the legend may well have contributed to the excellent condition of the finest of Yorkshire's wooden effigies.

At Middleton on-the-Wolds, the effigy stands in the churchyard beside a row of four medieval grave slabs, which appear to have been deliberately grouped together to display and preserve them (Plate 2). There is persistent local tradition that they were brought from a lost church at Kiplingcotes (Beresford 1952, p. 64). No documentary evidence of such a church has yet been discovered but Beresford thought its existence was supported by an account of a 1689 enquiry in the York Diocesan records (in 2017 this could not be located by the Borthwick Institute). Witnesses to the enquiry said they had heard of the transfer of a bell or bells from Kiplingcotes to Middleton but this hearsay does not outweigh Kiplingcotes' absence from the Archbishops' registers of the fourteenth century or the 1291 Taxation of Pope Nicholas. Since Kiplingcotes is within the parish of Middleton, which is known to have had a church since Domesday, it seems most unlikely that any church or chapel there would have enjoyed full burial rights. A possible alternative explanation for this tradition may be that part of the cemetery at Middleton was designated for the use of Kiplingcotes folk and that, when the slabs were gathered together as they are now, some or all of them came from that area of the churchyard. They could then justifiably be described as having been brought from Kiplingcotes' burial plot.

2d Conclusions

This account of the afterlife experienced by Yorkshire's effigies is not intended to be comprehensive but it does demonstrate the range of possibilities, including boundary markers, masonry blocks and hardcore. Given the long time period, sometimes turbulent history and occasional extreme violence, we are fortunate that so many have survived. Some have been helped by antiquarian interest and others better regarded because of the legends woven around them but the threat of an uncertain future is ever present. One final example will bring the story up to date. Arthur Mee records under Felkirk, 'A battered fragment is all that is left of an old stone knight' (Mee 1969, p. 91). The *Little Guide* (Morris 1911, p. 188) had earlier mentioned a fragment of a recumbent effigy but Mark Downing does not include it in his survey (2015). So it was with some expectation that we visited the church for the first time, only to find the cupboard was bare. A careful search inside failed to reveal any hint of an effigy. We exchanged pleasantries with a parishioner who arrived to attend to the flowers and asked if she knew anything of an old knight. She volunteered that an 'old stone' had been moved outside and put inside a tomb chest (Plate 21). Following her advice we discovered the tomb chest housing the battered and very weathered hulk of a *c.* 1400 military effigy, without arms or legs. Putting it inside the tomb chest would afford it some protection but it was clearly unloved and its unhappy afterlife had taken a turn for the worse.

Plate 1 Hull, Holy Trinity. The civilian's individual face.

Plate 2 Middleton on-the-Wolds. Group of churchyard tombs including the effigy.

Plate 3 Jervaulx Abbey. The active knight.

Plate 4 Kirby (in Cleveland). Hand-holding effigies carved together.

Plate 5 Hornby. Lady still in the churchyard.

Plate 6 Coverham Abbey. Both complete knights.

Plate 7 Birdsall. Shield of de Brideshale.

Plate 8 Kirklington. Perhaps Sir Alexander de Mowbray.

Plate 9 Pickering. Mail represented as double links on the de Bruce effigy.

Plate 10 Felixkirk. Sir John de Walkingham's mail-clad skull-cap.

Plate 11 Stillingfleet. The mail-clad skull-cap on the de Moreby knight.

Plate 12 Winteringham. The mail-clad skull-cap.

Plate 13 Ilkley. Sir Peter Middleton's mail-clad skull-cap.

Plate 14 Stillingfleet. Effigy in Nicholas and William de Moreby's chapel.

Plate 15 Winteringham. Poleyns of leather construction.

Plate 16 Eastrington. Small-scale male civilian reused in a tomb chest.

Plate 17 York, Hob Moor. A de Ros effigy, reused as a marker.

Plate 18 Moor Monkton. Small semi-effigial with rainwater drainage holes.

Plate 19 Patrington. Drainage holes seen underneath the lady's churchyard effigy.

Plate 20 Barnburgh. The wooden knight.

Plate 21 Felkirk. Damaged armoured effigy.

Plate 22 York Minster. Prince William of Hatfield.

Plate 23 York Minster. William of Hatfield's soul, borne up by an angel.

Plate 24 Goldsborough. Painted tomb chest panel, showing the Virgin.

Plate 25 Beverley Minster. Remains of painted figures on a tomb chest panel.

Plate 26 Goldsborough. Tomb canopy integrated with the chancel structure.

Plate 27 Kirkham Priory, gatehouse. The entrance gable design is comparable with the Goldsborough tomb canopy.

Plate 28 Goldsborough. Remnants of a painted scheme found inside the tomb arch.

Plate 29 Goldsborough. The chancel built at the same time as the tomb.

Plate 30 Bishop Auckland, South Church (Co. Durham). Late thirteenth century chancel, comparable in design with Goldsborough's.

Plate 31 Goldsborough. The face cloth stitched to cushion under the Series B effigy's head.

Plate 32 Coverham Abbey. Larger knight with ailettes and angels raising the face cloth.

Plate 33 Sprotbrough. Isabella FitzWilliam's south aisle.

Plate 34 Sprotbrough. Isabella FitzWilliam, d. 1348.

Plate 35 Sutton-on-Hull. Sir John de Sutton's college/choir, founded 1347.

Plate 36 Swine. A surviving misericord.

Plate 37 Kirby (in Cleveland). The double monument still in the churchyard.

Plate 38 Pickhill. Structure of the pisolitic limestone.

Plate 39 Adlingfleet. The Lincolnshire limestone's fossils and pisoliths marking the lady's face.

Plate 40 Bedale. Series B effigy of Sir Brian FitzAlan, d. 1306.

Plate 41 East Harlsey. The Series B effigy's distinctive face.

Section 3

Monuments in context

3a Introduction

Effigies were usually just one component of a commemorative ensemble and some appreciation of the entire scheme is necessary to better understand them. This Section focuses on their settings. Many Yorkshire figures are now divorced from their original situations but we can often infer something of what was intended. Close examination of the effigy details and surviving settings reveals much, while the interpretation of that evidence is greatly assisted by reference to more intact monuments elsewhere, and to sources such as wills and antiquarian descriptions. Only the most expensive memorials would have had grand and elaborate settings like those in York Minster, whereas some of the simplest effigies, set up churchyards, may have just enjoyed a favoured location. Some major elements such as canopied recesses and tomb chests, survive in reasonable numbers and provide a useful basis for understanding how the figures were originally presented. Polychromy provided most of the original detail, as well as bestowing much of the monuments' visual impact, but what survives is sparse and fragmentary, with the important Goldsborough tomb chest paintings providing a rare glimpse of what once was (Plate 24). It should not be overlooked that monuments often had a range of less durable adjuncts, such as covering cloths and candles. They have long gone but even here clues can remain, notably the hearse with prickets at West Tanfield and the enigmatic surviving supports around the Bedale lady. The different categories are reviewed below, with case studies to draw attention to a few of the more informative examples.

3b Freestanding monuments

Freestanding monuments were prominent features within a church, drawing attention to themselves and, thereby, to the commemorated's need for prayers. They could present an effigy to good advantage and gave opportunities for display including heraldry and devotional imagery. On the other hand, they could obstruct the conduct of the liturgy, impeding processional routes (Rogers 1987, p. 20). Consequently, sites were carefully chosen and they are mostly found in less busy areas, such as private chapels. A balance was needed between marking the status of the deceased while soliciting prayers to assist them through Purgatory and not impeding the business of the church nor, indeed, the process of their own commemorative liturgy.

The larger, more prestigious, freestanding monuments were often located in a special place within the church. This is certainly the case with the tomb of Archbishop Walter de Gray. When he died in 1255, he was buried in the centre of the middle bay on the east side of the south transept of York Minster, which had only just been completed under his aegis. This was the chantry chapel that he had established and was close to the altar of St William of York, in the adjacent bay to the north (Miller 2012; Brown 2003, pp. 36–41). The burial position was chosen with care for the grand, freestanding canopied tomb that would follow. It therefore took primacy within the major building programme which is his enduring legacy. The tomb is of a scale and grandeur befitting its powerful occupant. With its soaring canopy, it was at the forefront of innovation in the mid-thirteenth century. Whilst the design seems not to have been influential in Yorkshire, it did serve as something of a prototype for other grand episcopal English tombs, such as those of Bishop Giles de Bridport (d. 1262) in Salisbury Cathedral and Bishop Peter D'Aigueblanche (d. 1268) at Hereford. However, amongst these comparisons, the design of de Gray's tomb is particularly effective at displaying the effigy. It is set on a low plinth and visible from all sides, due to the slenderness of the Purbeck marble shafts supporting the canopy, affording a clear view of one of the finest monumental effigies of thirteenth-century England.

From the surviving evidence, some time seems to have elapsed before the freestanding effigial tomb was to appear again in Yorkshire, although the losses engendered by the destruction of the monasteries may have distorted this picture. For example, the late thirteenth-century military figure now lying on the site of the crossing at Jervaulx Abbey was perhaps on a freestanding tomb. The early fourteenth-century monument of Brian FitzAlan and his wife Muriel at Bedale certainly was freestanding. Both effigies were recorded as being originally set on a tomb chest in the south aisle but it was subsequently dismantled and rearranged elsewhere in the church (see below). By this time, many people of the highest status, particularly bishops, were choosing monumental brasses, and one of the earliest in Yorkshire commemorates Archbishop William Greenfield who died in 1315. This forms the lid of a tomb chest beneath a substantial freestanding, canopied, monument in York Minster. In the south transept chapel of Howden Minster, the de Metham monument has been drastically remodelled and elements incorporated into another tomb, so it has been necessary to attempt a reconstruction, to appreciate the original arrangement (Badham, Gittos & Gittos 1996). The armoured male effigy and female now reside in a recess in the north wall but were previously on a tomb chest in the middle of the chapel, crammed against a pillar and divided by a parclose screen running between them. Prior to that, and in what was probably their original arrangement, they were on a freestanding tomb chest within the chapel. The de Metham monument dates from soon after 1310.

Whilst freestanding monuments are not common, there are outstanding examples of the 1330s at Beverley and Stillingfleet. That at Beverley Minster commemorating Provost Nicholas Huggate (*2a.iii*) is now in the north transept (Fig. 104), where it has been since at least the time of Dugdale (1641), although it may have been moved from elsewhere in the church. The base slab of the effigy is too short for its tomb chest but this might be due to the loss of other elements. The long edges of the base slab are chamfered and decorated with roses, suggesting that he was to be viewed from both sides. The ends of the slab are left unchamfered so were not intended to be seen. A small area of carved rose diaper appears in the spandrels above two adjacent niches on the north side of the tomb chest, which Harvey noted is similar in character to that on the effigy itself, suggesting that the effigy and chest belong

Fig. 104 Beverley Minster. Priest's tomb chest.

together despite the disparity in length (Harvey 1955). Nicholas Dawton (2000) associates the carved decoration on the chest sides with that on the so-called 'Sisters' Tomb' in the nave, which also includes rose diaper of similar character, but believes the effigy is unrelated. He sees these panels and the canopy as remnants of Idonea de Percy's monument, missing a hypothetical alabaster effigy. The altar tomb-like assembly currently under the 'Sisters' Tomb' is unrelated to it. The authors believe that all three elements (canopy, chest and effigy) are most likely to belong together as, what was originally, a high quality freestanding tomb.

The military effigy at Stillingfleet now lies on a modern tomb chest close to the south wall but this is unlikely to be in its original location as it blocks access to the piscina (Plate 14). As the effigy is contemporary with the chapel and no recess remains to house it, it is likely always to have been freestanding and was probably originally positioned closer to the centre of the space. The knight's shield is carved with the arms of Moreby (on a bend, three mullets, pierced), differenced by a label to denote an eldest son. Unfortunately, the arms do not appear in any of the surviving fourteenth-century heraldic rolls, although two seals show heraldry sufficiently close to confirm that the effigy bears the de Moreby arms, differenced. Robert de Moreby's 1328 seal shows, on a bend, three mullets and a label of three points (Ellis 1981, seal P1780) whereas William de Moreby's seal lacks the mullets on a document of 1348 (Birch 1894, Item 11, 914). Both have labels of three points, whereas the effigy shows five and the published descriptions of the seals do not mention whether the mullets are pierced. However, there is a difference in scale and the number of points may not be significant. In 1336 two brothers, Nicholas (a priest) and William de Moreby, both founded chantries in the chapel of St Mary at Stillingfleet, which were intended to have separate chaplains celebrating at the same altar (Robinson 1978, nos 472 for Nicholas' charter, 481 for William's; William's licence is recorded in CPR 1327–1330 p. 362). In 1344–45 William augmented his (The National Archives, *Inquisitions Ad Quod Damnum*, C 143/273/3). Nicholas' charter says he had newly built the chapel of St Mary, where the effigy now lies, presumably as the de Moreby chantry chapel. The effigy has previously been identified as Robert de Moreby who was dead by 8th January 1336 (FR IV, p. 466) leaving his heir a minor (CPR 1334–1338 p. 270). Robert de Moreby was a knight of the household of Queen Isabella and served as Keeper of the castles of Knaresborough and Brecon, amongst many other roles. His royal service and marriage to a substantial heiress must have made him wealthy but, unfortunately, it is unclear what his relationship was to the founders of the chantries, or where he was buried. He is mentioned amongst the chantry beneficiaries and his death may have prompted their creation, but William must also be a candidate for the effigy. The Stillingfleet chantry chapel and its monument are important survivals of an arrangement that must once have been commonplace across the county. Approaching the church from the village, the chapel is a major feature, with a fine set of reticulated windows and a separate entrance at the west end, for the chantry priests. The presence of the de Moreby tomb, in a primary position in the centre of this purpose-built chapel, would have provided a constant reminder of the beneficiaries to the priests celebrating on their behalf.

Freestanding tombs are more frequent from the mid-fourteenth century. Sir John de Sutton's monument at Sutton-on-Hull is still the primary focus in the chancel (Fig. 129), where he was buried in 1357 (*3g.iii*). Now displaced to the south, his effigy lies on its tomb chest, but was originally in the centre of the chancel. Less dramatically situated in the north chapel at Aldbrough, but performing a very similar function, is the tomb of Sir John de Meaux (d. 1377) (Fig. 105). His tomb chest also has an heraldic display. Roughly contemporary with Aldbrough is the tomb to a knight and lady at Ripley. Now under a modern low arch at the east end of the nave, it was originally freestanding, as evidenced by the fact that the chest is fully carved on all sides (Fig. 106). The knight bears the arms of Ingleby on his coat-armour and must commemorate Sir Thomas Ingleby (d. *c.* 1378). It is said to have come from the previous church known as the 'sinking chapel' (Historic England Pastscape Record 51714) and may have been displayed there in a more prominent location (Pev:WR 2009, p. 633; Bishop 1999, p. 11).

When complete, freestanding monuments had considerable presence but their creation can sometimes be a more involved process than is first apparent. The remarkable late fourteenth century tomb at West Tanfield stands foursquare in the centre of the Marmion chapel before the site of the chantry altar. With figures of alabaster on a local stone tomb chest, it commemorates Sir John Marmion (d. 1387) and his wife Elizabeth St Quintin, who survived him. John was the last of the family's male line (Gittos 2002a) and the tomb seems originally to have been set up with a single effigy, presumably when he died. Elizabeth's effigy is stylistically different from her husband's, being some 9″ (23 cm) shorter and showing the work of a different hand in details such as the depiction of the eyes and the animals' fur. The edges of the slabs are handled differently too (Fig. 107), his being simply square-cut and unfinished, while hers are delicately moulded and clearly meant to be on view. In contrast, his base slab looks as though it were intended to be inset within a chest. Although laid quite close together, the figures overlap the top of the chest on both sides. The chest too is less coherent than might be expected. Made in three levels, it comprises plinth, sides and moulded capping, which has boldly cut denticulation at the top, seen elsewhere in the later fourteenth century. The chest is composed of quite regular blocks but smaller sections of stone have been

Fig. 105 Aldbrough. John de Meaux in his chapel.

inset into both ends, at all three levels. Whilst the quality of the material and carving is consistent across the joints, this seems to be the result of an alteration rather than being original. An expansion of the chest relatively soon after its creation in order to accommodate an additional effigy seems the most likely explanation. If it were intended that the effigies would lie on top of the chest rather than being inset within a surround, that would also account for the lady's figure being ordered with moulded edges. The sequence, therefore, seems to have been that the military effigy was set up first on a freestanding chest tomb, his effigy surrounded by a denticulated edging like the 1360s tomb at Berkeley (Gloucestershire) and the alabaster couple of *c.* 1370 at Swine. The effigy for Elizabeth was added later, which necessitated widening the chest. The new effigy was ordered from the alabasterers and set on the expanded chest, with the female on the south side and the man on the north. However, the width was still a little narrow and the rearrangement made the best of a difficult job. It must have been at this stage that the famous hearse was provided (*3f*), since its dimensions reflect those of the expanded tomb (Fig. 121). Expert opinion also dates the hearse to *c.* 1400 (Geddes 1999, p. 381). A further rearrangement during the 1859 restoration of the church saw the figures transposed (McCall 1910, p. 194), presumably to present their better sides to view, hiding the disfiguring graffiti. At some stage, the effigy of the lady appears to have been shifted slightly towards the head of the chest, leaving a witness on the chest top, below her feet. Elizabeth may have survived until 1400 (McCall 1910, p. 197) and it was probably her decision to alter the tomb and commission the wrought iron hearse. It seems to have previously gone unnoticed that, far from being an exemplary survival, the monument has effectively been cobbled together. Despite its difficult gestation, this centrally placed tomb, once glowing with colour (traces of which survive), surmounted by two finely carved effigies and illuminated with candles, would have been a striking reminder of the last of the Marmions.

Fig. 106 Ripley. Tomb chest carved on all sides, recovered from earlier building.

Fig. 107 West Tanfield. Alabaster husband and wife with different base slabs.

It is likely that there once were many more freestanding monuments in the county, particularly as the losses from the religious houses were so severe. But, from what remains, a picture emerges of such monuments being employed in special circumstances, Archbishop de Gray in his newly built transept, John de Sutton in his chancel and the tombs at Aldbrough and Stillingfleet in association with chantry chapels. The same is likely to have been the case at Bedale and Howden, while at West Tanfield, the end of the Marmion line demanded something special.

3c Canopied recesses

Freestanding tombs inevitably took up important space within the church and the fact that some have subsequently been moved demonstrates the problem. A practical alternative was the canopied recess, which certainly took up less space but also offered considerable opportunities for the display of imagery, heraldry etc. The effigies were usually set above a tomb panel, with potential for the display of weepers, saints or heraldry. Devotional images were frequently depicted on the rear walls and in the vaults, while the wall above could also be utilised. The resulting dramatic effect could be just as impressive as a freestanding tomb, if not more so.

The earliest of the canopied recesses still containing an effigy would appear to be that in the north wall of the chancel at Goldsborough (Plate 26). The design is appropriate for *c.* 1300, with its steep gable, spiky crocketing, the use of a little naturalistic foliage (maple leaf) and the big trilobe occupying the space between the cinquefoiled arch and the straight-sided gable. The significance of another, smaller, arched opening in the back of the recess is discussed later (*3g.i*). This recess forms the setting for the effigy of Sir Richard de Goldesburgh IV who was dead by 1303 (Gittos 1994a). The Decorated style canopied tomb in the south aisle at Bainton (Fig. 108) dates from *c.* 1330 and is rather different in form. Here the canopy has no depth but is in relief on the face of the wall, providing more of a backdrop. Consequently, the effigy intrudes somewhat into the aisle. Bainton's sweeping ogee arch is enclosed within a heavily crocketed, straight-sided gable with the spandrels filled by just two large angels, bearing up the soul of the deceased in a sheet (*5c.iv*). The canopy fills the width between the windows and the scheme continued onto the wall above, with a symmetrical group of relief de Mauley shields, clustered around the finial (Plate 67). This arrangement has been planned in relation to the fenestration so that the highest shield sits level between the uppermost lights. Bainton had to be rebuilt after the Scottish raid of 1322, the *Chronicle de Melsa* ascribing the work to William de Brocklesby who held the living from 1331 to 1352 (*Chron. Melsa.* III, p. 95). However, it is difficult to believe the church was abandoned for nearly ten years, so it may be that he simply completed work begun by his predecessor,

Fig. 108 Bainton. Monument of John de Mauley.

Fig. 109 West Tanfield. Wall-height canopied tomb recess.

Sir John de Mauley. This is the man commemorated by the monument, who was rector of Bainton from 1317 to 1331, so it is likely that he at least planned the rebuilding and the incorporation of his own tomb (see Section 5b.i for the attribution). There is also some evidence to suggest this part of the building was incomplete at John's death. The two components of the tomb seem to be of different materials, the stone of the effigy being more brown than the arch, which appears of similar material to the walling. The arch has to have been built at the same time as the wall and planned with it. The effigy and plinth are a single monolithic block of stone, a form more usually encountered amongst churchyard monuments (*3h*). So it is conceivable that John was buried in the churchyard and an effigy erected, pending translation inside when the designated position was ready.

Other Decorated period tombs vary radically. That at West Tanfield (Fig. 109), probably commemorating Sir John Marmion (d. 1335). It follows the general formula of a cusped arch within a crocketed gable, flanked by side shafts and pinnacles. There is also a narrow frieze decorated with flowers acting as a pediment across the top of the whole monument, which occupies almost the full height of the wall. The tomb canopy over the knight at Sprotbrough dates from 1340–50 and originally accommodated the lady now on the opposite side of the chapel (*3g.ii*). The ogee arch is devoid of all delicacy with heavy mouldings, almost oppressive in its bulk as if the Decorated style had finally lost its *raison d'être* (Fig. 125). However, the most dramatic canopied recess from this architectural period is the double-faced monument at Welwick, which must commemorate Provost William de la Mare of Beverley, who died in 1360. It is unlike any other and for a detailed appraisal see Section 6a.

A pair of adjoining recesses with slender mouldings at Kirklington house male and female effigies of *c.* 1360–70. They share a common central shaft and were probably configured to accommodate a lost painted scheme on their back walls. The design of the arches, with just two small cusps close to the apex, is difficult to parallel. However, the linearity of the Perpendicular style is clear, on the monument in the south choir aisle at Holy Trinity, Hull (Fig. 110), of the later fourteenth century. This large tomb uses carved detail sparingly, mostly confined to the canopy arch itself. Its spandrels have a regimented row of blank cinquefoil-headed niches, presumably once filled with painted figures

Fig. 110 Holy Trinity, Hull. Canopied tomb recess.

Fig. 111 York Minster. Britton's illustration of Prince William of Hatfield's complete tomb. (Britton 1819, Pl. XXXIV).

but starkly Perpendicular in form. Crossley (1921, p. 66) illustrates the Hull tomb alongside that of Sir John Wingfield (d. 1361) at Wingfield in Suffolk, which demonstrates that the Yorkshire monument is a standard design of the period and not something with a local flavour. Both employ a common formula in the design of the canopy and the decoration of the tomb chests with shields within quatrefoils. Another late fourteenth-century recess houses the knight at Walton. The extremely narrow side shafts that spring from modest corbels are in tune with the Perpendicular, while the lofty proportions of the arch recall those of the Hull tomb. The decoration is even more sparing than at Hull, being confined to the outer order of the arch and its small spandrels, consistent with the monument's late century credentials.

The tallest canopied recess in the county was created to house the only royal effigy within our compass (Plate 22). Prince William of Hatfield, the infant son of Edward III, was born in December 1336 and buried in York Minster on 10th February 1337 (Ormrod 2011, p. 174, fn. 113). As the result of a rearrangement, the present tomb was constructed *c.* 1400, to provide a new setting for his displaced effigy (French 1991). The tomb now occupies a whole bay of the north choir aisle wall and extends from the floor to just above the springing of the vault (Fig. 111). It comprises three canopied recesses, stacked one above the other. The two higher recesses are empty and would have had painted detail on the back wall but there would also have been room for sculpture. Indeed, the flat tops of the two lower canopies resemble plinths for statuary. That the upper recesses were part of the monument is demonstrated by the repetitive pattern they create and by the fact that one of the bosses in the vault of the second tier canopy is carved with an angel bearing up a tiny soul figure (Plate 23 and see also *5c.iv*). At the base of this assemblage is the tomb chest supporting his alabaster effigy, portrayed as a fashionably attired youth despite his early death. The chest below the figure is most unusual, with a deep central panel flanked by two slender niches. The panel is divided into what are effectively two blank three-light windows with complex curvilinear tracery in their heads. It may be all that remains from the original tomb chest. There is agreement about the identification of the infant Prince William but its date has been a matter of dispute, with claims that it was set up about 1337 (shortly after death) or retrospectively in the 1370s. Routh (1994) supports French's view (1991), that the effigy must have been added to an earlier tomb probably in the 1370s, whereas Sally Badham (2009; 2016) argued that William's costume and posture show the effigy was produced 'within a few years of his death'. This builds on Prior and Gardner's comments (Prior & Gardner 1912, pp. 673–74) about the stylistic links between his angel supporters and those of other Westminster products, such as John of Eltham (d. 1336). Prior and Gardner note their 'graceful modelling' and the distinctiveness of their form, especially the 'trick of exhibiting the flat of the feet half covered with the alb'. Whilst the former quality is a matter of judgement, the latter trait is so widespread during the fourteenth century, that it is unhelpful for dating purposes. By contrast, the comparison between Prince William and his brother – another William – in Westminster Abbey, seems so close it is difficult to believe they were carved forty years apart. The surviving contract for the Westminster tomb was placed with John Orchard in 1376 (HKW:I p. 485). Prior and Gardner also compare the York prince with the effigy of Bishop Hatfield (d. 1381) in Durham Cathedral, noting similarities between the 'embroideries' [damask?], cushions and the lions. This is even more persuasive following Budge's reassessment (2015) of the Hatfield tomb's date to the 1360s, following the Convent's permission for it in 1362. Comparisons for Prince William's tightly-fitting horizontal hip belt with contiguous heavy square mounts are quite widespread, but a particularly good example is worn by the effigy of Sir Thomas Cawne (d. 1374) in Ightham (Kent). They are also found on the weepers of Queen Philippa's tomb – work on which was commissioned from John Orchard at the same time as the Westminster prince's tomb. All this is entirely consistent with the York effigy having been made in the 1370s, as a retrospective monument. The original location of the tomb is not recorded but there is a tradition that it was on the north side of the high altar and may have been free standing. The need to relocate it was driven by the reconstruction of the choir and demolition of the old one from 1394. The current setting is part of the new north choir aisle wall. The effigy has been moved many times and was returned to its present position as recently as 1978. Nevertheless, the place where it now resides does represent a dramatic medieval presentation of William's effigy, albeit displaced from the position of honour.

Like William of Hatfield, not all effigies in recesses are in their original situation and other displaced figures include the Sprotbrough knight, the priest under a much later arch at Bedale and the two knights in Hazelwood Chapel. They are unrelated to the canopied recesses they now occupy, since they previously lay on a single tomb chest on the north side of the altar (*5b.i*). Although Yorkshire's fourteenth-century canopied tomb recesses exhibit a great variety of forms, for the most part, they reflect the prevailing architectural style. Consequently, when they house figures that belong to them, their details can be used as evidence for dating the effigies.

3d Tomb chests

Although most Yorkshire effigies are displaced from their original settings, it is likely that a significant number were on tomb chests. There were clear advantages of siting effigies on tomb chests. Elevating the figure would increase its prominence and make a stronger visual statement, which could be enhanced by utilising the vertical surfaces of the chest for heraldry and relevant imagery (religious or secular). It might also give the impression of the body being close at hand within the chest. In fact, the corpse was usually interred below ground, but examples of burial within a tomb chest are known, such as that which once stood beneath the Percy Tomb canopy in Beverley Minster, another below the effigy in the West Tanfield recess and the recently discovered lead-wrapped body of Blanche Mortimer at Much Marcle (Herefordshire) (Oliver 1829, p. 337 n.64; Gittos 2017b).

Many tomb chests continue to support Yorkshire effigies and more survive as fragments. The most common form of decoration is heraldic with shields set within quatrefoils, examples including the ladies at Adlingfleet and Aldbrough, knights at Sutton-on-Hull, Whorlton and the Magnesian Limestone pair at Swine. A panel with blank quatrefoils under the Kirkby Fleetham knight may have had painted heraldry. After about 1370 this continues but with the quatrefoil enclosed within a circle, as at Aldbrough, Holy Trinity, Hull and Darfield (Fig. 112). Two chests at Harpham and Hornsea carry this decoration, but they support incised rather than carved figures and are probably of the early fifteenth century. Both were commissioned by Anthony Saint Quintin before his death and both have the addition of central crucifixions flanked by the shields. In keeping with the artistic diversity typical of the first half of the fourteenth century, there are many variations of tomb chest design. The priest at Thorpe Bassett has flower heads set

Fig. 112 Darfield. Tomb chest detail.

within quatrefoils, and the Adlingfleet lady has her shields framed by four lobes with spiky buds between them. Of special note are the niches headed by curvilinear tracery at Beverley and York Minsters. The priest's tomb at Beverley has eight niches on each long side carved like two-light windows and the head of each has a different curvilinear design – an essay in Decorated window tracery (Fig. 104). If the panel below William of Hatfield's effigy does belong to his original tomb, then both can be dated to the late 1330s. An earlier incidence of window tracery on a tomb chest, albeit non-effigial, is in the churchyard at Loversall. Dating from *c.* 1300, it is topped by a cross slab. Window tracery patterns appear on cross slabs too. One at Coverham Abbey, which may be of a similar date to Loversall as both show intersecting tracery, has an arched base in the form of a window. An intriguing fragment, apparently once forming the head of a grave slab, is at Valle Crucis Abbey in north Wales (Gittos 2012b). It appears to copy the tracery of the chapter house windows, of about 1350. Like the canopies, chests show useful parallels with contemporary architecture.

Carved weepers on tomb chests are now rare in Yorkshire, although many more may have originally existed. The reset panels at Howden are an important survival, the figures probably represent the children or family members of the de Metham effigies of *c.* 1310, to which the tomb chest panels belong (Fig. 113). The panels represent one of the earliest Yorkshire tomb chests and the remains of another can be seen at Bedale, where all that survives are two defaced pieces from one side of the chest, now built into the base below the priest. They once supported the effigy of Brian FitzAlan (d. 1306) and his first wife and were recorded as such by Gale (1722, pl. facing 242). Blore engraved a reconstruction of one side of the chest, albeit badly damaged and partially hidden (1826, facing p. 1 of 2nd subject, 'Brian Fitz-Alan, Baron of Bedale'). It comprised a mixture of secular and religious figures in niches. Dodsworth (p. 237) saw the knight and lady in the south aisle in 1622 but did not mention the chest. They were in the same location in Dugdale's account of 1669, copied by Nathaniel Johnston, together with sketches of

Fig. 113 Howden. Tomb panel figures.

the effigies but again without the chest (Johnston C 31, fo. 124v). The monument was later repositioned and arranged with two others in the north aisle, the FitzAlan effigies end to end and the others behind them, against the wall. Gale says they had been moved into something like this grouping about twenty years before his time (so, *c.* 1700) and may already have been as Blore described them a century later. By Glynne's visit in 1842, the chest had been broken up and the FitzAlan effigies deposited in the chancel (Glynne 2007, p. 88). These examples have carved figures but it can be assumed that seemingly blank panels (such as at Kirkby Fleetham) originally had painted detail. However, Yorkshire is extremely fortunate in having a tomb chest with considerable remains of such a painted scheme. This is below the 1330s knight at Goldsborough (*4b.iii*). The sides of the alabasters' tomb chest at West Tanfield are now quite plain but they too are likely to originally have been painted. Painted detail may also have completed the composition in three cases where shields are shown in isolation, without any display framework: a late fourteenth-century lady at West Tanfield, the mid-fourteenth-century knight at Sheriff Hutton and the earliest of the alabaster tomb chests at Swine. The last has each shield on a separate piece of alabaster and there is just one carved figure, kneeling in a niche. Tomb chests were almost invariably exploited for display purposes, in a variety of forms, and even those that appear blank probably had painted detail.

Tomb chests could be a vehicle for the display of allegiances and kinship. Although the relationship between the figures and the effigies can only be inferred on the early Yorkshire example at Howden, it was made clear on the later tomb at Ripley, where each weeper was individually identified. They stand on pedestals under nodding ogee gablettes, alternating with stacked niches containing a shield in the upper compartment (Fig. 106). A prominent lawyer, Thomas Ingleby ceased to be a Justice of the King's bench in 1377 (Baker 1984, p. 520) so the tomb probably dates *c.* 1370–80. The weepers are fashionably dressed and well carved but have mostly lost their heads. Significantly, their names are cut above them and they must represent the children of Sir Thomas Ingleby and his wife Adelina. Five names remain. On the north side are: 'Wil[...]'; 'Johs de Ingilby'; 'Thomas' and 'Magister Henricus de [...]', while on the south, all that can be read is 'Alicia', above the only female. Magister Henry, a prebend of York, Lincoln and Southwell, certainly was one of their children because his will of 1375 survives (*Test. Ebor*. I, p. 94) naming his parents and also John de Ingleby (Fig. 230). Those on the south side include two ecclesiastics, one dressed as a monk and the other in mass vestments giving blessing and holding a crosier or staff (Fig. 114). There do not appear to be any English bishops named Ingleby at this time, although a William Ingleby was Abbot of Rievaulx for some ten years from 1322 (Smith & London 2001, p. 302), which is too early to be one of the children but, if he were a close relative, he might still have been included on the tomb chest. However, as very many heads of religious houses are known only by their Christian names, an unrecognised abbot is also possible. On the tomb of Michael de la Pole (d. 1415) at Wingfield (Suffolk), the children's names were painted (Badham 2015a). The Markenfield tomb at Ripon, from the end of the fourteenth century, has six shields in cinquefoil headed panels on the sides, flanked by narrow niches with

Fig. 114 Ripley. Tomb chest figure with crosier or staff.

Fig. 115 Amotherby. Tomb chest panel.

Fig. 116 Gilling East. Integral effigy and tomb support, now truncated.

figure pedestals. This demonstrates that there were other possible arrangements for displaying affinities.

Like their decoration, the structure of chests can also be revealing. The Markenfield tomb has a castellated top edge, something first encountered on Sir John de Meaux's tomb at Aldbrough (Fig. 105) and found on two late fourteenth-century chests at West Tanfield. Peripheral castellations were sometimes added to tombs in the later fourteenth century and throughout the fifteenth, a decorative feature with a military flavour that conveniently masked the junction between the effigy and the top of the tomb chest. On the early examples cited above, the castellations are carved on the capping slabs of the tomb chests, but at Ripon and on the earliest of the alabaster effigies at Swine, they are cut into the edge of the effigy's base slab. On some monuments (*e.g.* the later fifteenth-century alabaster effigies at Norbury, in Derbyshire) they are on the upper edges of the slabs that form the sides of the tomb chests.

Constructional methods vary to some degree with the type of stone and its properties. Alabaster tomb panels can be relatively thin and the carving quite delicate. On the other hand, the loose limestone piece at Amotherby is thick and chunky, probably an end panel, with a crucifix flanked by two shields and further shields in the spandrels (Fig. 115). There are holes in the top surface for metal cramps, probably to secure it to the rest of the tomb. In most cases, such as Sheriff Hutton, the base slab of the effigy closes the tomb chest. This direct relationship between the effigy and its chest is most marked on the mid-fourteenth-century semi-effigial monument at Gilling East. Not only is the effigy the lid of its tomb chest, with an under chamfer, the upper part of the sides is carved integrally with it. As the lower part is lost or covered, all that can be seen are the upper lobes of the quatrefoils that decorated its sides, now resembling an undulating frieze (Fig. 116). However, Torre sketched it when complete with full quatrefoils and a chamfered masonry plinth (Torre 1692, fo. 280). Another example of an integral plinth is below the de Mauley effigy at Bainton (*3c*). Archbishop de Gray in York Minster lies on a low plinth inside his canopy structure and they occur quite frequently, especially in conjunction with canopies or recesses. Examples are to be found at Goldsborough, below the canopied figure, beneath the knight at Felixkirk and the priest at Welwick, both of which are in recesses.

The priest's tomb at Thorpe Bassett has been reconstructed, so it is difficult to be sure of the original arrangement

Fig. 117 Thorpe Basset. Priest on tomb chest.

(Fig. 117). However, the effigy does appear to belong to the chest on which he now lies. Both are trapezoidal, with matching tapers. The sarcophagus rim is rebated and the effigy seems to be a reasonable fit. Although now cracked into two, the sarcophagus is made from a massive single block of stone, hollowed out, and may well have been used for an above ground burial, the effigy forming the lid. An earlier example of a sarcophagus intended for display can be seen at Kirby Grindalythe (E.R.), it perhaps dates from the eleventh century.

Tomb chests and plinths were not the only form of support. The badly weathered effigy at Middleton on-the-Wolds is supported on three trestles, graduated in size to fit the taper of the effigy and the slab on which it all stands, although it is currently wrongly assembled, with two of the trestles switched and one of them upside down. The ends of the trestles are carved with dog tooth ornament sandwiched between pairs of engaged shafts, complete with capitals and bases (Fig. 118). Dog tooth occurs in the Middleton area at Great Driffield and North Grimston, but used in a different way. However, dog tooth between shafts is a major feature of the shrine of St William, first abbot, at Rievaulx Abbey (Fig. 119), believed to date from *c*. 1250 (Coppack & Fergusson 1994, p. 20). Whether the Middleton on-the-Wolds monument was produced by the same masons is impossible

Fig. 118 Middleton on-the-Wolds. Dog-tooth detail on a support trestle.

Fig. 119 Rievaulx Abbey. Shrine of St. William, dog-tooth detail.

to say but it is probably of similar date. It is demonstrably important to pay attention to what supports the effigies, as it is often a significant part of the monument's overall message.

3e Glass and painting

Whilst in some instances it is only possible to infer the extent of the additional elements that constituted the commemorative scheme, in others, useful clues remain. The lady at Pucklechurch (Gloucestershire) lies beneath open canopy directly in front of a large contemporary window, which must once have held glass that formed part of the monument (Saul 2009, p. 162). It is also clear from historical accounts that glazing commonly formed either the monument itself or was an integral part of one. Little of this commemorative glass has survived in parish churches, although there are some notable exceptions in the city of York, but some indications can be derived from antiquarian sources, for instance at Howden (see below). However, the presence and positioning of windows can hint at what has been lost. Some suggestive elements survive and amongst the most positive is Swine, where a knight and lady occupy a recess in the south aisle wall directly below a contemporary late fourteenth-century window (Fig. 135). The recess is deep, witnessed by a low gabled outshot externally. Recently, stonework has been replaced beneath the window, both inside and out, which has probably maintained the external appearance but internally, has created a void where a vaulted canopy would have risen in front of the window. The bases of its substantial, lost side shafts remain, befitting a large canopy. It is likely to have been of an open design to frame painted images in the stained glass, as a dramatic part of the overall composition.

Somewhat earlier, in 1290, Sir Brian FitzAlan founded a chantry in the Lady Chapel in Bedale church (Nicolas 1832, II, p. 286 fn., quoting a record in the Augmentation Office). Still known as the Lady Chapel, it is on the south side of the chancel (Plate 53). The masonry of this part of the aisle is quite different from that further west, being constructed from ashlar rather than rubble, and contains a prominent east window with late thirteenth-century tracery. It was in this area, in 1622, that Dodsworth (p. 236) recorded heraldry in the glass for FitzAlan and Brittany (FitzAlan held Bedale from the Duke of Brittany and the Countess was amongst the beneficiaries of the chantry). Gale recorded these arms again, specifically in the east window of the south aisle (1722, pl. facing p. 255). He also illustrated the effigy of Brian FitzAlan on a tomb chest, together with a female figure and provided a description, which translates as '… he was buried with his wife in the south aisle of his church of Bedale, under a tomb…; which nevertheless today is by the north wall, where it was clearly removed about twenty years ago' (1722, p. 242 & facing pl.). So, the heraldry in the glass can be associated with the tomb. The east window was clearly an important feature of the chapel as it dominates the area, filling the wall. It is said that the window was brought from Jervaulx Abbey after the Dissolution (Pev:NR 1966, p. 75) but McCall had no doubt of its originality (McCall 1907, p. 83). The masonry around the window is undisturbed and, as we have seen, it once contained relevant heraldry. Perhaps a particularly large window was incorporated to accommodate a specific and impressive display of glass and this seems to be another case where the glazing was an important element of the commemorative scheme. FitzAlan's involvement with glazing is attested by the presence of his arms in glass at York Minster, in both the chapter house and its vestibule, so he was well aware of the possibilities.

Evidence from Yorkshire to illustrate the use of painting as part of a monumental design is scarce but sufficient survives elsewhere to demonstrate how widespread this practice was. At Winterbourne (Gloucestershire) the walls of the chapel bear the remnants of a mixture of heraldic, donor and religious imagery (Gill 1998). Recent conservation and archaeology at Puddletown (Dorset) has demonstrated that paint was used to replicate features usually perceived as being carved (Gittos 2014b, pp. 5–6). This *c.* 1360 monument has a carved arch over the tomb recess but lacks shafts to support it. Instead, the deficiency was supplied in paint and the conservation uncovered part of a side shaft and capital. There is no reason to suppose that Puddletown was exceptional and it is probable that other monuments had painted settings, in exactly the same way as details of costume and equipment could be depicted on the figures themselves. This means that ostensibly plain tomb chests and arches may not originally have been so.

Another key use of painting was to provide devotional and other images within arches. Puddletown also retained traces of a painted scheme on the rear wall of the recess, where the wall surface had been concealed behind the effigy. In some places, paintings survive directly above the effigy. A notable example is the painting of Christ with the five wounds over the effigy of Bishop Stapledon (d. 1326) in Exeter Cathedral (Hulbert 1991). Other survivals of paintings in this position are the tombs of the Black Prince and King Henry IV, both in Canterbury Cathedral (Wilson 1995). Paintings within a recess or above a tomb provide a subject on which the effigy can fix its eyes, just as the concept of a 'good death' anticipated that the dying person would gaze on a crucifix or other image with connotations of redemption (Duffy 1992, pp. 313–27). They are, perhaps, also a visual representation of the conventional invocations at the opening of contemporary wills. For example, in Johanna de Walkingham's will of 1346, she commended her soul firstly to Almighty God and then to the Virgin and all the saints (*Test. Ebor.* I, p. 16). Johanna is probably the person commemorated at Felixkirk (*4c.iv*). Two years later Isabella FitzWilliam (commemorated by the female effigy at Sprotbrough) entrusted her soul to God, the Blessed Virgin Mary and all the saints (*Test. Ebor.* I, p. 50). Perhaps paintings reflective of this sentiment were in the recess where she was buried. Evidence of painting inside a recess (Plate 28) has been found at Goldsborough (Gittos 1997), see Section 4b.iii. Given modern understanding of the extent of wall paintings in medieval churches, together with recorded or known survivals associated with tombs, it is reasonable to suggest that every recess or canopy would have carried a painted design and that the great majority of these would have been figurative and devotional.

Other architectural and sculptural elements of monuments would have been treated in the same way. Important remains of painted figures on tomb chests survive at Goldsborough (Plate 24) and, less clearly, at Beverley (Plate 25), see Section 4b.iii. They demonstrate that paint could be used anywhere to supply decoration that might often be carved and that, given carved figures would also be painted, the final effect might be more similar than now appears. This extends to the effigies themselves. The historical evidence at Bedale is detailed in Section 4b.iii and careful examination of the more protected parts of many Yorkshire effigies reveals some traces of colour. So it is clear that painting both of the monuments themselves, and of the areas surrounding them, was an integral ingredient of their original design. The degree of additional detail provided by the polychromy would have created a radically different visual effect and rendered the monuments far more interpretable.

3f Armour and hearses

Outside the monuments themselves and their architectural, painted and glazed contexts, other features might also be present, which added depth to the significance of the monument or provided for liturgical enrichment. The great bascinet from Aldbrough serves as a reminder that armour might be deposited in the church and displayed as an adjunct to a tomb (Fig. 120). Seemingly first noted in 1699 (de la Pryme p. 217), it would have been only one part of a more extensive display of Sir John de Meaux's

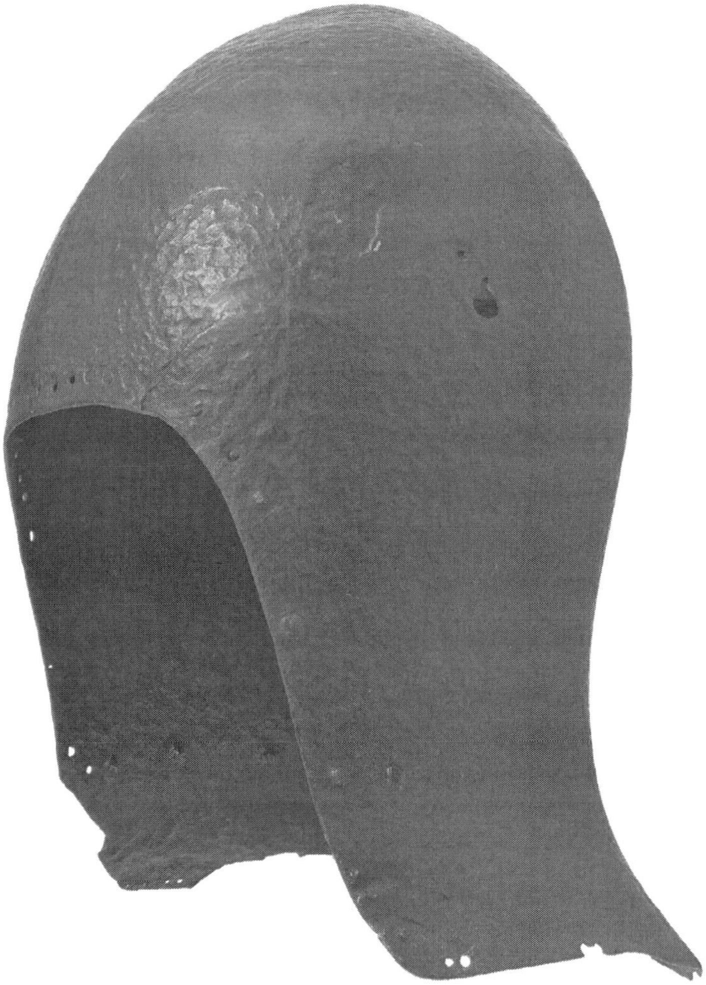

Fig. 120 Aldbrough, Sir John de Meaux's bascinet (Royal Armouries, Object No. IV 1677).

armour but the bascinet alone survives, perhaps because it was once used as a coal scuttle (Poulson 1841, II, p. 13). Dateable to the late fourteenth century (T. Capwell, pers. comm.), it is now in the collection of the Royal Armouries and a replica hangs above the tomb. The most famous example of armour deposited with a tomb is that of Edward, the Black Prince (d. 1376) displayed ever since by his tomb in Canterbury Cathedral. His will gives specific instructions for his funeral (Nichols 1780, pp. 66–77). He requested an heraldic funeral: his body to be preceded by two men wearing his armour and mounted on caparisoned war horses, one displaying his heraldry for peace and the other for war. When such heraldic funerals took place, the arms were then laid up in the church and, in the case of the Black Prince, the achievement has survived. A sketch of *c.* 1600 shows that the achievement then consisted of his great helm, cap of maintenance and crest, jupon, sword, dagger, gauntlets, shield for peace, shield for war and a targe – all hung around or supported above the tomb (reproduced in Wilson 1995, pls 120 & 118). Of these items, all but the shield for peace, the targe and the sword remain in the Cathedral. Heraldic funerals were frequently requested by knights and noblemen (Vale & Vale 1992; Marks 1994; Badham 2014). Yorkshire examples from this period include Gilbert de Aton (d. 1350), whose will implies an expectation of such an event when he left almost all his armour to his son, except what was needed for his funeral (*Test. Ebor*. I, p. 62), see Section 1. In 1399, Robert de Swylyngton asked for burial at Swillington and gave to the church his best beast with his coat-armour, helm, shield and a sword (*Test. Ebor*. I, p. 107). Amongst the more sumptuous Yorkshire instances is the funeral of Sir Brian Stapleton in 1394 who requested burial in Healaugh Priory (*Test. Ebor*. I, p. 198). He asked for his body to be covered with a cloth of blue say (a fine material, often of silk mixed with wool) and that there should be a hearse over his body carrying five large candles, each of five pounds of wax. A further thirteen torches were to be carried by men dressed in blue. He also specified a man wearing his armour (including his helm) mounted on a good horse and stipulated that whoever fulfilled this role should be a fine figure of a man. The armoured figure would precede the body in the procession, as for the Black Prince. There is little doubt that, at Healaugh too, the armour would remain in the church and be displayed around the burial place. Sadly, very little remains of Healaugh Priory and there is no indication of a tomb.

Other testators reacted against the expense and ostentation of such funerals, going as far as to expressly reject this type of ceremony in their wills. For instance, in *c.* 1391 Sir William de Mowbray of Colton (W.R.) stipulated five tapers around his body but no other lights, no feasting or any other vainglory around his vile body (*Test. Ebor*. I, p. 158). Sir Ralph Hastings, in 1397, left his best horse as his mortuary to Selby Abbey but did not want his body to be honoured after his death with anything other than three tapers and that he should be carried to the Abbey in a cart (*Test. Ebor.* I, pp. 216–19). The fact that these and other men wished to avoid elaborate ceremony, and felt it necessary to specifically guard against it, suggests that heraldic funerals were rather the norm at that level of society. Indeed, in 1400, Robert Constable left to Flamborough church, as his burial gift, his best horse with armour as was the custom ('Item legavit pro mortuario suo meliorem equum suum cum armatura, secundum consuetudinem patriae,' *Test. Ebor*. I, p. 264). The normality of heraldic funerals in the area is demonstrated at Aldbrough. Sir John de Meaux made no mention of his armour in his 1377 will (*Test. Ebor*. I, p. 100), being rather more concerned that he should be buried in the habit of the Friars Minors, that a black cloth should be laid over his grave and that four great torches should burn around his body. Nevertheless, despite this ostentatious display of humility, his tomb did involve a display of armour. His great bascinet is a precious survival of what must have been a common feature of Yorkshire's medieval churches.

Like armour, textiles were a vulnerable part of the monumental ensemble and, when a pall was to be used to cover a monument, a hearse would be needed to support it, as requested by Sir Brian Stapleton. These were often temporary structures erected for the funeral or for the celebration of obits and anniversaries but they could also be permanent. Even then, they rarely survive. The most famous remaining is that over the effigy of the Earl of Warwick (Marks 2010). This barrel-shaped latten structure was clearly designed to fulfill this function, with expanded terminals on each of the longitudinal ribs to ensure the pall stayed in place. Others, as implied in the Stapleton will, doubled as supports for candles. It is this type that survives over the Marmion tomb at West Tanfield (Fig. 121). This is the only surviving medieval hearse in the country, apart from Warwick, and is of the first importance. Made of wrought iron, it has upright supports at the four corners, joined at the sides by crenellated bars. There are plain stretchers at each end, which are, in turn, the bases for arched supports to hold a third crenellated rail at a higher level over the full length of the tomb. When covered by a pall, the effect would have been of a gabled structure. The hearse incorporates prickets for seven candles, with one positioned in the centre of the top rail. One implication of this is that it could not have been covered by a single pall. A single cloth over a double tomb, and held at some height, would have been very large so it may have been more practical to use two smaller cloths. The denticulated upper edges of the rails may be purely decorative but they may also have served to restrain the cloths from slipping to the side.

Some hints of the former existence of hearse-like constructions can be seen at Goldsborough, Bedale and Kellington, while Welwick may have had a temporary arrangement (*6a.ii*). When the earlier tomb at Goldsborough

Fig. 121 West Tanfield. Tomb with contemporary iron hearse.

was conserved, two sockets were discovered in each jamb of the arch. They seem likely to have held two horizontal bars to act as a simple, permanent, hearse (Gittos 1997). Another witness to the possible former existence of a hearse is on the effigy of the lady at Bedale. Here, three of the corners of the slab are shaped to act as supports (the fourth is broken). The positions are circular and stand outside the effigy but are fairly small. If these positions were to hold a hearse, then the upstands on the chamfer of the slab may have provided seating for additional uprights. However, the corner positions could also be sconces for candles and the surviving lead might have secured the prickets. Candle supports might also be incorporated into the structure of a monument and stumps or positions for them can still be seen at Welwick (Fig. 279) and beside the lady at Aldbrough.

A final aspect to be considered in connection with hearses is the provision of cloths to cover them. The few surviving cloths associated with tombs are richly decorated, for instance the early sixteenth-century Dunstable pall and the late thirteenth-century funerary cloth of Otto de Grandisson. The Fayre family pall from Dunstable is shaped to fit over the coffin rather than to cover a tomb, so is intended for use during the burial service. It is a sumptuous piece made in Florence and combines rich fabrics (cloth of gold silk velvet) and embroidery depicting members of the family and heraldic devices (Marks & Williamson 2003, pp. 57 & 454). The Grandisson cloth is relevant since despite being buried in Lausanne (Switzerland), Otto de Grandisson spent almost his entire career in England and was a very close companion of Edward I. This cloth was used in association with his tomb and is a simple rectangle of taffeta and silk made in Cyprus. Much of the embroidery is done in gilded silver thread and the design depicts a tiny kneeling figure of the donor before a Virgin and Child between angels and flanked by foliage. There are also two tiny shields of Grandisson's arms (Cormack & Vassilaki 2008, pp. 295–96 & 445). These two examples are at the most opulent end of the spectrum but the cloth of blue say requested by Sir Brian Stapleton is likely to have stayed in the church and been used to cover the hearse on anniversaries and obits. Whilst probably a frontal band for an altar rather than part of a pall, an embroidery in the V&A Museum (T.70–1923) may well have been used for funeral or obit services. From the first half of the fourteenth century, in addition to its lettering, it carries the arms of de Vescy and de Lacy with an inscription recording it was worked by a nun called Joan of Beverley. Given the embroideress' name and the heraldry, it is likely to be related to the county and is potentially the only surviving funerary textile from Yorkshire.

3g Dedicated locations

Monuments are often associated with defined sacred spaces, installed either as part of an integrated scheme or as an addition to an established space. Private chantry chapels, the choirs of collegiate churches and chancels in parish churches all served as fitting settings to pray for the dead and ease their passage to heaven. These dedicated locations would provide private remembrance spaces for the family and, where the line had died out, an associated chantry or college would stand in place of relatives, keeping their memory alive (Saul 2017, p. 284). The extent to which monuments were integrated with their locations varied greatly, with the family's burial history and the size of budget playing their parts. The following case studies demonstrate a range of relationships between some Yorkshire effigies and the positions chosen for them.

3g.i Goldsborough

St Mary the Virgin, Goldsborough is an outstanding example of the integration of commemoration with a contemporary architectural setting. The chancel still contains three fourteenth-century monuments commemorating two generations of the same family: two military effigies and the indent of a female monumental brass (Gittos 1994a). The earliest is the Series B knight in the north wall recess. He rests on a low plinth, beneath a cinquefoil arch with a steep and dominant gable set low over the effigy. There are tall side shafts flanking the crocketed gable and a large trilobe completely filling the spandrel. The trilobe contains a pedestal above a maple leaf but the image it once supported has gone. The Goldsborough gable (Plate 26) can usefully be compared with the facade of the great gatehouse at Kirkham Priory (Plate 27). There, the entrance is surmounted by a dominant gable, which has tall side shafts and is broad in proportion to its height. This gable has a close affinity with that of the Goldsborough tomb, as do the smaller gables in the upper stage of the façade, which are just as steep as at Goldsborough and have very similar crocketing. The gatehouse has been dated to the late thirteenth or early fourteenth century, on the basis of the carved heraldry and on comparison with work at York Minster, perhaps *c*. 1290–95 (Harrison 2010, p. 14; Pev:ER 1995, p. 590). The back wall of the Goldsborough tomb has a smaller cinquefoiled opening that only spans just over half the length of the recess. The form of this opening is a trefoil with two additional, smaller and pointed side lobes giving it the appearance of *c*. 1300 window tracery. A similar shape can also be seen, for example, in the heads of the niches on the side panels of the Cantilupe shrine in Hereford Cathedral, dating from the 1280s. So it is likely the Goldsborough tomb dates from the years around 1300.

The chancel itself is an interesting structure, with a dramatic east window (Fig. 122). For a short distance at its west end, the chancel abuts a north chapel, perhaps of the early thirteenth century, which is continuous with the north nave aisle and which Pevsner (Pev:WR 2009, p. 283) thought predated the chancel. The possible date of this chapel is best assessed from

Fig. 122 Goldsborough. The chancel and its monuments.

the large archway that still provides access from the chancel. This has a probably fourteenth-century chamfered arch, like those of both nave arcades, but it sits on two half round thirteenth-century responds. The half round capitals have mouldings sympathetic with those of the hexagonal capitals of the nave north arcade, providing a harmony between the two phases. The implication is that an existing opening to the north chapel was modified, probably when the nave arcade was built in the fourteenth century. This suggestion is corroborated by the fact that the responds are narrower in cross-section than the arch and the wall above. In fact, the capitals support only the central rib of the arch and the awkward junction between them has been accommodated by tapering the lowest blocks of the arch, on both sides, to fit the narrower responds.

So, when was the chancel constructed? From the exterior, there are two particularly notable features (Plate 29): the east window and a continuous string course at sill level that, on the south side, steps over the head of the priest's door and under the low side window. Inside, the sill level string course is also a prominent feature, crossing through the canopy of the tomb recess and stepping up to frame the head of the sedilia, although this area has to be treated with some caution since the sedilia were rebuilt by George Gilbert Scott in 1859 but said to replicate the original (Pev:WR 2009, p. 283). The east window comprises five stepped lancets, the outer two beneath small circles, all within a single arch, which is backed on the inside by two ribs that amount to a miniature vault. The closest comparison of which we are currently aware is the east window of South Church (Auckland St Andrew, Co. Durham), albeit lacking the circles and with more pointed heads to the lights (Plate 30). The chancel there also features a prominent string course that runs at sill level and steps both up and down around features in the same way as at Goldsborough. Auckland St Andrew was a collegiate church reconstituted and re-endowed in 1292 by Anthony Bek, Bishop of Durham, who is credited with its rebuilding (VCH:D:II, pp. 126–27; Pev:D 1985, p. 411). The links are so close, they are unlikely to be a coincidence.

But why should a West Riding parish church have any association with one of the most powerful men in the kingdom under Edward I? The answer lies with the family who held the manor, the de Goldesburghs. Richard de Goldesburgh IV married Eva de Bek, the daughter of a Lincolnshire landowner and Bishop Bek's sister. Two of Richard IV and Eva's sons, Thomas and Anthony, entered the church, under the patronage of their uncle (Fraser 1957, p. 47 fn.4; the fundamental family records are collected in Goldsbrough 1930). Anthony seems to have died young but Thomas became a Canon of Lincoln, Archdeacon of Durham and one of the executors of his uncle's will. The relationship with the de Goldesburgh family was clearly close and this is underlined by Dodsworth's account of the glass he saw at Goldsborough in 1620 (Dodsworth, p. 103). The chancel windows seem to have contained at least two shields of Bek undifferenced and one of Anthony Bek, in addition to an image of the bishop himself: 'A picture of a bishop with staff and miter; on his brest gu[les] a cross sarcele and border erm[ine].' This is very reminiscent of images on the obverse of his seals both as Bishop of Durham and as Patriarch of Jerusalem (to which he was elevated in 1305). They depict him blessing, with his cross moline on the front of his chasuble (Fraser 1957, frontispiece). Given this close association between the de Goldesburgh family and Bishop Bek, it is unsurprising that their building projects should also bear comparison but it does assist in interpreting the architecture of the chancel at Goldsborough. The comparison with Bek's work at Auckland St Andrew suggests a date of around 1300 for the rebuilding of the Goldsborough chancel, which is consistent with the comparison between the tomb recess and the gateway at Kirkham Priory.

The fact that the string course that runs around the interior of the chancel also passes through the monument's gable and side shafts, suggests that the monument was built at the same time as the chancel and is structurally a part of it. The construction of the tomb recess is revealing. It is made in two separate sections. The recess utilises a small number of very large stone blocks, which form both the soffit of the arch and the mouldings for the shafts and gable. In contrast, the smaller arch on the north side is made from fairly thin slabs on end that provide the shape and edge moulding but are just a facade. So it appears that the recess itself is integral to the chancel wall and is designed to be a load-bearing constituent of the original build. The facade on the north side can be interpreted as a means of integrating that face with the pre-existing chapel. It may even be that it was intended to blend with the style of the chapel as it then was. The architectural mouldings provide further evidence to support this. Those on the south face of the recess are all simple combinations of chamfers and hollows, akin to both the string course and the wall plate in the chancel. The north face moulding has a scroll backed by a deep three-quarter circle hollow, which divides it from a series of simple straight chamfers on the recess side (Fig. 123). This inner face is in sympathy with the mouldings of the main opening and the chancel but contrasts with the north face, within the chapel. Here, the scroll moulding recalls the capitals of the arch into the chancel. So the recess must have been built at the same time as the chancel but designed to blend with both the new work and the old.

The justification for describing the chancel and tomb recess in this level of detail is the need to understand the special care that has been taken in the siting of the earlier of the two effigies at Goldsborough. Lying as it does between the north chapel and the chancel, it is visible from both. The large opening towards the chancel clearly displays the effigy, reminding the celebrant to remember the commemorated. However, the plinth on which the effigy lies is not horizontal but slopes up towards the head, rising by some 3½ inches and increasing the animation of the cross-legged figure, as if to permit the representation of the deceased (and, by inference, the deceased himself) to participate in and, perhaps gain additional benefit from, the services at the high altar (Saul 2017, p. 171). The space in the chapel provided by the seemingly blank back wall beside the lower part of the figure would have provided a location for the chapel's piscina and allowed the monument to be placed as far east as possible with respect to the former altar in the chapel. Consequently, it is sited nearer to this altar than would otherwise be the case and the chapel's celebrant would have stood beside the effigy's head. A further benefit of the recess' unusual design is that the two arches would have acted together as a squint, allowing the line of sight between the chapel's celebrant and the high altar to run through the monument, across the effigy. All this suggests a deliberate attempt to integrate the monument with the church's liturgy. With a new-build chancel, there

Fig. 123 Goldsborough. Tomb recess and effigy from the north chapel.

Fig. 124 Goldsborough. Eva de Goldesburgh's memorial.

could have been no problem of finding a less tricky space to site the tomb. In this respect too, the lack of a tomb chest seems quite deliberate. To have raised the effigy would have interrupted the sight line between the altars, and the shallow plinth was probably a compromise to lift the figure while retaining the necessary visibility. However, despite the monument's relationship with the altar in the north chapel, its primary face is towards the chancel.

It is also important to consider the rectangular floor slab commemorating a lady, currently on the floor of the chancel, its design formerly incised or painted and partly inlaid with brass (Fig. 124). The indents for the brass letters allow the inscription to be read and it commemorates Richard IV's wife Eva, who is said to have died after 1313 (Dodsworth, p. 103 n. 3). It lies alongside the effigy attributable to her husband, emphasising that the chancel is more likely to have been the primary altar for commemoration, rather than that in the north chapel. This is reinforced by the existence of a further monument, another effigy of an armed man, bearing the de Goldesburgh arms on his shield. It commemorates Richard de Goldesburgh V and dates from the 1330s (Gittos 1994a). He lies on a tomb chest on the south side of the chancel, outside the altar rails. Nigel Saul has observed the increasing frequency at this period of patrons and holders of advowsons being buried in chancels, often near where they had worshipped (Saul 2017, pp. 178–79). All three monuments were described as 'in the same chauncel' in the record of a 1612 herald's visitation, making it highly likely that they are still in something like their original arrangement (College of Arms, RR14B/C fo. 200):

> There lyeth Sir Waulter Becke under a stone in the Chauncell but the arms and inscription is all gone away. There is in the same chauncel two lying pictures in stone very old cross leged with there sheilds and in male very fayre carved the one of them hath the coate of Goldsbrough's Arms on his sheild.

The identification of the slab as Walter Bek is a misreading, since the inscription describes Eva as 'FYLE : SIR : WAVTER : BEK'. In 1669, they lay as they are now, on opposite sides of the chancel (Johnston C 13, fo. 187r, 194r). So at Goldsborough, the chancel was built to double as a family mausoleum and the primary monument integrated in accordance with ideas current at the period. It is an extreme example of structure, monument and liturgy functioning as a unit.

3g.ii Sprotbrough

By contrast, the monuments surviving at Sprotbrough were designed to reflect their position in a chapel. Two tomb recesses stand on either side of the chapel, one containing a knight bearing the FitzWilliam arms on his shield and the other holding a female figure, likely to be his wife. The current arrangement is a result of extensive reconstruction work undertaken by Ninian Comper during 1914/15 (Carrington 2014a), when the demolished recess on the north side was rebuilt, using some surviving *in situ* fragments. The south arch appears to be largely original and the new north arch copies it, including the solid back wall. However, recently discovered pieces from the original north arch show that it was open to the nave (Carrington 2014a, p. 17; 2014b). The north arch must have been lost prior to 1670 when Henry Johnston recorded the monuments and the knight was already out of place, on the floor (Johnston C 14, fo. 237r). At the restoration, he was placed in the south arch (Fig. 125) while the lady, who had previously occupied it, was switched to the north (Fig. 126).

The Decorated arch of the south wall tomb (occupied by the armoured figure), appears to be an integral part of the structure. Inside the chapel, wall plaster conceals the structural detail but there is no disturbance (even thickening) of the wall outside and the tomb's eastern pinnacle has been curtailed by a window that must, therefore, be later in date. This window is one of a set along the length of the aisle (Plate 33). Externally, the weakening of the wall occasioned by the incorporation of the recess is handled by the addition

Fig. 125 Sprotbrough. FitzWilliam knight in canopied recess.

Fig. 126 Sprotbrough. Isabella FitzWilliam in reconstructed recess.

Fig. 127 Sprotbrough. Knight's crowned lion foot support.

of a buttress. This is of the same form as the corner buttresses and all incorporate the angle-topped plinth course that runs the full length of the aisle, interrupted only by the later porch. It seems likely, therefore, that the chapel was built as part of the aisle at the same time as the monuments were commissioned. Since the two arches seem to have been very similar, they were almost certainly contemporary and the architecture of the southern arch can be used to date both canopies. The complex cusping, pronounced ogee outline and big foliate crocketing combine to suggest a date towards the middle of the fourteenth century. The will of Isabella FitzWilliam (neé Deincourt) made in 1348 asked for burial in the chapel of St Thomas the Martyr in Sprotbrough and she bequeathed 100 shillings to the fabric of the chapel (*Test. Ebor*. I, p. 50). This suggests that the building was either unfinished or incompletely fitted out. Although her will makes no mention of a FitzWilliam chantry at this altar, the arrangement of the tombs in proximity to it strongly suggests that one existed. Her bequest of ten marks to fund four priests celebrating for a year after her death may simply denote her anxiety to be sped through Purgatory.

Isabella's husband, William FitzWilliam had predeceased her, 1340 × 1342. Their eldest son, William, was executed after supporting Lancaster at Boroughbridge in 1322 while their eventual heir, John, died the year after his mother, in 1349 (CP V, p. 519). The female effigy (Plate 34) is datable from her costume and that of her attendant figures Margaret Scott said that although 'This figure is sometimes dated *c*. 1310, … the cut of the clothes suggests a date not before *c*. 1340' (Scott 1986, p. 32). Scott concluded it was likely to date '*c*. 1340–50' and since the effigy is shown as a widow, it is likely to commemorate Isabella and to date from after William's death. The armour worn by the male figure seems rather old fashioned for such a date (*2b.iii*) except that the surcoat has a shaped hem that reveals the knees at the front. This makes it a variant of the mid-century short-fronted surcoat (*2a.v*), of which there are many examples on monuments dating from the 1340s. Similarly, the straight-legged posture suggests a date after 1340 since, from the mid-thirteenth to the mid-fourteenth century, cross-legged effigies were in vogue and it was only in the 1340s that the stance reverted to its earlier form. Why the knight should have been shown in this awkward manner, when the female figure straightforwardly wears the clothing of the day, is puzzling but likely to be intentional. That their depiction was given careful thought is clear from the fact that the lady's fillet decoration of lozenges matches that on her angels' amices, both reflecting the FitzWilliam's lozengy arms. Her husband's lion is crowned (Fig. 127), which also seems like an armorial reference.

During the early twentieth-century work on the chapel, a lead coffin was found below the north arch. This was the original position of the armoured effigy so it may well contain the remains of whoever was commemorated by that figure. Lead coffins and shrouds (where the body is wrapped

Fig. 128 Sutton-on-Hull. Sir John de Sutton's effigy.

Fig. 129 Sutton-on-Hull. Sir John de Sutton's monument.

in lead rather than placed in a container of lead) were likely to be employed when there was a need to retain the effects of bodily decay or agents used for preservation and whilst one might have been used for reasons of prestige, it is more likely that its presence implies an anticipated delay in consigning the remains to their final resting place (Gittos 2017b; Gilchrist & Sloane 2005, Section 5.2). It is not known what form the Sprotbrough burial took. It is possible, therefore, that Isabella intended her husband to be buried within the chapel but that the site was not yet ready. This may mean that the aisle was still under construction or that the scheme was not initiated until after his death. It appears that what Isabella FitzWilliam intended at Sprotbrough was a private chapel that could be used for family commemoration.

3g.iii Sutton-on-Hull

Although the building work most frequently associated with monuments was the creation of new chapels, other areas could also be subject to development. An outstanding case is Sutton-on-Hull, which seems to have been rebuilt in its entirety in the middle of the fourteenth century (Blashill 1900, pp. 90–101; Pev:ER 1995, pp. 565–66) and where the monument of Sir John de Sutton, who died in 1356 (CP XII, p. 575), survives in the chancel (Fig. 128). In 1347, despite its status as a dependancy of the mother church at Wawne, the church became a collegiate foundation with five priests and a warden. A new nave was created and a large chancel was built (Plate 35), which is believed to have been divided in two, to provide a small sanctuary for the parishioners (themselves accommodated in the nave) and, to the east, a substantial choir for use by the college (Blashill 1900, pp. 92–95). Apart from the conventional benefit to the king and queen, the college was for 'the good estate of John himself, and Alice, his consort, while living, for their souls when dead, and for the souls of Sir John's father and mother, their ancestors and heirs' (Poulson 1841, II, p. 331). Sir John's interment is unusually well attested in evidence associated with a local legal dispute. In 1402, John Dowson, an elderly parishioner, said 'that around fifty years ago he was present in the aforesaid church of Sutton, on a certain day which is not recorded, where he saw the body of Sir John de Sutton, … publicly buried in the choir or chancel of the said church of Sutton; whose body lies buried in the aforesaid chancel, as it appears by the witness of his tomb' (Luxford 2009). The tomb lay in the centre of the choir until it was shifted to the south side in the later nineteenth century (Fig. 129), 'about 1870' according to a notice in the church. What survives at Sutton is the tomb of the founder and beneficiary at the centre of his college.

Sadly, the depredations of the Reformation and more recent restorations mean that none of the college's fittings and furnishings have come down to us. However, glimpses of what might be expected in such an institution can be gleaned from survivals elsewhere. The major collegiate church at Ottery St Mary (Devon) was founded ten years before Sutton, its Statutes issued in 1338. It was far more lavish but the immense amount of detail about its foundation and operation casts some light on what Sutton has lost (Dalton 1917). The new church at Ottery was fully equipped by its patron (John Grandisson, Bishop of Exeter) and certain elements have survived while others are detailed in its Statutes. Some carved wooden stalls for the members of the College remain, as do a wooden eagle lectern, part of the great reredos, a few floor tiles and the vault with carved bosses. Its Statues, John Grandisson's will and the Dissolution inventory, taken in May 1545, provide further information on its vestments, plate, devotional images, books, bells, organs, window glass and metalwork. At Ottery these were all of the highest quality, which is unlikely to have been so at Sutton but, nevertheless, these are the kind of fittings and equipment that would have surrounded the monument as the chaplains went about their daily business of commemorating the dead and speeding their passage through Purgatory. Many of the items at Ottery carried the founder's arms or those of other beneficiaries and this would almost certainly have been the case at Sutton-on-Hull.

So, what indications are there of Sutton's fittings and furniture? When Abraham de la Pryme visited in 1700, to conduct a funeral, he noted, 'In the quire has been seats for the collegians, turning up like the prebendary's seats in collegiate churches, with the arms of the builders thereon, only one of which is now remaining, which is a cross flure, which I take to have been the arms of the Lassels' (de la Pryme, p. 234). A group of later fourteenth-century figurative stalls survives at nearby Swine (Plate 36) but Sutton clearly had heraldic misericords, like Ottery St Mary. The shield recorded by de la Pryme was not that of Sutton (or a lion rampant azure debruised by a bend goboney, argent and gules) but the use of heraldry other than that of the patron was clearly a feature of this building, as it often was in other contexts at this time (DBA 1, pp. 221–22). There are no wall paintings now visible at Sutton but those at Winterbourne (Gloucestershire) are possibly to be associated with the chantry founded there before 1352 (Badham 2008). Here shields and other heraldic devices with the family arms decorate the walls, with at least one kneeling donor figure shown with his knight's pennon (Gill 1998). The grand chancel at Norbury (Derbyshire), whilst belonging to a parish church rather than a college, was rebuilt in the early years of the fourteenth century and retains much of its original glazing. The height of the windows is largely filled with fashionable grisaille glass but each light features one or more large shields, again demonstrating the prominence of heraldry in such situations (Titterton 2012). There is evidence that something similar was in place at Sutton. De la Pryme noted two shields of arms, one in the east window and the other in a north window, but in 1584 Glover recorded twenty-five (Foster 1875, p. 445). He does not make it clear where the shields were located but Harvey has sensibly argued that they were ranged around the windows, potentially one in each light, citing the comparison of the contemporary chancel windows at Selby Abbey (Harvey

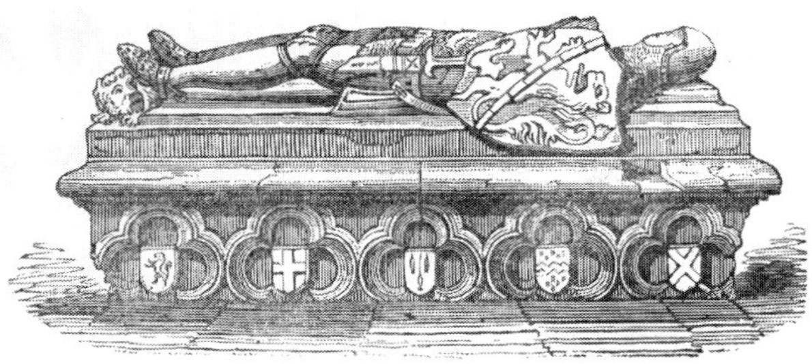

Fig. 130 Sutton-on-Hull. The tomb chest heraldry, from Poulson (1840 & 1841, II, p. 338).

1961, pp. 462–77). This arrangement would also be very akin to the surviving Norbury scheme, albeit on a smaller scale. The individuals represented at Norbury constitute a gallery from royalty, magnates and nobility down to representatives of the local gentry. The brass of Sir Hugh Hastings (died 1347) at Elsing (Norfolk) shows figures of warriors in the niches of the canopy surrounding him, identifiable by their heraldry. They can be interpreted as Sir Hugh's companions in arms, in various campaigns (Saul 2009, pp. 216–17). Shields on the tomb chest of Reginald, Lord Cobham (d. 1361) at Lingfield (Surrey) do the same job and such connections were also invoked on Sir John Sutton's tomb chest, by fourteen large shields (Fig. 130). The Sutton heraldry may have been intended to convey Sir John's career, as suggested by Saul (2009, p. 224). The chest displays the arms of Percy (probably), Lucy, Deincourt, Neville, Fauconberg (probably), Ros, Greystock, Welles (probably), Darcy, Cantilupe and Hastings, while the window glass seen by Glover included, in addition, de Mauley, de la Pole, FitzWilliam, Malbys and (probably) Ughtred. Many of these families were local and while some may represent intermarriages, this cannot be true of all, whereas Sir John fought alongside a high proportion of these people at the battle of Neville's Cross in 1346 and at the siege of Calais the following year. These are probably the associations being illustrated in a secular display within a religious setting. Sir John Sutton was childless and his brother, Thomas, who succeeded him left only daughters, so the male line became extinct. His may be the remains of the once impressive canopied tomb at Swine (*3e*). Late in his life, Thomas reformed the college statues, adding himself and his wife to the specified beneficiaries (Blashill 1900, p. 107). It seems as though this foundation, in its new-build chancel, was intended as a lasting testament to the Sutton family and its presence in the community, keeping the name alive (Saul 2017, p. 284). Sir John's effigy remained as a visual and virtual presence at its core, surrounded by evidence of his family's associations and achievements.

The case studies of Sutton-on-Hull, Sprotbrough and Goldsborough demonstrate the amount that can be gleaned through careful observation, in terms of the degree of planning, the extent of provision and the subsequent history of just five effigies. The studies also show the value of examining the historical circumstances and immediate environment, to understand their effects on the monument. Each example carries different resonances. While all involve the stimulation of prayer, Sutton kept the memory of the family and its achievements alive through the working of the college situated at the centre of their property, Sprotbrough provided a private space for remembrance and Goldsborough inextricably bound family members into the regular functioning of the liturgy. In each case the location should not be seen as just a setting for the monuments but as vital to their understanding. They are rich architectural contexts that enable interpretation of the effigies.

3h The churchyard

The broadest of all monumental contexts is the churchyard itself. Often believed to have been devoid of monuments in the medieval period, there is substantial evidence to the contrary. The study of external medieval monuments is still in its infancy but we published a summary of our research on this in 2013 (Gittos 2013a). The great majority of medieval churchyard memorials were not effigial but some were and many have been recognised countrywide. They are well represented in the county, a number still remaining outside, while others have been moved indoors for protection. There is a deeply-rooted belief that monuments have only become weathered because they were cast outside during church restorations but this seems unfounded. In a high proportion of cases, the weathering is a result of spending their lives in the churchyard. Effigies set up outside were subject to special problems and a number of features can help to identify them. They tend to be more robust, with little or no undercutting, making them less vulnerable to casual or deliberate damage. The base slabs are often particularly thick and heavy, so they would be difficult to disturb. They usually display an overall pattern of weathering, commensurate with long exposure to the elements. Since cavities would retain rainwater, sometimes tell-tale drainage holes have been provided to deal with the problem. Applying the above criteria to the corpus, as many as forty-eight effigies or one fifth of the total could be considered external. Two thirds are male and female civilians, with the remaining identifiable types almost equally split between military and ecclesiastics.

The chronology spans the period, with the table tomb at Middleton on-the-Wolds one of the earliest effigies in the county, while one of the latest is the double effigial tomb in the churchyard at Kirby (in Cleveland) (Plate 37). Between them are whole figures, such as the male civilians at Hedon and Weaverthorpe (Fig. 89), the bas-relief female at Patrington (Fig. 273) and many semi-effigials, such as Aldborough, Garton-on-the-Wolds, Moor Monkton (Plate 18) and Wadworth (Fig. 42), the latter having two busts on the one slab. Particularly good candidates for churchyard monuments include two of the ladies at Hornby, one of which still lies in the churchyard (Plate 5); the Hutton Cranswick priest; the low relief lady at Kirkleatham; all the very weathered figures at Forcett and Stanwick and the two figures inside the church at Garton-on-the-Wolds. Drainage holes occur on five semi-effigials, although curiously venting only the head area: Aldborough, Garton-on-the-Wolds, Goodmanham (the female), Moor Monkton and the double effigy at Wadworth. In addition, the bas-relief female at Patrington has holes either side of her neck that widen as they pass through the stone, presumably to enhance drainage (Plate 19). The holes at Wadworth and Aldborough have eroded into small channels, where water trickling through them has left furrows down the edges of the slab. However, those flanking the head of the Garton-on-the-Wolds lady are still intact, perhaps due to better weathering properties of the stone.

Wadworth is an example of a monument known to have been brought in from the churchyard (Hunter 1828, I, p. 254). Another is the small semi-effigial at Loversall (Fig. 29), which is now in the north aisle but in a nineteenth-century sketch appears next to the famous medieval chest tomb in the churchyard (Bloxham 1882, facing p. 352). Others known to have been brought inside include the Hedon civilian, Kellington (Fig. 131), the knight and lady at Hauxwell (I'Anson 1917) and both the Thrybergh ecclesiastics, all of which are very weathered. As well as Aldborough and Garton-on-the-Wolds, those remaining in churchyards include the male civilians at Batley and Weaverthorpe, the ecclesiastic at Great Mitton, the knight and lady (double effigy) at Kirby (in Cleveland) and Middleton on-the-Wolds. The complete lady at Garton-on-the-Wolds must be the heaviest and most robust (Fig. 132). Despite being carved in low relief, her massive base slab makes the block a remarkable 26 inches (0.66 m) deep and she is also very weathered. Another example may be the monolithic effigy and plinth at Bainton (*3c*). However, the robustness criterion cannot be used alone as a definitive indicator, since a seventeenth-century sketch records the very thick slab at Gilling East sited in a recess in the chancel (Torre 1692, fo. 280). Significantly, its carving is well preserved and it does not appear to have been exposed to the elements. The double effigy at Lowthorpe was probably also an external monument (*5c.ix*) and it must easily be the heaviest block in the corpus. One tomb that defies even the seemingly straightforward internal or external categorisation is Welwick, as it has a presence both inside and outside the church (*6a*).

Of those that remain outside, few if any can be claimed to be still *in situ*. The Weaverthorpe effigy has recently been set on a modern plinth and the figure at Batley lies on a plinth of

Fig. 131 Kellington. 'The Serpent Stone'.

Fig. 132 Garton-on-the-Wolds. Lady.

uncertain date but was formerly elsewhere in the churchyard The knight and lady at Kirby (in Cleveland) have been in their present location for a long time but their plinth does not look medieval. They are also some distance to the north of the church, which is an unlikely choice of medieval burial location (Plate 37). The Middleton on-the-Wolds table tomb has been disturbed and the supports wrongly reassembled. It is even rumoured to have been brought from elsewhere (*2c.ii*) and its proximity to three other medieval grave slabs suggests they have been deliberately grouped in more modern times (Plate 2). Often the degree of weathering makes it very difficult to judge the quality but, even so, few if any can be considered in the first rank, probably because they were commissioned by patrons with more limited resources. The local mason seems usually to have been tasked with fulfilling their ambitions. Nevertheless, Yorkshire does boast some very good examples of the genre, which strengthen the thesis that the medieval churchyard was populated with monuments and was far from being just an open space for unmarked graves.

Most parish churchyards have been in continuous use for centuries and the inevitable rise in ground level means that monuments laid down in the thirteenth and fourteenth centuries become buried. Digging for later interments can lead to their rediscovery. Usually they would be considered an obstacle and covered over, moved out of the way or even broken up. Occasionally they have been carefully placed on the surface, directly above the original location. This is so with a thirteenth-century grave slab in the Camery at Wells Cathedral (Somerset) (Gittos 2001). It may have happened to some of the Yorkshire monuments, such as the semi-effigial figures at Garton-on-the-Wolds and Aldborough. The latter is a particularly good candidate because its massiveness makes it difficult to move and it lies in a slightly elevated position, on the south side of the church, quite close to the path. Some medieval wills that call for churchyard burial specify a location near a recognisable feature, such as a cross or path, adding credence to the Aldborough monument as being in its original location.

There is very little evidence for how the Yorkshire churchyard monuments were intended to be seen. Set flush with the ground they would rapidly grass over and become hidden. Raised on plinths or tomb chests they would remain visible for much longer and a non-effigial example survives on a tomb chest at Loversall. Elsewhere in England some medieval churchyard memorials have crosses carved on their vertical end faces. Examples include an effigy at Leckhampton (Gloucestershire) and semi-effigials at Silchester (Hampshire) and Limpley Stoke (Wiltshire) (Gittos 2013a). These would only be visible if the slab were above the surface but end crosses are not present on the Yorkshire examples and so the question of their setting must remain open. The fact that they are mostly tapered or coffin-shaped could mean that they once formed the lids of stone coffins, but from evidence elsewhere this was not always so. Coffins might be buried with only the lid showing but sometimes they must have been above ground, as was probably the case with the Purbeck marble example in the churchyard at Sturminster Marshall (Dorset), which has arcaded sides (Gittos 1994b, p. 10). However, like the end crosses, few stone coffins can be associated with the effigial churchyard monuments in Yorkshire. As yet, we are not aware of any archaeological excavations in association with the Yorkshire effigies still in churchyards and this remains a potentially fruitful prospect.

3i Conclusions

Despite the large number of Yorkshire effigies surviving from the thirteenth and fourteenth centuries, it is often unclear how they were originally displayed. Many are still on tomb chests and some lie in canopied recesses but the majority have lost their context. However, through studying surviving fragments of evidence, antiquarian sources and drawing comparison with monuments elsewhere, it can be possible to glean something of the original intent, the circumstances prevailing when the monuments were set up and their subsequent, sometimes complex, histories. A picture emerges of effigies rarely employed in isolation and often only one part of elaborate commemorative displays, involving many different media. Occasionally the monument of which the effigy was a part might constitute a whole chapel or section of the church. At this end of the spectrum, the complexity of such instructions as chantry foundations and the extreme elaboration of the grandest funerals serve to illuminate a whole panoply of commemorative possibilities. Whilst only the most affluent could have afforded such lavish arrangements, those lower down the social scale might still commission an effigy. A comparatively modest outlay would have been required for a semi-effigial slab to be located in a churchyard but even then it could be carefully displayed in the most advantageous way. What is clear from this examination is that effigies cannot be understood in isolation from their context and history. Unless there is some appreciation of the thought and care that accompanied their presentation and the architectural, decorative and liturgical aspects of their settings, a crucial part of the original intent is missed and we see nothing more informative than a skeleton.

Section 4

Makers and making

4a Fundamentals

A major factor in the final appearance of an effigy was the person who carved it: their expertise, interests and individual ways of working. After surveying the corpus and the effigies' settings, attention now turns to this aspect, considering how the figures were produced, where they came from and what can be deduced about the sculptors. We explore the evidence for the techniques used to achieve the finished items and examine the mason's approach to realism, portraiture and posture. The Section concludes with a description of the groups of sculpture that can be recognised as the products of a single carver or workshop – the Series referred to through the book – but initially the focus is on the fundamentals: materials and patterns of production.

4a.i Distribution patterns

The geographical distribution of Yorkshire effigies largely follows what would be expected from the pattern of settlement (Endpaper Map). There is a large void in the north west corresponding to the sparsely populated Pennine/high dales region with its difficult terrain and low population. Other gaps include the North Yorkshire Moors and the western Wolds and another swathe of mostly high ground to the south west, bordering Derbyshire and Lancashire. The effigies at Great Mitton, Kildwick and Ilkley are notable outliers to the west and without them the whole of western Yorkshire would be an effigy desert. Low population density and difficult transport routes for heavy objects are both logical reasons for this but perhaps the relative poverty of the population may have been the key, since, with sufficient funds, most difficulties can be overcome.

A smaller and more surprising effigy void, lies immediately to the east of York. It extends across the lowland vale as far as the edge of the Wolds at Market Weighton and from Sheriff Hutton in the north down as far as Howden. Forming the western boundary of the East Riding, the river Derwent flows north-south through this region and was navigable at least as far upstream as Stamford Bridge in the fourteenth century (VCH:ER:III, p. 154) and should have provided a conduit for monument distribution. Given the closeness to York, it is difficult to account for the absence of effigies in this area. Perhaps it is a misleading distortion of the picture due to the random nature of losses but some significant families were resident. However, the Everinghams of Everingham seem to have had a tradition of burying at their Nottinghamshire property of Laxton (CP, V, p. 193) where some fourteenth-century effigies remain. There was a strong interest in the area by families based elsewhere, such as the Percy family (Fangfoss, Catton) and de Malbys (Wheldrake), while some land, such as parts of Wheldrake, were held by the church. It is also true that the monastic houses of the area have been swept away and their contents lost. There were three: a house of Gilbertine canons at Ellerton and Benedictine nunneries at Thicket and Wilberfosse. All were small, Ellerton with four canons and a prior while Thicket and Wilberfosse had between eleven and twenty nuns in addition to their prioresses. Inevitably, the male house at Ellerton was the best endowed, but the only testamentary burials recorded by John Burton are fifteenth century (Burton 1758, p. 262). He notes none for the nunneries. It may be that this void in the distribution is simply a combination of these factors and that the nearby major ecclesiastical establishments of York, Selby and Howden creamed off many of the wealthier interments.

4a.ii Major sources of imports

In terms of how figures were sourced, the corpus can be divided into two broad categories: effigies made from

Fig. 133 Welton. Purbeck marble knight.

material obtained locally with the minimum of transport cost, and those for which the stone was won further afield such that the cost of delivery might equal or even exceed the cost of production. Given this differential, only those who could afford it would choose something other than a local product and the evidence largely supports this, although it happens that the two that have travelled the furthest are widely separated on the cost spectrum. They are the figure of Archbishop de Gray and the military effigy at Welton, both carved in Purbeck marble from the south east coast of Dorset, 235 miles away as the crow flies and more than 400 miles by water transport. De Gray's mid-thirteenth-century effigy was the best available at the time and can be compared with contemporary products of the highest quality from the Purbeck marblers, such as Bishops Northwold and Kilkenny in Ely Cathedral. The Welton knight (Fig. 133), on the other hand, represents the final phase of Purbeck marble effigies, much more simply carved in modest relief with no undercutting. Produced at a time when Purbeck was no longer a highly fashionable material, it was a form aimed at customers lower down the social order but who aspired to a 'marble' effigy (Blair, Goodall & Lankester 2000; Gittos 1998). As explained in Section 4a.v, the wooden knight at Whorlton is likely to have come from a metropolitan source.

Somewhat closer were the midland workshops that supplied the effigies carved in alabaster, which would have been able to use the River Trent as a conduit (*5a.i*). They all date from *c.* 1370 or later and there are twelve, comprising five male and female pairs (Darfield, Hull, Pickering, Swine and West Tanfield) and two single figures, the military torso at Pickering and Prince William of Hatfield in York Minster. The Hull pair (Fig. 134) have been claimed to be of alabaster from Ledsham in Yorkshire (Badham 2015a, p. 144). They are highly individual carvings and the stone is darker coloured than typical midlands alabaster, but there seems to be no definitive evidence for their source. When midlands alabaster achieved popularity in the later fourteenth century some Yorkshire patrons continued to select local Magnesian Limestone alternatives and the region seems to have been more resistant to these ordinarily all-pervasive imports than is usual elsewhere. The process can be seen at Swine where the *c.* 1370 alabaster pair was followed by a couple carved in the Yorkshire limestone (Fig. 135). In addition to Swine, there are other examples of important and elaborate monuments made from Magnesian in the period at Ripon, Ripley and Kirklington. With a handful of notable exceptions, Yorkshire was not a fruitful market for imports from prestigious sources elsewhere, until the fashion for alabaster monuments took root in the fifteenth century. Patrons and sculptors preferred their local products.

4a.iii Stone sources within Yorkshire

Within Yorkshire, the carvers of Series B, C and D (*4c*) chose to work in Magnesian Limestone. Although no documentary evidence has yet been discovered for its use in effigy making, there is a great deal recorded about its employment for building work. This was well demonstrated by Eric Gee's 1981 study. The main quarries supplying York Minster were at Thevesdale (near Tadcaster) between 1225 and 1423 and at Huddleston (Sherburn-in-Elmet) from 1385 until 1544, but as early as the 1180s William le Vavasour granted stone from his quarry at Hazelwood (near Tadcaster) to Salley Abbey. The family also leased quarries to Howden Minster, Thornton Abbey and St Mary's Abbey, York, at various dates in the thirteenth and fourteenth centuries (West Yorkshire Archive Service, WYL245, Vavasour Family Records). The Vavasours granted many parcels of the lands near Tadcaster for quarrying and in 1291 the monasteries of Selby, Thornton

Fig. 134 Hull, Holy Trinity. The alabaster pair.

and Drax were extracting stone from adjacent areas (Gee 1981, p. 248). The two Vavasour effigies in the family chapel at Hazelwood can justifiably be described as being of local stone. Magnesian Limestone has a fine texture that can be exploited to achieve very good detail, but it can also contain flaws that manifest themselves as thin seams of carbonate and small holes, often also lined with crystalline carbonate (Lott & Cooper 2008, pp. 83–84). Such irregularities posed problems for the carvers but now serve as an aid to its recognition. We have no means of knowing what the opinion was based upon but a note published following the discovery of the Church Fenton lady, described it as from 'a single block of fine yellow Huddleston limestone' (Boyne 1855, p. 31). However, Church Fenton is marginally nearer to the site of the Huddleston quarry (currently an equestrian centre) than to Thevesdale, which is believed to be the still active Jackdaw Quarry just south west of Tadcaster.

A rare case of Yorkshire effigies being related to a quarry source by geological analysis was achieved when the condition of the mid-fourteenth-century FitzWilliam effigies at Sprotbrough were assessed. In view of its importance the following details from the geologist's report are given in full (Jefferson 2014, p. 2):

> The petrographic analysis of the stone confirmed that it is magnesian limestone, composed largely of small crystals of dolomite, although larger crystals of calcite are randomly scattered throughout the stone. Although essentially featureless and rather porous, …, it can be identified as being stone from Stapleton quarry five kilometres east of Pontefract and about 18 kilometres north of Sprotbrough. The quarry was in operation from about 1300 until at least 1448 when it was supplying stone to Eton College. Within this period Stapleton stone was used at Windsor Castle, Westminster Hall, the Tower of London and Westminster Abbey, as well as at York Minster. The time during which this quarry was important fits in well with the dates attributed to the monuments.

Extensive quarrying at Stapleton (east of Pontefract, between Womersley and Darrington) continued into the twentieth century and a huge area of abandoned workings still remains. Although it seems only to have had limited

Fig. 135 Swine. Magnesian Limestone monument, including bases for the lost canopy.

use at York Minster, as Jefferson indicates, it was much sought after for important building works elsewhere and was even handled by the leading master mason of his day, Henry Yevele. He supplied thirteen tons of Stapleton stone for Rochester Castle *c.* 1368 (Knoop & Jones 1933, p. 23). It is also the most likely source for the ninety-two stones of 'Pontefract stone' purchased for St Stephen's Chapel, Westminster in 1343 (Salzman 1952, p. 131). The effigies at Kellington and Womersley are both much nearer to the quarry site than Sprotbrough and so must be candidates for being of Stapleton stone, as they all appear to be Magnesian Limestone. However, despite Darrington also being in the same area, its effigies might be of stone from Thevesdale because they are members of Series C and that location seems a better focus for the Series as a whole. Another material from the Magnesian Limestone deposits has a loose open texture like a honeycomb (Fig. 136). The best example is the Patrington lady but the priest at Beeford is another, as may be the related Winestead priest – all three being members of the Wolds Series. A geological comment about Patrington saw it as 'like some of the dolomitised limestones within the Magnesian Limestone' and 'a replacement petrographic texture not an original limestone' (Tim Palmer, pers. comm.). The source for this holey material remains unknown. In selecting material, transportation costs were not necessarily paramount. Quarry ownership might dictate what stone could be made available, while the circumstances and preferences of the carver might influence the choice.

In the north east of the county, the Ingleby Arncliffe group (Series E) are carved from a fine-grained sandstone, which still awaits formal identification (Gittos 2002b). However, since Guisborough can be seen as a focus for Series E production, it is likely to be relevant that the stone used by the abbey masons was a local sandstone from the immediate area, described as of the Middle Jurassic period from the Ravenscar Group and specifically the 'Saltwick and Cloughton formations' (King 2012, p. 15). In that context, when a pair of Series E knight's legs were discovered below the Eston Hills during clay digging for the Normanby Brickworks in 1900 (Fallow 1900), it may not have been far from its source of manufacture.

Fig. 136 Patrington. Lady's honeycombed Magnesian Limestone.

The polishable limestones of the region seem rarely to have been used for making effigies. There are just two cross slabs/grave covers in the county fashioned in the coralline Frosterley marble from near Stanhope, Co. Durham. They are at Howden with an inscription for the viscera of Walter Kirkham, Bishop of Durham (d. 1260) and in the churchyard at Spennithorne (N.R.). Although effigies were made from this material, *e.g.* a female at Easington, an ecclesiastic at Ryton and an armoured man at Hurworth (all Co. Durham), none survive in Yorkshire if, indeed, any were ever set up. The crinoidal limestone quarried near Egglestone Abbey became popular for tombs and grave slabs in the fifteenth century but only two effigies are known, both now in store: from Denton there is a very low relief lady and, from Egglestone Abbey itself, part of a foot supporting animal (Fig. 30) (Badham & Blacker 2009, pp. 45–46). Very few Yorkshire effigies have been the subject of professional geological identification so there is still much to be done and discovered in this regard.

4a.iv Lincolnshire limestone imports

At a late stage in the recording process an unusual type of limestone was noted that contains very distinctive pisoliths of a darker colour than the matrix and thin black flakes of shell debris (Plate 38). Geologist Tim Palmer did not believe the stone was from Yorkshire saying that it 'contains fossils and petrographic features that are typically found within Middle Jurassic limestones of the Lincolnshire area' (Tim Palmer, pers. comm.). Five effigies in Yorkshire have so far been identified as carved from this material: the females at Adlingfleet and Harpham plus two knights at West Tanfield and another at Pickhill. The earliest knight at West Tanfield was certainly not a surprise as its strong similarity with that at Rippingale (Lincolnshire) had been recognised by Harry Tummers, who illustrated them both side-by-side to make the point (Tummers 1980, pls 110 & 111). On this basis we have long regarded it as a Lincolnshire import (Gittos 2002a). None of the other four effigies belong to Yorkshire stylistic groups and so are also plausible imports. The Adlingfleet lady is adjacent to the Lincolnshire border and the pisoliths are so marked on her face that it gives her the appearance of having contracted some dreadful disease (Plate 39). Personal examination has since confirmed that the comparable knight at Rippingale is indeed of the same stone, which is also true of an ecclesiastical effigy in the same church. Checking back through photographs it has been possible to identify two more Lincolnshire effigies in this stone, the knights at Harrington and Saleby. A cut-out for a major repair to the right arm of the knight at Scotton (Lincolnshire) recalls the repairs to the earliest knight at West Tanfield and suggests it may be another, as pieced-in repairs during carving are typical of effigies in this material. Fragments of a military effigy apparently in this material have been recognised in Newcastle (Northumberland), discovered by excavation on the site of the Blackfriars (Lankester 2019). Much more needs to be done to discover the source of this intriguing material and plot its distribution, with the prospect of shedding new light on the effigies involved.

4a.v Wooden effigies

Five effigies are made of wood: at Allerton Mauleverer (two), Barnburgh, Swillington and Whorlton (Fig. 137). The latter is probably the product of a London-based workshop – the related group comprising Ousby (Cumberland), Danbury (Essex), Pamber End (Hants), Abergavenny (Monmouthshire), Ashton, Gayton, Woodford (Northants) and Berrington (Shropshire) (Prior & Gardner 1912, p. 666; Blair 1994, n. 25). Prior and Gardner saw Abergavenny, Berrington, Danbury, Gayton, Ousby and Whorlton as 'almost repetitions, and evidently close versions of the "Crouchback" stone figure' in Westminster Abbey. This association with a prestigious royal tomb and the country-wide distribution, were their justification for attributing this group to a London source. Swillington is now too decayed to judge its quality but a 1669/70 drawing (Fig. 138) suggests it was a competent work (Johnston C 13, fo. 276r). The Allerton Mauleverer figures have also lost much detail but Barnburgh is well preserved (Plate 20) and can be compared with two of the Yorkshire stone effigies at Bedale and Pickering because all three wear the short-fronted surcoat, which is uncommon in Yorkshire but seen elsewhere in England on effigies of the 1340s. The wooden effigies of Yorkshire are a disparate group, with little in common, and there are fewer than might be expected in

Fig. 137 Whorlton. Wooden knight.

an area of this size but that may be because Yorkshire is a stone-rich county.

4a.vi Where effigies were made

Even more difficult than determining the sources of the different stones is the question of where the effigies might have been carved. This topic has been the subject of a survey by Sally Badham (2010b), some of which deals with the situation in Yorkshire. In the absence of contracts, inferences must be drawn from the distribution, material, carving, stylistic relationships, estimated dating and local context of the monuments themselves so that no more than informed conjecture is possible. However, it is unlikely that all were carved in the same kind of situation. For instance, it is probable that many figures were carved at the quarry, as may be the case with the Ham Hill stone quarries in Somerset (Gittos 2012a). This may also be true for Series C in Yorkshire (*4a.iii*). It is also possible that work was done at the destination, perhaps using a prepared blank.

Fig. 138 Swillington. Johnston's drawing (C13, fo. 267r) of the wooden knight before he decayed.

A partially carved fourteenth-century knight at Grosmont (Monmouthshire) may well be an example (Pickford 2001/2). There is also circumstantial evidence that carving took place in the masons' yards associated with major building works. The knight and lady in Selby Abbey are well carved but unlike any others. The chancel was completed *c.* 1315–35, so work would have been in progress throughout the period when the effigies may have been produced (Coldstream 1994, p. 34). At Guisborough Priory, rebuilding work began soon after the destructive fire of 1289 but then continued slowly during the fourteen century and could readily have provided a centre for the production of the Series E effigies in the 1340s (Gittos 2002b, p. 26). The priest at Beverley Minster is believed to commemorate Provost Nicholas Huggate, who died in 1338, when major work was in progress involving much high quality sculpture and he is a well carved one-off likely to have been produced by the Minster masons. This is also true of the tomb at Welwick for a Provost, which can be shown to have been carved by masons working at Beverley but at a later date (*6a*). The carver of Series A and B also produced architectural sculpture for York Minster and this may have become his base (*4c.ii*), although no monuments of his are known from the Minster.

To what extent there were urban centres of production is unclear. Effigy making at York might have been associated with work at the Minster but separate workshops may equally have functioned in the city producing carving for the numerous parish churches as well as monuments. Whilst the York city Freemen Rolls might be expected to provide a picture of those masons trading in York during the period under study, the situation is made far more complex by the presence of five Liberties within the city that lay outside the jurisdiction of the city authorities. These Liberties belonged to the Abbey of St Mary, the Hospital of St Leonard, the Archbishop, the Dean of the Minster and, perhaps most crucially, the Minster itself. Stoneworkers operating in these areas would not have had to become city Freemen in order to trade and the owners of the Liberties probably constituted the most significant local patrons.

Between the start of the records in 1272 and the close of the fourteenth century, some sixty-eight masons took out the Freedom (Collins 1896), together with one 'cementarius' and two 'rough masons' (an average of just over one every other year). Clearly most of these men will have been contractors in the local building industry, only a handful appearing in John Harvey's *English Medieval Architects* (1984). Amongst those that do are four of the Minster's master masons: Simon le Mason (free in 1315), Ivo de Raghton (free in 1317), Robert de Patryngton (free in 1352) and Hugh de Hedon (free in 1394) of whom at least de Raghton and de Patryngton appear to have taken out the freedom before assuming charge of the Minster. Simon evidently made tombs, since his 1322 will provided for the sale of his stock of 'lapides marmoreos pro tumbis' (*Test. Ebor.* I, p. 2) but though he lived in the Minster precinct, he must nevertheless have felt it worthwhile to take out the Freedom. De Raghton's involvement with monument production is unproven but since this prolific and inventive man is known to have been involved with everything from the great west window of the Minster to the earlier shrine of St William and the pulpitum at Southwell Minster, he may well have done. He is known to have lived in the parish of Holy Trinity Goodramgate and died *c.* 1339 (Harvey 1984, pp. 238–39). Patryngton's situation is clearer since he is known to have provided monumental brasses, including commissions to commemorate some of Archbishop Thoresby's predecessors, one for Thomas de Thwing at Kirkleatham and, probably, another retrospective group for the Abbots of Meaux (Gittos 1991a; Badham & Oosterwijk 2010, pp. 197–200). None of these men can be shown to have been involved in the production of sculptured monuments and even if they were, they probably employed masons to carry out the carving.

The loose grouping found in Holderness and elsewhere in the East Riding that we have termed the Wolds Series (Gittos 1989) is now known to include figures of both sandstone and limestone. The variation suggests production at an urban centre rather than quarry-based, with Beverley a plausible location. The craftsmanship of these monuments is not of the highest standard but can reflect that of better quality contemporary work. The designs are idiosyncratic and suggest an inventive mind but hands that lacked the skill to carry the work to the top. This may explain both the size of the group and its limited distribution (*4c.vi*).

The picture from Yorkshire is a mixed one. Many local products are likely to have been made at the quarry, as may some of the major Series. York is a possible centre for others while a case can be made for an urban workshop at Beverley. Finally, a number of good quality figures may have come from the masons' yards of major churches and monasteries.

4b Techniques

4b.i Carving

Many effigies retain evidence of their carving, most often as tool marks. Works such as Rockwell 1993 and Daniels 2012 are helpful in understanding stone-carving tools and the marks they make – an important area that can assist with understanding not only the carving process but also how the effigy was intended to be finished and set up. Butterwick (Series B) in particular is of great significance because of its partially finished state (Fig. 139), as though the carver were interrupted, leaving the paint to make it

Fig. 139 Butterwick. Unfinished Series B effigy, probably Robert FitzRalph.

sufficiently presentable to satisfy the client. Its condition demonstrates aspects of the sculpting process. The figure is fully modelled, including the drapery of the surcoat and the tooling largely smoothed away, but many of the belts and buckles are simply blocked out, left deliberately larger than the finished item, to allow material from which the detail can be cut. Although shaped and undercut where necessary, the shield too is thicker than usual, sufficiently so to carve the internal detail common to Series B. Its outer face is uncarved, like those at Goldsborough and Escrick, save for some lightly scored lines (Plate 47). Given the care and precision in the rest of the carving, they may have been initial setting lines, suggesting an intention to carve the heraldry. The knight's face is finished and the foot supports almost so but only one small area of mail has been carved. This is on the part of the hauberk seen in the surcoat split and may be where the mason was working when carving ceased. The area has been marked out with scored parallel guide lines and the topmost few rows fully carved. There is also evidence here of a curious alteration while the links were being carved (Plate 44). The right side of the surcoat has been cut back, leaving a narrow strip without either mail or its guide lines,both hauberk and surcoat showing residual marks of his claw chisel. This may have been done to remove an error or fault in the stone but, whatever the reason, the alteration was left incomplete and the mail never extended into the newly opened area of hauberk. In several places, including the area around the ring locket, the folds above the waist belt and the head of the surcoat split (Plate 46), there are small drill holes, made in preparation for deeper carving which was never carried out. For whatever reason the mason never completed the job but in failing to do so he has unintentionally demonstrated aspects of his method of working.

Butterwick is an exceptionally informative case but marks telling of the carving process are to be found on many effigies. Although caution is necessary not to mistake later reworking for original dressing, indicators such as the position and direction of the marks and trapped paint fragments usually help to distinguish between them. Retouching during restoration often meant scraping, leaving long marks that can fail to respect the form of the carving while re-tooling creates suspiciously crisp edges. Another point to be borne in mind is that different materials require different tools and techniques. In this respect the Yorkshire evidence provides some useful indicators.

The most common finishing tool for Magnesian Limestone at this period seems to have been a fairly fine claw chisel, used very lightly, as if almost skating across the surface, leaving short parallel lines. They might have been left to provide keying for paint. Good examples include the Norton knight's left hand gablette shield, Goldsborough Series B effigy (Fig. 140) and East Harlsey. Claw tool marks show particularly well on the Felixkirk knight, except

Fig. 140 Goldsborough. Series B knight, claw tooling on poleyn.

Fig. 141 Kirklington. Knight, different types of tooling behind poleyn.

his face, where they have been smoothed away to leave a much more skin-like surface, appropriate to the finishing process used on him (*4b.iii*). Similarly, despite the Series B effigy at Goldsborough's widespread claw chisel marks, it too has a smooth face. The Kirklington figures show remnants of coarse and subsequently fine claw finishing but also the use of a small flat chisel as an additional way of producing a smooth surface. Marks under the knight's left knee (Fig. 141) show a straight chisel cutting into tooling of a relatively coarse claw. His female companion has been less carefully treated but the presence of paint fragments trapped amongst the straight tooling argues the finish is original. McCall (1910, p. 86) thought these effigies must date from around 1369, a time when elsewhere in England alabaster effigies were popular. Because of the nature of the material, alabaster carving was a different process than for other stones, resulting in a very smooth surface (Cheetham

Fig. 142 Bedale. Lady's head showing contemporary repair.

Fig. 143 Norton. Seated lady wearing a textured veil.

1984, p. 24) and it may be that, by this time, expectations and methods favoured this appearance.

Surfaces can also be deliberately textured. The Series B sculptor seems to have skilfully used the corner of a straight chisel in a regular, shallow, 'V' pattern to differentiate between fabrics, as in the veils at Bedale and Norton and the face cloth at Fountains (Figs 142, 143, 144). A later man used the same pattern at Ripley, to represent fur on the lady's dog and hair on the neck of the knight's boar head crest. Very shallow relief decorative effects can be added when the stone is sufficiently fine grained, such as the ermine tails on the hem of the lady's *surcote ouverte* at Pickering. She is alabaster, as is William of Hatfield in York Minster, whose cote has been given an overall foliage scroll pattern, representing damask or embroidery.

The stone axe was also used. Although toothed, it leaves different marks from claw chisels as it is used differently and the marks more resemble lines of pits. They are frequently found in areas where fine finishing was unnecessary, such as slab edges. Examples such as the Felixkirk knight are useful, where the two patterns can be compared, but other good examples include the Yorkshire Museum knight known as William de Vescy and the Alne lady. The marks on Goldsborough's shield (Series B) might be either a broad claw or even a toothed axe, used at a relatively steep angle to the surface (Fig. 145). It contrasts with the well finished surface of FitzAlan at Bedale (by the same hand but with carved heraldry) and may have been done because a layer of gesso was expected to be applied to the surface. The

Fig. 144 Fountains Abbey. Knight's textured face cloth.

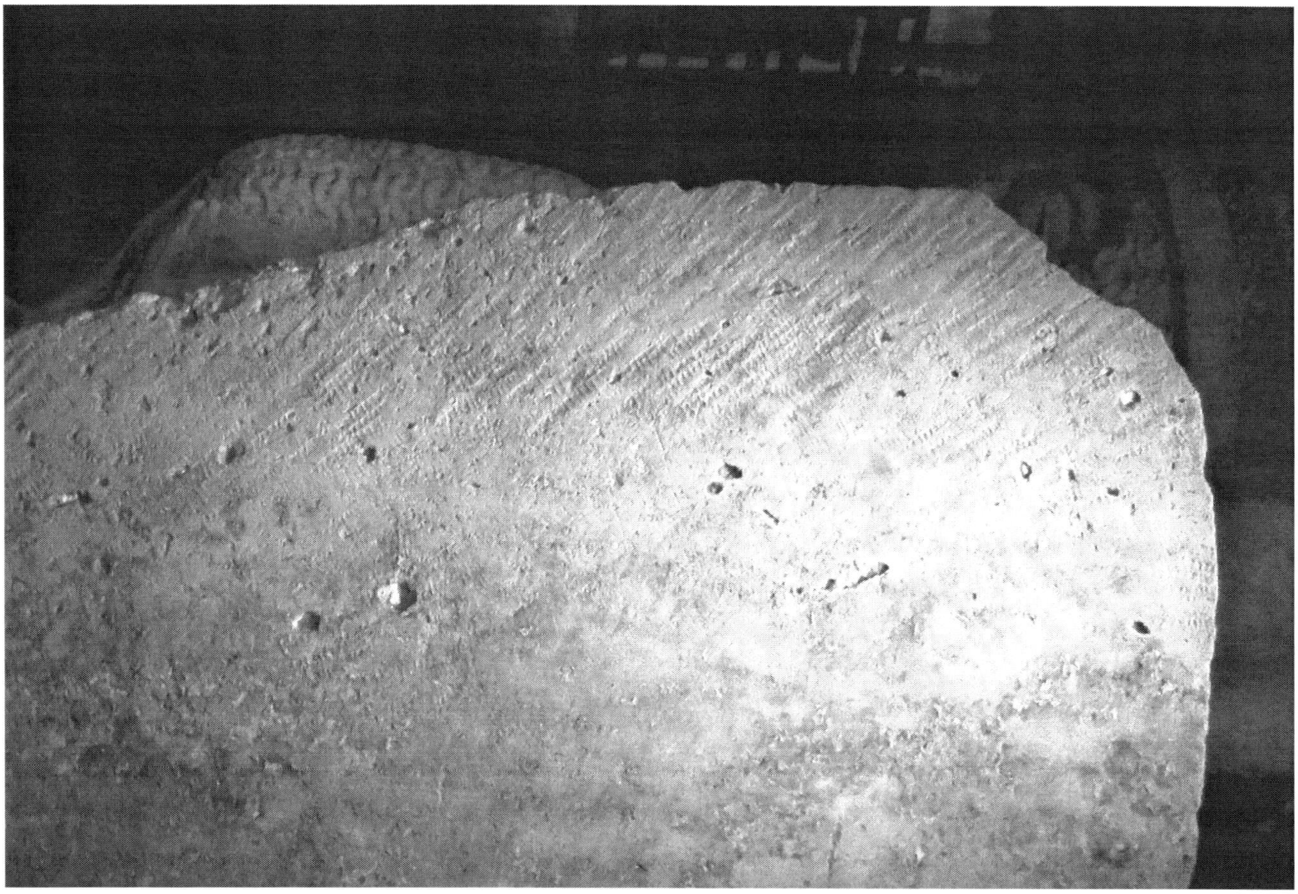

Fig. 145 Goldsborough. Series B knight, relatively coarse tooling on shield.

Hornsea lady combines a fine claw-finished surface with very coarse, broad chisel work on her underside where the block has been hollowed. Hollowed areas (*4b.iv*) are always coarse, the work done for practicality rather than finish and this is also true for undersides, where they can be inspected, as at Loversall.

Differences in tooling can help understand an effigy's original situation since areas to be hidden are often less well finished. The Fountains effigy has beautiful fine claw work, leaving combed lines, as has the surface of the slab, but its edge has lines of pits, made by either a broad claw or axe used acutely to the surface. It is not finished for display and this is also true of the top of the gablette, which is quite coarsely dressed with diagonal toothed axe or very broad claw chisel marks overlying even coarser diagonal tooling in a different orientation (Fig. 52). It is too rough to be a basis for paint and at odds with the fine quality of the rest of the figure, so it must have been out of sight against a surface. Other flat-topped gablettes, at Thornhill and Scarborough, also have unfinished tops, Scarborough being the smoother but the underside hollowing appears as a cut-out. Similar considerations affect Scarborough's foot end where the lion is not fully formed, the side away from the effigy only axe dressed and the hollowing again visible, so Scarborough may have been made for an arch. In contrast to the elaborate scene on the smaller Coverham's left side, the right edge of the slab seems still to have the marks of the block's original shaping by point chisel or punch. Presumably it too was to be hidden. The de Bruce effigy at Pickering has extremely rough slab edges and at the foot, the dog scarcely emerges from the block. As at Kilkenny (Fig. 17), the surface appears to be that left from the original squaring of the block (Gittos forthcoming). Often less obvious than Pickering, many effigies (*e.g.* the Kirklington man and Felixkirk lady) show the carver was fully aware of the monument's intended situation. Economy of effort also shows in the figure carving. The sculptors who left the mail uncarved on one side of Romaldkirk's head and the Swine Magnesian knight's neck, must have known no one would see them. It is commonplace to find very rough cutting in concealed areas, such as under the insteps of the Ormesby knight's feet or below the books of the Sprotbrough lady's praying attendants (Fig. 250). These areas are often very difficult for the sculptor to access, such as under Kirkby Fleetham's scabbard (Fig. 146), which lies close to the slab and preserves marks of the point tool that made the undercutting, or between the sword grip and shield at Darrington. Even the more easily carved alabasters

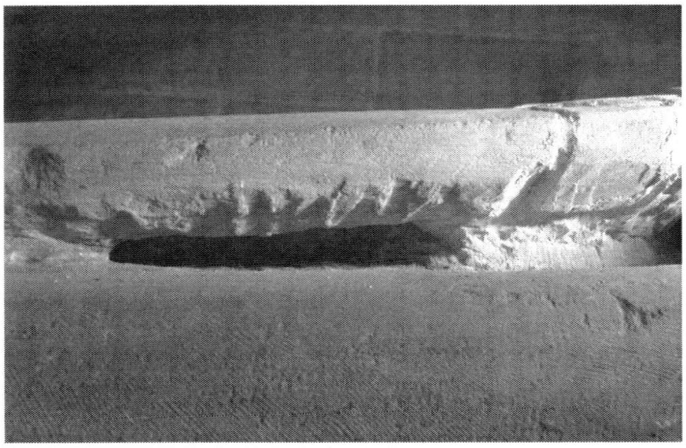

Fig. 146 Kirkby Fleetham. Rough cutting beneath scabbard.

Fig. 147 Melsonby. Mail laid out using a compass.

are not immune. There is rough cutting under William of Hatfield's arm and the damask pattern runs out. In a similar manner, the mail is uncarved under the Darfield knight's neck, running out neatly to a plain surface. These are hidden areas whilst other marks would be disguised by paint. Scribed setting-out lines occasionally show when sharply lit, such as on the Rievaulx Abbey lady's shaft bases, while part of Fountains Abbey's original laying out can just be discerned on top of its canopy (Fig. 52). Faint ruled lines run across the surface delineating the slab's chamfer, while the monument's centre line is ruled top to bottom but rather weathered out at the top.

Military effigies often have extensive areas of carved mail, the overwhelming majority of Yorkshire instances having each link laboriously carved in relief. On good quality figures, the link shapes are pretty consistent, perhaps varying in size and density, according to position. Some carvers seem to have developed shapes characteristic of their work. Series C's circular links are quite different from the shallower shape of Series B's. In both instances, examples remain to show work in progress (Plates 44, 45). Carved between marked lines as at Butterwick, Darrington's incomplete row ends make it clear each link is being developed individually rather than cut with a shaped tool. A rather different system was used at Melsonby and Newcastle Blackfriars (Lankester 2019) where the carver cut circular links around deep, freehand points (Fig. 147). The resulting pattern is erratic and the idiosyncratic method suggests the carver was not trained in figure sculpture. The sculptor of the Selby knight clearly used a compass to draw his links, achieving a very regular pattern with small holes at the centre of each.

Undercutting is another area where the mason needed skill, often avoiding it altogether or providing unobtrusive support. For instance, the lion at Sutton's feet biting the scabbard chape might be symbolic but it also supports the otherwise very vulnerable tip. Many carvers chose to rest the sword amongst the folds of a surcoat, supporting the entire blade length but when outer garments shortened, this was no longer possible. Support was often provided by leaving small columns of residual stone but the result was still vulnerable, so far fewer later fourteenth-century scabbards survive than earlier. Similarly, crossed legs might allow the sculptor to give movement to the drapery but they were also far more robust than undercut limbs. Such practical considerations undoubtedly influenced design. Some were willing or sure enough of their material and the monument's location to take risks, as in the deep drapery folds of the Alne (Fig. 148) and Felixkirk ladies that form high ridges of stone. The Hornsea lady's rosary has fared less well (Fig. 149), having formed an undercut arc of stone between her fingers and neck that has broken fully away. These examples serve to demonstrate how important the practical aspects of stone carving are in understanding effigies and what the evidence from Yorkshire can contribute. However, given that so many of the figures badly need conservation to remove surface grime and contamination, there is potentially much more still to be discovered.

4b.ii Original repairs

Post-medieval repairs have already been described (*2c.ii*) but, for a variety of reasons, some were made at the time of carving. There may have been an error, a fault may have appeared in the stone, the carving may have been damaged during transit and handling or there might even have been a change of plan for what was to be depicted. Repairs to correct carving errors were normal procedure for medieval masons and this was usually achieved by inserting a fresh piece of stone and carving it to blend in with the surrounding detail. This could be done very skilfully, using stone matching the original and with very narrow joints such that, when painted, the repair was invisible. This has been observed elsewhere, notably on the west front of Wells Cathedral, where recording during conservation revealed some 280 contemporary repairs on both the sculpture and

Fig. 148 Alne. Lady's deeply cut folds.

Fig. 149 Hornsea. Lady's undercut and broken off rosary.

the fabric itself (Sampson 1998, p. 103). The replacement pieces had been bonded in place using mastic blended with wax and stone powder. This created a very strong bond, which could withstand the carving process and was also weather resistant. The mastic was applied hot after it had been melted and, to achieve a good result, the stone was also warmed. At Wells this hot bonding process seems to have been an innovation of the early thirteenth century and previously joints had been achieved simply using lime mortar (Sampson 1998, p. 107). Similar and contemporary repairs have been noted at Salisbury Cathedral (Ayres & Sampson 2000, pp. 32–33)

Evidence of original repairs can be seen on several Yorkshire effigies. Muriel FitzAlan at Bedale has a very neat repair to the top right of her head, which includes part of the veil, fillet and hair (Fig. 142). At Ryther the whole of the sword grip was replaced by a rectangular insert, which has itself been later damaged and the end portion including the pommel is missing, leaving that part of the cut out exposed (Fig. 150). No mastic can be seen in this recess, so perhaps this was just a lime mortar repair. When we last saw it, the effigy was damp and the surviving joints green with algae concealing any bonding agent that might survive. The Magnesian Limestone from which this figure is carved has many visible flaws, which were probably the reason for the repair. The surviving angel attending the lady at Alne has lost his head, which is usually evidence of iconoclasm but, in this case, there is no fracture of the stone because the head was originally a separate piece. The hole where it was attached using a wooden or metal dowel is very clear. The dog at the feet of the lady in the recess at Swine has also lost his head and again without a fracture. The exposed surface is completely smooth and can be contrasted with the tip of the lady's left foot close by. The dog's head must have been separate and simply bonded in place for there is no dowel hole. These were all quite modest repairs but the accolade for the most heavily repaired figure unquestionably belongs to the earliest knight at West Tanfield (Fig. 151). It is impossible to be sure how many separate pieces were used because much is missing from the head end, including the base slab and whatever supported the head. The most obvious repairs are now lost: the two shoulders have deep right-angled cut-outs either side and there is another in the

Fig. 150 Ryther. Knight's sword grip – an original repair, now partly lost.

Fig. 151 West Tanfield. Eastern knight's multiple repairs, most now lost.

top of the shield, making it appear shorter than it really was. The inserted pieces were originally bonded, probably with mastic, to carefully prepared surfaces, by a process involving heat that has caused extensive reddening of the stone. An unsuccessful attempt was made to strengthen the vulnerable joint at the top of the shield with two metal cramps set in lead, some of which remains. The head itself is also an insert, its neck edges neatly tapered into the chest as might be done to achieve a good joint (a technique seen in classical sculpture). The top of the head was yet another separate piece. The surviving surface is flat, scored with a lattice pattern for keying and a dowel fixed in the centre to enhance the joint. The scabbard was an additional piece but since the drapery below is fully carved, this is likely to have been intentional, the sculptor not trusting the material to allow him to undercut it. His quest may have been for realism and the scabbard was probably in wood or metal (*4b.v*). Two related Lincolnshire knights at Rippingale and Harrington also had separate scabbards attached by dowels in a very similar way. The West Tanfield jigsaw creates an aura of desperation on the part of the carver to complete this effigy whatever it took. However, the figure is well carved and it seems that the problems lay with the stone rather than the competence of the mason. Other related figures carved in the same material show significant repairs and the stone must have been problematic. Perhaps it was difficult to source blocks suitable for effigy carving and the masons just had to make the best of it. What is strange is that different methods of attachment have been used at West Tanfield and this may be due to bonded pieces coming loose and subsequently being fastened back in place.

It is not always clear if a repair is original or not and the knight at Sutton-on-Hull is a case in point. His gauntlet-clad hands are carved on a separate square stone let into the middle of his chest (Fig. 152). At first sight they look like a later repair because the stone of the insert has reacted differently to the atmosphere and is now much darker, marking it out from the rest of the monument. Also, the broad dark fill around it looks as though it is roughly set in pitch and quite unlike the medieval repairs seen elsewhere. However, small surface breaks show that the stone is really very similar to that of the effigy and its appearance might be deceptive due to a slight difference in the mineralogy of the replacement piece. Further, the quality and detail of its

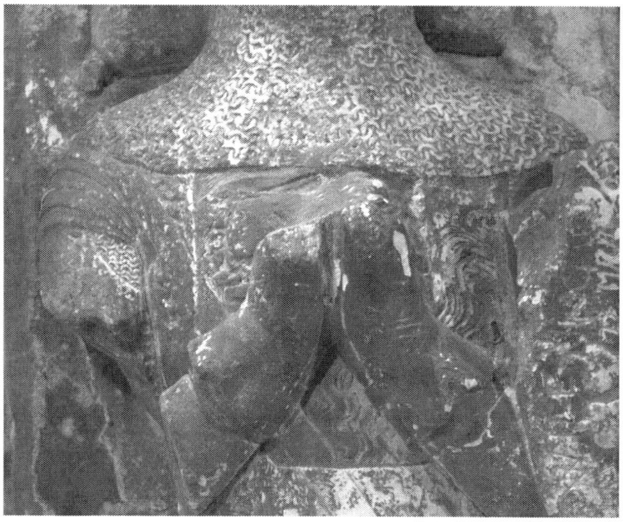

Fig. 152 Sutton-on-Hull. Major contemporary repair to hands etc.

carving suggests that it could well be original. A possible explanation is that it is an original repair that came loose and following a period out of position was put back in a different manner. The knights at Melsonby and Nunnington have similar large repairs, encompassing the shields' front edge and the left arm. Both inserts are lost but a small fragment of Melsonby's remains. The surfaces were carefully prepared and show local reddening of the stone. These effigies are very different in style, so the similarity of the repairs must be coincidental, but do demonstrate this was a common practice. When looking at monuments, one needs to be aware that repairs were sometimes made at the time of its creation as well as at any time in its subsequent history.

4b.iii Finishes

Although very few monuments survive in their original condition, one or two are sufficiently well preserved to demonstrate how they were intended to be finished. An outstanding but unusually elaborate later fifteenth-century example at Arundel (Sussex) has been studied in detail (Brodrick & Darrah 1986) showing the use of successive layers of paints and glazes applied over a ground. Completed by the addition of fictive jewels, the effect was sumptuous and life-like. Being the tomb of an earl, Arundel is an upmarket example, but such effects could be tailored to the budget available. A small proportion of effigies seem to have remained wholly or partly bare, the Abbot of Easby testifying in 1386 that Sir William Scrope (d. 1344) 'lieth sculptured on a high tomb, armed, and the arms engraved on a shield represented upon him without colours' (Nicolas 1832, II, p. 275). The lack of colour may have been to exploit the natural properties of the material or perhaps the colour had not been applied. Alabaster faces might have eyes, lips and hair painted and clothing picked out with colour in the way that is better preserved amongst the devotional images of the same material (Cheetham 1984, pp. 26–27). The stone was left bare to represent skin and white surfaces. Similarly, Purbeck marble and other polishable limestones might have relied on their polished surfaces for dramatic effect in the way those materials were used architecturally. Yorkshire examples are Archbishop de Gray and the Welton knight, although point tooling on Welton's shield may have provided keying for painted heraldry. Nonetheless, these are exceptions. Surviving traces of paint show that almost all effigies, together with their chests, arches and other settings were painted (Saul 2009, pp. 88–90). This was amply demonstrated in a detailed examination of the Westminster Abbey tomb of Aveline, Countess of Lancaster, probably of the 1290s, which showed that all its components carried decorative treatments (Houlbrooke 2005). Whilst this is exceptional, both in its survival and the use of expensive techniques, it does demonstrate a contemporary application of total polychromy. This means that the loss of original finishing treatments is a considerable handicap in understanding effigies. In general, what remains tends to be fragmentary, clinging on in corners and crevices but at least providing clues as to what was once there. It continues to disappear and the example of Brian and Muriel FitzAlan's effigies at Bedale is instructive. In 1722, Gale said the tomb had 'formerly been beautifully covered by various colours and gilt' (Gale 1722, translated from p. 242). In 1826, Blore could say, '… within the memory of persons now living, the original painting and gilding of the figure remained quite vivid …' (Blore 1826, p. 5 of section entitled 'Brian Fitz-Alan, Baron of Bedale'). Remains of the painted scheme still survived (Plate 48) when the Hollis brothers drew them in the mid-nineteenth century (Hollis & Hollis 1840–42, III no. 3; IV no. 4), including colour on the lady's clothing and on parts of the knight's equipment. No description accompanies the painted details but the dark red lattice and foliage pattern was on one of the cushions beneath his head. Faint traces of this were observed by the authors in one small area as late as the 1980s but these were not seen in June 2016, although some colour was noted elsewhere.

However, caution must be exercised since red colour, such as that traceable in the drapery folds and on the cushion of the Alne lady, may be the remains of an overall ground rather than the final surface. However, the ground tends to be a dull colour and, where bright red survives, it is likely to represent a finishing coat, as on the clothing of the crouching man supporting the left side of the gablette at Goldsborough. Gold leaf will almost certainly belong to the original finish. Some details on alabaster figures were picked out in gold leaf, as on the most protected edge of one mount on the front of the Pickering lady's *surcote ouverte*. Her angel too had golden hair and wings (Plate 49). Rich colouring would have characterised any display of heraldry, such as knight's shields, ailettes, surcoats and coat-armours. Some have the charges carved ready for painting, whereas

Fig. 153 West Tanfield. Alabaster pair, with overall carved heraldry.

a proportion of plain examples would have been rendered wholly in paint. Fully heraldic costume was also depicted on at least some females. The alabaster pair at West Tanfield have heraldry carved in very shallow relief, hers covering her entire supertunic (Fig. 153). Both the alabaster knights at Pickering had the Roucliffe arms on their coat-armours and others with carved heraldry on their surcoats or coat-armours include Saltmarsh (Howden), Bruce (Pickering), Sutton (Sutton-on-Hull) and an unknown coat on the mid-fourteenth century figure at Bedale. The seemingly plain surcoat at Nunnington supports the concept of heraldry being depicted solely in paint. He can be identified with confidence as Sir Walter de Teye, who died *c.* 1324 (*5b.i*). Dodsworth describes the arms carved on his shield as 'theron a fesse inter 2 chevrons 3 mollettes of 6 points perced' (Dodsworth, p. 181) and noted a shield of the same arms in glass where the tinctures were a gold field, red fesse and chevrons with silver mullets. No colour remains on the shield but what seems to have escaped previous notice is that his otherwise plain surcoat has gold leaf surviving from the field (Plate 50) and a little red from the charges. Providing a knight with a golden surcoat would have a very dramatic effect on his appearance. One Yorkshire knight (Crathorne) does have a painted shield (Plate 65), the arms being 'argent, a saltire gules bearing five crosses paté, or' (Gittos 2002, p. 29). Unfortunately, the colour has been renewed because some areas of surface damage have been over-painted, nevertheless it probably reflects the original scheme. Preparation for painting can be seen at Romaldkirk where incised setting out lines are still present on the shield for the arms of FitzHugh, 'azure fretty and a chief or' (Brault 1997, II, p. 168). A little colouration from the fret survives on both shield and surcoat. The shield of Butterwick is more puzzling (Plate 47). There are slight traces of some incised horizontal lines and three brownish features, which look as though paint from the charges has been absorbed into the stone (*5b.i*).

The shields of Yorkshire knights display an interplay between carving and painting, for instance Goldsborough, Fountains Abbey and Bedale were fully carved prior to painting, and others, such as all three at Coverham Abbey, were left blank for the detail to be rendered in paint. This interplay manifests itself in a different way at Church Fenton. The lady is the work of a highly skilled carver who has adventurously undercut her elbows and forearms but has left the inside of her wimple uncut as if it were a solid block. Here paint must have been employed as shadow, to create the illusion the wimple was indeed just thin fabric. However, given the multi-layers of paint that were sometimes necessary to achieve the final effect, it is surprising how far the carver might go in providing detail which might easily be masked by paint. The Pickering lady is now very worn but, where good detail survives, she can be seen to have been richly carved with fine detail, which includes shallowly carved ermine symbols to indicate that the hem of her *surcote ouverte* was trimmed with fur. Given she is carved from white alabaster it seems likely the stone was left bare in such areas and just touches of black applied on the tails. The question of whether an area was painted is most problematic on the Fountains effigy. The fine uniform texturing of the face cloth is so subtly done it would be masked by any application of paint, again suggesting the stone was left bare (Fig. 144). The Felixkirk knight provides another insight into careful finishing. His face has most of its original surface, which is very smooth with the appearance of having been waxed. If this were a final finishing treatment it is possible that any subtle flesh tone beneath may have faded with time but the fine texture of the stone is still apparent. Magnesian Limestone can adopt a translucent appearance when it has absorbed grease, a property that misled Nikolaus Pevsner into describing the FitzAlan effigy at Bedale as 'one of the earliest alabaster effigies in existence' (Pev:NR 1966, p. 76). At Bedale, the effect seems to have been caused by grease from passing hands but if the property were known, it may have been deliberately exploited and another Series D knight at Winteringham was possibly treated in the same way.

The same considerations apply to effigy settings (chests, arches etc) as the figures themselves and Yorkshire has an outstanding survival in the painted scheme on the tomb chest at Goldsborough (Gittos 1994a). It may be faded and incomplete but as a representation of how such tomb chests were originally treated it is of national importance. The tomb is against a wall but the three faces carry a sequence of double niches carved in relief, one at each end and six down the side. Painted figures occupied the sixteen locations with significant remnants of a Coronation of the Virgin at the west end (Plate 24) and some survivors of male saints along the side, which probably carried the twelve apostles. The east end scene is more fragmentary but may have been an Annunciation. The best preserved of the saints shows a nimbed figure giving blessing and is simply a well-drawn sketch in paint, which would have been worked up with additional colour, like the Coronation. There is white on the Virgin's robe and a darker finish on the side of the bench beneath her. All are painted directly on the stone without a base coat or background and what remains is probably still there because it has been absorbed.

The survival of the Goldsborough chest paintings is special but some ghosts of painted figures also remain (Plate 25) on the contemporary priest's tomb at Beverley Minster. They may have been more interpretable in the late eighteenth century (Gough 1786–1796, II.3, p. 312):

> ... the richly vested stone figure of a priest lying on an altar tomb, having eight niches on each side, wherein have been saints painted in pairs....

Further evidence of painted settings was revealed at Goldsborough during conservation in 1995, when the Series B figure was removed (Gittos 1997). A narrow strip of the painted scheme was revealed at the base of the recess, where it had been concealed by the effigy (Plate 28). Unfortunately it was too small to be readily interpretable, being a strange pattern of red and black lines, but it did indicate that the whole of the inside of the arch was originally painted. As a footnote to the subject of finishing techniques it is worth noting the effect of the piercings of the canopy etc. at Welwick, which might justifiably be considered 'painting with light' (*6a*).

4b.iv Hollowed out behind

The backs of wooden effigies were hollowed out as standard practice, done to achieve a stable block for the carver to work on and to ensure the wood dried out thoroughly, with charcoal added to the cavity as a desiccant. The conservation work on the wooden effigy at Abergavenny (Monmouthshire) revealed that it had been hollowed and the report by Carol Galvin gives a very useful description of how and why it was done (Lindley 2006b, pp. 87–88). Yorkshire's five wooden effigies of our period are most likely to have been the same, although only the pair at Allerton Mauleverer can readily be seen to be hollow. Swillington is too decayed and difficult to examine to make a judgement and, although it is not possible to inspect the undersides of Barnburgh and Whorlton, the hollow beneath the body of the former can be glimpsed through a gap below his right thigh. Whorlton emanates from the same source as Abergavenny and it would be surprising if it were not hollow. As a secondary consideration coring out the back of a wooden effigy would significantly reduce its weight and make transport and handling easier, probably also the motive for hollowing out the backs of stone effigies.

As with many aspects of medieval effigy carving this practice was found on the West Front figure sculpture at Wells, where nearly all the statues are hollowed (Sampson 1988, p. 110). The Wells masons had a special interest in minimising weight for hauling the figures into place and the coring is thought to have been done at a very late stage, just prior to painting. A great deal of stone was removed in large chunks using a stone axe, occasionally

Fig. 154 Egglestone Abbey. The hollowing underneath the priest.

Fig. 155 Catterick. Attachment hole for the lost scabbard.

too deeply, breaking through to the carved surface. It is rarely possible to examine the underside of recumbent effigies except in special circumstances, like a knight at Abbey Dore (Herefordshire), whose extensive hollowing can be seen because he is supported on blocks. Very few of Yorkshire's stone effigies have inspectible undersides but sometimes there is a gap that reveals a hollow, such as with the ladies at Hornsea and Bilton (in Ainsty). Three effigies held in museum collections (Scarborough, the 'de Vescy' knight at York and the Egglestone Abbey ecclesiastic) can be seen to be hollowed (Fig. 154), as can the broken knight at Pickhill and that from Upleatham. The male civilian at Loversall and the lady at Alne are both raised up on supports and neither is hollowed, showing this was not a universal practice. Clearly, lower weight would have been a particular advantage for those effigies that needed long distance transportation from the source to their final resting place.

4b.v Separate pieces & inserts

The practice of adding details in other materials to carved stone has a long pedigree, the use of inset bronze crosses onto carved Chilmark stone settings on Salisbury Cathedral in the early part of the thirteenth century being a notable example (Ayres & Sampson 2000, pp. 43–47). It was employed to enhance some of the figures on Wells Cathedral west front as early as the 1240s. The additions no longer survive and can only be inferred from the evidence of their locations but examples include a knight (No. 197) who had parts of his sword belt, his scabbard and his sword added and a seated man (No. 195) who held an object in his right hand, probably a sceptre (Sampson 1998, pp. 227–28). Two knights in Westminster Abbey (Crouchback and Aymer de Valance) had separate shields indicated both by attachment points and by the guiges that supported them, as did others at Englefield (Berks), Halstead (Essex) and Bures (Suffolk). The Halstead shield may survive (Bayley 1955) but the others are lost. In Canterbury Cathedral, the wooden effigy of Archbishop Pecham (d. 1292) had a separate mitre, attached by a horizontal pin through a surviving integral lug. Some Yorkshire effigies also have indications that separate items, likely to be of wood or metal, were attached to them. It was both a means of avoiding difficult carving challenges (particularly undercutting) and enhancing realism. The majority of Yorkshire separate adjuncts were of military equipment, most often scabbards. Butterwick and the earliest figure at West Tanfield have integral sword grips but separate scabbards, held in position by several pins or dowels. Nothing was carved integrally at Catterick, where the sword and dagger (presumably in their scabbards) were separate in their entirety. They were secured just below the belt on either side, where single circular holes remain to take some form of fixing (Fig. 155). The different construction and handling at Catterick may, conceivably, have been because they were actual weapons. Maybe the person commemorated requested his own weaponry as a part of his monument, which would be one way of laying up his arms (as discussed in Section 3f). In the other two cases, it was the greater part of the scabbard that was an addition and they were probably wooden. Both effigies have drilled holes for attachment and the drapery of their surcoats is fully carved behind where the scabbard would have lain. A wooden scabbard attached in exactly this way can be seen on a stone effigy, now at Edington (Wiltshire) but originally from Imber (Fig. 156). The wooden knight at Whorlton must have once had a shield because part of its guige remains and his left arm is locally flattened where it would have rested. However, the heavy surface coating applied to Whorlton makes the evidence for its addition less positive. No fixing points can be made out and the flattened part of his arm might be a fracture where the shield broke away.

Fig. 156 Edington (Wilts.). Separate wooden scabbard.

The most notable example of added equipment in Yorkshire is at Darrington where the knight once held a lance (Plate 51). This is not immediately obvious and has not previously been recognised but the evidence is very persuasive. Although he has lost both hands and most of his right forearm, a broad scar remains centrally on his chest in a position where the hands would normally join in prayer. This is much wider than usual and aligned with the left forearm as if that hand were flat on the chest. The surviving portion of the right forearm (attached to the elbow) is not symmetrical with the left and must have been unsupported and broke off because of its vulnerability. The fully finished drapery on the chest beside the left hand's position reinforces the asymmetry of the arms and also confirms that the right hand did not meet the left, so must have been otherwise employed. It seems to have been raised, a pose that would make sense for a bishop giving blessing but is uncommon for a knight. However, it is interpretable if he were holding something in his right hand and there are two further clues as to what this might have been: a drilled hole below the sword belt that looks like the location for a support and a small broken feature like a bracket on the lion's side between the knight's feet. These positions share a diagonal alignment and the only satisfactory explanation to account for all the evidence is that the Darrington effigy originally held a lance in his right hand. It was supported in the middle where a spigot hole bears witness, the butt located on the bracket. This would make Darrington comparable with the famous contemporary brass of Sir John d'Abernon (*c.* 1327) at Stoke d'Abernon (Surrey), although there are differences. Sir John's lance is upright, cradled in the crook of his right arm and in the jaws of the lion at his feet. Nicholas Rogers believed that Sir John's lance-carrying pose 'was unknown in contemporary monumental effigies, but can be matched on incised slabs, as well as in stained glass and painting' (Rogers 1996, p. 148). However, it now appears that at least one effigy did adopt this pose and a similar weapon lies on the base slab beside the Shurland effigy at Minster in Sheppey (Kent) (see Stothard 1832, pl. 41). Also relevant are three of the knightly statues on the west front of Wells Cathedral, which are believed to have held lances (Nos 125, 126, 145). Their right arms are in a similar attitude to Darrington and 145 also retains a socket for the butt beside his foot (Sampson 1998, pp. 210 & 214). Geographically closer to Darrington, the contemporary image of St George in stained glass from St Peter, Barton-Upon-Humber holds a lance in his right hand, angled across his body in a very similar stance (Plate 52). The armoured statue in the triforium of York Minster has a broad hole through his left hand, which almost certainly grasped an upright lance. He is most likely to have been carved in the 1320s or early 1330s (Brown 2003, pp. 125–29), so the three are also close in date.

Wooden effigies could also be enhanced with additional pieces. Whorlton retains small upstanding pegs on either side of the lower cushion. This is where angels are often positioned so the pegs may have been fixings for them. The wooden knight at Barnburgh has a complicated construction for his sword and scabbard (Fig. 157). Only the top of the scabbard with its two belt mounts are carved integrally with the body. The remainder of the incomplete scabbard is a separate piece of wood. The sword grip and crossguard are two more separate pieces located by six pins some of which have caused the grip to split. Henry Johnston's sketch of *c.* July 1670 (C 14, fo. 189v) shows the scabbard complete, passing beside the left knee where there are now two small holes, which probably mark an attachment point. Bloxham's very accurate drawing (Bloxham 1849) shows the sword and upper part of the scabbard as they now appear but the scabbard is missing below the lower attachment point. However, a rebate and pin location are shown where the missing part was attached, confirming that what is there now is a modern replacement, despite being incomplete. Why so much of this assemblage was not integrally carved is difficult to understand unless metal pieces were added originally for realism and, having been lost, they were replaced in stages in wood.

Much more subtle than added elements but also very effective were the sword belt insets that decorated the alabaster knight at Swine (Fig. 77) and that in the recess at West Tanfield (*2b.iii*). Usually termed 'fictive jewels', small decorative inserts survive occasionally, for instance in mounts on the effigy of John Sheppey, Bishop of Rochester (d. 1360) at Rochester Cathedral, while their settings are seen more frequently. A recent study of the Coronation Chair shows it has many areas where a combination of glass and painting was used to imitate enamelling (Sauerberg 2013, pp. 93–99). A series of shields on the slab edge at West Tanfield have deeply cut fields that leave the major charges in sunk relief. With the fields filled with colour there would still have been sufficient depth to set glass over the top, in imitation of enamelling (Fig. 158). However, the indents for the shields on his sword belt are plain, suggesting they

Fig. 157 Barnburgh. Sword grip repair.

were inserted complete (Fig. 71). Swine has deep sockets and, although nothing remains, they too probably held fictive jewels, most likely false-enamel plaques, that would have appeared as life-like versions of the carved mounts seen elsewhere.

All the forgoing relates to military figures for whom their equipment provides ample scope but it does seem likely that the female figure at Holy Trinity, Hull had something clasped between her hands as well as the tiny heart held by her finger tips (*5c.ii*). Something similar may have been the case with the Catterick knight who has a smooth horizontal platform where the rest of his gauntlets should be and where an object could have been positioned, although a lost repair is also possible.

Close study of the Yorkshire material reveals much evidence to show how these effigies were made and set up. None are in their original condition but the carving techniques and traces of their original finishes demonstrate that what remains are just the cores of much more elaborate designs. The dull looking knight at Nunnington who once had a golden surcoat, provides a tantalising glimpse.

4b.vi The masons' intent

Medieval Yorkshire was blessed in its masons, amongst whom were some of the finest in the land. One of the most accomplished worked on Series B (*4c.ii*) but others turned out memorable works, such as Ripley, Sutton-on-Hull, Alne, Kirby Sigston and Welwick. Whilst monument designs would have been approved by the people commissioning them, the masons must have brought their own ways of working to the finished items. Indeed, the most highly accomplished (and well known) are likely to have been chosen by reputation. Differentiating between the respective influences of the patron and the sculptor is difficult, but certain aspects must be fundamental traits of the carver, betraying their interests, preferences and skill.

Realism and portraiture

Certain Yorkshire masons seem to have been acutely interested in depicting what they saw. This requires a high level of both observation and representational skill. It shows, for example, in the use of different drapery styles to signify a range of fabrics, the successful depiction of the weight and

Fig. 158 West Tanfield. Shield inlays on base slab chamfer (knight in recess).

behaviour of mail and the naturalistic portrayal of objects, such as animals and foliage. A case in point is the Series D carver's ability to distinguish between items of leather and metal armour (*2b.iii*). A desire for realism extends to showing how clothing and equipment were made, at which the Series B carver excelled. Examples not seen elsewhere include details of the padded backing of shields, complete with their dome headed rivets, and the way the leather is dished behind the belt mounts (Fig. 184). Some extremely characterful faces were also depicted. The bulging eyes at East Harlsey (Plate 41), the wild hair and worried face of the Hull civilian (Plate 1), the long hair and beard of the Beverley civilian (Fig. 85) and even Robert Haringel's spade-shaped beard at Hickleton (Fig. 39), are unlikely to have been figments of the carvers' imagination. Portraiture is not often identified at this period but faces such as these must have been acceptable to the patron, unlikely if they were just generic caricatures.

Stance

The traditional image of a medieval effigy is of a knight with crossed legs and his hands joined in prayer. For a proportion of figures, this is true – but only for a proportion, as posture alters over time and between types of figure. It could also be adapted to suit the circumstances. A response to a particular setting might be required; it could convey a message to the intended audience; it might reflect the patron's wishes or just be a matter of practicality, such as having to deal with an awkward space. Cross-leggedness is a posture that was favoured in the later half of the thirteenth century and the first half of the fourteenth century, for most military and several civilian figures in Yorkshire. However, the attitude is rare amongst women and we are unaware of any ecclesiastics depicted cross-legged. The origins and significance of the posture have been debated at length (Harris 2010) but are outside the scope of this work. Nevertheless, its country-wide popularity generally coincides with that of Decorated architecture and the complex drapery patterns often created are in tune with its flowing lines.

The only cross-legged lady is at Howden (Fig. 16), where the drapery very clearly defines the stance (*2a.iv, 4c.ii*). However, several women have one leg shown straight and the other slightly flexed, producing a related effect in the drapery patterns. The Alne lady's right foot is against her dog's head, the angle of the leg and bent knee dictating the pattern of her skirt drapery, while her straight left leg is invisible, its position betrayed only by the asymmetrically placed toe of her shoe against the dog's flank (Fig. 148). A similar posture can be found at Church Fenton and Hornsea (Fig. 159). In a subtle form it is shown at Harpham, Ormesby and West Tanfield (the alabaster). In all these cases, the posture is exploited to dramatise the drapery and this may even have been the primary motive for depicting the stance.

This consideration cannot have applied to the cross-legged male civilians, where little or no visual interest was to be gained, due to the narrower cut of their clothing. Those that come nearest to the effect of the ladies' leg positions are Birkin (Fig. 160) and Stonegrave, wearing loose unbelted garments, while Skerne, wearing shorter clothes, shows the legs clearly crossed quite high. The opposite is true at Garton-on-the-Wolds, where the thighs are straight and parallel, while the drapery at Hornsea indicates a similar posture, although the lower legs are lost. Batley too is legless but the position of the upper legs suggests something similar, confirmed by Henry Johnston's 1669 drawing (C 13, fo. 41r).

The cross-legged pose seems to persist in Yorkshire for armoured effigies right up to the middle of the century (Gittos 2002b). In many instances, the sculptors have used the attitude and the looseness of the surcoat to create exciting and inventive drapery that is often characteristic of a carver's work. The great majority of the cross-legged knights wear full surcoats but the 1340s examples at Barnburgh, Pickering and Upleatham combine short-fronted surcoats with crossed legs. Overall there appears to be a trend for the knights of earlier date to have their

Fig. 159 Hornsea. The lady's drapery showing her posture.

Fig. 160 Birkin. A cross-legged civilian.

legs crossed higher, while later examples tend to have their thighs more parallel and knees slightly apart. This change seems to have begun during the 1330s. Effigies late in the century are almost ubiquitously straight-legged in Yorkshire. The 'Sheffield' knight at Bedale varies this by moving the lower body, to create a swayed or hip-shot posture (Fig. 161). The stance is found in all artistic media but rarely met in Yorkshire.

Fig. 161 Bedale. The 'Sheffield' knight's swayed stance.

Fig. 162 Church Fenton. One of the lady's deeply undercut arms has been lost and repaired.

Posture

Just as leg positions vary, so do the arms, influencing how the hands are occupied. The simple palms together attitude of prayer is the most common, with many variations. Where hands touch the chin, elbows are close to the body (as at Beeford) but if the hands are held low and the wrists turn through more of an angle, the elbows can be well away from the body and require adventurous undercutting, as at Church Fenton (Fig. 162). The mason's confidence and the integrity of his material would be important factors since anyone less competent, or working with poor stone, might seek to avoid such flamboyance. A few of the armoured figures handle their swords, notably Jervaulx Abbey (*2a.v*) where the energy invested in drawing it yields a posture unparalleled in the north (Plate 3). It contrasts starkly with the passive hand on hilt attitude at Welton, a late Purbeck marble product that gives the impression the sculptors had lost sight of the militant message the sword-handling gesture could convey. Other objects held in the hands might also influence stance. Mostly, they are held with praying hands but the lance-holding posture at Darrington (*4c.iii*) means the knight rests his left hand on his breast while the right elbow is sharply bent to provide a stable grip. Archbishop Walter de Gray's right hand is held up in blessing and he controls his crosier with his left, leading both hands to be raised.

The final influence on posture to be considered is the effigy's response to its surroundings. This is most evident through inclined heads and turned bodies. Examples include the more complete lady from Rievaulx Abbey and the smaller of the two complete figures at Coverham. The Rievaulx lady's whole body is turned to her right,

Fig. 163 Rievaulx Abbey. The lady's side-turned attitude.

resting on her right shoulder, with her left arm uppermost (Fig. 163). Whilst her head seems less angled than her body, there is no doubt that the figure was carved as facing outward from her canopied position. This recognition has made it possible to suggest that this previously unprovenanced monument was originally sited against the north wall of the Presbytery (Susan Harrison, pers. comm.). In such a location, the figure must have been conceived as responding to the solemnities of the high altar. The Coverham Abbey figure's head is both turned and twisted towards his left and he is consequently likely to have been located against a south wall. The twist of the head may be towards the altar or respecting a devotional image close to his setting: a statue, wall painting or glass. Rather more obvious than either of these two is the kneeling, backward swayed posture of the small lady at Wistow (Plate 42). Although now lost, her hands were held high and away from her body, perhaps in prayer. She kneels on a small bracket and appears to be a three-dimensional equivalent of the donor figures so frequently found in medieval glass and painting, this is certainly not an attitude normally in the repertoire of English fourteenth century monument sculptors. However, Sally Badham (2015b) has conclusively demonstrated the extent to which donations to church fabric were considered to be commemorative and it is in this context that the figure is included in the corpus. Currently set in the eastern part of the north chancel wall near a carving of Christ displaying his wounds, which may well be related, she gazes outwards and upwards and was very likely part of a larger composition. It is possible that she originally offered up an object (*e.g.* a window or part of the structure) like the window being offered by Robert Skelton in the mid-fourteenth-century glass at St Denys, Walmgate, York (Plate 43). A donation marked by such a large and striking carved composition ought to be substantial, so it is worth noting that the chancel itself is a rebuilding of the fourteenth century and incorporates an impressive Decorated tracery east window. If the gift to the church were a new chancel, it may be that she is not too far from her original position and that she is not only drawing attention to her gift and seeking prayers in return for it but is actively reminding the priest to pray for her at the high altar (see also Appendix A1).

Posture is not easy to use as an indicator of date (although it may offer clues) but it is a vital element in understanding a monument and interpreting the intent.

4c Relationships and series

4c.i Introduction

The surviving total of 231 effigies demonstrates the number of masons who were capable of turning their hand to commemorative figure sculpture at this period but not all of them were accomplished and it is to be expected that only the best should have received multiple commissions. Surprisingly few figures in the corpus can confidently be seen as related to each other, but a proportion does seem to cluster into groups, based on shared characteristics. These groups (termed Series A–E and Wolds) are the main focus of this section. It is important to appreciate that judgements about whether an individual figure belongs to a Series are based primarily on how the carving is done and the character of the work, not simply on what is portrayed.

The Yorkshire Series differ from each other in many respects. The largest is A/B, with more than twenty members and the smallest, Series D with only four. A to D are widely distributed, whereas E and the Wolds are more locally based. What they all share is the benefits of being considered together, which can greatly assist in understanding the monuments and can help to make sense of effigies otherwise difficult to place. One of the reasons we have termed these groupings 'Series' rather than the more conventional 'workshops' or 'ateliers' is that the number of hands involved differs. Series A/B appears to be the work of a single individual. Series C, in contrast, probably represents the work of two or more closely associated people. Both these groupings have a sufficiently long working life to show stylistic development. The four effigies of Series D are so closely related, they must be by the same hand while the Wolds figures may be the work of a number of associated sculptors. Inevitably, there are a few figures that, despite having some characteristics of one of the Series, are too badly damaged or for some other reason not quite close enough to be sure of their status. The Yorkshire Series are described below but first it is worth considering briefly the great majority that have not been categorised but for which there are some relationships to be noted.

Even when the Yorkshire Series are combined with those imported from production centres elsewhere, they represent only 29% of the 231 total. So, who made the remaining 71% of the effigies? Most appear to have been produced by local men using material that was close at hand, probably on an opportunistic basis both for the carver and the patron. Examples are Filey, Forcett, Great Langton, Great Mitton, Kellington, Slingsby and Yarm. Judgement of their quality can be difficult since the lesser quality stone is often quite vulnerable to decay but, whilst usually conforming to the standard arrangement of their day, they tend to be quite perfunctorily carved, with little detail or modelling of form. Sometimes two or more similar figures occur in the same church and nowhere else, such as the two head slabs at Melsonby, the two later females at West Tanfield or the quartet at Stanwick. They may be of good quality as, for example, the male and female pair at Kirklington. Occasionally, a particular feature can suggest local sharing of ideas, such as the unusual placing of a book in the crook of an arm at Acklam (two figures) and only two miles away at Stainton. However, we have judged these low levels of comparison as more indicative of local influence than of effigies from the same source.

During major building programmes, masons might also fulfill private commissions, which could explain the smaller-scale knight and lady in Selby Abbey. She wears a sleeveless supertunic with deep armholes, which suggests the effigies were probably carved during the protracted work at the east end, when this style was fashionable. Similarly, the good quality effigy of Provost Nicholas Huggate in Beverley is like no other and was presumably made by someone working at the Minster (*4a.vi*). It is suggested below that Series E may be associated with building at Guisborough and there are some fine individual figures in parish churches, which may have been created in this way. High quality effigies that cannot be associated with groupings or building projects include the knights at Kirkby Fleetham (Fig. 164) and Aldbrough, together with the Alne, Felixkirk and Kirby Sigston ladies (Fig. 165). Some relationships are tenuous, like the knights at Bedale ('Sheffield') and Pickering (Bruce) who both have mail depicted as double rings but are probably not by the same carver, since in other respects (including proportions, attitude and layout) they are quite different. At Melsonby (Fig. 147) the mail has been worked up laboriously around a series of irregularly set points (*4b.i*). Surprisingly, this highly unusual method is replicated on a fragment of mail discovered during excavations at the Dominican Friary, Newcastle. Perhaps the mason using this strange technique was itinerant, as was common amongst medieval masons.

Fig. 164 Kirkby Fleetham. Finely carved thongs of the knight's scabbard attachment.

Fig. 165 Kirby Sigston. The lady, a high quality carving not part of a Series.

This also may account for some of the high quality figures, which lack a sculptural context.

4c.ii Series A and B

Background

The initial 'Classification of Early Yorkshire Effigies' (Gittos 1980) distinguished the earlier sandstone figures (then called Group A) from those immediately succeeding them in Magnesian Limestone (Group B). Apart from henceforth terming them 'Series', the 'A' and 'B' labels have remained, despite it becoming apparent material was the only distinction in a coherent sequence, but for continuity and to avoid confusion, we have chosen to maintain this nomenclature. The dating and possible identifications followed some years later (Gittos 1992) with detailed appraisals of Howden and Goldsborough (Badham, Gittos & Gittos 1996; Gittos 1994a; Gittos 1997). The full detail given in these earlier publications is not repeated here but the conclusions are brought forward to this discussion. Here the Series is considered in relation to the rest of the corpus and key messages are drawn out through the medium of the career of the man responsible. There have been some criticisms of this Series, mostly in respect of dating, and they are addressed in Appendices A7 and A8, but one red herring also needs comment. I'Anson assigned most of the Series B effigies to his 'Cheyne atelier' at York, apparently on the basis of what he took to be a rebus of the carver's name on the chamfer of the Norton slab. It takes the form of a letter 'I' followed by three rings interlinked like a chain (Fig. 166). Hunter Blair suggested this was for John Cheyne (Hunter Blair 1929, p. 24) but Sir James Mann was rightly sceptical (Mann 1928, p. 234) and, as the device has been cut in sunk relief, it could have been added at any time. It appears nowhere else and signatures on English effigies of this date are unknown, so it would be unique. It may just be graffiti or possibly, given its situation below the shield, relates to re-carving of the heraldry.

Fig. 166 Norton. 'I Chain' cut into slab near shield.

All the A/B effigies appear to show the work of a single individual, with common traits and idiosyncrasies. They are intelligent works springing from an observant mind and talented hand, described by Claude Blair (1995) as an 'exceptionally gifted artist'. Realistic depictions (such as distinguishing between the behaviour of different materials) and the capture of innovations (*e.g.* equipment and architecture) were important to him, coupled with a love of symbolism and detail. His carving is dense, filling the available room and contrasting with the sparse elegance and space accorded some Series C works.

Series A

The earliest figures are in the North Riding, at Bedale and Coverham Abbey, depicting two knights, a lady and a priest. Since the Bedale lady almost certainly commemorates Muriel FitzAlan who was dead by late 1290 (*5b*), our man must have completed his apprenticeship by the last decade of the thirteenth century at the latest. The cluster of early works within ten miles and the use of a potentially local stone, suggests he was working in the area, even if not native. The effigy is carved with great sensitivity (Fig. 167) and already exhibits his hallmark understanding of how different fabrics behave, her veil textured in a 'V' pattern with a narrow fringed edge (Fig. 142) and falling differently from her stiffer cote. She is also unconventional, with flexed knees twisted to the side and hands not at prayer or holding the cloak cord but displaying a long scroll. Another commission soon followed at Bedale for a priest (Fig. 243). Large naturalistic leaves and shields punctuate the base slab margins, the composition filling its surface with additional detail fused into a whole, including scroll-bearing angels and four heads around a gablette. Two of these heads are craggy-faced and elderly (one male, the other damaged) accompanied by a knight and lady, all so characterful they may depict individuals, mourners rather than grotesques. A seated Christ, blessing and book-holding, fills the end panel (Fig. 168). The priest holds a crucifixion tablet (not a book) in an unusual manner, using both hands from below. The only other effigy in the area known to hold something in this way was Dean Langton (d. 1279) formerly in York Minster, pictured in a seventeenth century sketch (*2c.i*). This is unlikely to be a coincidence and suggests the sculptor was fully aware of an exceptional and prestigious monument at York. Double commissions for contrasting but contemporary knights at Coverham Abbey (Plate 6) enlarged his repertoire and military monuments became a speciality. His versatility produced monuments of contrasting character but with strong similarities in planning and the treatment of mail, knees and surcoat drapery. The larger lies flat and composed, while the smaller is vigorously attentive under a steep sided gablette. The difference may result from their original situations. The smaller has far more additional sculpture (*5c*) and is likely to be the later, since the proportions, modelling of the figure,

Fig. 167 Bedale. Series A effigy of Muriel FitzAlan.

Fig. 168 Bedale. Series A priest, panel with blessing Deity.

Fig. 169 Goldsborough. Series B knight's eye.

Fig. 170 Bedale. Naturalistic leaves on priest's slab.

Fig. 171 Coverham Abbey. Naturalistic leaves on smaller knight's gablette.

handling of the drapery and liveliness are close to Series B figures. However, they do share features the carver was to use elsewhere. Both have ailettes economically disposed against the cushions behind their shoulders, where they are protected from breakage. Two more sandstone knights complete Series A, both much further afield, at Routh in Holderness and on the coast at Scarborough. The former is very weathered and has lost most of its detail but traces of an ailette laid flat behind the right shoulder can be made out. All four have face cloths drawn back on their heads, a feature they share with several early Series B figures at Escrick, Fountains and Goldsborough (its significance is discussed in Section 5c.v). In the case of the larger Coverham effigy (Plate 32), the cloth is held up by two angels. Scarborough has been crudely recut for a seventeenth century appropriation (*2c.ii*), hampering appreciation of his original appearance (Fig. 95), but comparisons can still be made with the Coverham knights and the drawn back face cloth is quite clear, spreading from the top of his head across the cushion. Apart from these Yorkshire figures, we know of only one other effigy depicted with a face cloth (Fig. 260), the later thirteenth-century lady at Wolferlow (Herefordshire). Like the larger Coverham figure, hers is held back by angels.

The carver's drawing of eyes develops through this period, always very elongated and quite narrow. They seem, in the earliest figures, to be upward tilted, *e.g.* the Bedale lady and larger Coverham knight. They gradually assume his standard pattern with the eyeball deeply modelled, the upper lid marked by a double line extending well onto the side of the face and the lower lid straight or even convex (Fig. 169). Another feature that crosses this period is the use of maple (acer) leaves. The Bedale lady's headdress frontal is worked with them, large single leaves sit on the chamfer of the Bedale priest (Fig. 170) and a trail of them forms the forest to which the stag flees on the smaller Coverham knight (Fig. 171). Leaves of this character can

Fig. 172 Goldsborough. Series B knight, padded shield interior with enarmes.

be found in the 1290s at, for instance, Southwell Minster and again at York Minster, on an eastern nave pier capital. The two Bedale effigies and Coverham belong to the Series A (sandstone) phase but a single, slightly modified leaf of the same form nestles in the Series B Goldsborough canopy, in the spandrel between the main arch apex and the gable trilobe, as if supporting the image pedestal. This has more pointed and elongated main lobes that fit it to the space but its overall form links the Series B tomb with the earlier Series A sculpture. A lively interest in military equipment also spans the sequence, with almost obsessive depictions of fittings and fastenings. This is most graphically shown in his careful carving of the interior padding, lining and enarmes of many Series B shields (Fig. 172).

Series B

Probably in the late 1290s and very soon after producing Scarborough, came a major change in the mason's career. One effect was that he migrated to the close-grained Magnesian Limestone, which better suited his skill and opened increased opportunities for fine detail, such as the rivets shown consistently on buckle plates and strap ends. Significantly, he seems to have become involved with the programme at York Minster, where hallmarks of his work can be seen in some of the architectural sculpture. Notable amongst these are the two armoured label stop figures on the nave walls (Oosterwijk 1990), stop b east of window sXXXIX, stop c west of window nXXVII and two of the heads on the arcade piers (eastern sides of first and third piers, north arcade). The two fighting men have all the character and proportions of Series B knights, with similar surcoats, drapery, sword pommels, poleyns and belts (Fig. 173). The pattern of the female head stop's forward-combed wavy locks over the top of her head (Fig. 174) is akin to the bare headed knight's at East Harlsey (Fig. 175), where the hooded male face of the other head stop (Fig. 176) also appears, between the shield and the cushion (Fig. 177). Sarah Brown (2003, p. 90) says that 'By 1300 the two easternmost bays of the new nave appear to have been fully accessible and in use'. This includes one each of the heads and label stops. She goes on to argue (2003, pp. 105–106) that the first phase of the nave was being glazed *c.* 1306–15 and that even some of the westernmost head stops on the south side must have been carved prior to 1307. The structural breaks that define the first phase encompass all four of our comparative sculptures, which must have been not only carved but positioned by the time work stopped. Another key Minster sculpture, although a little earlier,

Fig. 173 York Minster. Nave label stop, St George in sleeved surcoat. Crown copyright.

Fig. 174 York Minster. Nave, female head with forward-combed hair. Crown copyright.

Fig. 175 East Harlsey. Knight's forward-combed hair.

Fig. 176 York Minster. Nave, hooded man. Crown copyright.

Fig. 177 East Harlsey. Small male hooded head.

bears comparison with Series B work, the trumeau Virgin and Child at the entrance to the chapter house. The Virgin's face, right hand, the child's head and orb have been replaced but otherwise the carving is original, including the fight at her feet (Fig. 178). Wrapped around one another, locked in mortal combat, a lion and dragon sink their teeth into each other's necks, just as at the feet of the Series B knight at Norton (Fig. 179). In both cases the dragon is two legged and, unusually, wingless with a thin mane along the length of its neck. The B sculptor's dragons are always the stuff of nightmare, with hairy legs, vicious claws and teeth, ridged snouts, sunken eyes and heavy brow-ridges. The luxuriantly curling hair of the Norton dragon's bifurcated tail (Fig. 180) is closely related to the opposing curves in the hair and divided beards of other nave head stops, *e.g.* a male head on the same pier (Fig. 181) as the lady (Fig. 74) and other

Fig. 178 York Minster. Fight at the feet of the Chapter House Virgin.

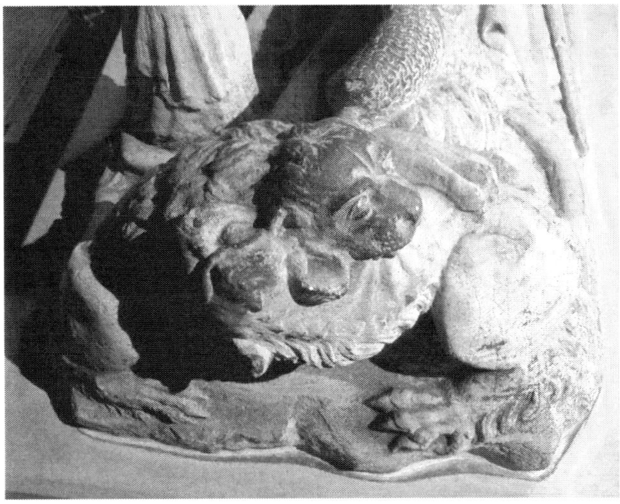

Fig. 179 Norton. Series B knight's fight.

Fig. 180 Norton. Series B knight's dragon with curled, divided, tail.

Fig. 181 York Minster. Nave, man with curled and divided beard. Crown copyright.

comparisons can be made with sculpture from the earlier phase of the nave.

Such very close links between details of the Series B effigies and sculpture in the Minster indicate that the carver was working there when he produced the effigies, so York is also likely to be where they were made. He was working in York at a time when it was the functional capital of the country (*5a.ii*) and consequently thronged with opportunities to observe the great and the good, their fashions and, because there was a war on, their equipment. Combined with his inside knowledge of the new work in the Minster, it was a fertile mix that can account for much of his originality.

Perhaps through his involvement at the Minster, he gained access to supplies of Magnesian Limestone, which he seems to have used consistently for the rest of his career. Three very closely related figures can be seen as marking the transition: from the final use of sandstone at Scarborough to Magnesi Limestone at Fountains Abbey and Escrick. Their position in the Series means that all three were probably carved around 1300. The Fountains knight may have been the first in Magnesian (Fig. 182) and there is a strong case for it commemorating Lord Mowbray who was buried there in 1299 (*5b.i*). This effigy is similar in layout to Scarborough (Fig. 183) and they both have wide gablettes with flat tops

Fig. 182 Fountains Abbey. Series B knight.

Fig. 183 Scarborough. Series A knight.

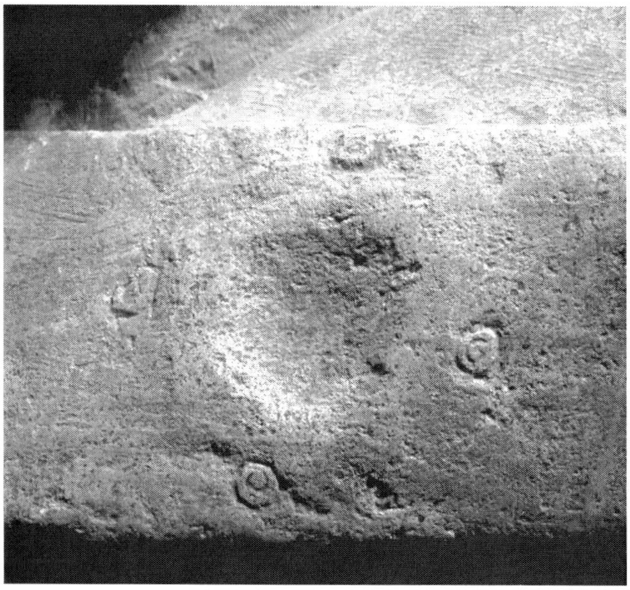

Fig. 184 Bedale. Brian FitzAlan's sword belt, position of lion mask mount seen from behind.

and additional side arches framing the cushion. The praying hands are held at the same angle and the waist and sword belts are arranged similarly. Both have face cloths drawn back and there can be little doubt they must have been carved within a short time of one another but Scarborough is sandstone, while at Fountains, the carver could fully exploit the superior qualities of Magnesian Limestone. This is perhaps best appreciated in his delicate texturing of the face

Fig. 185 Fountains Abbey. Elaborate strap end on sword belt.

cloth (Fig. 144) that is better preserved than on the Bedale lady but shares the 'V' patterning and narrow fringed edge. The 'V' texturing occurs again on the veil of Norton's seated figure, with a more wavy pattern of strokes on her wimple (Fig. 143). This is reminiscent of the surface treatment of the unworn parts of the York Virgin's veil. The sculptor has exploited the Magnesian Limestone's capabilities to produce a level of detail beyond what might be expected. A trademark example is to show the mount positions on the back of turned-over sword belts (Fig. 184), marked by four rivets around a depression (where the leather was relieved of its tension). Remarkably, he even represents the tiny rivets as fabricated from rolled-up sheet. A special feature of Fountains is the sword belt strap end, which, although worn, seems to have been moulded with a man and a bird inside a crocketed frame under a finial (Fig. 185). It is handled in a similar way to a pilgrim badge and we know of nothing like it. A bird was also carved on the edge of his base slab. The damaged and displaced knight at Escrick lacks the gablette of Scarborough and Fountains but shares their modelling of the head, with its depressed chin, chunky but narrow-wristed arms, and the upper knee as the high point of the composition (Fig. 186). Their broad belts are arranged in the same way and all have drawn back face cloths, clearly indicating Escrick's place as the third member of the carver's output of *c.* 1300. Escrick is also the first figure to show the sleeved surcoat, a feature unique to Series B knights in Yorkshire and rarely shown elsewhere in the country.

Fig. 186 Escrick. Series B knight.

Fig. 187 Goldsborough. Series B knight.

Fig. 188 Norton. Series B knight.

In the early years of the fourteenth century, the Series B sculptor, then at the zenith of his powers, was commissioned to create the three military effigies, at Goldsborough, Bedale and Norton. The wonderfully preserved Goldsborough knight's setting and context are the subject of a case study in Section 3g.i. It is one of the Series B sculptor's finest works (Fig. 187), carved with outstanding realism in the draperies of his sleeved surcoat and the weight of the mail coif around his neck. His ridged gablette is like Bedale's but lacks the ballflower. He also shares the lion masks on his sword belt with Bedale and with Norton the single seated person by his knees (*5c.vii*). Goldsborough is the last of these figures to have the drawn-back face cloth, only in this case it is shown stitched to the top cushion (Plate 31). In contrast to the nobility of Goldsborough's face, Norton's is unflattering with a large nose, as if the caver were creating an honest rendering of the rather podgy face of a man of mature years (Fig. 188). To offset that, he has a fine head of hair, revealed by his coif being shown folded down. Bare-headedness is yet another speciality of the Series B sculptor, with a total of five of his knights shown like this, while in Yorkshire, the only other bare headed military is Bainton. The identity of Norton is problematic as the heraldry on his shield is from a sixteenth-century appropriation for the Blakiston family, while the two shields behind the gablette (Fig. 189) are original but

Fig. 189 Norton. Original shields on gablette.

Fig. 190 Bedale. Brian FitzAlan's carved shield.

ambiguous, lacking their tinctures (Coss 1996). The traditional attribution to Sir John Lythegraines may be right as one of the gablette shields could be his but he is not known to be associated with Norton. However, in the absence of pre-Reformation records it is impossible to be certain the effigy belongs to the church. If, as suggested by Peter Coss, it was appropriated out of antiquarianism, because it was believed to be part of the family's history, it may have been brought from elsewhere, as with several effigies at Chester-Le-Street (Coss 1996). It could possibly commemorate Lythegraines because he was associated with a number of men commemorated by Series B effigies and he died in 1303 when the sculptor was working on monuments (*5b.ii*). The second gablette shield may be for Bek, the Bishop being a primary patron of Lythegraines.

There is no doubt the Bedale effigy (Plate 54) commemorates Brian FitzAlan (d. 1306) and this identification is discussed in Section 5b. It was fitting that his memorial should have been created by the same sculptor who had carved that of his first wife Muriel, about a decade previously. The sculptor's work had developed greatly in the interim and combined with a difference in material, the new effigy was quite different. There are two seated figures by the knight's feet (Plate 55), first seen at Coverham, and a wingless, feather-legged dragon with a spiny backbone claws its way up his surcoat to bite the shield (Fig. 264). The completely revised style of the gablette is innovative, decorated for the first and only time with embryonic ballflower and topped with Decorated style crocketing, both examples of the very latest fashion in architectural motifs. Ballflower makes an appearance in Yorkshire on the Kirkham Priory gatehouse in the years around 1300, as discussed in Appendix A8. Outside, two angels hold on to the gablette for balance, like footmen riding behind a coach. Even the depiction of FitzAlan's barry heraldry on his shield shows originality (Fig. 190). Instead of plain bars of simple rectangular cross section, they are finessed with back-to-back concave hollows either side of a central ridge. The Lord of

Fig. 191 Beverley Friary. Series B lady.

Bedale was an illustrious client (*5b*) and his splendid effigy is rightly one of the most well-known from Yorkshire.

During the first decade of the fourteenth century the Series B carver continued to accept tomb commissions, including two female figures at Appleton-le-Street and Beverley Friary (Fig. 191). The latter was a popular church where many wealthy women were buried (Young 1837) but the shields behind her gablette are too eroded to be read, so it is impossible to suggest whom she might represent. The Appleton-le-Street lady has heraldic mounts for her cloak cord and is a member of the de Bolton family who held the manor (Fig. 192). The uppermost of the three lions on the chevron is horizontal but the outer two more nearly respect the edge of the shield, as they are depicted on the Bolton shield in York Minster nave (Brown 2003, p. 124). She shares the rare detail of a bushy-tailed squirrel with the knight at Fountains Abbey although both creatures are mutilated (Fig. 269). Several more military effigies were produced but, although still of high quality, the sculptor seems to have spent a little less time on them. The figures at East Harlsey and the Temple Church are exquisitely carved but excepting their boldly worked heads of hair, generally lack the additional details (Plate 56, Fig. 193). As noted above, East Harlsey's hair and the miniature head by his left shoulder are close to work in the Minster. It would seem that when this effigy was carved, the sculptor was also working on the heads at the east end of the Minster nave where both heads are located. The characterfulness of the Minster heads is carried through to East Harlsey's face, which is most individual: pop-eyed, rounded and pudgy, it is difficult to believe something so idiosyncratic is not an attempt at portraiture (Plate 41). Sadly, his identity is unknown as the heraldry (a label of four points) is problematic. I'Anson (1927) thought he commemorated Sir Geoffrey Hotham of Cranswick (d. 1320 × 1322) but did not publish the reasoning and the authors have been unable to follow his trail. Saltmarshe's rigorously compiled Hotham family history (Saltmarshe 1914, especially pp. 191–95) does not associate him with the area, nor did he know how this branch differenced the Hotham coat (Or, on a bend sable, three mullets argent). East Harlsey's label is properly carved, so it is difficult to believe the coat itself would not have been, suggesting it was very simple. The difficulties of identifying the de Ros effigy in the Temple Church are covered in Section 5b.i and the problems of its restoration in 2c.ii. The Yorkshire Museum torso, which stood for many years by the roadside at the edge of Clifton village and was known as Mother Shipton's stone, appeared in the initial (Gittos 1992) Series B list. It is incomplete, broken and extremely weathered but does show characteristics of the Series in the way the figure blends into the base slab and how the very broad sword belt is handled. It is a great pity that it lacks so much detail. Two of the military effigy fragments found

Fig. 192 Appleton-le-Street. Series B lady.

Fig. 193 London, Temple Church. Knight of the de Ros family.

amongst the ruins of Rievaulx Abbey may perhaps also belong to this grouping on the character of the carved mail but the pieces are too small to be certain.

A larger commission was the tomb at Howden Minster for Thomas de Metham (d. 1311/12) and his wife Sybil (Badham, Gittos & Gittos 1996). Effigies were made for both (Fig. 16) and a tomb chest provided, comprising panels with figures in niches portrayed in a lively manner with animated postures and some gesturing to the onlooker. They could not be more different than the formal representations on some later tomb chests. Much detail has been lost from the effigies themselves but the carver's innovative approach is still apparent, as unlike any other Yorkshire effigies, they both lie on draped material, as if on a covered funeral bier (Fig. 261). Like the Beverley lady, their gablettes carry shields but while hers are large and unsupported, theirs are smaller and hang from crockets either side of a prominent rib. The rib is like Goldsborough's and all three (with Bedale) have base slabs pointed at head and foot (Fig. 47). After Howden, just four further military figures complete the Series. The knight at Amotherby carries otherwise unrecorded heraldry (DBA 1) that are probably canting arms

Fig. 194 Amotherby. Series B knight.

for Boresden (Fig. 194). The effigy's heavily whitewashed state masks detail of what appears a rather restrained figure, compared to the earlier works but he may originally have had a tomb chest. Although neither of the interpretable shields are Boresden, the church has a damaged tomb panel (Fig. 115) consistent in its proportion with those at Hazelwood, Howden and Bedale. These panels also share elements of their design. John Boresden leased land in the parish from at least 1293 (Slingsby 1956, p. 108), William paid tax in Amotherby in 1301 while John paid for adjacent Neusom (Brown 1897, pp. 51, 56), Robert Boresden occurs in 1306 (Prestwich 2003) and William son of William was active by 1329 (Baildon 1910, p. 21) preventing any certainty about identification or date of death.

As explained in Section 5b.i, the two Vavasour knights at Hazelwood (Figs 195, 196) were originally together on the same tomb and are very likely to commemorate Sir William (d. 1312) and his son Sir Walter (d. 1315). Together they provide evidence that, some twenty-five years after Muriel FitzAlan's effigy, the master carver was experiencing some difficulty. For some reason the master was unable to complete the commission himself and a less able mason became involved, probably with little supervision. Now separated in individual recesses and severely damaged by damp, one panel of their single tomb chest remains. Superficially they appear alike and previous commentators have treated them as almost identical but there is still sufficient detail to make telling comparisons.

Fig. 195 Hazelwood. Knight (east).

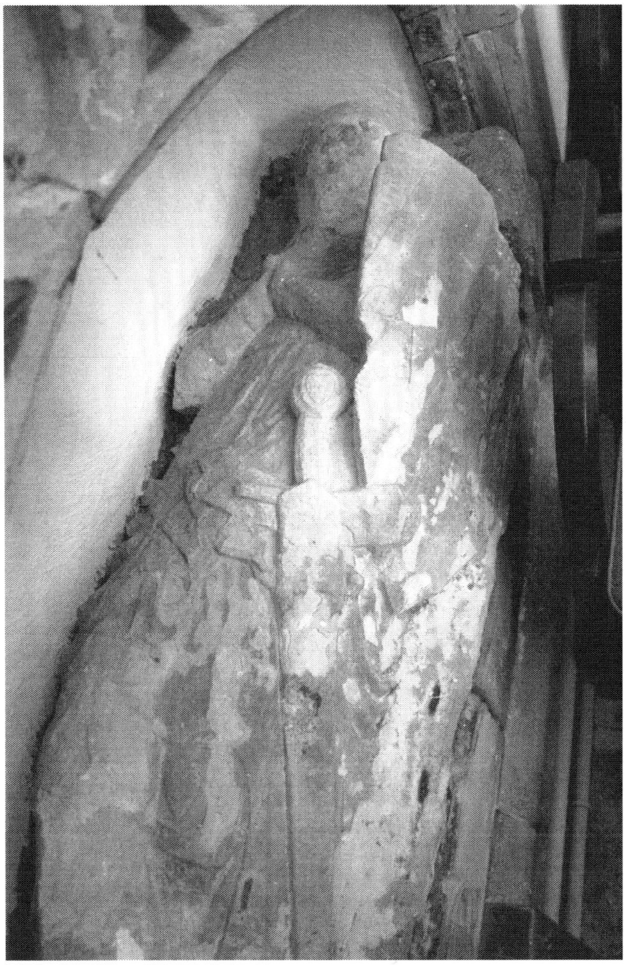

Fig. 196 Hazelwood. Knight (west).

Fig. 197 Hazelwood. Erratic mail on the western knight.

The layout of both figures conforms to the standard Series B pattern (Gittos 1992), with the knees a high point and the legs crossed so that the toes point towards each other and their heads propped on cushions in such a way as to depress their chins. The Vavasour's fess dancetty has been carved on the face of each shield in a very comparable manner, while the detail of the poleyns is almost identical and similarly of high quality workmanship. However, making allowance for the damage to both figures, in most other respects, the eastern effigy is of far better quality than the west. The carving of the mail is markedly different, with the eastern very uniform and closely cut, typical of Series B, while the west's mail is quite erratic (Fig. 197). The eastern spur arms are of modelled section while the west's are just cut square. East's scabbard mounts are finely carved, whereas west's are completely unmoulded (Figs 198, 199). The differences are many but nowhere are they more marked than in the treatment of the lions' tails,

Fig. 198 Hazelwood. Eastern knight's scabbard attachment.

Fig. 199 Hazelwood. Western knight's scabbard attachment.

Fig. 200 Hazelwood. Eastern knight, lion's tail.

Fig. 201 Hazelwood. Western knight, lion's tail.

which both occupy the space between the knights' feet. East has a realistic curved tail culminating in three tufts of fur, but west's looks more like a pattern of three leaves with serrated edges (Figs 200, 201). No effort has been made to represent fur and it is only interpretable by reference to the other figure. There can be little doubt that the eastern effigy was the original and the western its later companion. Why its quality is so inferior can only be guessed at. Perhaps the master was preoccupied by other work or possibly his health was failing after a demanding career spanning at least a quarter of a century.

End game

The last act of this drama is played out with the unfinished knight at Butterwick (Fig. 139). The arms that were painted on his shield can just be discerned (*5b.i*), identifying him as Robert FitzRalph (d. 1317). In keeping with the later figures generally he lacks additional features but has unusual foot supports of an adorsed dog and grotesque, half-man, half-feathered creature (Fig. 202). Butterwick is also the only Series B knight to show a fully developed ring-locket scabbard attachment, with the intermediate link that later became standard, suggesting that even late in his

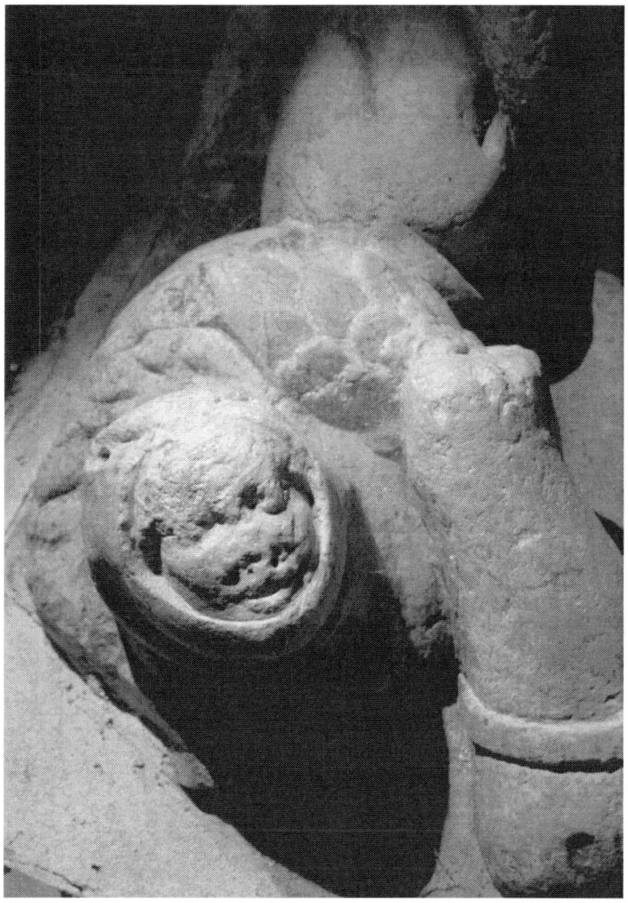

Fig. 202 Butterwick. Grotesque as a foot support.

Fig. 203 Goldsborough. Series C knight.

career the Series B carver was still aware of the very latest developments. The layout conforms to Series B norms in its planning, with a very broad guige and sword belt (Plate 46), the crease in the mail under his chin, elongated eyes and the mail hanging heavily below the forearms. However, the carving is unfinished and appears to have been abandoned part way through. The evidence it provides for the sculptor's working methods is discussed in Section 4b.i but here it is worth noting the attempt to retrieve the situation by painting the heraldic charges over the marking out for what was probably intended to be a carved shield, to judge from its thickness. Presumably the effigy was still needed and the sculptor unable to finish his work, as he would have wished. It is impossible to know but there seems to be no later work than Butterwick. Perhaps our talented carver was nearing his end because, to use Hamlet's dying words, 'the rest is silence'.

4c.iii Series C

The basic outline of Series C was published in 1980 and further detail added in discussion of the Goldsborough effigies (Gittos 1994a) but the group has still to be fully described. The cessation of Series B seems to have been followed by a hiatus of a decade or more before a new flagship Yorkshire workshop emerged, producing a sharp stylistic break. Gone were the flamboyant draperies, the bare heads with their thickly combed locks, the plethora of additional figures and features and the ground-breaking innovations. Conservatism was back with a much sharper focus on the essentials and only an occasional carvers' indulgence. Having said that, Series C is anything but second rate. The best preserved, such as the later Goldsborough knight (Fig. 203) and the Church Fenton lady (Fig. 54) are beautifully carved, with both an artistic elegance and a delicate attention to detail. The exuberance might be lacking but a high degree of skill is only too apparent. However, whereas Series B betrays the hand of a

Fig. 204 Series C distribution map.

single talented carver, Series C can be seen as a workshop with more than one craftsman involved. Magnesian Limestone is used throughout and the distribution pattern is an interesting one as they are all located in the West Riding except for the knights at Burton Stather (across the border into Lincolnshire) and Sheriff Hutton (just into the North Riding). The centre of gravity is to the west of York (Fig. 204), where the quarries providing the stone are found, perhaps pointing to a quarry-based workshop (*4a.iii*).

Of the thirteen members originally identified (Gittos 1980), none has been added and two deleted. The casualties are the distant lady at Bottesford (Leicestershire) and the Birkin male civilian (Fig. 160). The Bottesford carver may have been aware of Series C products but the quality of workmanship is inferior. Perhaps the strong de Ros family connections between Bottesford and Yorkshire engendered the influence. The treatment of Birkin's shoes and buttoned sleeves does show the delicacy of carving characteristic of Series C but the drapery and facial features are inconsistent. Taken as a whole, he is more of a good quality singleton. That leaves a contingent of eight knights and three ladies, running through the 1330s to the mid-1340s. Over such a period, some development is to be expected, especially when comparing what is probably the earliest knight at Darrington (Fig. 205) with the latest at Kildwick (Plate 61). Darrington, who originally held a lance (*4b.v*), is mail clad with only poleyns (unusually secured by thongs) as additional protection. In contrast, Kildwick has plate armour on all his limbs and wears gauntlets. Darrington and Goldsborough have straightforward mail coifs but the other six wear bascinets. Five have aventails attached by the normal method, using exterior vervelles and a cord but Ryther has an earlier form of bascinet with no vervelles although a narrow strip along the lower edge may relate to a concealed means of attachment (Plate 57). Claude Blair believed this form was used before the standard method was adopted, probably in the 1320s (Blair 1958, p. 68). Again at the two extremes, Darrington has prick spurs and Kildwick the large rowel multi-pointed variety (sometimes referred to as chrysanthemum spurs), popular in the 1340s. All show the thong attachment of sword belt to scabbard, except Ryther

Fig. 205 Darrington. Early Series C knight.

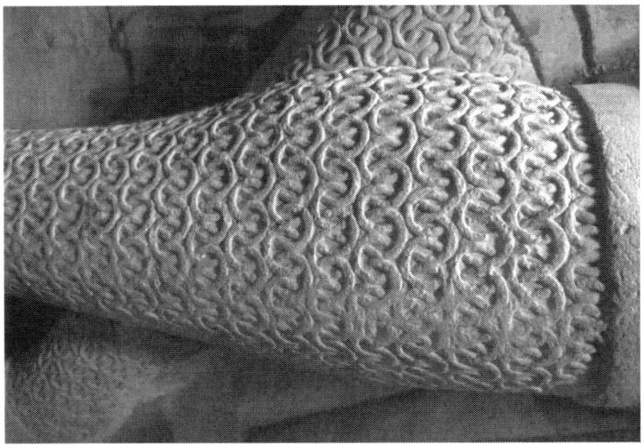

Fig. 206 Goldsborough. Archetypal Series C mail.

Fig. 207 Spofforth. Series C knight.

who has ring lockets complete with the intermediate ring. So, of the Series, Ryther exhibits both the earliest method of securing the aventail to the bascinet and the latest form of scabbard attachment, which makes this group a good illustration of the lack of any simple sequence of armour development in this period.

Darrington and Goldsborough clearly show the overly large circular buckles on both belts and straps that are characteristic of the earlier Series C knights (Fig. 205). An important unifying feature of all the knights is the carving of the mail, with well-rounded links larger than Series B's and more deeply cut, which can be fully appreciated at Goldsborough, due to its excellent state of preservation (Fig. 206). In contrast, the less fortunate Leeds knight is battered, rubbed and caked with dirt, a combination that makes the comparison unfavourable. Nevertheless, the similarities between the two are remarkable, saving their head protection and heraldry, they are almost identical. The layout and details of the belts and their buckles replicate one another (Figs 69, 70). The sword belts both have raised edges and circular mounts while both waist belts have bar mounts. It is not just the details that are replicated, it is the way they are carved, which is particularly noticeable with the complex scabbard attachment of split, woven and knotted thongs. Given also the comparability of such features as the disposition of the surcoat split and the knees shown side by side because the legs are crossed at the ankles, there can be no doubt that Leeds and Goldsborough are contemporary figures carved by the same man. Consequently, it is inexplicable that Mark Downing placed Goldsborough in his chronological group six and Leeds in group seven, seemingly because the latter has a bascinet (Downing 2010, pp. 94–96). The same combination of belt details are seen again at Spofforth but with a difference in quality (Fig. 207). Goldsborough and Leeds are the work of a master who thoroughly understood his subject but Spofforth was produced by a less accomplished and knowledgeable team member. This is apparent in the

Fig. 208 Sheriff Hutton. Later Series C knight.

contrasting approaches of the two carvers in handling the scabbard attachment and the absence at Spofforth of the creases in the surcoat due to the pressure from the waist belt buckle. Spofforth also shows one of the rigid belt mounts as unnaturally flexible but, if subsequently painted to a good standard, such points of detail would be much less apparent.

A key aspect common to both male and female Series C figures is the modelling of the head and shoulders. Most of the earlier members have relatively long necks (shown as quite flat across the front) and flattish rounded faces, sloping down to the chin. The knights have a crease in the mail to either side of the head, which adds width and produced the flat-necked appearance (Fig. 205). This feature is repeated on the females' wimples, especially at Church Fenton (Plate 60). However, the later knights at Sheriff Hutton and Kildwick have lost the slender shape and developed a more hunched appearance (Fig. 208), which may to a degree reflect the fact that these figures wear their aventails drawn higher up the side of the face. Burton Stather provides something of a link between the earlier and later military figures, sharing with the latter the sagging crotch of the hauberk and a more hunched attitude. His special feature is the form of his bascinet, which seems previously to have escaped notice. Multi-faceted rather than rounded in shape, it is the only one of its type in the corpus (Fig. 209). A more elaborate, fluted variant is on the Creke brass at Westley Waterless (Cambridgeshire) dating from the 1340s.

Fig. 209 Burton Stather. Faceted bascinet.

Fig. 210 Leeds. Carved heraldry.

The skill of the Series C master can be seen in the subtle modelling of the faces of the couple at Ryther. They have very similar eyes but the lady is unmistakeably female with the merest hint of pouting lips (Plate 58). The three ladies all wear wimples, veils and have very similar hair, arranged with plaits laid over cauls at the side of the head. The plaits are carried upwards to cross over on the top of their heads, at Church Fenton outlined under her veil. Despite this, the carver has imbued each one with a different character. If Ryther is rather seductive, Darrington is more shy and demure and, in contrast, Church Fenton is confident, aloof, almost imperious (Plates 58, 59, 60). This is reflected in her elbows-wide posture but, when viewed from the side, she has the flatness of face and forward inclination of the head that firmly establishes her as a member of the Series. A clever carver might just be ringing the changes but possibly he was reflecting some knowledge of the people concerned. Church Fenton also exhibits the greatest indulgence by Series C in the almost comical fight (Fig. 262) at her feet between a lion and an amphisbaena (*5c.vi*). Her clothing would suit a date in the 1330s but there is nothing at all to indicate whom she might be.

Another unifying aspect of the Series C knights is that all their shields have carved heraldry. This ought to assist with both identification and dating (particularly as two of the females are paired with the men) but unfortunately there are many difficulties. Whilst the families of all eight are identifiable, the particular people and their biographical details are often illusive. However, identities can be confidently given for both Goldsborough and Sheriff Hutton. The former commemorates Richard de Goldesburgh V, who is believed to have died between 1331 and 1334 (Gittos 1994a) and the latter Edmund de Thwing of Cornbrough, who died 15th October 1344 (VCH:NR:II, p. 179; IPM VIII, pp. 367–68). Leeds appears to carry the Manston coat but shown cotised on the effigy, a variant that has not been traced (Fig. 210). However, John de Manston who is last mentioned in 1337 has been suggested (Downing 2015, p. 74). The arms at Kildwick have not been traced and are assumed to be Stiveton by Lawrance (1946, p. 43). Darrington has the Scargill arms but the pedigree is not well understood for this period. There were several branches with a confusing succession of Warin and William Christian names. Ryther is claimed to be Sir Robert de Ryther who died in 1327 but unfortunately this is the date of a later dower apportionment and his death seems to have been in 1322 when his heir is first described as a minor (FR III, p. 201). This date seems too early for the effigy and his son William may be a possibility but nothing is known about him. Burton Stather has the arms of Sheffield but was apparently brought from Owston by 1717 (*A6*). Lawrance's suggestion (1946, p. 41) that it might be Sir Robert Sheffield was based on a misassumption that it came from Butterwick (Lincolnshire). A good case can be made for Spofforth commemorating Sir Robert Plumpton whose son William succeeded in 1324 and lived until 1362, even though the broken shield can only have had four fusils against the family's recorded five (DBA 3, p. 464). However, even this more positive attribution provides a date that is too early for Spofforth's place in the Series, suggesting that if it did commemorate Sir Robert, there was some delay in its commissioning.

There is some uncertainty over when Series C may have begun. Lacking bascinets, the men at Darrington and Goldsborough seem likely to be the earliest, with the possibility that the person Darrington commemorates may have died in the 1320s, while Goldsborough is probably from the early 1330s (Gittos 1994a). The plate armour at Kildwick marks him out as probably being the last of the group and dating from the 1340s, with Sheriff Hutton and Burton Stather a little earlier in the same decade. The remainder probably all date from the 1330s. So, there is good evidence for a workshop producing fine quality, dramatic effigies from perhaps the late 1320s and operating for some twenty years. Its distribution has a West Riding focus and it may have been quarry-based.

Fig. 211 Ilkley. Series D knight of the Middleton family.

4c.iv Series D

When we first set out the 'Classification of Early Yorkshire Effigies' in 1980, the smallest grouping was the four knights that constituted what we now call Series D at Felixkirk, Stillingfleet, Ilkley and Winteringham (Plates 62, 14, Figs 211, 212). That analysis still holds good today and although it was suggested in 1980 that other figures such as the ladies at Felixkirk and Kirby Sigston might belong, it has proved not to be the case. The four figures are all set out in a similar manner with hands at prayer, their legs crossed with their feet resting on a lion and heads resting on two cushions. Ilkley and Winteringham have angels holding the top cushion (although Ilkley has lost one of his). All are carved from Magnesian Limestone and for the greater part are finished with a delicately wielded fine claw chisel. Extensive areas of such tooling survive at Felixkirk, more limited ones at Winteringham and small patches at Stillingfleet (the surface at Ilkley is masked by paint). As discussed in Section 4b.i, Felixkirk's preservation shows the carver has removed all traces of tool marks on the face, leaving a completely smooth surface (Fig. 213). This has the appearance of being polished (repeated at Winteringham on both knight and surviving angel), which may be due to the application of wax or some other finishing treatment (*4b.iii*). This suggests that the pale colour and fine texture of the stone may have been exploited to represent flesh. A characteristic is the way the eyes are carved. Felixkirk, Ilkley and Winteringham all have a similar form, with an extended outer corner to the lid. Felixkirk has a pronounced, smooth, supra-orbital margin (which appears in a less exaggerated form at Winteringham and Ilkley). Stillingfleet's eyes are more rounded but uncharacteristic tool marks indicate his face has been tampered with (Fig. 214).

The knights carry a shield on the left arm, supported by a narrow guige over the right shoulder but only Stillingfleet and Ilkley have their arms carved on their shields. All wear wrist thongs tied in looped knots. The pendant ends of their waist belts are looped back through the belt itself. Only Felixkirk has mounts on his sword belt but all their scabbards attach to their sword belts by the split thong method. This can be portrayed in many ways but these are almost identical. All split the front belt into two, the upper thong threaded around the scabbard just below its lip and the lower split again, both parts being used to secure the rear belt around the scabbard before being tied together in a sennit knot below. A special feature they all share is the mail-clad skull-cap (Plates 10–13), which was also depicted on the lost figure of Sir Robert de Mauley in York Minster (*2b.iii*). The poleyns are another unifying feature, apparently formed of moulded leather with small shields on each side, which in the case of Felixkirk, Ilkley and Winteringham are enclosed in a shallow circular moulding. Stillingfleet is less well preserved and has lost detail due to wear but does not appear have had the mouldings. Winteringham's poleyns have additional detail showing how they were constructed (Plate 15). There is stitching round the lower edge, indicating that they were not metal and two straps can be seen behind each knee fastening the poleyn in place (*2b.iii*). Felixkirk's and Winteringham's surcoats are shorter than the other two, coming just below the knee, rather than mid-calf length. The left edges of the front splits are all turned back on themselves, Stillingfleet and Ilkley lying over the scabbard while Felixkirk and Winteringham lie under it. The wide splits display not only a substantial amount of the hauberk but the hem of

Fig. 212 Winteringham. Series D knight.

the aketon is also prominent, in a band two to three inches wide. Ilkley and Stillingfleet have prick spurs whereas Felixkirk's have short necks and small rowels of eight points (Fig. 215). So even in such a closely related group there are differences. These were probably just a matter of choice by the carver and/or the patron. They are not likely to be indicative of a chronological progression. Series D demonstrates that both forms of spur and different surcoat lengths all coexisted.

I'Anson recognised the relationship between Ilkley, Felixkirk and Stillingfleet but then broadened the scope of the York atelier he consider responsible for them to include two of the Series C figures (Goldsborough and Sheriff Hutton) and the very individual knight at Kirkby Fleetham. He did not consider Winteringham because it was over the border in Lincolnshire. More recently Mark Downing included all four Series D figures in his Group 6, together with the Series C figures at Darrington and Goldsborough. There is no justification for these arbitrary additions, which both lack the characteristics of Series D, as outlined above. If, for example, the faces of Felixkirk and Goldsborough are put side by side, the difference in carving is immediately laid bare.

The most useful dating evidence for the Series D effigies is at Stillingfleet where the heraldry on the shield is likely to be either Robert or William de Moreby's. Robert was dead by 8th January 1336 (FR IV, p. 466). It was probably his death that prompted the establishment of chantries in the church later in the same year by Nicholas and William de Moreby (*3b*). The carved arms at Ilkley were identified by Lawrance (1946, p. 31) as of Sir Piers Middleton II, citing 'Nicolas R. of Edw. III' as his source for 'd'argent fret sable a une quarter de sable'. They are described as 'Argent fretty sable a canton of the last', on the family pedigree published in 1878 (Whitaker 1878, I, facing p. 280). Peter de Middleton died between June and October 1335 (CPR 1334–1338, pp. 158, 174) and his inquisition post mortem was taken at York the following July revealing that he held the manners of Stobbum (close to Ilkley) and Stokkeld near Wetherby (IPM VIII, p. 4). The latter subsequently became the main family seat (now known as Stockeld Park) but his other manor would provide a good reason for Peter being buried in Ilkley and there seems little doubt that the effigy is his.

There are no arms on the shield at Felixkirk but assistance is provided by the heraldry in the stained glass window

Fig. 213 Felixkirk. Face of Sir John de Walkingham's effigy.

above the tomb (Plate 63, Fig. 216). The significance of the heraldry is described in a useful account of the church (Hamilton Thompson & Brown 1912), the arms including those of Walkingham and Cantilupe. The link seems to be Eva de Bolteby. She married three times and her son by her first marriage, John de Walkingham, who inherited from his father, was knight of the shire for Yorkshire in 1325 and died without male issue in 1332 (Brault 1997, II, p. 444). His burial at Felixkirk is confirmed by his widow Johanna's will of 1346, in which she requested burial at Felixkirk, 'juxta sepulchrum domini Johannis de Walkingham quondam viri mei' (*Test. Ebor.* I, p. 16). This attribution seems logical and his 1332 death means that three of the people represented by Series D effigies died within the space of five years. Before leaving Felixkirk, it is worth noting that this is one of the best preserved effigies of the corpus with most of its original surface remaining.

That just leaves Winteringham for which there are no heraldic clues. From as early as 1240 the Marmion family had possessions in this Lincolnshire parish (CP VIII, pp. 515–16). In 1292 John Marmion was granted free warren in his demesne lands in many places, including

Fig. 214 Stillingfleet. Partly recut face of the de Moreby knight.

Fig. 215 Felixkirk. Finely-carved rowel spur.

Fig. 216 Felixkirk. The knight in his setting.

Winteringham, and in 1298 he was elected Knight of the Shire for Lincolnshire. In 1310 he had licence to alienate in mortmain, land and rent in Winteringham and Beelsby for the maintenance of a chaplain to celebrate divine service daily in the chapel of St Nicholas, Winteringham for the souls of John, his wife Isabel, Alexander Peck, their ancestors and successors (CPR 1307–1313, p. 271). This marks a very significant Marmion involvement with the church. John died in 1322 and his successor, another John, in 1335. Given the dates of the other Series D effigies, the latter would be a good candidate but unfortunately there are effigies for both Johns at West Tanfield where most of the Marmions seem to have been buried. It is possible that there were two effigies for the same person as a way of maximising prayers for his soul, perhaps related to a divided burial. But this seems rather unlikely considering that the West Tanfield effigies are made from Lincolnshire stone while Winteringham is a Yorkshire product. Curiously Mark Downing assigns both Winteringham and the earliest knight at West Tanfield to the John who died in 1322 (Downing 2010), even though the latter is in his chronological group 3 (1315–30) and Winteringham in group 6 (1335–45). It would seem best to admit that Winteringham remains an unidentified but fine example of the Series D carver's repertoire.

Alone amongst the four, Felixkirk remains in its original location (Fig. 216). Its slab is the upper surface of a low plinth within a tall cusped and gabled arch. The prominently underchamfered line of the base slab continues across the side shafts to form a visually strong platform

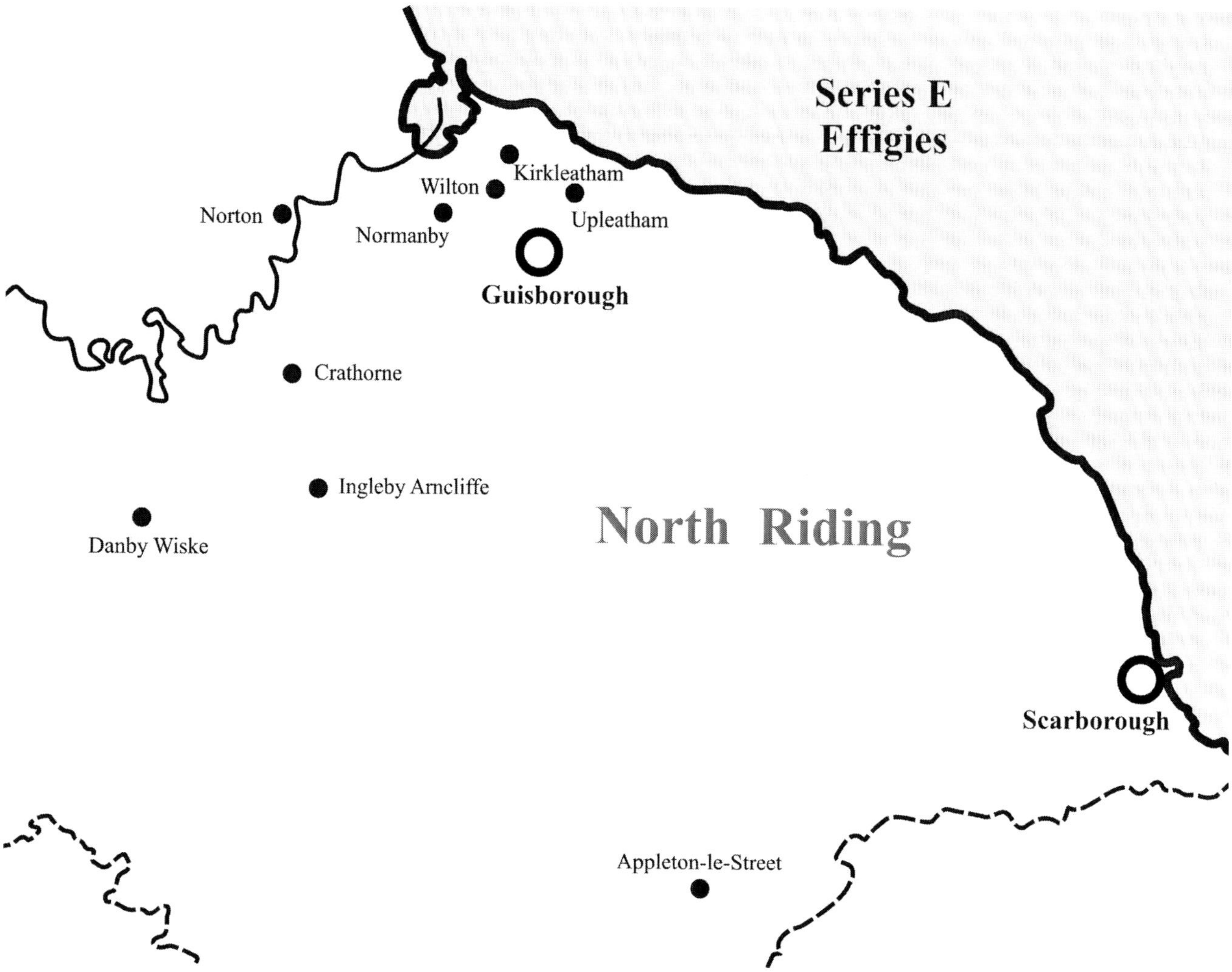

Fig. 217 Series E distribution map.

for the figure itself. The gable rises in front of the window with the heraldic glass, the block at its centre shorn of its carved decoration. The whole structure is built in front of the existing chancel wall. The design is simple but very effective, carefully fitted to an awkward space but of sandstone rather than the effigy's Magnesian Limestone. Although the arch has a complex moulding it is almost devoid of additional decoration, with the apex clumsily botched. It is in stark contrast to the skilful and fastidious representation of fine detail on the effigy. It would seem that the Series D carver was responsible for the effigy but not the setting. This is supported by the choice of what appears to be local stone (like the rest of the church) for the construction of the arch. Nevertheless, there is a coherence of design to the tomb and effigy, which suggests a well conceived plan was being followed. Since, as seems certain, the sculptor made only the effigy, he probably worked some distance from Felixkirk. The Series' wide distribution hints at a manufacturing focus centrally within the county. This may have been the Magnesian Limestone quarries around Tadcaster or even York itself. There he would have had the opportunity to develop his art, in an environment populated with other talented practitioners. Apparently created during just a few years in the 1330s, this carver's work exhibits high levels of craftsmanship, amongst the very best of the day.

4c.v Series E

Series E is a tightly-knit grouping both chronologically and geographically (Fig. 217). They are distributed on the northern side of the Cleveland Hills with two outliers, one just across the Tees, the other further south, near Malton. The centre was probably in or near Guisborough and the iron-rich sandstone from which they are all made may well be local to that area. The full date range is probably confined to the 1340s. They share a feature that makes them instantly recognisable as members of the Series. This is a decorative incised line about half an inch inside the edge of garments and equipment on both male and female figures. Other common features include: surcoat skirts with

Fig. 218 Norton. Series E lady, cut down for reuse.

convoluted hems and straight folds for the males; a 'Y' pattern of folds across the fronts of the ladies' skirts and cloak cords that are beaded between edging lines. Flower heads are frequently used as decorative motifs, sometimes punctuating the hollow-chamfered edges of the base slabs. A full catalogue and detailed account of Series E appeared in Gittos 2002 but during the resurvey process, one further effigy was identified. This is a lady deeply set in a wall at Norton (County Durham), so it is another export from

Fig. 219 Upleatham. Sir Robert de Capon's short-fronted surcoat.

Yorkshire, albeit just over the border, and the northern outlier (Fig. 218). It was 'discovered during alterations to the church in 1875–76' (Longstaffe 1892, p. 12) and has been cut down on all sides, presumably for reuse as masonry, so most of her head (except her chin) and any foot support have been lost and the top surface has spalled off across the front. The figure is carved from the usual material but with reddish seams of iron-rich deposits. She holds her hands at prayer and wears a veil and wimple, her cloak gathered up under both elbows. The carving that does survive shows stylistic traits including the drapery pattern of the skirt and the characteristic incised edging lines (especially on the cloak), which identify her as Series E.

The eleven figures of Series E comprise five ladies and six knights and some important messages can be gleaned from them. They show remarkable variation of both detail and form. The knights are evenly split between crossed legs (Crathorne, Upleatham and Wilton) and straight legs (Normanby and both at Ingleby Arncliffe). The Capon knight at Upleatham (d. 1346) is the only one to wear the short-fronted surcoat fashionable at the time (Fig. 219). Three of the ladies are close in both detail and layout but two are carved in high relief (Appleton-le-Street and Wilton) whereas Danby Wiske is done so shallowly her praying hands have had to be shown spread rather than palms together. The Kirkleatham lady differs again, with deeper relief at the head than the foot. In having closed eyes, Danby Wiske is not only unique amongst Series E but the only one in Yorkshire to do so (Fig. 220). This all points to considerable adaptability on the part of the carver, both in terms of the details required and what could be produced with the budget (or the material) available. Nevertheless, the range of features serves as a cautionary tale for anyone seeking to employ particular aspects of costume and carving practice as a means of grouping figures in isolation from other evidence. Like Series D, this group had a short life, lasting perhaps no more than ten years and may also have been accomplished by a single carver. The distribution is within a restricted area but the Series' richness and diversity belie its ostensibly provincial nature.

Fig. 220 Danby Wiske. Lady FitzAlan, with closed eyes.

4c.vi Wolds Series

We first proposed the existence of a Wolds Series at the BAA conference of 1983 (Gittos 1989, pp. 96–99), suggesting they were 'probably produced by a less accomplished workshop at Beverley'. Located on the Wolds themselves and the Holderness plain, they are characterised by very simple draperies, praying hands with the forearms held close together and, when present, gablettes fitting closely to the head. In some cases, large, distinctive angels accompany the composition. After thirty-five years, the core of the analysis remains valid but certain aspects have needed revision. One concerns the material from which the figures are made. Whilst it is true that some of the Wolds Series are carved in 'a relatively fine grained brown sandstone', this is not so in every case and at least two, or probably three, closely-related Wolds effigies (the Patrington lady, the Beeford priest and, probably, the priest at Winestead) are now known to be carved in a distinctive honeycombed limestone (Fig. 136). Fresh examination of the Patrington lady has revealed the stone to be limestone of a creamy colour, with a very open texture. A full petrological examination is still needed but it is believed to be a type of Magnesian Limestone, in which the dolomitic transformation is incomplete (Tim Palmer, pers. comm., based on photographs). The source of this intriguing material is sadly unknown but it could provide an insight into where these figures were produced.

Another point concerns the gablettes that fit snugly around the heads and shoulders of Beeford (Fig. 221), Winestead and Patrington (Fig. 273) because the arch shape can be recognised as a 'pinched trefoiled ogee' (Budge 2015, p. 116). This features in the canopy of Bishop Hatfield's tomb in Durham Cathedral, the reredos of the Lady chapel in York Minster (Fig. 222) and the sedilia in

Fig. 221 Beeford. Wolds Series priest, with pinched ogee gablette.

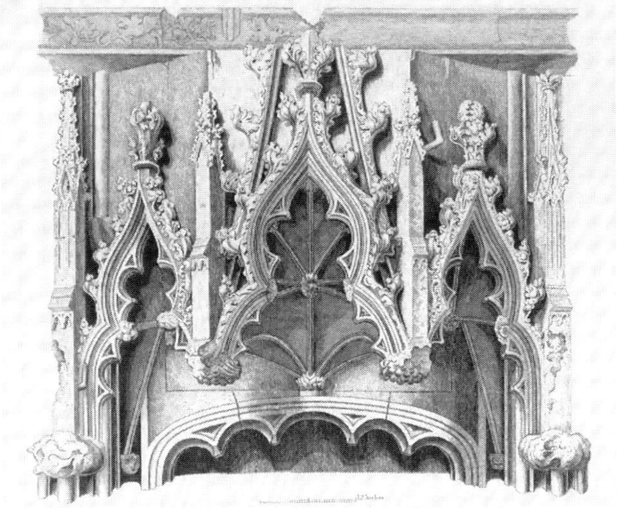

Fig. 222 York Minster. Reredos with pinched ogee arches (Browne 1839/47, p. 137).

Beverley Minster. The earliest of these is Beverley, for which a recent detailed study has demonstrated that the wooden sedilia were carved by members of the same team that produced the Percy Tomb (Woodworth 2011, Ch. 6), suggesting a date in the 1340s. It is extremely unlikely that the masons carving the modest Wolds figures would pre-empt innovative work at the Minster but it would have been fair game to imitate. Hence these three figures, which we previously regarded as dating back to the 1320s must now be considered as no earlier than the 1340s. This would place the tomb at Bainton, of *c.* 1330, as perhaps the beginning of the Series (*3c, 5b.i*).

A significant change is the number of figures now considered members of the Series, which currently stands at seven. In 1983 we suggested that six more effigies might belong to the group: the ladies at Aldbrough (Fig. 21) and Garton-on-the-Wolds (Fig. 132); male civilians at Hedon, Hornsea and Skerne (Fig. 100), plus the Thorpe Bassett priest (Fig. 117). However, detailed inspection has failed to identify clear relationships with the other Wolds figures and they are probably better regarded as individual pieces, perhaps produced very locally in each case. The seven effigies that now constitute the Wolds Series can be divided into two subgroups, the first of which comprises the Beverley Minster male civilian, the Birdsall lady and the Bainton knight, together with his canopy, which all have large, distinctive angels with spread wings, prominent feet and ankles revealed below their albs (Figs 223, 224, 225). At Bainton and Birdsall, their albs are split to the waist and fringed. Their postures vary: Bainton's carry the soul aloft on the canopy, Birdsall's stand alongside the lady but also support the soul, whereas Beverley's recline in a more conventional position beside the effigy's head. The second subgroup includes the Patrington lady plus the priests at Beeford (Fig. 221) and Winestead, all with their pinched ogee gablettes and distinctive limestone. Although the headless priest at Hutton Cranswick lacks the gablette, he shares similar drapery patterns with the other two priests and so is the fourth member of this group. However, his stone has not been identified.

The overall effect of this reassessment is to significantly reduce the size of the group and narrow the date span from the original estimate of some forty years to just the 1330s and 1340s. Consequently, the Wolds Series is now more coherent, with a strengthened impression that it was centred on Beverley and serving the local community. This is where one of the figures is situated and where inspiration for aspects of some of the others was probably drawn.

Whilst only a proportion of Yorkshire's effigies can be grouped according to who made them, the results set out in this Section are revealing, the most obvious conclusion being that availability was erratic. The A/B carver was supplying effigies for twenty years or so from the 1290s but there then seems to be a gap of about ten years before the C workshop began, perhaps in the late 1320s, lasting well into the 1340s. The Series D products date from the 1330s, so overlapping with C. Series E, probably all made during the 1340s, would again have been an alternative to C. However, while D's distribution overlaps C's West Riding territory, Series E is complementary, concentrated in the far north east. In terms of its area of influence, Wolds is also restricted as the effigies seem not to have

Fig. 223 Bainton. Wolds Series tomb canopy angel.

Fig. 224 Birdsall. Wolds Series angel.

Fig. 225 Beverley Minster. Wolds Series angel of the male civilian.

travelled outside the East Riding. Their period of activity in the 1330s and 1340s coincides with Series C, D and E but only a single figure seems to have penetrated the East Riding. All this means that in the long periods when no major supplier was operating in the county, patrons had to employ individual craftsmen on an ad hoc basis or seek sources elsewhere. This pattern of behaviour goes some way to explaining why such a high proportion of Yorkshire's effigies fall outside the recognisable Series. It also makes good sense that most of the imports occurred when the Series products were not available. A surprisingly low *c.* 8% were imported, comprising two of Purbeck marble, nine or eleven from the midland alabaster suppliers (depending on the source of Hull's material), five from Lincolnshire and two from London. Yorkshire was strikingly self-sufficient.

Grouping effigies by source allows developmental trends to be discerned, which can assist with interpreting effigies that are otherwise hard to understand. It allows cases, such as Spofforth and Leeds, to be dated in relation to their fellows. Spofforth might otherwise be considered up to a decade too early and Leeds would have been given quite a broad date range. It also enables a judgement about where the figures were made. The geographical patterns suggest a mixed situation with Wolds likely to be urban, while C was probably quarry-based. The distribution of Series A might suggest someone based in the North Riding, with Scarborough and Routh being outliers, while the Series B locations appear more York-centric. Given the sculptor's work at York Minster, the difference may well be due to the career move of joining the Minster's lodge. Series E seems most likely to have been fashioned in the Guisborough area, either in the town or associated with the Priory. However, given the find location of the Normanby legs, which might be close to the source of the stone (*4a.iii*), it is not impossible that the work was carried out at the quarry.

4d Conclusions

Section 4 as a whole has dealt with the work of the masons, examining how the effigies were made, the material used and considering those that can be related. This has shown something of the working methods of the sculptors and the elements of design that are probably attributable to them. The study of materials and groupings has shown that most Yorkshire effigies of this period were individual commissions and not the products of large-scale workshops. However, those masons who did receive repeated commissions for monuments turned out some fine work. The craftsman responsible for Series A/B was a thinker, bringing to his work a broad knowledge and interest in the world around him, artistic flair, great skill and the ability to translate ideas into stone.

Section 5

Patrons and patronage

5a Historical context and Yorkshire society

5a.i Economic background

The geography of Yorkshire is extremely diverse, providing areas of rugged high ground, fertile lowland, reclaimed land maintainable only through artificial drainage and a long coastline. A major waterway reaches deep into the county, making the capital accessible to the sea-going vessels of the middle ages. The result was an economy that spanned the extremes. As David Palliser has demonstrated, at the apex stood York (Palliser 2014, esp. Chapter 5). York's wealth probably ranked third in the country, after London and Bristol, based on a taxable value of perhaps £1620 in the 1334 Lay Subsidy (Dyer 2000) and Bartlett (1959) provides a useful portrait of the city's economy in the fourteenth and fifteenth centuries. York's pre-eminence in the region should not cast its fellow Yorkshire urban centres completely into shadow as Beverley, consistently the second most wealthy town in the county, was assessed at £500 in 1334 and was twentieth in the national rankings, while Hull stood at thirty-fourth; Scarborough, thirty-fifth; Pontefract, forty-fifth; and Doncaster, fifty-first. The 1377 Poll Tax assessment, made after the mid-century famine and plague episodes provides population figures for those over the age of fourteen (except the very poor). At that time York had 7,248 souls, representing the second largest population after London; Beverley was eleventh; Hull, twenty-fourth; Scarborough, thirty-first; Pontefract, thirty-seventh (Dyer 2000). Yorkshire had another eight places in the top one hundred, including Doncaster, Selby, Hedon and Wakefield. So, while only York and Beverley could be counted amongst the first rank of places in fourteenth-century England, a significant number were of reasonable size and wealth. Such towns were home to a range of potential patrons well able to finance commemoration, drawn from the merchant, artisan, legal and ecclesiastical communities. They also provided foci for the monument makers.

Amongst these towns were some significant ports trading with the continent. Hull was the headport for York's staple, the Humber estuary, the coast of north Lincolnshire and Yorkshire as far north as Scarborough. Its surviving customs accounts demonstrate its reach:

> Hull's direct trading area in the Middle Ages stretched along the entire coast of Western Europe, from Norway in the north to Portugal, and across the northern sea to Iceland. (VCH:ER:I, pp. 11–85)

At the beginning of the thirteenth century Hull ranked third amongst the country's headports, carrying 15.4% of English international trade (Kowaleski 2000). It declined in relative terms during succeeding centuries but it still ranked fifth at the end of the fifteenth century and was the busiest east coast port. Even measured just in terms of cloth and wine, it never ranked lower than sixth between 1350 and 1500. To this, Hull's coastal and local fishing trade must be added, together with its role as a principal supply port for the Scottish military campaigns (VCH:ER:I, pp. 11–85). Although the headport, and therefore accountable for customs, Hull was only one of many ports of varying size along the Yorkshire coast. All will have handled coastal trade and many supported their own fishing fleets, which could be substantial (Hey 1986, p. 81). The local trade was not only around the coast but also penetrated deep into the county and hinterland, eloquently sketched by Richard Morris (2018, p. 140). The great river systems that combine to form the Humber estuary drain more than 9,000 square miles, which equates to about one fifth of England (Pethick 1990). The consequence being that much of this area (and therefore the places within it) was accessible by water craft, via the Humber/Ouse system.

The Yorkshire countryside contained large areas where the land was highly productive, such as much of the East Riding and the Vale of York, counterbalanced by great tracts of poor quality farming land with consequent under population. The average wealth of the Yorkshire countryside seems to have been far less than might be anticipated from the status of the towns. Using the 1334 Lay Subsidy assessments, out of forty-one counties, the East Riding (the most affluent) ranks in the middle but the North and West Ridings are very close to the bottom (Glasscock 1976, p. 141). These figures have been rationalised as assessment per square mile, so the sheer size of Yorkshire and proportion of unproductive uplands inevitably skew the picture. Because a much higher proportion of the East Riding is thriving lowland, it may be that its middle-ranking position is indicative of the true status of the productive areas of the other Ridings. This suggestion is supported by the great wealth of the county's major monastic houses. Underpinned by massive estates, great houses such as Fountains, St Mary's (York), Selby and Guisborough were amongst the wealthiest in the kingdom. Fountains is likely to have been the richest Cistercian foundation in the country with a net annual income of £1115 in 1535 (Knowles & Hadcock 1953) while Byland, Jervaulx, Kirkstall, Rievaulx (Plate 64) and Meaux ranged between £230 and £330. Of the Benedictines, St Mary's Abbey (York), with £1650 could be counted amongst the ten richest establishments in the country, following such places as Westminster, Glastonbury and Canterbury Cathedral Priory while Selby had £606, Whitby £437, Monk Bretton £239, York (Holy Trinity, Micklegate) £169 and Snaith £110. Mount Grace was the third wealthiest Charterhouse in the country with £323. The Augustinian house at Guisborough was amongst that order's ten most valuable foundations with £628 followed by Bridlington on £547, Nostell £492, Newburgh £367, Bolton £213, Marton £151, Warter £143 and Haltemprice £100. The Gilbertine's Watton Priory was their wealthiest house with £360. The extent of these riches testifies to the very substantial patronage of the major landowners in the region.

5a.ii Royal administration in Yorkshire

York's long-standing importance and prosperity made it wholly exceptional, standing head and shoulders above any other centre in England apart from London. It was the seat of an archbishopric, housed one of the wealthiest abbeys in the country, a range of other monastic houses and, in St Leonards (Fig. 226), the largest hospital outside London (Cullum & Goldberg 1993). York's society has been succinctly described by Jennifer Kermode (2000, p. 678):

Fig. 226 York. Part of the great medieval hospital of St Leonard (Halfpenny 1807, pl. 17).

> The needs of sophisticated consumers were met by an unusual agglomeration of highly skilled craftsmen: bell-founders, bookbinders, embroiderers, glaziers, jewellers and upholsterers for instance. At their peak before the 1430s, York's international merchants accounted for over half the wool and cloth traded through Hull, and one third of wine and miscellaneous imports. They supplied the city and region with textile requirements such as dyestuffs and teasels, with wine, Mediterranean fruit and spices, silks and brocades, all financed from their sales of wool and cloth. Continental luxuries, like overseas travel, coloured the lives of provincial townsfolk. York was a cosmopolitan city importing ideas alongside almonds and liquorice, and, on one occasion, the text of a play from northern Europe.

York was very far from the remote backwater it is sometimes perceived to have been. Instead it had a vigorous, thriving economy, a cosmopolitan flavour and stood at the forefront of national affairs. During a substantial part of the fourteenth century it was arguably acting as the country's capital, hosting the great offices of state. The evidence has been assessed by Mark Ormrod (2000, p. 82) who demonstrated that the city hosted major parts of the royal administration for nearly seventeen years between 1298 and 1338, and felt that, 'in these years at least York became very much a second home for the English royal government'. This was a crucial period in the development of the area's monumental and related sculpture. It opened with a period of continuous residence between 1298 and 1304 on the part of the Exchequer, the Treasury and the courts of Common Pleas and King's Bench, together with four sittings of Parliament or the Great Council. York was 'the hub of [Edward's] war administration' (Miller 1961, p. 54). This necessitated major improvements in the infrastructure, for instance the Sheriff was required to fit out the Castle hall for sessions of the Exchequer; to erect and equip a new building for the Court of Common Pleas; while Clifford's Tower (Fig. 227) was to have new security measures appropriate for housing the Treasury (HKW:II, p. 891).

Fig. 227 York. Clifford's Tower, where the Treasury lodged (Halfpenny 1807, pl. 12).

> [York] was a rendezvous of armies and made its own contributions to them... In the year 1299–1300 alone, money was sent from York to Lochmaben (Dumfries.), Berwick, Carlisle, Caerlaverock (Dumfries.), and Roxburgh; commissioners were sent out from York to levy troops in the western counties; the king's counsellors ordained there for the provisioning of various places in Scotland; horses were collected there and the king's wine put in cellar; meat was salted and grain was stored there for victualling the armies. As a centre of affairs the city had been transformed. (Miller 1961, p. 54)

The benefit to the local economy may be judged by the findings of a 1337 inquiry into the adverse effects on the city of Westminster of a later removal:

> ... the men thereof do not sell merchandise or other saleable things, except when the king holds his parliament there, or when the Exchequer, the King's Bench, or Common Bench are there. ... On account of the absence of the courts the men of the town with their goods have departed and dwell at York and elsewhere, following the king and the courts ... (CIM II, p. 381).

The effect must have been similar during 1298–1304, since a similar complaint was made by London over the 1327 removal, when they maintained that '... their livelihood depended on a constant flow of magnates, government agents and litigants' (Ormrod 2000, p. 86). London's loss was York's gain and in the years around 1300, York was where it was happening.

Greater analysis has been done and more light shed on what happened when the administration moved north again in the 1330s. In 1332 the situation in Scotland precipitated a further episode of hostilities. Chancery moved north in the October, staying for seventeen months and returning for several periods (totalling a further sixteen months) between then and December 1336. The Exchequer was there continuously for more than five years; the Court of King's Bench sat in York for twelve of its twenty-nine terms during that period and the Court of Common Pleas from May 1333 to the end of 1339, lingering even after the Exchequer had departed. The workload of the Common Pleas in 1327–28 has been studied by Robert Palmer (1984, pp. 7–9) showing that it handled over 13,000 cases, providing an inkling of the numbers of individuals flocking to York for that body alone. The judges and their retinues, in addition to the court bureaucracy, lawyers, litigants and witnesses, of this court alone would have been a substantial influx in a city with a population estimated by David Palliser as at that time in the region of 20,000–30,000 (2014, pp. 128–29).

During both migrations, all the offices taken together plus the occasional presences of the King, the royal household, Parliament and the Great Council, means the incomers must have been highly visible. A cross section of society, amongst them the highest and wealthiest in the land, would either have been directly involved or drawn by business with the various administrations. Palliser and Ormrod have both noted the resulting boost to York's economy and the latter has suggested that in some instances, the transfer was partly inspired by the King's wish to subdue the recalcitrant Londoners, using the economic effect as a weapon (Palliser 2014, p. 142; Ormrod 1997, p. 19). Whatever the motivation, the newcomers cannot have gone unnoticed by anyone with an observant, enquiring and impressionable mind. Unquestionably, the best of the northern sculptors fell into this category, adding to their repertoire new ideas, attitudes and fashions, an effect that shows in their work.

5a.iii Domestic military involvement

The reason for moving the offices of state to York was conflict with Scotland, which involved the military machine as well as the administration. After a period of relative calm for the county during the reign of Henry III (1216–72), matters entered a new phase with the failure of the Scottish succession in 1290. This had serious and wide-ranging consequences, lasting for some sixty years, for both Yorkshire and its inhabitants who had been involved in Edward I's previous enterprises, notably the warfare in Wales. With the advent of conflict on the country's northern border, Yorkshire came to the forefront. For the duration of the problems, the county was on the primary arteries to the north (whether by road or sea) and witnessed a constant procession of supplies, munitions, armies, administrators and commanders. There were, however, other direct effects on Yorkshire society since the northern counties were expected to bear the brunt of finding the necessary manpower. Repeated calls for service on the part of the knights and barons, some responding with

Fig. 228 Fountains Abbey. Sir Roger de Mowbray.

substantial retinues, and levies of infantry from the towns and countryside alike, meant that many would have had experience of the fighting. Many of Yorkshire's effigies commemorate those who were involved, including some who lost their lives in action.

The conflict had its roots in the failure of the Scottish succession, so a brief resumé of the conflict may help set Yorkshire's involvement in context. By the time the offices of state moved to York in 1298, Edward had mediated the succession problem caused by the death of the young Queen Margaret in 1290, awarding the crown to John Balliol and administering the country during the interregnum. Balliol subsequently turned against King Edward and eventually abdicated. Scotland was taken back into royal administration, prompting revolt. Disaster struck in September 1297 when an English army, under the command of the veteran John de Warenne, was heavily defeated by Wallace's forces at Stirling Bridge. At the time, King Edward was out of the country, leading an expedition in Flanders. Some Yorkshiremen joined the King rather than staying guard in the north and it was in Ghent that Roger de Mowbray died (*5b.i*). His body was returned in 1299 for burial in Fountains Abbey, where he was probably commemorated by the surviving effigy (Fig. 228). In the aftermath of the king's return (in the spring of 1298) and a renewed determination to sort out the problem with Scotland, substantial English forces re-entered the field and the administrative base was moved to York. Conflict in Scotland continued until Edward's death in 1307, during which time engagements such as the Battle of Falkirk went some way to reassert English authority. Although Robert Bruce was crowned King of Scotland in 1306, his hold was shaky and years of conflict ensued before his position was secure (Brown 2008), the brunt of it borne by the northern counties.

Edward II's attitude towards Scotland was somewhat different, pursuing the conflict with far less vigour on a small scale until, in late 1313, a group of loyal lowland

Scots sent an appeal for assistance (Brown 2008, pp. 104–105). This demonstrated the need for Edward to reassert his dominion and came at a time when he was better placed to respond than in earlier years. The subsequent major expedition culminated in the disastrous defeat at Bannockburn. Prominent amongst the reported dead from a Yorkshire standpoint were: Sir Edmund de Mauley (Steward of the King's Household, Plate 68), William de Vescy of Kildare and Sir Miles de Stapleton (Hall 1722, pp. 14–15). Sir Robert Clifford, a veteran of the Scottish wars who commanded part of the main battle was another high-profile casualty. He had recently acquired and strengthened Skipton Castle, making it a primary residence. Although unattributed, Hugh Clifford (1987, p. 59) records the possibility that he may have been buried in Bolton Priory. Sir Robert Clifford's was one of only two bodies known to have been repatriated, the others said to have been buried on the battlefield (Brown 2008, p. 130). However, an effigy now in the collection of the Yorkshire Museum (*2c.ii*) may, on heraldic grounds, commemorate William de Vescy. Neither burial site nor monument are known for either Sir Miles Stapleton or Sir Edmund de Mauley. The effigy at Bainton has traditionally but erroneously been attributed to him but in fact commemorates his younger brother John (*5b.i*). Another de Mauley brother, Robert, was captured at Bannockburn (Hall 1722, p. 15) along with other Yorkshire knights including Sir William Latimer and Sir Marmaduke de Thwing. Robert eventually died in 1331, being commemorated by the now lost military effigy once in York Minster (Fig. 64) and when Latimer died, he was buried in Guisborough Priory (Oxford Dictionary of National Biography; Appendix A6c.v). Surprisingly, given the scale of this military disaster, the number of associated Yorkshire effigies is very modest and all the more so when one widely claimed to represent a member of the fallen (Bainton) turns out to be a case of mistaken identity.

In the wake of Bannockburn came persistent and widespread Scottish incursions (McNamee 1997, Ch. 3). Marauding Scots were nothing new in northern England but the raids of the ensuing eleven years were the most severe, extending as far south as York and Beverley. Of relatively short duration, the raids were targeted to inflict maximum harm, through the destruction of property and theft (including crops and livestock), using the fear engendered to extort protection money from towns and institutions. In the words of a contemporary source, in 1318 the Scots 'destroyed the town of Northallerton, burnt the church and adjacent countryside and then wasted and plundered on all sides as far as the abbey of Bolton' (translated in Cutler 2003). In 1319, the threat to York was considered so severe that a citizen army was organised by Archbishop Melton and the Chancellor of England, Bishop Hotham, to confront the invaders. The encounter took place at Myton-on-Swale (just east of Boroughbridge) but the inexperienced and ill-equipped people of York were routed by the battle-hardened Scots, leaving many dead, including Nicholas Fleming the Mayor of York. Three years later, in October 1322, King Edward came close to capture when a Scottish army confronted and defeated a small English force at the Battle of Byland (now believed to have been on the hilltop at Sutton Bank). The King was forced to flee eastward in haste, leaving his baggage at Rievaulx Abbey to be seized by the Scots. The raiders carried on south as far as Beverley and it was during this raid that Bainton church was damaged or desecrated beyond repair. Sir John de Mauley was the incumbent at the time (*5b.i*) and his effigy survives (Fig. 108). It testifies to the problems created by the raids since it appears to have been initially set up in the churchyard, presumably because the rebuilding of the church was incomplete at his death *c.* 1331 (*3c*). Given that the raids were aimed at fund raising as much as demonstrations of power, it is even conceivable that Bainton was deliberately targeted, if the incumbent were known to be a member of the wealthy de Mauley family. On the same raid, Beverley Minster paid £400 to the Scots for 'protection', while in 1320 men from the Vale of Pickering had given them 300 marks and in 1318 Ripon had agreed 1,000 marks, with an initial instalment of 240 marks and six hostages (McNamee 1997, p. 139). McNamee and Cutler (Cutler 2003) have demonstrated the extent of the damage sustained through successive tax assessments. Although the claims are likely to be exaggerated and incomplete, the geographical concentrations clearly show the extent of territory affected. By an unfortunate twist of fate, the Scottish incursions coincided with a period of agricultural calamities: harvest failures and livestock epidemics affecting both sheep and cattle, that led to prolonged famine (Kershaw 1973). The combined result was a population decline and widespread impoverishment. It is probably little wonder that there appear to be few effigial monuments set up in the years around 1320.

The eventful year of 1322 saw a major action in Yorkshire – the Battle of Boroughbridge. Unrest amongst the nobility had been seething through most of Edward II's reign and Thomas Earl of Lancaster was the natural leader of the dissidents. It culminated in March when Lancaster's forces fought the royal army over the river crossing at Boroughbridge. The cross (Fig. 229) which originally stood in Boroughbridge market place, before being moved to Aldborough, is believed to be a rare medieval battlefield memorial. The royal party prevailed but with representatives of major Yorkshire families on both sides. One of the executed leaders was Sir John de Mowbray, son of the man commemorated by the Fountains effigy (CP, IX, pp. 376–80). Sir Nicholas Stapleton was captured at Drax Priory (of which his family were patrons) and paid a fine of 2,000 marks. The factionalism, as so often, split

Fig. 229 Aldborough. Cross believed to commemorate the Battle of Boroughbridge.

families. For instance, John de Ryther remained loyal, taking prisoners and their goods on behalf of the King (CIM II, p. 132) while his elder brother Robert is listed in the same account as being in 'the custody of the bailiffs of the city of York, and … delivered to the sheriff' (CIM II, p. 133). Later that year, Sir Robert, who is a candidate for the effigy at Ryther (*4c.iii*), agreed to a fine of 400 marks and a group of local men stood surety for his good behaviour: John de Ros, William Malbys, Thomas de Heslerton, John and Walter de Fauconberg (FR III, p. 155). These men are all of families with surviving effigies.

A peace treaty with the Scots was agreed in 1327 during the minority of Edward III, shortly before the death of Robert Bruce and accession of his four-year-old son. However, it failed to satisfy all those who had been awarded lands and titles in each other's countries, giving rise to festering dissent, which spawned renewed hostilities from 1332. These men, led by John Balliol (the son of the man awarded the throne by Edward I), invaded in 1332 (MacInnes 2016, pp. 12–14). Their short-lived success and swift ejection followed by Balliol's willingness to acknowledge English overlordship, gave Edward III the opportunity to capitalise on the renewed hostilities and he launched his own offensive in 1333 (Ormrod 2011, Ch. 6). Conflict continued but after 1337/8 had to compete for resources with the operations against France. A resounding victory over the Scots came on 17th October 1346 at the Battle of Neville's Cross, just outside Durham. The royal administration had been aware that the 1346 invasion of France was likely to prompt Scottish opportunism and in recruiting for the French expedition had encouraged northern magnates to stay behind to counter any incursion (Ormrod 2011, p. 283). The hastily gathered army included William de Crathorne of Crathorne whose nuncupative will survives (*Test. Ebor*. I, p. 21). A contemporary letter not only lists him amongst the few English fatalities but says that he had served with Lord Neville and been knighted on the day of the battle (Aravangian & Leopold 1998, pp. 134–37). The names recorded as taking part constitute a roll-call of Yorkshire families who had previously favoured effigies: Mauley, Metham, Middleton, Mowbray, Neville, Scrope and Vavasour. However, only William de Crathorne (Plate 65) seems to have been commemorated by one (Gittos 2002b) and those who died subsequently must have had less robust memorials, which seem to have left no trace.

5a.iv Military service abroad

Whilst many northerners stayed behind to man the border in 1346, the main English forces were active in France, with the victory at Crécy (26th August) only eight weeks before Neville's Cross. Nevertheless, some northerners accompanied the king, with others joining them after defeating the Scots (Wrottesley 1898, p. 7) in time to participate in the long Siege of Calais. The army included many Yorkshire men amongst the rank and file, for instance William son of John de Malton of Pickering, Robert Tyrwyghte of Beverley and the splendidly named William son of Roger Rasoursmyth of Otley in Wharfedale (Wrottesley 1898, pp. 234, 265, 247). There were also representatives of many prominent county families amongst the knightly participants. Monuments remain for few of these men, with the notable exceptions of Sir John de Sutton at Sutton-on-Hull and Sir John de Meaux at Aldbrough. Sir Edward Saltmarshe died *c.* 1350 (Saltmarshe 1910, p. 105) and was buried in the Beverley Blackfriars (Young 1837, p. 129) although nothing is known of a monument. Henry de Ingleby (of the Ripley family) figures on his parents' tomb as a weeper (Fig. 230) but willed in 1375 to be buried in York Minster (*Test. Ebor*. I, p. 94), making no mention of a monument, instead abjuring secular pomp. Sir Walter de la Pole, who served with Prince Edward (Wrottesley 1898, pp. 36, 201, 206) was the son of William, who did much to finance the

Fig. 230 Ripley. Tomb chest figure of Magister Henry Ingleby.

Fig. 231 Ripon Cathedral. Magnesian Limestone knight, probably Sir Thomas Markenfield.

campaign. Walter died 1346 × 1354 (Horrox 1983, p. 30) but nothing is known of either a burial or monument. Sir Thomas Ughtred of Scarborough and Kexby was a career soldier, retinue leader and Sub-Marshal of the army during the Crécy-Calais campaign who died in 1365 and was buried at Catton in the East Riding. Ughtred might have been expected to have had a commensurately splendid tomb. In fact, his monument was not put in place until after 1398 when his son left provision for a figure brass (*Test. Ebor*. I, pp. 241–45). Sally Badham (2016) has recently argued that shared service in the Crécy-Calais campaign was a factor in the dissemination of alabaster monuments amongst the veterans, encouraging their popularity. Whilst this may hold good in other parts of the country, it does not appear to be so in Yorkshire. The veterans whose tombs survive are few and those that do chose a more local source than the midland alabasterers. However, the authors have been unable to substantiate Sir Robert Hilton of Swine's participation in that campaign (Badham 2016, p. 58). Sir William Latimer did serve in the Crécy-Calais campaign, as a sixteen-year-old. His choice of alabaster for his monument at Guisborough in 1380 (*A6c.v*) is more likely to be the result of the fashions of that time rather than a memory of his elders' preferences. Sir John Sutton's memorial chapel does, however, appear to be an example of the extravagant chivalric displays noted by Saul (2009, pp. 216–24) amongst the Crécy-Calais veterans and Sir John de Meaux's memorialisation at Aldbrough appears also to have followed this trend. These two memorials are the meagre legacy of Yorkshire's involvement in these campaigns.

Towards the end of the century, the military focus remained on the continent but whilst relatively few Yorkshiremen are identifiable amongst the Black Prince's retinue (Green 1998, II), a high proportion of John of Gaunt's retinue was drawn from the county where he had extensive holdings. Three men who served together were Sirs John Bosville, Thomas Markenfield and John Marmion and the first two gave evidence to the Scrope/Grosvenor Commission in 1386 (Nicolas 1832). A career soldier of the 1370s and 1380s, Sir John Bosville, may be the man commemorated by the alabaster monument at Darfield (Plate 66). He was dead by 1402 but in the 1380s had become a retainer of Gaunt's (Armitage-Smith 1911, II, pp. 295–96). His career included the 1350 naval engagement with the Spanish off Winchelsea, service in France with the King in 1360 and probably also in the Black Prince's expedition to Spain in 1367. The heraldic evidence at Ripon clearly indicates the Markenfield family. They had their own chantry in the Minster, to which Sir Thomas' widow presented in March 1398–99 (Fowler 1908, pp. 177–78). Capwell (2015, p. 300) dates the Magnesian Limestone monument *c.* 1398, by which time Sir Thomas was dead (Fig. 231). He had served with the other two under Gaunt in his 1373 French chevauchée and by 1386 had accrued twenty years of military experience across Scotland, Normandy and Guiennes (Nicolas 1832, II, p. 318). Sir John Marmion's monument is at West Tanfield and he was one of the Commissioners in Scrope/Grosvenor (Nicolas 1832, II, p. 163). He died in February or March 1387 (IPM XVI, Nos 414, 415) seemingly while on campaign with Gaunt in Spain, being last mentioned taking out protection prior to embarkation (Medieval Soldier Database). He occurs with Bosville and Markenfield on the payroll for Gaunt's French chevauchée in 1373, having become an indentured retainer (for peace and war, for the term of his life) the previous August. The rare surviving indenture was published by Armitage-Smith (1911, I, p. 323). Other Yorkshiremen in Gaunt's service included both of the later fourteenth-century generations of Roucliffes, based near Pickering where the alabaster effigies of two, together with one of their wives, remain. Given their close similarity and dates of death, it will probably never be possible to be certain which effigy represents which Roucliffe. The elder Sir Richard died in 1393 and Sir David, his heir, in 1406 (the younger Sir Richard's date of death is unclear). The trio are described by the History of Parliament Online as 'loyal and committed servants of John of Gaunt', although the family land holdings were relatively modest. Alongside his work in the county, David, like his father before him, was Constable, Steward and Master Forester of the Honour of Pickering but also saw military service, participating in Gaunt's attempt to take the Spanish throne. His allegiance embraced Henry Bolingbroke (later Henry IV) and it was to Pickering that Bolingbroke hastened in July 1399, immediately after landing at Ravenser to depose Richard II (Saul 1997, p. 408). So whilst the focus of political and military activity mostly shifted southward in the later part of the century, the people represented by effigial monuments in Yorkshire were taking part in national and international events throughout.

5a.v The Black Death

Aside from almost constant warfare, plague was a major influence on fourteenth-century society, not only during the Black Death of 1348–49 but also its subsequent recurrences. It created long-lasting economic effects, including inflation. Yorkshire was badly hit and David Palliser thinks the death toll for York during the 1349 outbreak is likely to have been within the 40–50% range estimated for the country at large (Palliser 2014, p. 189). Contemporary records illustrate the problem. Meaux Abbey (E.R.) lost its abbot and thirty-two inmates out of fifty while new burial grounds had to be consecrated to accommodate the dead, *e.g.* in the East Riding at Beverley and Fulford, while in the North Riding new consecrations were ordered at Barton near Gilling, Brotton, Wilton (in Cleveland), Cleasby near Stanwick, Easby near Stokesley, Egton and Seamer near Rudby (Horrox 1994, pp. 68, 269–71). Such a drop in population clearly had severe economic repercussions but the extent to which its effect can be detected in artistic works has been subject to debate, summarised by Phillip Lindley, 'But what is unequivocal is that the Black Death did have a dramatic effect on cultural production in England' (1996, p. 146). Very few Yorkshire effigies can be confidently assigned to the period 1350–70 so that, by this yardstick, the trauma appears very marked. Significantly, all the Yorkshire stylistic Series (*4c*) seem to have finished by the middle of the century, although there is some doubt about the final figures of Series E, the pair at Wilton (in Cleveland). They can confidently be assigned to Sir Ralph Bulmer (Fig. 232) who died after August 1349 (when plague was raging in Yorkshire) and Lady Alice, his widow who died in 1356. They might have ordered their monuments in advance but it is worth noting that the commission to consecrate the chapel and churchyard of Wilton was not issued until 17th July 1349. It was authorised 'on account of the pressing pestilence or mortality of men now waxing strong' but the privilege of burial there was to last only until the following Christmas (Horrox 1994, p. 270). Sir Ralph's burial may date from this time but with appropriate funds, special permission might have been negotiated at any time.

Another relevant monument is the priest's tomb at Welwick, which commemorates someone who died in 1360. As the case study in Section 6a establishes, it is likely to have been designed by William de Malton, master mason at Beverley, who is not recorded after the plague (Petch

Fig. 232 Wilton (in Cleveland). Sir Ralph Bulmer who died on the cusp of the Black Death.

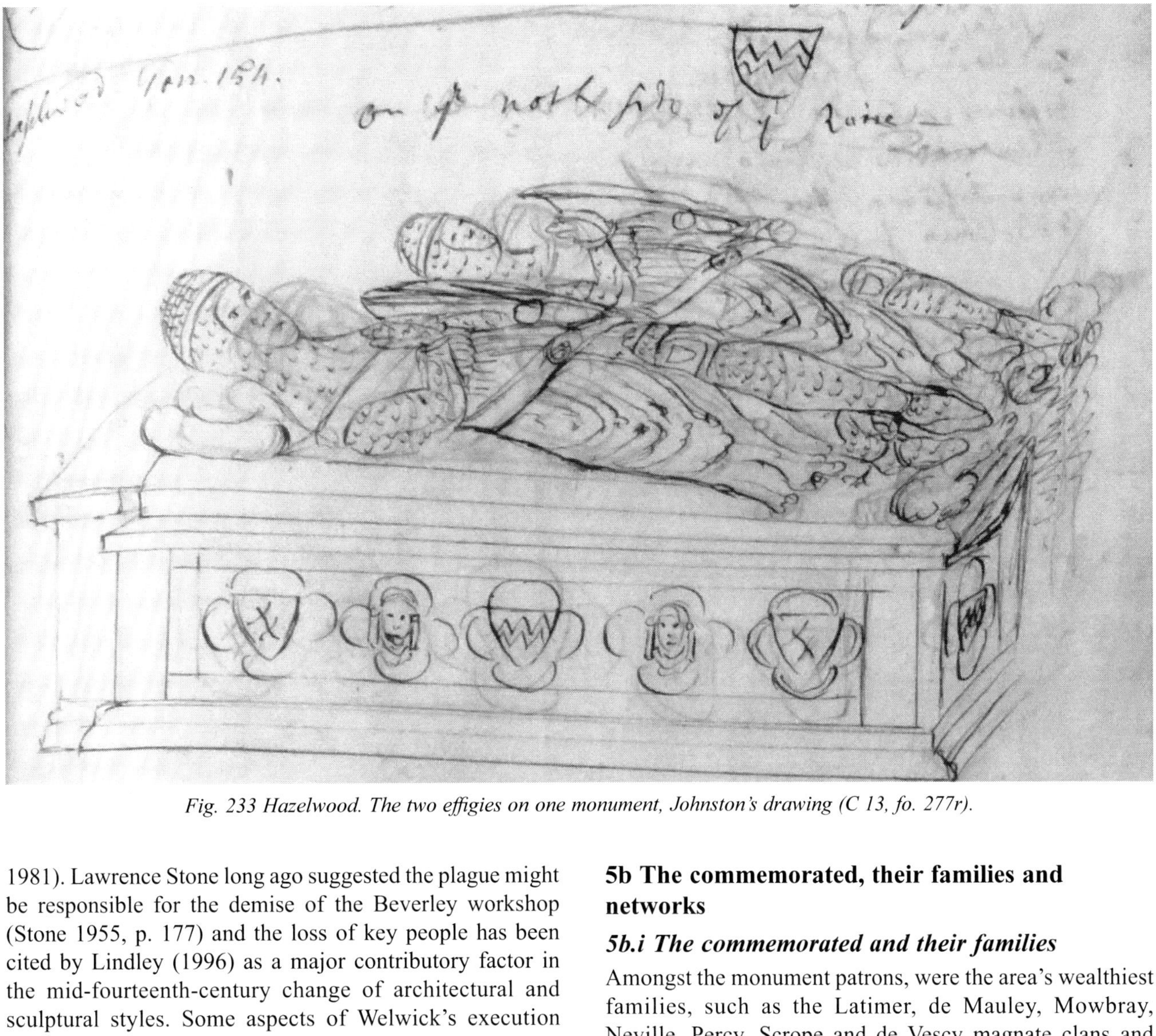

Fig. 233 Hazelwood. The two effigies on one monument, Johnston's drawing (C 13, fo. 277r).

1981). Lawrence Stone long ago suggested the plague might be responsible for the demise of the Beverley workshop (Stone 1955, p. 177) and the loss of key people has been cited by Lindley (1996) as a major contributory factor in the mid-fourteenth-century change of architectural and sculptural styles. Some aspects of Welwick's execution suggest that a sculptor who worked on the Percy Tomb at Beverley carried out the work without Malton's direct involvement. His untimely death is one explanation for the way the monument was made and would set its creation in the 1350s. If so, it might be the final work of the Beverley masons and the Yorkshire evidence can be seen as supporting Lindley's views.

Yorkshire's effigies are best understood in their historical context. Viewed in isolation they are a fascinating group of carvings but like so many worthwhile objects, they take on an additional dimension when seen against the backdrop of the time they were created. York's temporary role as the nation's capital was a major and beneficial influence on the effigies produced at that time. Some witness of people's involvement in military campaigns can be detected and there was a dramatic decline in production during the two decades that followed the Black Death.

5b The commemorated, their families and networks

5b.i The commemorated and their families

Amongst the monument patrons, were the area's wealthiest families, such as the Latimer, de Mauley, Mowbray, Neville, Percy, Scrope and de Vescy magnate clans and below them was a strong stratum of gentry families, including Bruce, FitzAlan, Hilton, Malbys, Markenfield, de Meaux, Roucliffe, Stapleton and Sutton. All of them organised commemoration in the county. A great deal is known of these families that not only demonstrates their activities and the extent of their wealth but also materially assists in understanding their monuments. The following studies illustrate specific problematic instances where such background is the key to dispelling myth and mistakes. This technique is only occasionally of use for the more modest monuments as insufficient information survives about families of lesser means but for the more historically visible, it can be crucial.

Hazelwood

Hazelwood Castle chapel has remained Roman Catholic, so escaping Protestant iconoclasm. It contains two effigies that at first sight appear identical but are not. They are usually regarded as a pair but their resemblance and situations have been misinterpreted. Housed in separate canopied recesses in the south wall, they have suffered badly from damp, that to the west being the more decayed. They were originally on the same tomb, on the north side of the sanctuary, where Henry Johnston drew them, probably in January 1670 (Johnston C 13, fo. 277r) when the tomb panel now below the more easterly formed part of their chest (Fig. 233). Torre (1691, fo. 219) noted them in the same position, 'Within the altar rayles on the north side is an old monument raised of white stone, having on the sides these escocheons 1 & 3 a lion rampant, 2 & 4 Vavasour. There lies thereon two portraitures of knights in solid stone.' I'Anson (1927, pp. 36–37) was unaware of their former location, claiming they were 'in situ' and considering them so similar that one description could serve for both. Mark Downing (2010, p. 92) fails to mention the double tomb and provides near identical descriptions, so the original arrangement has occasioned little comment. Neither I'Anson nor Downing mention the discrepancy in workmanship between the two effigies (*4c.ii*).

The dismantling of the double tomb is not recorded but despite a mid-eighteenth-century remodelling of the interior (Pev:WR 2009, p. 327), it must have survived into the nineteenth century (Hargrove 1809, p. 305). Following the Catholic emancipation legislation of 1829, the chapel's congregation grew rapidly, perhaps prompting alterations before the creation of Tadcaster's church. Some work was undertaken in 1845, since two skulls were discovered (identified as martyred recusants and now in Leeds Roman Catholic cathedral). At some stage, perhaps then, the knights were placed under later canopies (probably medieval in origin), both too small for them. One shaft of the eastern canopy has been cut back to accommodate the figure's feet, while part of the southern side of the western effigy's coffin-shaped slab has been let into the wall as the recess is rectangular and too shallow.

Both shields bear the Vavasour arms, an extremely important family in this part of the county. Sir William le Vavasour held Hazelwood from 1284 until his death in 1312, being militarily active throughout his adult life. He invested in the property, obtaining a licence to crenellate in 1290, five years after a mortmain licence to fund a chaplain to celebrate divine service at Hazelwood (CPR 1281–1292, pp. 383, 237). His will survives (Raine 1835, pp. 13–16) in which he asked for burial in the new chapel of St Leonard of Hazelwood, suggesting he was responsible for its construction. His eldest son Walter succeeded but died in 1315 (CCR 1313–1318, p. 259), another brother (Robert) inherited but died in 1322 (IPM VI, pp. 244–45), and the property passed to a third brother, Henry, who survived until 1342 (IPM VIII, p. 239). Henry died at Louth Park Abbey, where he was buried (CPR 1345–1348, pp. 1–7; CP XII/II, p. 236). In the context of three deaths in ten years, a double monument is understandable. I'Anson believed it was Sir William and Robert who were commemorated but quoted the wrong date for Robert's death and seems not to have appreciated he was in Holy Orders. 'Robert le Vavasour, subdeacon, son of Sir William le Vavasour knt. [was instituted] to the church of Freston' and had leave for study (Brown 1925, pp. 42, 103). This is Ferry Fryston, a family living until 1322 when Sir Henry gave it to the Vicars Choral of York Minster (Lawton 1840, I, pp. 124–25). Consequently, the only logical candidates for the double tomb are Sir William (d. 1312) and his son Sir Walter (d. 1315). This example shows how poor and incomplete our understanding can be if effigies are just assessed at face value.

Thwing

The need for commemoration was most urgent when the male line failed and we discussed the 'last of the line' phenomenon (Gittos 2002a). This problem was faced by the de Thwing family of Thwing, where the anonymous effigy of a priest survives (Fig. 234). Marmaduke de Thwing (d. 1322/3) had 6 sons, the eldest was killed at Sterling in 1297 and the next brother died childless in 1340,

Fig. 234 Thwing. Priest with chalice, perhaps for Thomas de Thwing.

when it must have been clear the line would end as three more were clerics and the sixth was probably already dead (CP XII/I, pp. 741–43). One of the clerics, Thomas, made a concerted effort to assist his family through Purgatory, founding a chantry in their parish church, dedicated to St Thomas (Lawton 1840, II, p. 314) and conceivably connected with his 1343 mortmain licence for gifting land to enhance the parsonage (CPR 1343–1345, p. 331). In 1344 he became head of the family and four years later went further, founding a college of twelve priests at Kirkleatham, where he was Rector. Its ordinances named his great grandparents, grandparents, parents, brothers, sisters and other relatives, in proper chronological order (Torre 1692, fo. 61). Still not content, in 1352/3 Thomas initiated a chantry at Lythe and in 1362/3 added another chaplain to Kirkleatham (IQD II, pp. 467, 526). Thomas survived until 1374 and was eventually commemorated at Kirkleatham by a monumental brass, commissioned in 1381, the slab for which survives. Torre's abstract of the contract was published by Badham & Oosterwijk (2010, pp. 197–200) although the accompanying account of Thomas puts him in the wrong generation and much too old. The effigy at Thwing seems beyond the pocket of the priests serving chantries there or the parish clergy, especially as the living was divided. It probably commemorates one of the clerical de Thwing brothers and may even have been commissioned by Thomas himself, perhaps before his creation of the Kirkleatham college. Since the monumental brass to him at Kirkleatham was not made until seven years after his death, whoever commissioned it believed he should be commemorated at his college. Double commemoration did occasionally happen when circumstances changed, for instance, William Canynges has two consciously contrasting effigial monuments in Bristol, one as mayor and the other as a cleric (Williams 1950).

Butterwick

The armoured effigy at Butterwick (Fig. 139) discovered under the floor in 1883 (I'Anson 1927, p. 8), is both instructive and puzzling, providing a rare insight into the carving process (*4b.i*) and challenging heraldry. It is widely attributed to Sir Robert FitzRalph, the son of Ralph FitzWilliam of Grimthorpe who succeeded his father in February 1317 but was dead by 22nd April (IPM VI pp. 22, 26). His burial at Butterwick is mentioned in his widow's will of 1346 (Borthwick Institute, Archbishop Zouche's Register, fo. 305v) and corroborated in an unidentified source 'called the Greystock Roll' (*Test. Ebor.* IV, p. 20 n.). His father was interred at Neasham Abbey (CP, V, p. 516) while his son Ralph, who only survived until 1323 was buried in Newminster Abbey (CP VI, pp. 190–91). Sir Robert's elder brother William had died earlier (Brault 1997, I, p. 172). The Butterwick shield has some scored horizontal lines, presumably guides for the painter, together with three brownish features arranged as charges (Plate 47). The family arms were barry, argent and azure, three chaplets gules, and traces of blue survive on the surcoat between the pommel and the waist belt. Chaplets are usually shown as wreaths (cf the Hilton arms at Swine). Sir Robert's arms appear on three rolls, one of which, the First Dunstable Roll of 1308, recording the charges as 'buckles' rather than chaplets (Brault 1997, II, p. 172; Long 1837, p. 71). The same charges were recorded for his elder brother William who predeceased Ralph. William appears on the Charles Roll of *c.* 1285 with buckles (Brault 1997, I, pp. 257–80), which the editor (following Perceval 1863) thought was a copyist's error, since no original of the roll survives. If Anthony Wagner's contention that there were two separate medieval copies (Wagner 1950, pp. 21–23) were correct, this is less likely. In the light of what can be seen on Butterwick's shield, the charges' appearance on the Dunstable Roll for Robert and the possibility of two separate records on copies of the Charles Roll, it may not be a mistake. The charges on the shield do somewhat resemble double oval frame buckles, such as the mid-thirteenth-century example from London (Egan & Pritchard 1991, no. 346) but do not appear fully closed, curving inwards at the top. If these are what the heralds saw, 'buckles' may be their best approximation and the case for the effigy representing Robert FitzRalph is a sound one.

Fountains Abbey

The Fountains Abbey effigy (Figs 182, 228) is normally seen as Sir Henry de Percy's (d. 1314) but how secure is this identification? The heraldry provides a starting point but the effigy's original location in the choir and its style of armour, that would have been outdated by the middle of the fourteenth century, are particularly helpful. The shield bears a single lion rampant, boldly carved in relief and without tinctures (Fig. 235). The field is not marked out in any way, nor is there any indication of a difference so, given the attention to detail shown in the carving of the lion, it is unlikely any variation from a plain field would have been left to the painting. Such a simple coat is impossible to identify with certainty, but the families who bore it and were most associated with Fountains Abbey were Mowbray and Percy. However, Stapleton – another Yorkshire family that used a lion rampant – has been postulated (Downing 2010, p. 91) and this suggestion will be examined first.

The Stapletons made relatively few gifts to Yorkshire monasteries, to judge from Burton (1758) and they were widely scattered: Monk Bretton, Byland, Jervaulx and Kirkham. Roger Stapleton made their only known gift to Fountains, probably to secure burial there (Burton 1758, pp. 171, 211) but he died before June 1246 (CP XII/I, pp.

Fig. 235 Fountains Abbey. The knight's lion rampant heraldry.

260–61). This is far too early for the monument and at that time they bore different heraldry. Tonge, writing in 1530 (Longstaffe 1862, p. 2), believed Sir Miles 1st Lord (d. 1314) was the first to use the lion rampant (see also Chetwynd-Stapylton 1897, pp. 33–34). This Miles died at Bannockburn and his body was probably not repatriated (Brown 2008, p. 131) but his two wives were buried at York's Dominican Friary (Oxford Dictionary of National Biography). Later, there was a family tradition of burial at Drax Priory, adjacent to the family's southern Yorkshire holdings, for instance Isabella, wife of Nicholas 2nd Lord who died in 1343 (Burton 1758, p. 103) and their son Miles in 1372 (*Test. Ebor.* I, p. 88). Since no family member is known to have been buried at Fountains Abbey in the fourteenth century and their interests lay elsewhere, it is highly improbable the effigy commemorates a Stapleton.

The strongest candidates are Sir Roger de Mowbray (d. 1297) who bore gules, a lion rampant argent and Sir Henry Percy (d. 1314) who bore or, a lion rampant azure. Sir Henry Percy, a distinguished soldier, had adopted these arms by 1299 (Brault 1997, II, p. 337). In 1309, he bought the barony, castle, manor and town of Alnwick (Martin 1909, p. 241), which became the centre of the family's interests, transforming them from major Yorkshire landowners into one of the most powerful forces in the north. He died in October 1314 (FR II, p. 214) and was buried at Fountains Abbey. His father had died in 1272 and been buried at Salley Abbey, while his son and successor, Henry 2nd Lord, survived until 1351/2, being buried at Alnwick (CP, X, pp. 456, 462). Henry 1st Lord's well attested burial at Fountains was described by Tonge in 1530, prior to the Dissolution (Longstaffe 1862, p. 51):

> Also, be yt notid, that in the Churche of Founteyns lyeth buried, Henry, the ijde [sic] Lord Percy, in the middes of the quere before the high aulter, and the said Lord Henry Percy was a great benefactour to the said monastery.

It is also mentioned in two early Percy genealogies (Atkinson 1879, pp. 682–696). One, a document by a monk of Whitby, gives the position: 'before the high Alter'. Sadly, no one mentions the nature of his memorial.

Heads of the de Mowbray family died in 1266, 1297, 1321/2 and then not until 1361 (CP, IX, pp. 376–83). The last is far too late for the effigy, while the first was buried in Pontefract. The 1321/2 death is of John 2nd Lord Mowbray who was executed for treason after the battle of Boroughbridge. The body is said to have hung in chains for three years before being buried at the Friars Preachers in York (*Chron. Melsa.* II, p. 343). So the only de Mowbray candidate is Roger, 1st Lord, who died in Ghent in 1297 while on active service. His body was later repatriated and buried at Fountains in 1299, 'Qui Rogerus obiit in Gant ultra mare, & delatus est ad abbatiam de Fontibus, ibique sepultus anno 1299' (*Monasticon* 1661, II, p. 193, from a medieval genealogy). Glynn Coppack (2004, p. 86) says de Mowbray's was the first recorded burial in the presbytery, perhaps because of the family's munificence, thirty Mowbray charters being listed by Burton (1758, pp. 148–209). In 1530, Thomas Tonge (Longstaffe 1862, p. 51) observed:

> Also, in the said quere lyeth buried the Lord Moubray, who was a great benefactour to the said monastery.

The precise location was omitted but from the phrasing, it was probably not in the centre of the choir.

Mowbray and Percy are the only burials given by Tonge, while Coppack (1993, pp. 64–66) says that no abbot was interred in the church until 1384. It is notable that all but the earliest of the abbatial burials marked on Coppack's plan of the later medieval church are on the processional route along the centre line of the choir. The exception is in the Chapel of the Nine Altars. This raises the question of who might have been buried in the surviving stone coffin, which the excavators believed was in situ, to the side of the main space, under the north choir arcade. It is difficult to avoid the conclusion that this must have been Mowbray. The mid-nineteenth-century investigations found 'the coffin stood in its original position on the floor' (Walbran 1854, pp. 57–58), *i.e.* not buried but above ground. Whilst above ground interments did occur, for example Archbishop Hubert Walter (d. 1205) in Canterbury Cathedral, the practice was uncommon – for obvious reasons. It was occasionally done where there was no risk of putrefaction (Gittos 2017b, pp. 15–17). The lead-wrapped body of Blanche Grandisson was interred above ground at Much Marcle (Herefordshire) and bones were discovered in a chest at Boyton (Wiltshire). Mowbray had been dead two years by the time he was brought to Fountains, so would have posed no problem if deposited in a tomb above ground.

Walbran conjectured that the effigy came from the coffin, partly because the figure's earliest recorded position was close by (*2c.ii*). One helpful feature of its design is the coarsely-finished flat top of the gablette, which was not meant to be seen (*4b.i*). If the effigy were centrally positioned, this would face those entering the choir. When such surfaces were displayed, they were usually decorated, like the deity on the Bedale priest and the heraldry at Birdsall, so Fountains must have been intended to be against something. If the effigy covered the coffin under the arcade, the gablette top would have been far less visible. The monument might even have had its own arched canopy, fully hiding the blank top. The concentration of detail on both sides of the figure also suggests these were the intended viewing angles. A further point is that a three-dimensional effigy in the centre of the choir would disrupt processional routes and the liturgy. This was a major concern. Situated under the arcade, it would have been far more acceptable to the community. Given his central position, Percy may even have had a floor brass to avoid the problem. Brasses were gaining popularity by 1314 and in the following year Archbishop Greenfield was commemorated by one in York Minster, but since his was in a side chapel it could be located on a canopied chest.

To sum up, the Fountains Abbey effigy must commemorate either Sir Henry Percy or Sir Roger Mowbray. Percy was buried centrally within the choir where a raised monument would have been problematic. Since the coffin is believed to be in situ and not centrally placed, it cannot have been his and must therefore be Mowbray's. The coffin's position would permit it to be topped by the effigy and its location above ground means the body must have presented no risk of putrefaction, while the effigy's gablette shows it was designed for a restricted space. The effigy is a fine example of the Series B work and its relationship to the other members of the group means a date of *c.* 1300 would be appropriate. So, the date of the effigy, its design, the location and level of the coffin all indicate that Sir Roger de Mowbray was the person commemorated.

Temple Church and Hob Moor

Sometimes, knowledge of the families involved can dispel myth and presumption. The effigy now in London's Temple Church commemorates a de Ros, and has attracted much attention, but some comments have failed to consider the family's complexity. Two Yorkshire effigies of the de Ros family survive, identifiable by carved heraldry although neither retain paint. Both are of armoured men: a fragmentary figure upright on Hob Moor in York (Plate 17) and a complete effigy in London's Temple Church (Figs 193, 236). The latter is a Series B product, so must date from the early years of the fourteenth century, while the former may possibly be another. The de Ros family presents particular problems for those wishing to understand their effigies and previous attempts (I'Anson 1923; 1927; Park 2010) have been less than satisfactory, making it worthwhile examining the issues.

The Temple effigy is known to have been brought to London in the seventeenth century, the account of its transfer indicating a York origin (Hatton 1708, II, p. 574). Describing it some twenty or more years after the move, he simply states it:

> … was brought from York, by Mr Serjeant Belwood Recorder of that City about the Year 1682, and is said to be the Figure of one Rooce of an honourable Family.

Robin Griffith-Jones (2010) has argued convincingly the circumstances that made a de Ros effigy an acceptable addition to the Temple church in the 1680s. Both I'Anson and Park were convinced the figure derived from Kirkham Priory. I'Anson (1923) envisaging it had been moved to York 'at some unknown date subsequent to the desecration of the Priory church' but without offering a reason. Griffith-Jones

Fig. 236 London, Temple Church. Stothard's drawing of de Ros knight (Stothard 1832, Pl. 38).

tentatively suggested the Duke of Buckingham's influence might have helped procure the figure direct from Kirkham. However, the primary account mentions only York, so the Kirkham association is just supposition. It was presumably rooted in a misapprehension that Kirkham was the only de Ros mausoleum in Yorkshire and fuelled by Leland's description (*A8*).

The de Ros family were a complex clan. The two major Yorkshire branches being Ros of Hamlake and Ros of Ingmanthorpe. The short-lived Watton branch was based in Lincolnshire, the Wark branch in Northumberland, while a fifth (of Kendal) was based on the western side of the Pennines. All branches bore fundamentally the same heraldry (three water bougets) differenced only by the tinctures (DBA 2, pp. 208 *et seq*). I'Anson assumed the Temple effigy represented the head of one of the Hamlake or Ingmanthorpe houses, presumably because there is no mark of difference carved on the shield. Whilst this is probably the case, it is impossible to be certain since any cadency distinction may also have been managed in the paint. This seems to have been a favoured method within the family and it is noticeable that while the *Medieval Ordinary* lists well over 140 records of varying combinations, there are only thirteen instances of a label and two of other cadency marks (crescents), both of which are late fourteenth century (DBA 2). Consequently, the absence of tinctures makes it impossible even to be sure to which branch either of the surviving effigies belonged.

Appendix A6c.v discusses the documented de Ros burials at Kirkham Priory and Rievaulx Abbey. Late medieval documents (Atkinson 1889, pp. 359–62) record four named de Ros burials at Kirkham, all from the Hamlake branch. However, despite some clearly being notable tombs, no effigies are mentioned. The same source names another five burials at Rievaulx, although those documented are either earlier or later than the effigies in question. A late medieval source records the burial of Sir William de Ros of Ingmanthorpe (d. 1310) and his wife in the Greyfriars at York (Young 1837, p. 78) but also notes (p. 76) the burials of both Sir Alexander de Ros and Sir William de Ros in the Dominican Friary at York. The true identity of these two is unclear since no branch is quoted but their burials, and those of some de Ros ladies, brings the known total of de Ros burials in York to six. In his assessment of the two effigies' identification, I'Anson noted only burials at the Franciscan Friary in York, Kirkham Priory and a lady at Thornton Abbey (Lincolnshire), seemingly unaware of those at either Rievaulx or the York Dominican Friary, so had a less complete picture of the family's burial history than is now available.

I'Anson (1923) dated Hob Moor to '*c*. 1310–15', considering it appropriate for a 1310 death and decided that it must be William of Ingmanthorpe from the Greyfriars, a conclusion reasserted by Park (2010). I'Anson was convinced the Temple figure came from Kirkham Priory. Having considered the possibility of the York Greyfriars, he concluded (1923):

> … the Temple effigy is 18 to 20 years later than the death of Sir William [in 1310] and such a lapse of time between the interment and the erection of the memorial is unusual.

He went on to decide that it could only be for 'William 2nd Lord Ros of Hamlake and must derive from Kirkham where he was buried'. However, there must have been some confusion in I'Anson's mind about this individual, since he quotes the date of death as 1316 in the text and describes him as 'William ii, 2nd Lord Roos of Helmsley and of Belvoir', whereas the *Complete Peerage* clearly designates him 1st Lord. The first lord died in 1316, but the second not until 1342/3. I'Anson continued with the remarkable statement, '… it is beyond dispute that it dates *c.* 1318–20', despite having previously argued on the same page, for a date of 1328–30 and captioned the illustration '1317'. David Park (2010, p. 91) followed I'Anson in believing the effigy came from Kirkham, commemorating William of Hamlake (d. 1316), opting for the latest of the three dates (thus disputing that which I'Anson designated 'beyond dispute'). He accepts I'Anson's work on Yorkshire effigies as a 'systematic study' and his identification of the Temple effigy as 'plausible'. However, I'Anson's superficially systematic work is seriously flawed. In the first instance, since it considers only armoured effigies, it ignores more than two thirds of the evidence and eschews that afforded by the monuments' physical context. Even amongst the military effigies, his comments relate only to the armour pieces depicted, coupled with identification and dating, usually unsupported by references. The user must also beware that, as demonstrated, his publications are strewn with errors and inconsistencies. I'Anson's work can be a useful starting point for the restricted selection of effigies that interested him but it is not a systematic study of Yorkshire's monuments.

Casting aside supposition, there are regrettably few solid facts to assist in understanding these two effigies. In the absence of painted heraldry, all that can be said is that they are de Ros family members. Which branch they belonged to cannot be deduced nor whether they were senior or junior members. Both effigies have an association with York, one because it is still there and the other because it was there once. The documentary evidence for this family logs four burials at Kirkham Priory, five at Rievaulx Abbey and six at two sites in York, none of the records mentioning effigies. The places of interment for most members of this complicated family are unknown but given the range of burial sites it would be unwise to assume a stray figure came from any specific one of them. In the case of these two figures, the problems are insoluble without additional evidence. However, there is no doubt that Temple is stylistically related to the work of the Series B sculptor (*4c. ii*) and for that reason we think it dates from the first decade of the fourteenth century.

Bainton

The Bainton effigy is usually identified as Sir Edmund de Mauley who died at Bannockburn in 1314 but this is based on a misunderstanding of the heraldry, the effigy and the family history. The tomb at Bainton (Fig. 108) has been mentioned previously because of damage to the church in the Scottish incursion of 1322 (*3c, 5a.iii*) and published comparisons with the Percy Tomb in Beverley, but Bainton presents other challenges. The effigy at first appears to be a straightforward 'knight' but the absence of his coif reveals his tonsure (Fig. 237), which would have been more prominent when the effigy had its original paint. His shield bears three wyverns on a bend, while three shields on the wall above comprise: the same arms, de Mauley (or, a bend sable) differenced by a label and, at the apex, de Mauley ancient (Plate 67). The ascription to Sir Edmund de Mauley, follows I'Anson (1927, p. 51) and Lawrance (1946, p. 29). The identification is derived from the Parliamentary Roll of *c.* 1312 and the Stirling Roll of 1304 that survives in a sixteenth century copy (Wagner 1950, pp. 42, 36). Amongst the latter's many scribal amendments, the wyvern difference (originally ascribed to Sir John de Mauley) was altered to apply to his brother Edmund (Brault 1997, I, pp. 492–93). Although Sir John appears only on these two rolls, Sir Edmund's arms are also in the Harleian Roll of Edward's II's reign (DBA 2, pp. 29, 68; Wagner 1950, p. 52) depicted as 'Or, on a bend Sa, betw. two Lions ramp, of the second, three dolphins embowed Arg' (Greenstreet 1886, no. 71). In addition, Richardson (2016, p. 192) notes an heraldic gambeson bearing the black bend with three gold dolphins listed in a royal Armoury account for the years 1325–44. It must have been left from Sir Edmund's time as Steward of Edward II's household and there is no reason a garment with Sir John's arms should have been there. There has been much confusion about how these brothers differenced their arms (Plate 68) but Sir Edmund must have borne the dolphins, while the wyvern difference shown on the effigy was John's.

Fig. 237 Bainton. Sir John de Mauley's tonsure.

Mulgrave Castle (N.R.) was a seat of the wealthy de Mauley family but they had extensive estates across

Yorkshire, including the area around Bainton (*Feudal Aids* VI, *e.g.* pp. 148–49, 165–66, 219) and the advowson of the church. John and Edmund had three other brothers, Peter (the eldest and third of the name but also first baron), Robert and Stephen. The generation played a significant part in military affairs, all but Stephen being knighted. He was a cleric with many offices and benefices in Yorkshire and Durham (Burton 1888, pp. 51–52), including Bainton from 1271, the prebend of Bugthorpe in York Minster (1298) and the archdeaconry of Cleveland (1289). He died in 1317 but was buried in York Minster rather than Bainton and differenced the de Mauley arms with three cross crosslets (DBA 2, p. 21). Robert provided extensive military service and in 1314 was appointed Steward of the future Edward III's household and as late as 1330, a grant to his son was partly on account of his deceased father's 'good service … to the king in the king's youth' (FR III, p. 177). Robert, who differenced the family arms with three eagles displayed, was also buried in the Minster (*2c.i*). Edmund was even more prominent in royal circles, but his close association with the king and his successive favourites incurred the opprobrium of the Lancastrian faction (Phillips 2010, p. 200). He was killed in 1314 at Bannockburn, probably during the king's retreat (Phillips 2010, p. 233). His property in Yorkshire, as recorded in his Inquisition, was minimal and his most lucrative holding was in Oxfordshire (IPM V, p. 286). He seems to have had no association with Bainton and there is no evidence that he was in holy orders, to justify a tonsure. In contrast, John had both attributes. After a military career (CP VIII, p. 560 n.), he followed his brother Stephen as Rector of Bainton in 1317, the record of his institution describing him as a knight and an acolyte, 'militi & acolyto' (Borthwick Institute, Abp Reg 5A f. 135r). He remained Rector until his death, in 1331 (IPM VII, p. 367) but by 1300, he already held some of the family's lands in the area (CChR II, p. 489). So John was a knight and a cleric, he held the living of Bainton and was a local landholder. He is, therefore, much the most likely person to be commemorated. The heraldry above the arch provides a further clue. John's elder brother, Peter III, died in 1308, the inheritance going to his son, Peter IV who emerges from the records as impetuous, immoral and lacking in judgement. Three times he did penance for adultery, raided Watton Priory's property and had to beg on his knees for absolution from the Provost of Beverley for flouting his authority. He was also constantly deep in debt and even more seriously, became embroiled in the politics of Edward II's reign, to a point where he seems to have jeopardised his entire inheritance. As a solution, the de Mauley estates passed to John (12 December 1322, CPR 1321–1324, p. 223). Within days of the regime change, on 13th February 1327, John obtained a licence to regrant it all back to Peter IV (CPR 1327–1330, pp. 15–16) but by June, there was a change

Fig. 238 Catterick. Sir William Pert.

of policy as an amended licence was granted to allow the property to be passed directly to the heir, Peter V (pp. 128–9). For whatever reason, the handover had not taken place by the time of John's death but the intention is set out in a further licence (CPR 1330–1334, p. 369), that Peter IV had granted the property '… to John de Malo Lacu in fee, upon condition that the latter granted them to Peter the son and Margaret his wife, a condition that was not fulfilled in consequence of the death of the said John.'

At the time of John's death he was holding the family property in trust for the head of the family's heir. At this point, during his father's lifetime, Peter V would have used the de Mauley arms differenced with a label and this is the third coat that appears in the canopy. So the canopy can be read as a record of John's role in resolving the family's difficulties. In light of this there can be no doubt that the Bainton monument commemorates John, the knight and cleric who saved the family from disaster.

Catterick

As at Bainton, there has been consensus about the identity of the Catterick knight (Fig. 238) since Whitaker suggested he was Sir Walter Urswick on the basis of the heraldry on the tomb (1823, II, p. 29). But is this valid? The one dissenter was the distinguished antiquary Sir Nicholas Harris

Nicolas who refuted the identification in his edition of the Scrope and Grosvenor dispute (Nicolas 1832, II, p. 170), proposing Sir William Pert instead. Sir Walter Urswick was a professional soldier of long and distinguished service. He had been an esquire of John of Gaunt's who knighted him after the battle of Najera (Goodman 1992, pp. 214–15). From 1362, he was his master of game and was still alive in the 1390s, long after 1372, when Collier and Lawrance believed he died (1928, pp. 206–207). Although Urswick was Constable of Richmond Castle and had other grants in Yorkshire, his interests seem to have remained in his homeland of Lancashire, for which he served as a Knight of the Shire in 1383 (Richardson 1938). Crucial to the identification are the three carved shields on the arch over the effigy. The central shield bears three mascles on a bend, to the east is a bend with a label of three points while to the west, these two coats are impaled (Plates 69–71). The bend with the label is for Scrope of Masham while the coat with mascles is what has been taken for Urswick, although the *Dictionary of British Arms* (DBA 2, p. 62) makes it clear that Urswick bore lozenges on the bend, with a crescent in chief. One record says each lozenge was charged with a saltire but none mention mascles. Collier and Lawrance (1928, p. 207) assumed the impaled coat represented a marriage between a Scrope and an Urswick but Nicolas failed to find such a union. All witnesses to the Scrope/Grosvenor inquiry were asked to state the nature of their knowledge. Urswick's testimony catalogued the campaigns and battles in which he had encountered various members of the Scrope family (Nicolas 1832, II, p. 51), whereas if he had married one, he would undoubtedly have mentioned it. As Nicolas knew, Joan Scrope, the daughter and sole heir of Stephen (of the Masham branch), married William de Pert. Pert bore argent, on a bend gules 3 mascles or (DBA 2, p. 45, from Jenyns Book *c.* 1410). The mascles are pierced lozenges, so superficially similar, and he did not have the crescent in chief. The coats on the arch show mascles and no crescent. Although the shields are currently painted with the Urswick tinctures, this is unlikely to be original, instead reflecting the mistaken identification. There is little doubt that a Scrope-Pert marriage is signified and that since the most prominent coat is the simple Pert arms, the effigy must represent Sir William. Glover recognised the Pert arms in his 1585 description of the effigy (Foster 1875, p. 462):

> AN OULD KNIGHT LYING IN HIS ARMOUR, CUT IN STONE, Wth THESE ARMES ON HIS SHIELD, AND THIS BADGE UNDER HIS HEAD. Argent, on a bend gules 3 mascles.... Crest, on torce, a ram's head couped, barry of 6 pieces, argent and gules. "Perte."

The marriage between William Pert and Joan Scrope is attested by her Inquisition Post Mortem of 1427 (Mapping the Medieval Countryside). William, who seems to have been from Lincolnshire, died between 20th May 1394 and 24th June 1395 and the couple had had three daughters (IPM XVII, pp. 109–19). After Pert's death, Joan married Roger de Swillington, but by 1427 was again a widow. At the time of her death, Joan had extensive property in Yorkshire, including some in the Catterick area. Catterick was the mother church of the nearby chapelry at Bolton-on-Swale (VCH:NR:I, p. 155). The Scropes had a manor there and anyone who died at Bolton is likely to have been buried at the mother church. Whatever the reason for his burial at Catterick, there is a sound case for effigy commemorating William Pert and not Sir Walter Urswick. Furthermore, William's demise without a male heir, is a classic circumstance for commissioning an effigial monument.

Fig. 239 Nunnington. Sir Walter de Teye's arms.

Nunnington and Stonegrave

The earlier effigy at Stonegrave and that at Nunnington are usually seen as linked by an heiress, the daughter of the former marrying the latter. Whilst Nunnington's identification is straightforward, Stonegrave's is not. The identity of a particular effigy is often a matter of weighing the evidence but with Nunnington this is scarcely necessary. Although part of the knight's shield was a separate block of stone, pieced in and now lost (*4b.ii*), what remains carries carved heraldry that can only have been a fess bearing three pierced mullets between two chevrons (Fig. 239). Or, on a fess, between two chevrons gules, three mullets pierced, argent (DBA 3, pp. 490–91) was borne by only one man linked with the village, Sir Walter de Teye, who died in 1324 (IPM VI, pp. 345–47) and his surcoat retains evidence it was painted with his heraldry (Plate 50; Section 4b.iii). Teye's family seems unconnected with the area and he rose to prominence in the Scottish wars through his ability. In 1295 he was designated only as 'King's yeoman' (CChW, p. 51) and in June 1297 retained the same status (CCR 1296–1302, p. 35) but he appears on the Falkirk Roll (fought July 1298) so must have been knighted by then and was summoned to Parliament from 1298/9 (CP XII/II, pp. 98–100). He was a knight of the King's household by 1300 (Ingamells 1992, II, p. 182) and in June that year, was in charge of the key border town of Berwick (CPR 1292–1301, p. 522). In 1301 his retinue was sufficient to include a man capable of fulfilling the office of county coroner and to take at least one knight bachelor to war with him (CChW, pp. 146, 144). In June 1297 he had already married Isabella, heiress of Sir John de Stonegrave (her father), through whom he acquired Nunnington. A curious note in his Inquisition Post Mortem records the marriage was 'by command of King Edward I'. If the king wished to promote a man of ability, the newly widowed heiress would have been a ready means of paying him and supplying de Teye with the resources to take a more prominent role. Isabella did not survive long in the arranged marriage, being dead before February 1300/01 (CPR 1292–1301, p. 573) and there were no children, the estates passing to her son by a previous marriage (CP XII/II, p. 100). So Teye is the only possible identification for this effigy.

The extinction of the de Stonegrave line led I'Anson to identify the civilian effigy at Stonegrave (Fig. 10) as Sir John, Isabella's father (I'Anson 1927, p. 28 fn. 1) but this is simply an assumption. Nothing about the effigy identifies him as a de Stonegrave and, rather, his depiction in civilian garb is at odds with Sir John's military career (CP XII/I, p. 276). It seems more likely that, as with the later fourteenth-century figures in the same aisle, it commemorates someone holding one of the other manors in the parish (VCH:NR:I, pp. 561–63).

Bedale

There is no dispute that the knight and lady who lie together in Bedale church commemorate Brian FitzAlan, Lord of Bedale (d. 1306) and his first wife. The only doubt concerns whether the knight was carved around the time of his death or retrospectively by up to two decades. To resolve this issue it is necessary to examine the historical background, his immediate family and the relationship of the effigy with other sculpture.

Brian FitzAlan's first wife, Muriel, was dead by 1290 and was commemorated by an early work of one of the areas's finest sculptors (Figs 142, 167), probably commissioned at the same time as FitzAlan instituted a chantry and built, or refitted, the south chapel to accommodate it. Her effigy was later incorporated into his tomb. FitzAlan (Plate 40) was a man who rose to prominence during the Scottish wars through his own capabilities rather than inherited wealth, although he seems to have been amongst the traditionalist bannerets who campaigned for the King out of feudal duty rather than for pay. In 1291/2, he was appointed an Auditor in the Great Cause and then the English representative amongst the Guardians of Scotland (Stones & Simpson 1978, II, pp. 80–81), working directly for Edward I and alongside John Comyn (Earl of Badenoch), James Stewart (the hereditary Steward of Scotland) and the Bishops of Glasgow and St Andrews. FitzAlan's eighteen months in office culminated in his presence when John Balliol did homage to King Edward for his kingdom of Scotland (Stones & Simpson 1978, II, pp. 260, 263). He was called again in 1296 to help resolve the issues around the end of Balliol's kingship, so he was present when Balliol abdicated and his seal was broken (Stevenson 1870, II, p. 61). Briefly, in 1297, he took Warenne's place as Governor of Scotland, for Edward I. When asked to accept the latter position he at first refused, protesting the inadequacy of his resources but accepted when the King agreed to increase the allowance (Stevenson 1870, II, pp. 222–24, 225–27; *Rot. Scot.* I, p. 45; *Fœdera*, I.II, pp. 785, 874, 877). FitzAlan died in 1306 (FR I, p. 537 records the order to the Escheator on 8th June) but must have been ill for some time, since a month previously the custody and marriage of his heirs had been granted in the belief he was dead (CPR 1301–1307, pp. 431, 432). They had to be regranted in June. In the interim, he managed to 'render' to the young Mowbray heir the lands he held of him, an action recorded on the same day as Mowbray's receiving his lands from the king despite still being under age. Such an action of a man close to death, smacks of the punctiliousness and sense of rectitude that emerges from the records as a fundamental character trait. FitzAlan had no male heirs, his sons having predeceased him and been commemorated in the Bedale chantry along with his wife. Only two daughters (from his second marriage) survived him, the eldest coming into her inheritance in 1317 (CCR 1313–1318, p. 517). He must have been at least in his sixties when he died and well aware that the male line would die with him. He already had a track record of commemorating his relatives. The Bedale chantry of 1290 (*3e*) was administered by Jervaulx Abbey to remember his parents, his first wife, his three dead sons, his overlord, himself 'and his special friends' during his life (Nicolas 1832, II, p. 286). At the Suppression it was said to have three chaplains. In addition, he had arranged for Sinningthwaite Priory to hold an annual commemoration for his mother and his first wife (CP V, p. 394). He had created a large and expensive chapel for the chantry (Plate 53), complete with an effigial monument for his first wife. His second wife later arranged with Egglestone Abbey for a chantry foundation of her own (CPR 1343–1345, p. 459), to pray for her good estate in life and her soul after death, for one of her sons-in-law and FitzAlan. Against this background, it would be surprising if he had not arranged his own commemoration. Indeed, the provision of a chest to support his own new effigy and his first wife's existing one, rather than simply create a separate monument for him seems unlikely to have been a decision made either by his second wife, or his heirs, as they were her children not Muriel's.

Conclusion

The examples investigated here are all drawn from more wealthy families because they have left the most visible traces in the documentary record. They were the people with the resources to fund higher quality, larger and more impressive monuments that are more likely to have survived. But they were not the only people to be commemorated. It is simply that there is no documentation to support, say, the forester at Wadworth, the semi-effigial figure at Aldborough or even the Purbeck marble armoured figure at Welton. A recurrent theme has been the erection of monuments at a point when the male line comes to an end and with it, the family name. In such cases, there was a desire to elicit prayers for the souls not only of the commemorated but also of their relatives and, often, their associates. An allied strand seems to be the wish to memorialise the family and its honour, most readily seen where heraldry or weepers were deployed to illustrate relatives, alliances and allegiances. The tomb at Bainton uses heraldry to associate the man commemorated with the family and his role in the family rescue plan. The Bedale tomb in its chantry setting seems designed to memorialise the family and its honour, in a place they had held for generations. Nunnington and Catterick preserve the memory of transient individuals who could claim no such deep association with their final resting place. But what every patron desired above all else was to be remembered in a manner that most benefited the future of their soul.

5b.ii Neighbours and colleagues

Whilst the people commemorated by the effigies might have contacts across the British Isles and abroad, it is fair to say that Yorkshire's was quite a small and closed society. In administration, in marriages and when going to war, there was a tendency for people to associate with those they already knew. Within this circle and at this time, there was a propensity for commissioning effigial monuments. The following limited survey is intended to demonstrate the kind of connections that were formed. These are men who knew each other, were related, sat on commissions together and had campaigned as comrades in arms. Their comparatively similar monuments, sometimes commissioned from the same sources, are a visible legacy of a network of intricately connected families. The numbers in square brackets relate the people mentioned to known effigies, as set out in 'Effigial representation' (p. 169).

Sir Brian FitzAlan's fairly long career is a useful tool for the years around 1300 since he saw some prominence in the affairs of the day, was summoned to every Parliament between 1295 and his death in 1306, but was also active locally and had substantial land holdings. FitzAlan's [1] appointments in Scotland put him into a working relationship with the royalty, nobility, higher clergy, administration and judiciary of both countries. From at least 1291, he was an advisor to the powerful Bishop Bek of Durham alongside Ralph FitzWilliam and John de Lythegraines (Fig. 240), a relationship encapsulated in the foundation of the college

Fig. 240 Norton. Series B knight perhaps commemorating Sir John de Lythegraines.

at Leysingby (near Northallerton) in 1291. It was founded by John Lythegraines [2], confirmed by Bek and the deed witnessed by FitzAlan, Ralph FitzWilliam [3] and William le Vavasour [4], amongst others (Fraser 1953, pp. 28–29). FitzAlan's dual position, working for both Bek and the King, put him in an ideal situation in 1304, as a guarantor that the royal justices would be permitted to carry out their investigation into a dispute within the Bishopric of Durham (Fraser 1953, pp. 101–102). In this he was joined by Ralph FitzWilliam and William le Vavasour. Sir John de Lythegraines worked as a justice for both Bek and the King, as did Alan de Walkingham [5] (Fraser 1957, p. 83 n.). As demonstrated in the case study (*3g.i*), the de Goldesburgh family's commemorative choices [6] were influenced by their close relationship with Bishop Bek. The clerical de Goldesburgh sons of Richard IV were favoured by Bek's patronage, especially Thomas who worked closely with his uncle. This seems a likely route through which the de Goldesburghs would have forged links with others who worked with and for Bek, men such as FitzAlan, FitzWilliam and Vavasour.

Andrew Spencer has demonstrated that many of those summoned for military service were less than enthusiastic, with the greater gentry and nobility forming the basic corps (Spencer 2011), a fertile ground for the formation of networks. Brian FitzAlan must be counted amongst this group, responding assiduously to summons from at least 1277 in Wales (CPR 1281–1292, pp. 189–90). His abilities had clearly attracted attention by 1287 when he was summoned to a military council in Gloucester (*Fœdera*, I.II, p. 675), for which the roll call of Yorkshire names reads like a *Who's Who* of Yorkshire effigial families: Roger de Mowbray [7], Ranulph de Neville [8], Walter Fauconberg, Nicholas de Meynill [9], Roger de Lascelles [10], Richard Malbys [11], Hugh FitzHenry of Ravensworth [12], Peter de Mauley [13], William de Ros of Hamlake [14], Henry de Percy [15], Marmaduke de Thwing [16], Ralph FitzWilliam [3] and John de Stonegrave [17]. FitzAlan's last summons was for 1303 in Scotland (*Fœdera*, I.II, p. 947–48) where he was to serve with Ralph FitzWilliam and John Marmion [18]. Sir Brian had been in Bek's division at Falkirk in 1298 with, amongst others, Peter de Mauley, William de Ros of Hamlake and Ralph FitzWilliam (Brault 1997, I, 'Falkirk Roll'). In 1300, FitzAlan took part in the siege of Caerlaverock (Brault 1997, I, 'Caerlaverock Poem') where his fellow bannerets included Vavasour, Percy, FitzWilliam and Ros of Hamlake, serving under the King, alongside many of the higher nobility but also William de Ryther [19]. A few weeks later, he again fought under the King, as recorded in the Galloway Roll (Brault 1997, I, 'Galloway Roll'; Simpkin 2009), where the same division included Ryther, Sir Henry FitzHugh [20] and Sir Robert Plumpton [21]. In 1303, Plumpton was again in Scotland (CChW, p.187), in the company of William son of William de Ros of Ingmanthorpe [22]. The next year John Mauleverer [23] was in Scotland. Not yet knighted, he accompanied Miles Stapleton [24], Vavasour, Adam de Swillington [25] and Robert de Ros (CChW, p. 223). In 1301 (CChW, p. 144) one of the Robert de Colvilles [26] went with his brother William and three de Mauley brothers: Peter, Robert [27] and John [28]. William de Vescy of Kildare [29] went to Scotland with Piers Gaveston and 'William ... of Butterwick' [30] (CChW, p. 328). Similar military connections can be demonstrated throughout the period under study and some have been noted elsewhere, for example between members of John of Gaunt's retinue and between participants in the Crécy–Calais campaign (*5a.iv*).

Alongside his work for the King, Bek and military service, FitzAlan and his fellow landowners played their part in the administration of local affairs, for instance in 1291 he received a commission for delivery of York gaol (CPR 1281–1292, p. 455), which he was to carry out with William de Ryther and John de Meaux [31]. Those who spent less time away on active service could develop networks through this route, in small groups of two or three, investigating such issues as breaches of the law or the state of the river banks, collecting taxes and raising levies for the army. John de Meaux and William Ryther must have known each other when they carried out a commission of Oyer and Terminer with Lythegraines in 1291 (CPR 1281–1292, p. 344) as must Thomas de Metham [32], Simon le Constable and John de Stonegrave, the previous year (CPR 1281–1292, p. 344). Extended families, estate management interests and sheer proximity were other routes, such as when John Lythegraines rented land from Nicholas de Meynill (CPR 1281–1292, p. 25). Brian FitzAlan was a close neighbour of Jervaulx Abbey and he left the patronage of the Bedale chantry to the Abbot, so he may have seen the surviving effigy there when it was new. When FitzAlan died in 1306, it was Miles Stapleton (some of whose lands adjoined parts of FitzAlan's estate) who gained the hand of the eldest daughter for one of his sons (CPR 1292–1301, p. 431). Stapleton was one of those who stood surety for Sybil de Metham [33] in 1312 (CCR 1307–1313, p. 542) when she was imprisoned on suspicion of misappropriating taxation collected by her husband John [34]. The Stapleton south Yorkshire estates were close to the Metham land and another of her mainpernors was Peter de Saltmarshe [35], also a close neighbour. The picture that emerges from this limited survey of a welter of information is of a society where the greater families all knew each other, were aware of their compatriots' activities and were often related. This is a large subject and cannot be examined here but must also have been a major cohesive force within the community. Against this background, there is little wonder that such people made similar commemorative choices.

Effigial representation

1	FitzAlan's effigy is at Bedale, where it joined an earlier one for his first wife, in his own chantry (*5b.i*). His second wife is the lady at Danby Wiske.
2	Lythegraines may be the man commemorated by the effigy at Norton, he and his wife founded a collegiate chapel at Leysingby.
3	FitzWilliam is almost certainly commemorated by an effigy at Hurworth (just over the Tees in County Durham) while his son has the Series B figure at Butterwick (*5b.i*).
4	Vavasour has an effigy in his new chapel at Hazelwood Castle, his home, as has one of his sons (*5b.i*).
5	The Felixkirk knight almost certainly represents his son Sir John Walkingham (*3e, 4c.iv*).
6	Sir Richard de Goldesburgh IV has the Series B effigy, in the new chancel at Goldsborough beside his wife's brass (*3g.i*). His eldest son has the later figure there.
7	Roger de Mowbray is almost certainly the Fountains effigy (*5b.i*).
8	Ranulph de Neville's first wife is likely to be the earliest of the females at Staindrop (Co. Durham).
9	Nicholas Meynill must be commemorated by the wooden effigy at Whorlton.
10	Roger de Lascelles is almost certainly commemorated by the Escrick effigy.
11	There is a surviving Malbys effigy at Acaster Malbis and another knight, seemingly of similar workmanship from Rievaulx Abbey may be associated (*A6c.v*). One of these may be for Sir Richard.
12	Hugh FitzHenry of Ravensworth is probably Romaldkirk, where he was buried (*2a.v*).
13	Peter III, the father of Robert (effigy lost from York Minster) and John (Bainton). His wife is believed to have been commemorated by an inscribed floor slab in Hazelwood Chapel (Foster 1875, p. 452).
14	William de Ros of Hamlake, was buried in a marble tomb at Kirkham (*A6c.v*). If Temple did come from Kirkham Priory (*5b.i*), then it probably commemorates him.
15	Henry Percy, the less likely candidate for Fountains (*5b.i*).
16	Marmaduke Thwing was the father of Thomas de Thwing who had a brass at Kirkleatham and may well be the effigy at Thwing (*5b.i*)
17	John Stonegrave's daughter inherited the Stonegrave & Nunnington estate and married Walter Teye, the Nunnington effigy (*5b.i*).
18	John Marmion is almost certainly commemorated by the earliest effigy at West Tanfield.
19	William de Ryther, of the same family as the effigies in Ryther church.
20	Sir Henry FitzHugh (of the same family as the Jervaulx and Romaldkirk effigies).
21	Sir Robert Plumpton, identified by Simpkin (2009) and therefore commemorated by the Spofforth effigy (*4c.iii*).
22	The elder William, d. 1313, was buried in the Greyfriars at York (Young 1837, p. 78), so either the Hob Moor effigy, or Temple Church if it originated in York (*5b.i*) may be his.
23	John Mauleverer is probably the later of the two wooden figures at Allerton Mauleverer.
24	The Kirkby Fleetham effigy probably represents his son Gilbert who married Brian FitzAlan of Bedale's elder daughter.
25	Adam de Swillington, d. 1328. Either he or his son (another Adam) are likely to be the wooden Swillington effigy.
26	May be one of the Colville effigies at Ingleby Arncliffe (Gittos 2002b).
27	Robert de Mauley's effigy was in York Minster (*2c.i*).
28	Bainton (*5b.i*).
29	William de Vescy of Kildare is probably the complete effigy in the York Museums' collection (*2c.ii*).
30	This is likely to be the William FitzRalph, son of Ralph FitzWilliam, commemorated at Butterwick (*5b.i*).
31	John de Meaux, grandfather of the Aldbrough knight.
32	Father of the Series B knight at Howden.
33	The female effigy at Howden.
34	The earlier knight at Howden.
35	The later knight at Howden.

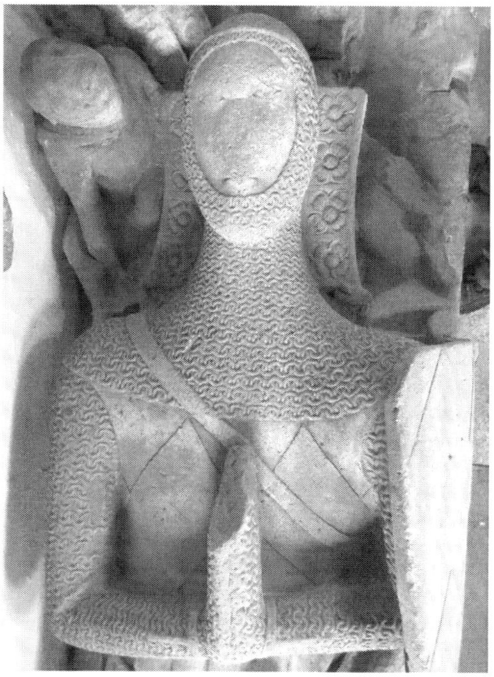

Fig. 241 Sprotbrough. FitzWilliam knight with supporters beside his head.

Fig. 242 Sprotbrough. A supporting figure's tonsure revealed in a mirror.

Fig. 243 Bedale. Priest holding a devotional image.

5c Symbolism

5c.i Introduction

The creation of a monument required many decisions, involving both craftsman and patron. One aspect likely to have particularly concerned the latter was its symbolism – the subject of this section. The most obvious iconographic features are beasts at the figure's feet and angels at the head, which were commonplace from the later thirteenth century, sometimes subject to variations, *e.g.* at Sprotbrough where the knight has monks in their place (Figs 241, 242). However, a fair proportion also have a gamut of additional features that are not just decorative but are imbued with meaning and symbolism. The messages intended by these adjuncts are a significant aspect of understanding Yorkshire effigies. Strong religious imagery is a particular feature of the Bedale priest. As well as the tablet displaying the crucifixion that he holds (Fig. 243), at the head end of his monument is a lozenge-shaped, cusped panel enclosing a seated figure holding a book and giving blessing, which is almost certainly another manifestation of Christ (Fig. 168). So the Bedale priest appeals directly to Christ for both his

Fig. 244 Wadworth. The forester's horn suspended from straps.

protection and salvation. Images of the four Evangelists are not common amongst Yorkshire effigies but they do appear at Welwick and at the four corners of Joan de Lellay's monument at Goxhill (Figs 280, 2). There were probably four on the slab at Yarm originally but only two remain. These later fourteenth-century monuments anticipate the great popularity of the Evangelist symbols on Yorkshire brasses of the next century.

As well as religious imagery, there is considerable use of secular symbolism, some of which can be regarded as representing the deceased's 'tools of his trade'. The knights display an appropriate array of arms and armour and a few male civilians have indicators, such as the forester at Wadworth with his hunting horn (Fig. 244) and the fabric maker at Batley with his weaver's sword (*2a.ii*). Two decayed male civilians at Stanwick have what appear to be extremely large and robust mittens, which may be hawking gloves, perhaps indicative of falconers. Their left hands supported additional objects, now extremely weathered but plausibly the remains of birds. The male civilian effigy in Holy Trinity, Hull has two objects suspended from his belt, which are likely to be implements of his trade but both are worn and the larger object damaged (Fig. 245). This has been seen as a tool for testing the quality of baled wool (Routh 1976, p. 74; Badham 2015a, pp. 144–48) but if this were true, it would cast doubt on the attribution to Robert de Selby (*2a.ii*), who was primarily a vintner (Kermode 1998, p. 177). In what follows, aspects of the symbolism found on Yorkshire effigies are examined together, categorised by type. This is a representative rather than exhaustive treatment, but it demonstrates the range of allegory employed. Whilst a concerted effort has been made to interpret the medieval thinking behind it, this remains a fertile area for future research.

Fig. 245 Holy Trinity, Hull. Male civilian with tools hanging from his belt.

5c.ii Religious objects

Some of the clergy have chalices, used in celebrating mass but also indicative of their ordained status. The chalice is held rather awkwardly between the hands at Thrybergh, Hutton Rudby (Fig. 12) and Great Langton (Fig. 15); steadied from above and below at Egglestone Abbey; beside the head at Ingleby Greenhow and lying on the abdomen at Thwing (Fig. 234). The Ingleby Greenhow arrangement, with chalice and book either side of the priest's head (Fig. 246) reflects what is sometimes seen on cross slabs, such as Marrick (Yorkshire) and Barnard Castle (Co. Durham) (see Boutell 1854, p. 59 & facing p. 56). These may reflect the postures of bodies in tombs and many mortuary chalices have been discovered in excavated ecclesiastical burials (Gilchrist & Sloane 2005, pp. 160–65), placed in a variety of positions. Most were on the chest but some were clasped in the priest's hands, as at Stratford Langthorne Abbey (Essex), Much Wenlock Priory (Shropshire) and

Fig. 246 Ingleby Greenhow. Priest with chalice and book.

Fig. 247 Holy Trinity, Hull. Lady holding heart with cavity between her hands.

Hulton Abbey (Staffordshire). Amongst parish churches, two excavated burials at St Peter's, Barton-Upon-Humber (Lincolnshire) preserved chalices, one clasped in the hands, the other upright on the chest (Rodwell & Atkins 2011, pp. 620–22). A slightly lower position is sometimes found too. The Thwing chalice is set oddly, simply lying on the priest's stomach below his praying hands. This curious portrayal also occurs on the Flemish brass at South Mimms (Hertfordshire), while another at Wensley (N.R.) shows it placed above the hands but Gilchrist and Sloane note two chalices placed on the corpse's midriff at Bristol (St James) and another at Tavistock, which was found by the pelvis. They conjecture this might have slipped and so could reflect Thwing's abdominal position. Four stone coffins at Wells Cathedral are equipped with carved recesses to support upright chalices (Rodwell 2001, pp. 497–501). In most excavated instances, the chalices were accompanied by patens but none are depicted on the Yorkshire effigies, although they appear with the host on the cross slab at Sproatley (E.R.). Chalices occur regularly on grave covers and in at least one instance, a slab so marked covered a burial containing a chalice. This grave was excavated at Monk Bretton Priory (W.R.) where the chalice was held between the hands on the chest (Walker 1926, p. 86). Interestingly, the chalice on the cover is centrally placed, perhaps intended to denote the burial arrangement. Philip Lankester (2011) comments that depictions of chalices on effigial memorials were infrequent in England and Wales at any time during the medieval period, listing only thirteen, two of them in Yorkshire. The remainder are widely spread, with a decidedly north midland and northern bias, now emphasised by the addition of a further five from Yorkshire. In general terms, this reflects the area where symbols most frequently occur on cross slabs. One other symbolic variant of ecclesiastical effigies is the crosier-holding and blessing pose common to most bishops, although the only Yorkshire example is Archbishop de Gray.

Not everything that was held survives, for instance the Holy Trinity, Hull lady's praying hands are cupped and hollowed around an empty cavity with a rebated rim (Fig. 247). At first glance this could be for a heart casket but, as she already holds a small heart between her finger tips and the cavity is too small for a casket, it is more likely to be a socket for an upright devotional image, probably of wood or metal. There may have been something similar at Catterick where the knight's gauntleted, praying, hands are carved quite wide with a smooth, horizontal platform cut into them, where something could have been bonded in place.

The Hornsea lady shows a different approach. She holds a rosary between her palms and her fingertips are broken off, but above her hands the rosary must have lain in an undercut loop, with a small witness of it remaining on her wimple (Fig. 149). In each case the hands have been arranged to accommodate the additional feature.

5c.iii Books and scrolls

Books, especially those associated with ecclesiastics, are customarily interpreted as sacred texts, but this is not always so. The deacon at Rippingale (Lincolnshire) carries a large open book, the pages outward as he would for the priest to read from, but rather than a text, they carry an inscription naming him and requesting prayers. In secular hands, the range of possibilities is greater, encompassing psalters, books of hours and devotional writings but they may not always have a religious connotation. Three civilians in the north of the county (a male at Stainton and a male and female at Acklam) are shown carrying a book in the crook of their arm (Fig. 248). There is no way of knowing what type of work was intended but if, for example, the males were lawyers, then their books might represent the law. Reading literature for pleasure was practised in Yorkshire at the time and an unassuming volume in the Bodleian Library (MS Hatton 82) once belonged to Brian FitzAlan whose effigy is at Bedale. This is a version of *Perlesvaus*, an Arthurian romance in Old French concerned with the Holy Grail. It has the words 'Le seinti Graal; Le liuer Sire Brian fiz Alayn;' at the head of the first page of what must then have been a popular, relatively inexpensive, copy. On either side of his effigy's feet are two seated figures holding books but, as they are dressed as monks, they will be reading from holy texts rather than a romance, however allegorical its character (Plate 55). Although badly mutilated there appear to have been two similar seated figures with books at the feet of the smaller knight at Coverham Abbey. The symbolism of reading from books reflects contemporary funerary inscriptions asking for prayers on behalf of the deceased. In effect they are a visual reminder of what the patron of the monument wished those who passed by to do and, cut in stone, also create an image of eternal commemoration.

Fig. 248 Stainton. Male civilian with heart and book.

Seated figures with books (Fig. 249) can also be seen beside the knight at Norton (female with veil and wimple) and at Goldsborough (probably also a woman). The Norton lady is a prominent feature of the monument and a possible interpretation is that she is the knight's grieving widow (Coss 1996, p. 23). Michael Clanchy (2004) argued that manuscript depictions of women reading religious books demonstrated their owners' active participation in personal worship. This must have more general applicability and relate to carving as much as illumination. He cites the example of the lady Landine who, in Chrétien de Troyes's romance *Yvain* (probably composed in the 1170s) remains alone and grieving after her husband's funeral 'as she reads her psalms in her gilt-lettered Psalter'. This symbolism can be read across to the seated, book-reading figure in the same position beside the Goldsborough knight, perhaps intended to represent his widow Eva (whose own monument is set in the floor by her husband's, Fig. 124). Two females wearing veils at the feet of the Sprotbrough lady are kneeling whilst holding open books (Fig. 250). Another female with an open book kneels by the Birdsall lady. Insufficient of the lady near the head of the Womersley knight is shown to reveal whether she is kneeling or sitting but her finger points most emphatically to a page of the book she holds, stressing the importance of its message (Fig. 251).

While tiny books held by attendant figures could at best carry only a few words, fuller texts could be displayed using a scroll, as is demonstrated by Brian FitzAlan's wife at Bedale. She has a long scroll, one end of which reaches to her ankles and holds it so as to present the words to her audience (Fig. 252). The painted text has not survived but would once have been clear for all to see and a few to read. Elsewhere, two notable earlier effigies hold similar scrolls: Avon Dassett (Warwickshire) and Scarcliffe (Derbyshire). The Avon Dassett ecclesiastic holds the scroll rigidly straight down in front of him but Scarcliffe is more informative (Fig. 253). It probably dates from the earlier thirteenth

Fig. 249 Norton. Seated lady beside the knight, holding an open book.

century and depicts a lady holding a child (Oosterwijk 2010). It is the child who holds the scroll and sufficient of the incised inscription still remains to recreate it in full. We are grateful to Jerome Bertram for providing us with the following translation of the Latin verse:

> Here lies a woman buried flat under the earth,
> Constantia, rightly named so being constant and pleasing.
> The child she was given rests buried with its mother;
> May their sins be buried at her [head?].
> Purged of guilt, with her blessed child John,
> May she live through fate, located in the seat of the saints.
> Amen

The phrase 'may their sins be buried at her head' is fascinating because, unusually, her head rests on a lion, presumably symbolising sin in this instance. Given the length of the inscription it is surprising for what it does not

Fig. 250 Sprotbrough. Women kneeling at Isabella FitzWilliam's feet, resting books on a grotesque head.

say. There is no mention of her husband or her family name, no request for prayers and no appeal for the protection of the saints, etc. There is not even a reference to the monument on which the words appear – just that she is buried under the earth. Scarcliffe provides at least an indication of what the scroll held by Muriel FitzAlan at Bedale might have said. Given the sad circumstances of her death following the loss of three sons, similar sentiments may have been expressed. Elsewhere in Yorkshire (Howden Minster) a fourteenth-century statue of St John displays a scroll with the message incised upon it, 'IN PRINCIPIO ERAT…', the opening words of St John's Gospel. In contrast to Scarcliffe, it reads upwards since the words emanate from the symbolic eagle at his feet. At Pickering the task is performed by the lion at the feet of the alabaster knight (Fig. 254). The scroll that it holds in its mouth hangs down and lies on the base slab presenting its message. So, while texts are usually handled in a conventional manner, the carver can always produce something out of the ordinary.

5c.iv Hearts and souls

Most Yorkshire effigies that hold something between their praying hands have representations of hearts or heart caskets. They are held by nine military figures, the male civilians at Birkin, Goodmanham, Hickleton and Stainton plus the ladies at Hull and Sprotbrough, while the couple

Fig. 251 Womersley. Lady pointing to her text.

Fig. 252 Bedale. Muriel FitzAlan presenting her scroll.

Fig. 253 Scarcliffe (Derbyshire). Lady with child holding scroll.

at Lowthorpe share a single heart, placed between them (Fig. 255). The heart-holding attitude is seen widely on English monuments and is not clearly understood. There may well be no single explanation. A hand-held heart, incised with 'Credo' and surrounded by scrolls with a text from Job XIX: 25 & 26, is used on some fifteenth-century brasses to demonstrate the deceased's faith, for example, Loddon (Norfolk), commemorating Denis Willys (d. 1462). However, Danielle Westerhoff (2008, pp. 53–54, 88) considered the heart 'represented humanity's inner

Fig. 254 Pickering. Alabaster knight's lion with scroll in its mouth.

being' and the location of 'interiorised spirituality' so that a heart-holding effigy might be offering up their spiritual record for judgement. Images of the soul are less common and less prominently displayed. However, four Yorkshire examples of tiny soul figures have been noted. At Thornhill an angel beside the knight's head bears up his soul in a sheet (Fig. 256). Its elevation to heaven is more graphically shown at Bainton where two large angels in the canopy hold a sheet containing the knight's soul (Fig. 257). Two angels perform the same duty for the Birdsall lady and her tiny praying soul figure has very long hair (Fig. 258), like that of the female soul in the canopy of the Percy Tomb in Beverley Minster (Fig. 259). The fourth example associated with a Yorkshire effigy is also the most elevated. When Prince William of Hatfield's tomb was re-sited in the north ambulatory of York Minster just after 1400, a whole bay of the north wall was configured to accept it. This dramatic, floor to vault construction is divided into three compartments, the lowest for the chest and effigy and the upper two probably for lost statuary. Each stage has a vault, the second with some angels at intersections. One holds a sheet containing a soul figure, huddled up like a swaddled infant (Plate 23). William lived for a very short time and, although the effigy shows him as a youth, the designers of this fine tomb setting were clearly aware of his infant death. Despite all that has been written about this royal monument, this telling detail seems to have previously gone unnoticed. Considered together,

Fig. 255 Lowthorpe. Couple with heart between them.

Fig. 256 Thornhill. Angel (now headless) bearing up knight's soul.

these Yorkshire soul figures express different stages of the soul's journey to heaven, from close to the body at Thornhill and Birdsall, rising aloft at Bainton and York Minster and culminating at Beverley Minster in its reception by Christ.

5c.v Face cloths and sheets

English effigies typically differ from their Continental counterparts in being shown with open eyes and it could be that the English carvers (and their patrons) intended portrayal not as the dead but as they would have appeared in life. Only the Danby Wiske lady bucks this trend and there is no obvious reason for her uniqueness (Fig. 220). Another interpretation is that the effigies with open eyes are prepared for the Resurrection. Support for this idea comes from six of the military figures that are shown with cloths draped over the tops of their heads, all made by the Series A/B sculptor (*4c.ii*). An explanation for this puzzling feature is to be found on the larger knight at Coverham Abbey, where two angels hold the cloth as if they have lifted it from his face (Plate 32).

Fig. 257 Bainton. Angels carrying Sir John de Mauley's soul in a sheet.

Fig. 258 Birdsall. The lady's praying soul figure carried in a cloth by the angels.

Fig. 259 Beverley Minster. Percy Tomb, with female soul's reception into heaven.

What seems to be represented is the sudarium (or sudary). This term (meaning napkin) has been applied to a cloth used to cover the face as part of the preparation for burial. Remains have been found in a number of high status burials, including Edward I (Ayloffe 1775). Philip Lankester examined the subject in an unpublished lecture to the Church Monuments Society in 2001 (private communication), finding other high status examples from England, France and Spain. He had found little evidence related to nobility or gentry burials but was able to cite examples for the clergy from the Russian Orthodox church. He also pointed out that the burial of Christ recorded in St John's Gospel had involved a sudarium, which was found in the empty tomb. There is evidence for its use in the Cluniac Customary (Paxton 2013, pp. 55–172):

Fig. 260 Wolferlow (Herefordshire). Angels drawing back the lady's face cloth.

> The washed body is dressed in a coarse woolen shirt, cowl, night shoes, and a sudary that is of the same material as the woolen shirt. The shoes are ones that are not open at the toes but stitched together. The chamberlain having supplied needle and thread, the hood of the cowl is then sewn down over the sudary and the face on both sides. The hands are folded together on the breast outside the cowl and sewn in place. Everything is so drawn together that none of the limbs is loose. The night shoes are sewn together as well.

In this arrangement the sudary lies immediately over the face, assisting the monk's habit to substitute for a shroud. Something similar was stipulated in the eleventh century at Canterbury Cathedral Priory and St Alban's Abbey, except that the cloth over the face was to be in the shape of a hood (Lanfranc 2002, pp. 183–85). In the Yorkshire examples and the only other currently recognised instance, a thirteenth-century lady at Wolferlow (Herefordshire), the cloth appears flat and is shown directly on the head (Fig. 260). The larger knight at Coverham also shows the cloth lying between the head and the pillow (Plate 32), while at Goldsborough, it is stitched to the cushion (Plate 31). The double effigy at Lowthorpe shows a sheet or cloth under both heads and over their bolster. Its edge has been drawn forward and lies in folds over the tops of their heads and around them (Fig. 255), with the faces shown revealed (*5c.ix*). Both the larger Coverham knight and the Wolferlow lady have their cloths held up by pairs of angels, which are depicted as if they have just drawn back the cloth from the effigy's face, revealing the person alive. At Lowthorpe and Routh the faces are obliterated but all the other face cloth effigies have open eyes, refuting any possible interpretation of the figures as dead. We have previously suggested (Gittos 1994a) this symbolism might represent 'the knight as he was when alive or as he might be when resurrected'. However, a problem with interpreting this as Resurrection imagery is that medieval representations of last judgement scenes

Fig. 261 Howden. Metham effigies on what may be draped biers.

almost invariably show the resurrected as naked. However, we have not found any satisfactory alternative explanation.

It is worth noting here that the Metham pair at Howden are both shown lying on draped cloths or sheets (Fig. 261). This is difficult to parallel in England and the most obvious comparators are the four royal effigies at Fontevraud Abbey (France) where, as at Howden, the draped sheets also underlie the cushions. The Fontevraud depictions have been described as representing 'the dead person on a draped bier as if lying in state' (Clanchy 2004, p. 116) and, while the Metham pair could hardly be considered as 'lying in state', draped biers would make good sense. So monuments can tell us about rituals associated with the preparation of the body and also ideas about the afterlife.

5c.vi Beasts and birds

Creatures of all kinds appear on the monuments. They are most commonly found as foot supports where lions predominate, followed by dogs (*2a.i*). The subject of animal foot supports has been discussed by Sophie Oosterwijk (2016), while Malcolm Norris provided a useful overview (1978, pp. 71–72). The employment of lions in particular for this role has been widely taken to be a reference to Psalm 90 (91):13 (*e.g.* Meara 1990), 'Super aspidem, et basiliscum ambulabis: et conculcabis leonem et draconem', translateable as 'Thou shalt walk upon the asp and the basilisk: and thou shalt trample under foot the lion and the dragon'. Yet this seems not to accord with the lion's function on Yorkshire effigies, some of which have peaceful, even smiling faces. In most cases the effigy's feet are positioned in a relaxed manner with no indication of aggressive trampling and the lion sometimes appears braced as if using their strength to take the pressure of the knight's feet. Lions could also signify courage, determination and vigilance, which seems to fit better (Payne 1990, p. 19), and their purpose at the feet of effigies has more appropriately been described as watchful, guarding 'against sin and devils' and being 'alert on the dreadful Day of Judgement' (Tisdall 1998, pp. 158–59). However, in three cases (Church Fenton, Normanby and Norton) the lion is shown in action, fighting the forces of evil. The Church Fenton lady retains her elegant poise despite the mayhem at her feet (Fig. 262). The lion's adversary is a two-headed dragon (amphisbaena) who is sinking his razor sharp teeth into the lion's ear. The lion takes this discomfort in his stride, gazing hopefully heavenwards whilst gripping both the throat and second head of his foe. The amphisbaena seems confused because he is also aggressively gripping his other head. Perhaps he is trying to wrest it back from the lion. It is difficult to imagine how the contract for this monument was worded but the carver seems to have enjoyed considerable freedom to indulge himself. The fight on the Normanby fragment is more intense with the lion sinking his teeth into the dragon's back while he attacks the lion just below the ear. Similar ferocity is displayed in the Norton fight (Fig. 179).

Fig. 262 Church Fenton. Mortal combat beneath the lady's feet.

Beside the smaller knight at Coverham is something approaching a nest of dragons. The detail is badly eroded but what can be made out is up to three dragons in addition to another animal (lion?) supporting the feet. One bites the tip of the shield and another bites the scabbard while the third (the most badly weathered) follows them. Their bodies are intertwined but this is a melee rather than a fight, a concentration of evil. In contrast, the two dragons supporting the earlier Acklam lady's feet are extremely passive. They lie on their sides, back to back with their tails knotted together as if acknowledging good triumphant over evil (Fig. 263). The remaining five dragons all act alone. Four bite the shields of knights: Bainton, FitzAlan at Bedale (Fig. 264), York ('Kildare' effigy) and Nunnington (assumed because, although the head is lost, the body is positioned for this purpose). The symbolism of these shield-biting dragons is unclear but could mean that the knight's protection from evil is encapsulated in his shield. A related message may be carried by the disembodied hand that emerges from the slab to grip the tip of the shield of the larger Coverham knight (Fig. 265). Perhaps the hand of God is guaranteeing the effectiveness of the shield's protection. Such disembodied hands occur on a number of grave slabs like those holding crosiers at Romsey Abbey (Hampshire). Walter, chaplain of

Keyingham is commemorated on the Sproatley (E.R.) slab, with a hand holding the host on a paton above a chalice. The hand could be his but divine involvement would be more powerful imagery. The fifth single dragon is biting the base of Archbishop de Gray's crosier but this is more appropriately interpreted as the Archbishop thrusting his crosier down the dragon's throat and vanquishing him, in a pose often used for St Michael (Fig. 266). Aside from the dragons, another expression of evil is the grotesque foliate head at the feet of the Sprotbrough lady. His staring eyes and open mouth provide the drama and the substitution of oak leaves for his hair adds to his surreal appearance (Fig. 250). Fortunately any evil intent is countered by the calmness of the two kneeling ladies who rest their books on his head, using the power of their prayers to counteract his distress. Another foliate head appears beneath the feet of the priest at Harpswell (Lincolnshire). Joan de Lellay at Goxhill has a similar hooded face with a protruding tongue, sandwiched between the rumps of two lap dogs, although he has less impact on account of his diminutive size. A mythical creature with a man's head wearing a hood and a feathered, bird-like, body supports the right foot of the Butterwick knight. His left foot rests on a small dog, so the message is unclear. The dog at Thornton Dale is unusual, resting its chin rather awkwardly on a prominent male head. Several crouching men act as corbels to gablettes and two grotesques crouch beside the shields hanging off the back of the Norton gablette. They have human heads with hoods and liripipes but the legs of animals with cloven hooves (Fig. 267), the type of imagery popular as contemporary manuscript marginalia.

Fig. 263 Acklam. Lady (west) with dragons back to back at her feet.

Whilst mythical creatures are well represented, real creatures are less common, although two stags with very different roles are notable. One, now mutilated but once a fine beast, is the Birdsall lady's foot support. As it is so unusual, it may have held a special significance for the

Fig. 264 Bedale. Dragon biting Brian FitzAlan's shield.

Fig. 265 Coverham Abbey. Hand holding tip of larger knight's shield.

patron. The other stag has taken flight – racing past the smaller Coverham knight's shield to escape a pursuing hound and reach the safety of natural cover represented by a spread of leafy branches ahead of it (Fig. 268). The drama of the chase is heightened by the stag glancing anxiously over his shoulder and a hunting scene might have been requested by someone fortunate enough to engage the talented and innovative Series A/B carver. But the scene might also be allegorical, as deer were symbolic of the faithful leaving the world for the new pastures of heaven (Barber 1992, p. 51). The gablette foliage might then represent the new pastures. Deer were also famed for seeking out the plant dittany, to counter their wounds. It is even possible all three meanings were intended, as a visual triple *entendre*. The other creatures are more modestly handled. A squirrel crouches beside the earlier of the two ladies at Appleton-le-Street, its bushy tail curled over its back (Fig. 269). In a modern context it recalls the mouse trademark of the Thompson woodworking firm at nearby Kilburn. The second squirrel is more tenuous as only the tip of his bushy tail remains,

Fig. 266 York Minster. Archbishop de Gray's crosier impaling a dragon.

close to the cushion of the Fountains Abbey knight. It is only the comparison with Appleton-le-Street which makes it interpretable. One of the effigies in London's Temple church (RCHM No. 9) has a squirrel under the corner of his shield. It is shown standing with paws together devouring a nut and something similar may have once existed on RCHM No. 8 (Lankester 2010, p. 109). Although apparently just supports for vulnerable under-cut areas, they do indicate squirrels were a part of the repertoire of metropolitan carvers in the later thirteenth century. Just below Fountains' right elbow are the remains of a bird carved mostly on the base slab chamfer but with its tail extending onto the top surface. These two may be no more than decorative features added by the carver. Another bird seems to have greater significance because it is held carefully between the praying hands of the lady at Bilton (in Ainsty). The tail feathers and wings survive but the neck and head are broken off. It is quite a small bird and so a dove is a possibility. They feature in the bestiaries and, if coloured red, a dove could represent Christ (Payne 1990, p. 78). The large bird acting as a foot support for the Adlingfleet lady has lost its head but looks rather like a goose. Its meaning is unclear but a complete goose supports the feet of a later fourteenth-century maiden at Clehonger (Herefordshire). Two tomb chest figures at Howden hold birds, probably related to hawking and similar to the impression given by the male civilian effigy at Willoughby-on-the-Wolds (Nottinghamshire). The bird he once held with his left hand is lost but it is shown in an antiquarian sketch (Lankester 1989). Another damaged bird helps support the shield of one of the knights in the Lord Mayor's Chapel (Bristol) but they are not commonly seen on medieval effigies. The horse's head on the semi-effigial

Fig. 267 Norton. Crouching grotesque on knight's gablette.

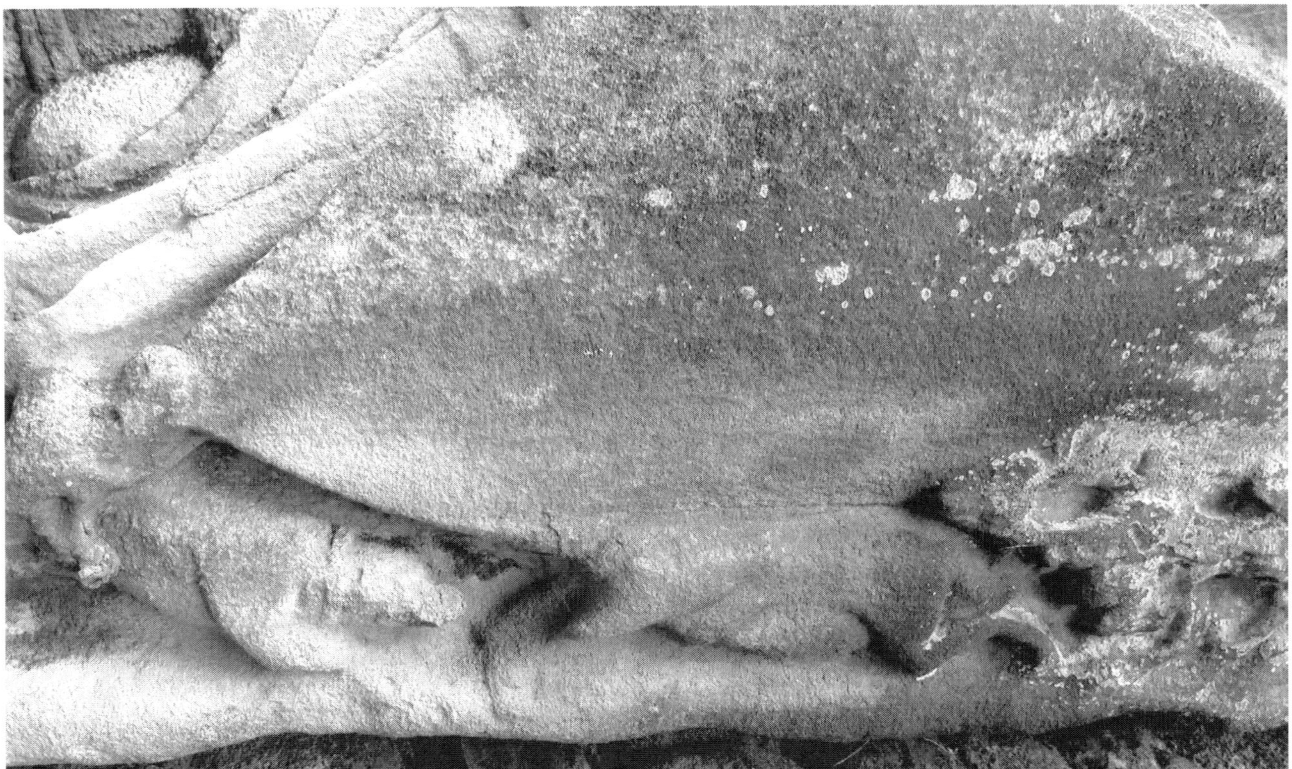

Fig. 268 Coverham Abbey. Stag pursued by a hound, on the smaller knight.

Fig. 269 Appleton-le-Street. Series B lady's squirrel.

Fig. 270 Thornhill. Kneeling ecclesiastic.

slab at Gilling East is probably heraldic, signifying a badge or crest and thereby complimenting the display of arms on the opposite side of the slab.

5c.vii Attendant figures

Some attendant human figures seem to have special significance. Despite its mutilated state, one of the kneeling figures by the feet of the Thornhill knight can be seen to be an ecclesiastic with a staff or crosier, blessing with his right hand (Fig. 270). This must represent a bishop or abbot, perhaps someone with whom the knight had a special relationship. The appearance of monastic figures alongside effigies (including those at Sprotbrough, Bedale and Coverham) probably refers to a close association with a specific religious house. For instance, the Bedale chantry was administered by Jervaulx Abbey.

A small figure of a man wearing a long robe stands beside Sir Walter de Teye at Nunnington (Fig. 271). He has lost his head and left arm but holds the top cushion with his right hand, like a supporting angel, the tip of his hood hanging down his back. He carries a scrip over his right shoulder and the remains of the staff he held run across the cushions in front of him. He must be a pilgrim and could signify that Sir Walter himself went on a pilgrimage. In 1285, William de Percy the younger of Kildale (a distant neighbour of de Teye, from the northern edge of the Moors) sought protection for three years as he was going on pilgrimage to Jerusalem (CPR 1281–1292, p. 159). At the same time, Brian FitzAlan from Bedale intended going abroad on pilgrimage, but on a shorter journey (CPR 1281–1292, p. 159). However, it is equally possible that the Nunnington figure represents someone going on his behalf. This might have happened during his lifetime or after his death, as such provisions do occur in wills. In 1429 John Scot (*Test. Ebor.* I, p. 420), a bowyer of York was determined to maximise his benefit. His provisions may be paraphrased as:

> Four marks to a good, true man going in pilgrimage to Rome, namely two marks for his trouble and two to have masses sung for me in Rome. That is to say at the altar before St Veronica's veil in St Peter's and also Santa Maria Scala Cœli and one at the altar of St Fabian or St Sebastian, wherever most need is. Also, he should arrange for thirteen masses to be sung for me at various places in Rome.

Whether the pilgrim represents de Teye or a surrogate, it symbolises the process of pilgrimage supporting de Teye's passage to heaven.

In contrast with such an individual attendant, a few effigies are accompanied by an ensemble. At Ripley, for example, the tomb chest supporting Thomas Ingleby and his wife had eight figures in canopied niches (Fig. 106). Most if not all of them represented the couple's children (*3d*). The Metham tomb chest panels at Howden lack names but the twelve figures comprise nine males and three females who have veils but seemingly no wimples to signify widowhood. They show youthful exuberance turning, swaying and even waving to the audience, two carrying birds and the majority holding books or scrolls to provide the necessary prayers. Children are almost certainly what is represented in a very different manner at Lowthorpe, just as heads (*5c.ix*).

A group of relatives is also likely to be represented at Birdsall where the lady lies on a deep integral plinth, as if on top of her bed or a bier, but most prominent are the six figures kneeling beside her, three on either side. The five men are all down on one knee (Fig. 272), with three holding books and two scrolls, while the female is on both knees holding a book. The impression is of a group of family mourners presenting prayers for the deceased. All are fashionably dressed for the mid-fourteenth century, which is the date of the monument. The combination of an effigy on a raised platform and the kneeling mourners clustered round reciting prayers is strongly suggestive of a deathbed scene, as on seven sacrament fonts, such as Nettlecombe

Fig. 271 Nunnington. A headless pilgrim beside Walter de Teye's three cushions.

(Somerset), where the mourners are joined by the priest giving extreme unction. The *Ars Moriendi* recommends the recitation of the Creed around the dying person as a defence against the 'Temptation of the Devil concerning Faith' and enjoins those in attendance at the deathbed to assist by saying the prayers for them if the person is incapacitated (Campbell 1995, pp. 31, 72). Camille has sketched the scene vividly (Camille 1996, pp. 156–57):

> The deathbed would normally have been surrounded by many onlookers, servants, friends and family, all taking part in an elaborate ritualised process of leave-taking. Clambering around the deathbed too were a thousand possible spiritual intercessors as well as devils and angels waiting for the separation of the soul from the body and for the fight over the soul to begin... It was also not so much 'the hour of our death' but the hours and even days of long drawn out waiting, during which the sick person would be the focus of prayers and readings from the Gospel.

The Birdsall tableau can be read as a narrative, the onlookers praying (those with scrolls) and reading from sacred texts (those with books) around the dying woman but with the angels portraying the outcome (*5c.iv*), having won the battle for her soul.

Fig. 272 Birdsall. Man kneeling beside the lady and holding a book.

Comparison has been made between the Birdsall assemblage and the Harrington tomb at Cartmel Priory but, although James Cameron (Cameron 2011, p. 26) correctly observes they are both examples of additional figures carved from the same block, his description of Birdsall is inaccurate. Furthermore, the imagery is completely different. At Cartmel, thirteen figures, identically dressed as monks stand either side of the knight and his lady, each holding an open book. These are the monks of the Priory in procession, chanting prayers for the deceased, as they were contracted to do. The regimented presentation at Cartmel makes a stark contrast with the filial devotion of the Birdsall lady's fashionably dressed offspring.

These figure groupings are all carved in stone but it is important to appreciate how much has been lost because the accompanying figures were originally only painted. The Goldsborough tomb chest arches retain tantalising fragments of their painted religious imagery (Gittos 1994a), including the twelve apostles and two biblical scenes: one, the Coronation of the Virgin (Plate 24) and the other, probably the Annunciation (*4b.iii*). Little now remains of the carved panels of the FitzAlan tomb at Bedale but antiquarian drawings suggest they had a mixture of secular and religious imagery with figures in niches displaying the FitzAlan arms, flanking what in one case could be the death of the Virgin (Gale 1722, p. 242; Blore 1826, facing p. 1 of section entitled 'Brian Fitz-Alan').

5c.viii The cross

Some monuments are designed to utilise the symbolism of the cross. The two semi-effigials at Melsonby both have the deceased's head placed at the centre of a leafy cross (Fig. 33). The involvement of the head or bust with a cross is more subtle on the memorials at Gilling East and Hickleton. Paired branches grow from the stem at Hickleton but the cross head has been entirely replaced by Robert Haringel's bust (Fig. 39), sunk within a large square panel (*2a.vii*). As a token gesture to the leafy cross heads of the Melsonby type, two small sprigs of leaves have been positioned in the spandrels of the trefoil headed recess within its square frame. At Gilling East, the role of the quatrefoil opening containing the bust of a knight as the principal element of the cross head is confirmed by foliate terminals at the apex of each lobe. There are more leaves on two branches at the base of the shaft, which has a ribbed circular knop (Fig. 34). Knops are a very frequent feature of cross slabs but not amongst this group of monuments. The only other example is at Throapham where part of a small lozenge-shaped knop remains on the incised shaft just below the quatrefoil opening displaying the bust of a man. Such features serve to strengthen the cross imagery and here, the quatrefoil represents the cross head. The cross plays a dramatic role in the design at Hutton Rudby (Fig. 12) where the complete figure of a priest rests his head on a cross composed of leafy branches (*2a.iii*). It gives the superficial appearance of leaves issuing from his ears and the top of his head, rather like a green man but the symbolism must be his protection by the cross. This message is unequivocal in the case of the bas-relief Patrington lady who has a cross actually resting on her body and is the only example of such imagery in Yorkshire (Fig. 273). The cross is carved in low relief complete with a stepped calvary and so there is no question that it might be a decorative feature of her gown. Such a deliberate placement implies a specific iconographic intent. The brass to a priest at Chinnor, Oxfordshire puts his head in front of the cross and other cross brasses, such as Taplow (Buckinghamshire) and Wimbish (Essex) employ the cross head as a kind of frame for complete figures. So, Patrington appears conceptually different but one monument that may have been comparable is an incised slab at Romsey Abbey (Hampshire), claimed to represent a fourteenth-century abbess. It is now so worn that it is extremely difficult to make out the detail. However, an antiquarian drawing (Liveing 1906, facing p. 120) shows what could be the stem of a cross with branching leaves overlaying the figure. The top of the slab is broken and even from the sketch it is unclear if there were any form of cross head. A more positive example of an overlying cross is at Preston Gubbals (Shropshire). The slab's top half survives with an ogee-topped, elongated, opening displaying the bust of a male civilian, the head of a straight arm cross with fleur-de-lys terminals carved on his chest. A straight arm cross with foliate terminals overlays the top half of a praying woman at Penshurst (Kent). The carver has avoided the cross obscuring her face and hands by tilting her head backwards and showing her hands in profile. Finally, an incised figure of unknown type is wall mounted in the ruined church of Tullylease (County Cork). It is worn and damaged but the outline of the upper part of a figure can still be made out around the head of an incised cross. These examples serve to illustrate that, although uncommon, crosses overlying both male and female figures do occur quite widely. The rarity of this arrangement suggests that something more might be intended than simply the person being under the protection of the cross. One possibility is that the person was a religious recluse. When they were formally shut up in their cells (enclosed), it was as if they were buried there, being considered dead to the world. The surviving enclosure rites for anchors and anchorites all include elements from the funeral liturgy (Jones 2012). Some called for an open grave within the cell, in which the last rites were administered before the door was blocked. Henceforth, the recluse's only communication with the outside was through a curtained window. The thirteenth-century *Ancrene Wisse* (Hasenfratz 2002, part 2, lines 16–27) said the curtain should be black and marked with a white cross as symbolic of chastity, but it would also have recalled the funeral pall and meant the recluse would always be separated from the world by a cross. An effigy shown beneath a cross might be a means of signifying an anchor or anchorite.

Fig. 273 Patrington. Lady with cross carved on top of her.

5c.ix Lowthorpe: case study

The interpretation of the extraordinary monument at Lowthorpe (Fig. 274) has exercised the minds of many scholars and, because of its uniqueness in Yorkshire and beyond, it warrants special attention. There are many facets to its iconography that merit further consideration. In contrast to the Howden figures shown lying on sheets, the couple at Lowthorpe are covered as if in bed, their heads on a bolster. However, the arrangement is more complicated than that because of the drapery that overlaps the tops of their heads (Fig. 255), giving the misleading impression that the man is wearing a night cap and the lady a veil. It could be the under sheet gathered up but seems more likely to be a separate face cloth or cloths, draped over their heads

Fig. 274 Lowthorpe. Double effigy for Sir John and Marjorie de Heslerton.

Fig. 275 Lowthorpe. Female head attached to the tree.

and drawn back to reveal their faces (*5c.v*). Between their shoulders is a single heart and from both figures emerge the roots of a tree, which curl over the bed covering and unite to become a single trunk with branches all the way to their feet. The branches leave the trunk alternately left and right, and at the end of each is a human head, six on the female's side and seven opposite. There are eleven male heads in all and just two female (one on each side). Five of the male heads are tonsured. High in the canopy of the tree (bottom of the bed) are two much smaller branches bearing five shields and above them some sprigs of foliage.

The symbolism of this remarkable assemblage is very powerful. The couple appear fused together with one heart and only one foot of each showing through the coverlet. Their heads (particularly the woman's) incline towards each other in an attitude of tenderness and their depiction resembles Jesse and the ancestors of Christ, displaying the fruits of their union in the form of a tree of life that springs equally from both bodies. The thirteen heads must be their very male dominated offspring, none of which are shown as infant deaths. The shields at the top of the tree may represent family alliances. The best dating evidence is afforded by the style of the children's heads, which would suit a date in the second quarter of the fourteenth century (Fig. 275). In the context of Lowthorpe, this suggests a very strong candidate, Sir John de Heslerton. In 1333 he founded a college at Lowthorpe, comprising six perpetual chantries each served by a chantry priest. Collier 1923 (pp. 32–35) quotes the full details of the college foundation from the Patent Rolls, which make it clear that two of the six chantries were for Sir John, his wife Marjorie, their children, heirs, etc. because of his role as both patron of the living and founder of the college. The college was later augmented by his son Thomas with the addition of a seventh chantry in 1364, (VCH:ER:II, p. 323). John was dead by 1348 and Thomas by 1376 (Saltmarshe 1914, p. 50) but the latter would be too late for the style of the monument. In the same year as the college foundation licence, a dispute over who held the advowson of the church was settled by a fine in favour of Sir John and Margery (Baildon 1910, p. 60). This also mentions their children (to whom the advowson would pass by succession), naming them as Thomas, Walter, John, Simon, Nicholas, Agnes and Marjorie. Interestingly, this includes only two daughters, which is the same as the number of female heads on the monument. However, there are only five sons compared to eleven carved male heads so the monument may include sons who had died.

It might be expected that such a key monument to the founder of the college would be set up in the chancel where the liturgical business of the college took place, and most writers have assumed this to be the case. It is now inside the nave and the chancel has been a roofless ruin for several centuries, falling into neglect when the college was dissolved at the Reformation (Plate 72). The move of the slab into the nave seems unrecorded but evidence of its history comes from an unlikely source, an 1846 travel guide written by J. Furby for visitors to Bridlington. One of the places covered was Lowthorpe, for which he provided the following information (Furby 1846, p. 40):

> A cross in the Church yard at the East end of the building, and in good preservation, is said to have been brought from Harpham Field; and close by it two recumbent figures in Stone said to be from Ruston Parva. They appear to be the effigies of a male and female, with the trunk and branches of a tree running between and over them—the root being placed between their heads and the branches bearing fruit on each side, in the shape of three distinct hearts near their feet. It has been highly ornamented with heads round the margin, but no inscription is perceptible.

Furby is clearly describing the same monument that was then in the churchyard, near the east wall of the chancel beside an ancient cross, which is still there. His comment that it was 'said to be from Ruston Parva' is strange because in the fourteenth century the church at Ruston Parva (one mile to the north east) had the status of a chapelry of Lowthorpe and would not have enjoyed burial rights (VCH:ER:II, p. 323). However, the tradition of the monument coming from Ruston Parva is repeated by Bulmer (1892, p. 236) who appears to describe the monument as being in the ruined chancel. If it were just outside the east wall as Furby describes, Bulmer's account might be a loosely worded description of the same situation.

There is a good case for the monument's original location being the churchyard. Although the collegiate chancel was lofty with impressively large windows, particularly when seen from the north, it was not especially large in floor area and with all that was needed by the college priests, allocating room for a tomb of this size would have been difficult. However, this problem would have been solved by placing it outside, whilst still being sited close the principal altar. Moreover, its design would suit an external situation as it is robustly carved, devoid of undercutting. It is also uniformly weathered, with much detail being lost, such as from the faces of the couple and their children. The chancel arch was eventually bricked up and the roof removed, apparently in the eighteenth century. Once the arch was blocked, it would have been extremely difficult to have moved such a massive object out of the chancel as the only doorway is very small, nor would there have been any great need to do so. It therefore seems likely that this highly individual memorial was originally set up by John de Heslerton in the churchyard, some time before his death (probably in the 1340s), immediately outside the college that he had founded. Its purpose was to commemorate John, his wife Margery and their children.

5c.x Conclusion

Most patrons of effigies were content with something straightforward and uncomplicated but others sought designs more laden with meaning and these are likely to have been collaborative projects. The selection of such elements as the religious imagery would almost certainly have been down to the patron but it was for the mason to realise the ideas. Whilst the best masons would have been able to contribute ideas, patrons are unlikely to have approved designs and authorised payment if they were unhappy with what was projected. Quite how complex an effigial monument might be is not always readily appreciated as the messages vary greatly and multiple meanings can be layered in a single monument. The differing approaches to salvation imagery demonstrate the range of possibilities. While one monument may depict the deathbed (*e.g.* Birdsall), another shows the soul's journey to heaven (*e.g.* Prince William of Hatfield in York Minster) and a third depicts the moment of resurrection (*e.g.* the larger knight at Coverham Abbey). The Series B knight at Goldsborough is an example of multiple messages, invoking the Resurrection theme, involving the figure with the liturgy taking place around him and perhaps even including his widow's participation. The extended case study that follows in Section 6 explores an extreme application of imagery. It combines many of the main themes of the book in an analysis of one of Yorkshire's most fascinating and enigmatic monuments.

Plate 42 Wistow. The kneeling lady.

Plate 43 York, St Denys. Donor presenting a window, mid fourteenth century.

Plate 44 Butterwick. Series B effigy's unfinished carving.

Plate 45 Darrington. Series C knight's partly carved mail.

Plate 46 Butterwick. The unfinished carving: drill holes, blocked out sword pommel and lack of mail on the arms.

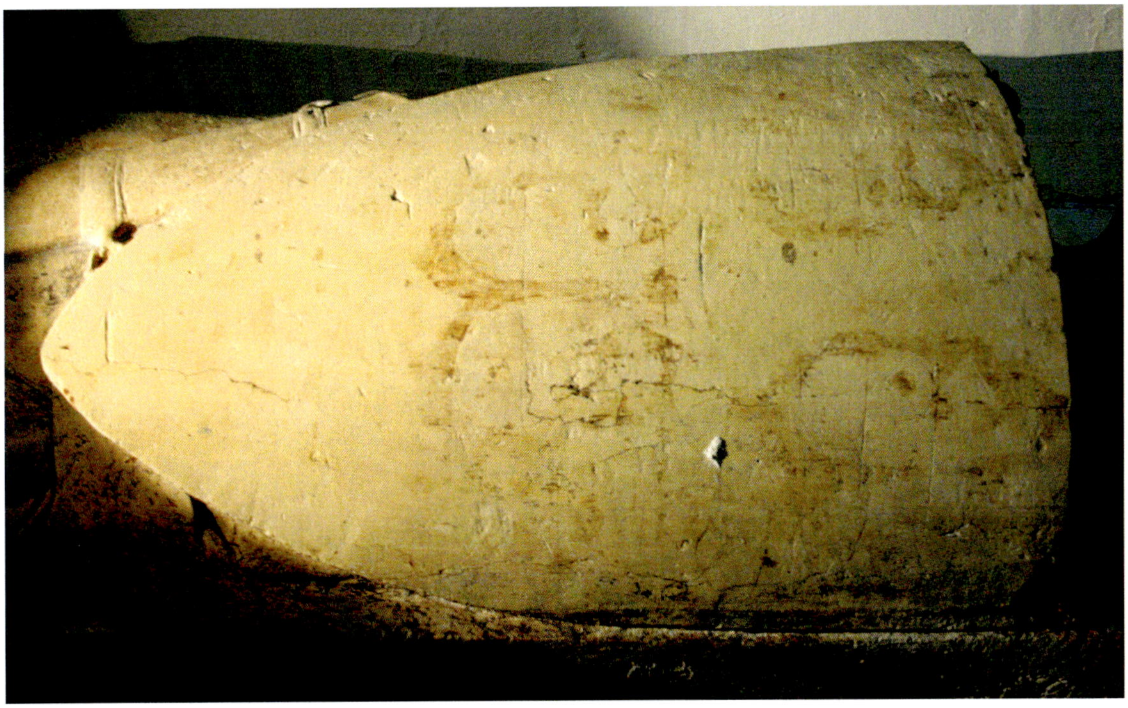

Plate 47 Butterwick shield, traces of scored guide lines and painted heraldry.

Plate 48 Bedale. Painted details on Brian FitzAlan surviving in 1841, from Hollis.

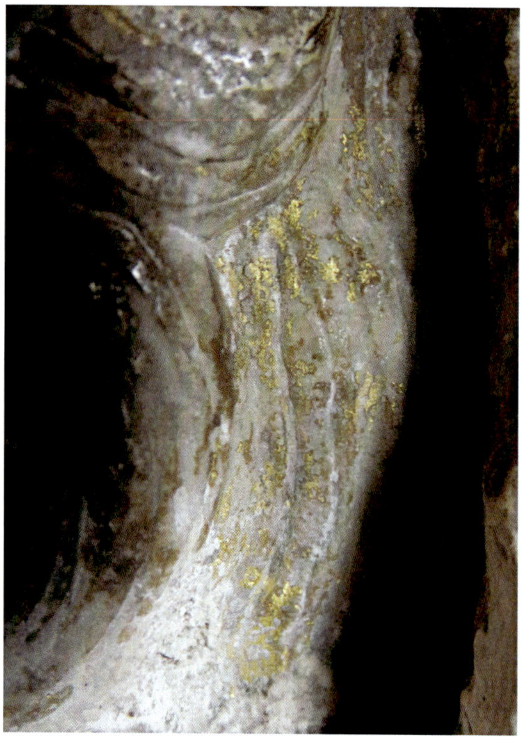

Plate 49 Pickering. Roucliffe lady, gold on an alabaster angel's wing.

Plate 50 Nunnington. Gold on Sir Walter de Teye's surcoat.

Plate 51 Darrington. Reconstruction showing how he held his lance, using I'Anson's drawing.

Plate 52 Barton-Upon-Humber, St. Peter (Lincolnshire). Lance-holding St George. © English Heritage Trust.

Plate 53 Bedale. Brian FitzAlan's late thirteenth century south chapel.

Plate 54 Bedale. Series B effigy for Sir Brian FitzAlan, d. 1306.

Plate 55 Bedale. Headless monk reading from a book beside Brian FitzAlan's figure.

Plate 56 East Harlsey. Series B effigy.

Plate 57 Ryther. Series C knight's bascinet.

Plate 58 Ryther. Series C lady's hair arrangement.

Plate 59 Darrington. Series C lady's hair arrangement.

Plate 60 Church Fenton. Series C lady's hair arrangement.

Plate 61 Kildwick. A knight from late in the Series C sequence.

Plate 62 Felixkirk. The Series D effigy of Sir John de Walkingham, d. 1332.

Plate 63 Felixkirk. Family heraldry. Some surviving medieval glass in the window above the knight's tomb.

Plate 64 Rievaulx Abbey. A rich foundation of which the de Ros family were patrons.

Plate 65 Crathorne. Series E effigy of Sir William de Crathorne, with his painted shield. © Martin Stutchfield.

Plate 66 Darfield. Probably a de Bosville, c. *1400.*

Plate 67 Bainton. Family heraldry above the tomb canopy.

Plate 68 York Minster. From the early fourteenth century de Mauley window showing Sir John and Sir Edmund.

Plate 69 Catterick. The arms of Pert at the tomb canopy apex.

Plate 70 Catterick. Scrope of Masham on the canopy.

Plate 71 Catterick. Pert impaling Scrope of Masham, indicating a marriage.

Plate 72 Lowthorpe. Ruined chancel.

Plate 73 Welwick. Interior face of the tomb.

Plate 74 Welwick. Exterior face of the tomb.

Plate 75 Welwick. Image niche with its Virgin and Child.

Plate 76 Welwick. South porch in relation to the tomb and south aisle.

Plate 77 Welwick. William de la Mare.

Section 6

Complexity and conclusions

6a The enigmatic priest's monument at Welwick

6a.i Introduction

Given the scope of what has been covered in this assessment of Yorkshire's effigies, it should be a daunting task to choose a single monument, as a worked example, to encapsulate the key ideas of the book and provide a fitting conclusion. Fortunately the extraordinary priest's tomb at Welwick more than satisfies this demanding requirement. It has already been aired under many different headings because it is by far the most complex and ambitious design of the corpus. Its interpretation greatly benefits from an archaeological approach, supported by its building history, sculptural comparisons, architectural context and the significance of its likely identification. The tomb demonstrates how a mason might respond to a patron's wishes, bringing together design, carving and finishing techniques to create a visual interpretation of abstract ideas. This case study interprets the puzzling evidence presented by this multi-faceted tomb and, in more ways than one, sheds light on the thinking behind its creation.

The parish church of Welwick, far out on the plain of Holderness, houses a truly remarkable monument. The effigy of a priest wearing mass vestments lies within a recess in the south wall below a large, elaborate canopy, which has been partly dismantled, revealing the window behind it (Plate 73). Located at the east end of the south aisle, close to the altar position and a piscina of related design, it dates from the mid-fourteenth century, like the aisle itself with its arcade and windows. The floor has been lowered, exposing the monument's irregularly coursed foundations. There are reasons for believing the canopy may not originally have been completely symmetrical but its interpretation is hampered by the severe damage, although some idea of its former height can be gauged from the side shafts. Most unusually, the tomb has a second face outside the church, which was also seemingly in conflict with the window and is correspondingly damaged. Two intimately associated features are a piscina immediately east of the tomb and a niche with a Virgin and Child over the south porch externally. These four elements provide the visual evidence. They pose multiple questions, including how the elements relate to one another, the way they were intended to function, when they were constructed and who might have been responsible.

6a.ii Description

The effigy depicts a priest with curled hair and a close-cropped beard, wearing mass vestments, with richly carved rose diaper on his amice, maniple and alb apparel, while individual flowers powder the chasuble and its lining (Fig. 276). His hands are at prayer and his head rests on a small cushion beneath a crocketed, ogee gablette. The surface within the gablette, beneath both cushion and effigy, is carved with a curvilinear pattern (Fig. 277). Akin to the blind tracery in the panels of the Beverley Minster reredos, it is recognisable as an abstraction from the chancel east window at Welwick, of which the sculptor must have been aware (Fig. 278). Consequently it assists with dating the effigy. This may just be an architectural adjunct to the gablette but it could also represent the decorated interior of a coffin, examples of which are known from excavations, such as the rare fabric-lined case discovered at Lichfield Cathedral (Gilchrist & Sloane 2005, p. 119) and numerous painted cists on the near Continent (Bergmans & Hans-Collas 2013). The figure is in low relief and contained, along with the gablette, within a tapered (coffin-like) box, no part transgressing its margins. It seems, despite the gablette over his head and the priest's open eyes,

Fig. 276 Welwick. Priest's effigy.

Fig. 277 Welwick. Priest with blind tracery behind him, matching the chancel east window.

Fig. 278 Welwick. Chancel east window showing matching tracery.

Fig. 279 Welwick. The stumps and sockets for candle prickets beside the priest.

Fig. 281 Welwick. Angel at the priest's feet.

Fig. 280 Welwick. Eagle for St. John the Evangelist.

Fig. 282 Welwick. Angels holding hands, a vault springer.

as though he is lying in an open coffin. This means, for instance, the angel sitting at his feet is not upright but laid back and the effigy's praying hands are depicted not palms together but almost flat on the breast. A comparable adaptation occurs on the bas-relief lady at Danby Wiske, where a design elsewhere carved in high relief has been modified to suit a shallow block (Fig. 18). The box is coffin-shaped in plan but both ends have a slight gable, making it effectively coped. Along the front edge are some iron pins (Fig. 279) from an original row of twelve, presumably candle prickets. Set within the box rim and on the front edge, are castellation-like features. Those on the inner edge may be functional rather than decorative, since they could have acted as seating for a hearse or cover. Such a cover would have created the appearance of a coffin with a coped lid like those depicted in a Remiet manuscript of 1390–1400 (Pierpont Morgan Library, MS M.526. ff. 043r & v, illustrated in Camille 1996, pp. 190, 191). It would have left the prickets exposed and still available for use whenever the monument was covered, *e.g.* for obits or other commemorative services.

The front face of the coffin is deeply cut with a full-length wave moulding, punctuated by medallions bearing Evangelist symbols (Fig. 280). The effigy is also accompanied by five angels. Two keep vigil by his shoulders like corbels for his gablette, two steady themselves above it holding the crocketing, looking anxiously about them, and a fifth has perched on the priest's feet (which lack a support). Even this unusually placed angel has spread wings, in tune with the animation of the others on the monument (Fig. 281). Immediately above the effigy, hovering in close attendance is a squadron of eight angels, acting as vault springers within the recess. Two hold hands in the centre of the back wall (Fig. 282) and there are three individuals at each end, one of each group with their right hand raised in blessing (Fig. 283).

These angels support a vault with ribs forming a pattern of two pairs of elongated Xs, which are starkly straight, in contrast with the sinuous curves elsewhere (Fig. 284). However, comparison of the two sides of the vault shows inconsistences in how the rib joints are handled, as if pieces were being carved freehand to suit, rather than in accordance with a strict plan. Similarly, the sides are awkwardly handled, not properly following the XX pattern. Between the springers each wall surface is carved into two panels, with those at the rear being much larger than those at the

Fig. 283 Welwick. Angel giving blessing.

Fig. 284 Welwick. Ribbed vault of tomb arch.

Fig. 285 Welwick. St. Margaret of Antioch slaying the dragon.

ends. The end panels have trefoil heads and V-shaped bases, like mouchettes stood on end, while the back panels are the only significant blank spaces on the whole monument and probably carried painted scenes.

The segmental arch framing the recess has two surviving angel label stops. Deeply moulded and encrusted with bubbly foliage crocketing, its sweeping curvilinear tracery culminates in a modest ogee, flanked by two mouchettes and just three cusps. Curiously, the arch is constructed independently from the vault behind it and there is even a small gap between the two (visible in Fig. 284). On the front under edge of the latter are four positions where carving has broken off. They are too complex to have simply been cusping but would make sense as locations for something, such as yet more angels. Here they would be seen immediately below and behind the tracery as if in free flight. It is also possible that two may have been carrying the priest's soul aloft. Such a dramatic arrangement would provide some justification for the unconventional construction.

Above the recess arch is a richly decorated but damaged canopy. Much of its centre and east side has been torn away to reveal more of the fourteenth-century window behind than would originally have been visible. The canopy is given a gable shape by two sloping ribs running through intermediate shafts, buttressing the central arch that rises above them. The whole composition is bounded by side shafts, topped by canopied standing figures, both mutilated but still recognisable as female saints, St Catherine (with her wheel) and St Margaret of Antioch (slaying the dragon, Fig. 285). The canopy is divided into sections by four smaller shafts and between them are two low canopied niches and an incomplete, tall, central arch. There is lavish crocketing with more bubbly foliage and every panel is filled with carving, comprising blind curvilinear tracery, foliage and angels with spread wings. Four carved shields on the wall above and west of the canopy, bear: (from the top) the emblems of the passion, England (three lions passant gardant), St Edward the Confessor and St Edmund King and Martyr. They seem an ad hoc arrangement and without a clear relationship to the monument, but their predominantly religious theme would be appropriate for the tomb of an ecclesiastic. They may have been rearranged

Fig. 286 Welwick. Tomb canopy, central position missing its image, with window behind.

Fig. 287 Welwick. Deep piercings above an angel in the tomb canopy.

when the eastern part of the canopy was dismantled and other lost features could have provided a more balanced composition.

The canopy's centrepiece was a moulded arch framing a pedestal-mounted image, flanked by traceried panelling filled with adoring angels (Fig. 286). The figure has gone, together with much of its setting, but four of the angels survive on the west and one on the east. The highest remaining portion of the arch curves forward and was of nodding form. The surface behind where the lower part of the figure would have been is plain and whitewashed. Its upper courses are brick infill and the lower part is probably also blocking but concealed by plaster. Above the fill, the inner side of the opening is smoothly finished, with some cusping and other remnants, possibly of tracery or more angels. So this area was open, enabling at least the upper part of the lost figure to be backlit with something akin to a corona.

A surprising and hidden feature of the canopy is the way it has been selectively pierced. As with the central image, its purpose seems to be the provision of back lighting for dramatic effect. Without taking the canopy apart, it is impossible to recapture the extent to which light was channelled. The disruption of the canopy and subsequent consolidation, coupled with centuries of neglect, have blocked the pathways but torchlight and gentle probing shows that places which appear just deeply cut are, in fact, through holes. The piercings are widely spread, beside angels, through tracery and around the crocketing. The largest are just above the angel on the extreme left of the canopy (Fig. 287) and more are beside the two diving angels in the ogee headed niches. The eastern has openings either side and under the body, while the other lacks the slot below (Fig. 288, 289). They seem to be also around the higher angels beside the central arch. The piercings vary in size and their orientation seems to respect their position relative to the window, with none at all furthest away from it. Their depth is difficult to assess but an inflexible probe can be inserted to a depth of greater than eight inches (20 cm). Their purpose must have been to create points and rays of light. This is corroborated by their distribution as they are more concentrated in the eastern half (in front of and close to the window), with the paths behind those to the west seeming to be angled towards the window. Much has been said about the use of paints and glazes on monuments, but at Welwick, they seem to have been painting with light. The position of the window, eastward and above the tomb, means its light would have been strongest in the early part of

Fig. 288 Welwick. Tomb canopy, eastern swooping angel.

Fig. 289 Welwick. Tomb canopy, western swooping angel.

Fig. 290 Welwick. Piscina of a design matching the tomb.

the day, the time when services are most likely. Since only part of the window was needed to light the canopy, some two thirds remained open to view and we should expect that this was filled with appropriate stained glass, creating a seamless vision.

As a consequence of partly dismantling the canopy and opening up the window, some brick repairs were made to damaged areas. The window was given a new sill, up to three courses deep, including the bricks visible in the central arch. Some of this may have been done because cavities associated with the light channels had been exposed. Mortar from the repairs has fallen into the cavities (visible with the aid of a torch), blocking off their original courses.

Immediately east of the tomb is a contemporary piscina, the bowl a projecting half octagon with a moulded under chamfer (Fig. 290). Its deeply moulded, pointed recess has chamfered cusping and its undamaged hood mould rested on two corbels. The left is lost and incongruously replaced by a brick but, although headless, sufficient remains of the other to show it was an angel matching those acting as corbels of the tomb arch (Figs 291, 292). This crucial evidence links the piscina directly with the tomb. The substitution of a brick for the missing corbel looks a clumsy repair, although it would have been less obtrusive if whitewashed. However, it is consistent with the other repairs and alterations made in brick throughout the church, probably in the late eighteenth century. The presence of a piscina and the monument's position suggest the east end of the south aisle was intended to function as a memorial chapel, perhaps even as a chantry. The fact that no documentary evidence survives does not

Fig. 291 Welwick. Piscina angel corbel.

Fig. 292 Welwick. Tomb canopy angel corbel.

mean that one was not intended. It may simply never have been implemented or the records lost.

Outside, the tomb is truncated and partly rebuilt (Plate 74). A gabled outshut accommodates a shallow recess flanked by short shafts with pinnacles, which spring from extremely weathered angel bust corbels, the eastern carrying a scroll. The pinnacles are not symmetrical, the western being set at an angle against the buttress while the eastern stands foursquare. This is capped by a gabled block in good condition while its western counterpart is badly eroded. This may be because the roof drained down this side of the buttress over a long period (a new rainwater-head and down spout currently carry it well to the west) or, the eastern cap may be a replacement.

At first sight, the wall to the west of the window seems a clumsy repair of randomly assembled stones. However, it is actually cleverly joggled ashlar, which is so carefully fitted and closely jointed it can only be original (Fig. 293). The curved pattern mirrors the location of the canopy inside and it may originally have been hidden as the design of the exterior upper sections is unknown. An iron staple almost halfway up the western window jamb and another, somewhat lower, in the eastern are likely to have been fixings for lost elevated elements. Such fixing points suggest the upper part of the canopy stood independently, forward of the window and requiring metal stays. It may have been a delicate structure of pierced work that would not have prevented light reaching the window and may have mirrored the internal construction. Such a structure might readily decay and eventually have been dismantled for safety. The composition is currently topped by the remains of an embattled gable, now mutilated and disordered. The two western blocks are in situ since they are coursed with the joggled masonry of the wall. There is too much crenellation to have come from the simple outline suggested by them. Displaced blocks (almost twenty in number) have been packed together as infill below the window and their original configuration remains uncertain.

The outshut's focus is an image niche (Fig. 294). Its shaft, bracket and canopy remain, with the offset moulding at the base of the wall carried up, to create an emphatic outline around it. The missing figure was separate and its iron fixing pin set in a lead plug remains. The outline preserved by a plain backing area, suggests it was probably seated. It was encircled by Evangelist symbols, echoing their representation alongside the effigy inside, set against quatrefoil diaper. Although its regularity is masked by partial rebuilding, decay and over-pointing, this backdrop is still much as intended, just lacking a little of the diaper and most of St Mark's lion. The right jamb of the niche incorporates a stray curved piece of moulding but the left shows the original intent.

A noticeable feature of the tomb's exterior is the use of distinctive, pink Roman cement. It can be seen in the more disturbed areas, notably in the fill below the west corner of the window and around one of the Evangelist symbols in the central niche. It can also be detected in other joints and patches, which have been subsequently over-pointed with a different, grey cement or mortar. Without removal of the later pointing, the extent and role of the Roman cement is unclear. It may have been applied as weather proofing because of its water-resistant properties, perhaps some time after the alterations to the tomb were made. Roman cement was patented in 1796 (Clifton-Taylor 1972, p. 367) but there was significant use in Yorkshire by 1808 (Davey 1961, p. 105) and

Fig. 293 Welwick. Tomb exterior, joggled masonry.

even local manufacture on the Humber by 1821. However, the disturbance to the tomb may predate Roman cement coming into use, see below (*6a.iv*).

The miniature canopy is much more damaged, shorn of its pendants, pinnacles and any finial, capped off by what appears to be an over-mortared stone tray but may be seating for the upper stage. Made from a single hollowed block, the canopy underside is intricately carved into a complex ribbed vault, the webs pierced and cusped, and it seems the gablette's exterior arches and tracery were also pierced (Fig. 295). The result is that a solid block of stone has been rendered able to transmit light in multiple directions. Lumps of Roman cement can be seen on and behind the capping, in the roof of the cavity above the vault and blocking some of the apertures. The rear of the central chamber has a semi-circular cut-out (now blocked) that could have connected with the back of the internal canopy.

Two bays west of the tomb is a post-medieval brick porch, which is the main entrance to the church, since there is no west door (Plate 76). It incorporates a doorway and image niche from a demolished medieval two storey precursor. The aisle masonry above the current porch is of rubble rather than ashlar, its extent suggesting the medieval porch was no wider than its replacement. In the western part of this area is a high level doorway (also visible inside) blocked by brickwork of similar character and bonding to the porch walls. It seems to have given access to a lost upper level but was not related to the unobtrusive ground level door just west of the porch. In the early nineteenth century this gave access to the school room, which had been created by

Fig. 294 Welwick. Tomb exterior, image position.

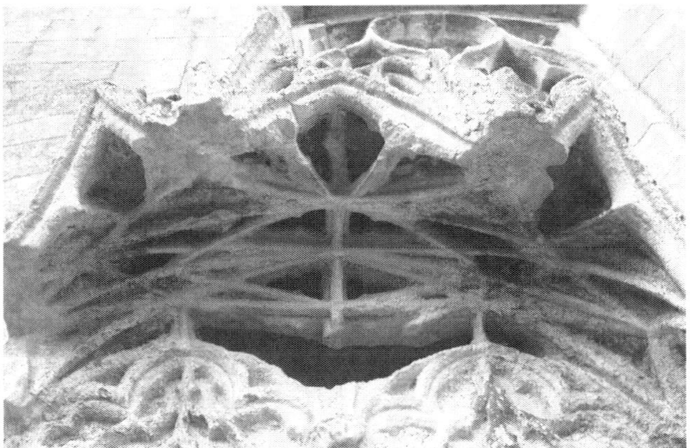

Fig. 295 Welwick. Tomb exterior, piercing of vault above the image position.

partitioning off the west end of the south aisle, an area still delineated by a platform of brick and tile. The close affinity between the doorway/niche and the tomb, together with the seeming integration of the lost upper porch structure with the ashlar walls of the south aisle, strongly suggest that the medieval porch, the aisle and the tomb were all components of the same ambitious scheme.

Sitting atop the porch gable, there is an image niche comprising a pedestal and canopy housing a contemporary Virgin and Child, the church being dedicated to St Mary (Plate 75). Structurally and conceptually, it is of a piece with the doorway below. The hood mould does not join at the apex but turns upwards to form the shafts of the niche above. The concept of a moulding rising to embrace a niche was also used on the exterior face of the tomb. Above the door

Fig. 296 Welwick. Porch niche, Virgin and Child.

apex, the uprights clasp a rose diapered block that fills the space below the image bracket, which has a band of foliage spilling across the side shafts. The Virgin has lost her head but appears to be of the right scale for the niche, although its base seems too large for its pedestal. However, the front edge of the underside is carved with a hollow chamfer, punctuated by small eroded devices that appear to be four petal flowers. The under chamfer dies away at the sides so that the width becomes the same as the pedestal and its front edge was meant to be seen. Consequently the sculpture must be in situ, tailored to its position over the entrance where people arriving would see the underside as they entered the church. The figures are extremely eroded and encrusted with lichen but some features are still discernible, such as the undercutting of the Virgin's left arm (behind the Child), the pattern of drapery over her legs and her cloak's double cord with its large, openwork, central buckle (Fig. 296). This buckle is strongly reminiscent of that worn by the shield-bearing spandrel lady of the Percy Tomb in Beverley Minster, another version of which is worn (without the cloak and double cord) by St Catherine on the Welwick tomb canopy. The drapery across the knees and legs of the Welwick Virgin can also be parallelled on the Percy Tomb, for instance on three figures of Christ. All have their knees apart with a sharp 'V' shape between and a strong pattern of splayed linear folds emanating from each knee.

Fig. 297 Welwick. Pierced vault above the porch niche.

Structurally, the niche is a stack of blocks intended to be coursed in with the original masonry of the porch but now looking incongruously lumpy. However, the structure is sufficiently coherent to understand the intent. The top is truncated, capped off with a block of bricks rendered to masquerade as a stone, under what looks like the stump of a small-scale gable cross that may be a remnant of the original. Inside the niche, one block is carved with four angels, close kin to those on the tomb, flying above the Virgin. Overhead is another ribbed, cusped and pierced vault similar to that of the tomb exterior, carried on rosette springers (Fig. 297). It is hollow and daringly pierced in two directions: through the little gable spandrels on its front face and underneath, where every web of the vault is open. Like the exterior tomb niche, it becomes a net of stone capable of transmitting light, which must surely be the purpose. It is difficult to believe that such elaborate measures were taken simply to utilise daylight. However, in twilight or at night, it would have been a different matter. A stone trough protrudes behind the vault (Fig. 298), carried on two brackets that belong to the intermediate course between the angels and the vault. In the porch's earlier, two storey form, it would have been accessible from the upper level, allowing a lamp to be set behind the open fretwork of the canopy. Its filtered illumination would provide points of light to shine above the Virgin: a real equivalent of the star-painted canopies over roods and other statuary. It must have been a striking feature in the darkness of Holderness, perhaps lit for obits, for vigils, for the church's dedication feast or for All Souls. This arrangement helps explain the exterior tomb niche, as its pierced vault must similarly have been intended to function in the dark. The now blocked semi-circular aperture in the rear wall above the vault, probably allowed light through from a lamp in a comparable light box, accessible from inside the church. This cavity is likely to have been lost or blocked in the dismantling and consolidation of the interior canopy.

Fig. 298 Welwick. Porch, possible lamp position behind pierced vault.

6a.iii Fourteenth-century building work

Before considering other aspects of the tomb, it is important to understand it in the context of the building's history. The church at Welwick was substantially rebuilt in the fourteenth century (Pev:ER 1995, p. 743). What survives is largely the result of this campaign, including both nave arcades and most of the windows, although traces of earlier phases remain. Rough masonry of local cobbles remains in the tower itself and locally elsewhere. The lack of a stair is evidence that the tower was not rebuilt in the fourteenth century, necessitating a substantial wooden ladder (dated 1846). Before the fourteenth-century campaign, the building must have been substantially of the previous century but some of the structure may be earlier, since a church is recorded in Domesday (VCH:ER:V, p. 146).

The coherence of the fourteenth-century work is apparent in the window tracery and the good limestone ashlar. The south aisle windows east of the porch have the same tracery: a relatively simple curvilinear design (Plate 76), with the east window more elaborate but identical to the chancel side windows, indicating all this was part of a single scheme. The tracery of the large, five light, chancel east window is clearly related, although more elaborate and showing a consciousness of the Perpendicular, which should mean the work was completed after about 1350 (Fig. 278). Fortunately there is documentary evidence relating to this final phase, which is likely to have been underway in or soon after 1358 when Thomas de la Mare allocated ten marks in his will for the renewal of the great window of the chancel at Welwick (*Test. Ebor*. I, pp. 68–70, 'Item ecclesiae de Welwik, pro renovatione magnae fenestrae cancelli ejusdem, x marcas'). Ten marks was £6 13s 6d, convertible to £3,323 at the 2017 rate (http://www.nationalarchives.gov.uk/currency, calculated March 2018), probably insufficient to cover the full cost of the window and its glazing. In 1338, the glazing alone of the west windows of York Minster nave aisles (nos 30 & 36) cost eleven marks each (French & O'Connor 1987, p. 4). Since these windows are probably smaller, and certainly simpler, than Welwick's, the bequest must be a contribution to a project already in hand. The proportions, rough walling and clasping buttresses of the chancel suggest the windows were a modernisation of an existing structure. The chancel itself seems likely to have been built in three stages, the masonry of the eastern half (lower parts) and of the east wall being substantially different in character from that to the west. The upper masonry on the north and south sides is different again and may indicate a heightening of the walls, as suggested by a change of roof line visible on the exterior of the east nave gable. This may have been done when the new windows were installed as their heads lie within the heightened zone. The residual lancet and short clasping buttresses suggest a thirteenth-century date, at least for the last pre-refurbishment phase.

Some post-medieval fabric repairs have been made in brick, see above. They include the new sill for the window adjacent to the tomb, blocking the priest's door, rebuilding the porch and blocking the upper doorway, a new parapet for the south aisle and reconstructing the westernmost window head in the north aisle. Some indication of when the medieval porch was replaced is an 1837 reference to the present porch being 'a comparatively modern addition, from the connecting brick work' (de Sawtry 1837, p. 13). Brick has been a relatively common building material in Holderness for many centuries, so its use cannot be taken as conclusive of a single campaign. It is, nevertheless, suggestive of repairs and alterations in the late eighteenth century, when they may have been necessary because the church had become dilapidated.

Little attention has hitherto been paid to the complex design of the Welwick tomb. Poulson saw it as a badly reassembled collection of disturbed material and only Bob Petch (1981) seems to have appreciated some of its intricacies. He described the tomb in more detail than anyone else, seeing the clever and subtle hand of a master mason in some aspects of the design, in which he claimed to have detected a 3, 4, 5 rhythm. He was also the first to suggest that light from the window was deliberately channelled to enhance the focal image. We share Petch's regard for the cleverness embodied in this unique monument. One of the keys to understanding the Welwick tomb is its relationship to the adjacent window. The present arrangement appears clumsy, with the window only properly visible because major sections of the canopy (inside and out) have been torn down. This has been interpreted as evidence the tomb was brought from elsewhere. The current orthodox view holds the tomb to be a later insertion into an existing wall 'blocking the early C14 S E window of the S aisle which when later unblocked destroyed the top left section of the monument' (Pev:ER 1995, p. 743). However, a range of features confirm the tomb must be in situ. It is sited next to a closely related piscina and in an ideal position to benefit from services at the related altar. When the floor was lowered, its original foundations were exposed and the curious masonry adjoining the window externally is undisturbed. Crucially, the tomb has been carefully designed to utilise the window as a light source for dramatic effect. Consequently, the tomb, window and aisle must be regarded as inseparable components of a unified composition.

6a.iv History of the tomb

Welwick's geographically isolated position must always have deterred antiquaries from visiting the church and the tomb seems not to have attracted attention until the early nineteenth century, when it is mentioned by Thomas Thompson (1822, p. 261) as unpublished. He added that the shields on the wall would have remained 'covered in dirt and foul whitewashing, if they had not been cleansed and brought to light by the antiquarian zeal of Mr Child of Easington' (p. 259). A very creditable drawing by Mr Child of the tomb's north elevation was published by Poulson (1841, II, frontispiece) showing the tomb, window and piscina very much as they are today (Fig. 299). Only minor losses have occurred, such as the up-raised wing of the highest angel and some small details from the side shafts. Poulson and other nineteenth-century commentators believed the tomb had been brought from Burstall Priory (*e.g.* Baines 1822/3, II, p. 398; Allen 1828/31, IV, p. 315), which has been lost to the Humber but lay just south of Skeffling, a neighbouring parish. It was presumably thought too grand for a parish church. The Burstall Priory tradition remained current (*e.g.* Crossley 1921, p. 36 n.) but no basis for this supposition has been discovered. The tomb's significant constructional aspects have been under-appreciated but its close relationship with the piscina is by itself sufficient to demonstrate the implausibility of the tomb being brought from elsewhere, particularly in the post-Reformation period.

Fig. 299 Welwick. Tomb, drawing from Poulson.

6a.v Identification

The supposed association with Burstall provoked wild speculation about the identity of the person commemorated, exacerbated by the then widely held view the effigy was female. Poulson himself, overlooking the priest's vestments and closely cropped beard (Plate 77), described him as 'an effigy of a woman, in flowing robes' (1841, II, p. 511). Bilson (1909) presented a carefully reasoned assessment of the possibilities, concluding that William de la Mare, Provost of Beverley (d. 1360) was the most likely. Goldberg (1984, p. 71) rejected Bilson's identification, proposing instead William of Beverley, rector of Welwick 1317–27 but still living in 1335. However, such an expensive tomb, coupled with a major modernisation scheme, would have been beyond the purse of the average parish clergy. More recent assessments have favoured William de la Mare or possibly his brother Thomas, Canon of York (d. 1358) who left the money for the east window. Thomas' candidature was also based on the assertion he was Vicar of Welwick (Pev:ER 1995, p. 744) but this seems without foundation and, as he specifically requested burial in York Minster next to the tomb of Archbishop Melton (*Test. Ebor.* I, p. 68), the monument is most unlikely to be his. Pevsner mentions both

(Pev:ER 1995, p. 744) but subsequent writers have favoured William (Dawton 2000, p. 144; Saul 2009, p. 159; Badham 2011, p. 49).

In the medieval period, Welwick (both the advowson of the church and the manor) was owned by Beverley Minster and retained as the personal prerogative of the Provost, lying at the heart of one of the Provost's estates (VCH:ER:V, p. 142; McDermid 1990, map facing p. 1). It was the Provostry's primary sheep-rearing centre (McDermid 1980, I, p. 56). Since the Provost was *de facto* lord of the manor, the monument is likely to commemorate one of them. The only Provosts dying in office in the fourteenth century were Robert Aberwick in 1306, Nicholas Huggate in 1338, William de la Mare in 1360 and Adam de Lymbergh *c.* 1373 (McDermid 1980, II, pp. A19–22). Nicholas Huggate was buried in the Minster and since the work at Welwick dates from the mid-fourteenth century, Aberwick is too early and Lymbergh too late, leaving William de la Mare as the only candidate. It seems likely that he was responsible for all the fourteenth-century work at Welwick.

William de la Mare took office in 1338 and remained in post until he passed the Provostship to his relative Richard de Ravenser on 4th October 1360, within a month of his death, presumably to ensure that the position stayed in the family (McDermid 1980, II, pp. A21–22). William's career has been detailed by McDermid (1990, pp. 8–9; 1980, II, pp. A21–22). He was part of the great network of Yorkshire clergy families which included the de la Mares, the Meltons, the Thoresbys, the Ravensers and the Ferribys (Grassi 1970). He was briefly Treasurer of York Minster, a King's Clerk and worked for Archbishops Melton and Thoresby. He was also a canon of both Southwell and York, holding (successively) the prebends of South Newbald, Wilton and Ulleskelf, which he retained until his death. It was William's brother, Thomas de la Mare who bequeathed money for the Welwick window. He had been an Oxford academic (Emden 1957, I, p. 562) before spending twenty years as a Canon and Prebendary of York where he was Sacrist of the chapel of St Mary and the Holy Angels (Jones 1963, pp. 84, 88). The two must have been quite close. The bequest for the window is the first item after the provisions for his burial. He also left much plate to William, the first of the personal bequests and probably the most valuable. A minor point, perhaps illustrative of their relationship, is the bequest to a more distant relative of a horse called Morell of Welwick. This suggests that not only were the brothers close but they also kept in contact to such practical effect that a horse bred on one brother's manor was owned by the other. On 13th March 1360/61, six months after becoming Provost, William de la Mare's successor Richard de Ravenser impropriated the church of Welwick to the Provostry of Beverley (Bilson 1909). Everson and Stocker have recently identified a pattern of chancel enrichment by wealthy incumbents immediately prior to impropriation (Everson & Stocker 2014) and it may be that Welwick is another example, intended not only as a setting for William's own tomb but an enriched gift to his minster at Beverley, the deed finally enacted by de Ravenser acting as his proxy.

William de la Mare came from an interesting background: a family closely associated with the East Riding aspiring gentry and leading craftsmen. He was related to two Archbishops of York (Melton and Thoresby), together with other leading churchmen, including two Provosts of Beverley, Nicholas de Huggate (a King's Clerk) and Richard de Ravenser (Prebendary of York and King's Clerk). Provost William's relations also encompassed leading craftsmen – another brother, Richard, was Goldsmith to Beverley Minster while his father may well have been William de la Mare, Master Mason to Beverley Minster *c.* 1325–1335 (Pacey 2008, p. 84; Harvey 1984, p. 196). The next Master Mason at Beverley, William de Malton of Huggate, may also have been a relation (Pacey 2008, p. 84; Leach 1903, pp. 2, 3). William de Malton was presented by Nicholas de Huggate and admitted by the Chapter as Master Mason on 28th October 1335, on the death of William de la Mare the mason (Leach 1903, p. 114). The new Master Mason and his patron must have been quite close since in his will (proved July 1338), Huggate left de Malton a horse and a piece of plate with a cover (Leach 1903, p. 124). Huggate's is an orderly will and this was the first of the personal bequests, ahead of his sister and niece. In July 1340 Provost William de la Mare similarly organised the adoption of his brother Richard as Goldsmith to the Minster (Leach 1903, pp. 133–34). So Provost de la Mare seems to have been the son of a master mason and the brother of both a goldsmith and an academic. He was probably related to the then master mason at Beverley and through his associations with Beverley, York, Southwell and the court, exposed to some of the finest craftsmanship in the country. At Beverley, he will have seen the completion of the reredos and the creation of the Percy Tomb so it is little wonder that he sought the assistance of these craftsman when he was rebuilding the Provostry church at Welwick and planning his own tomb as part of that work.

6a.vi Contexts

In recent years, the Welwick memorial has prompted comment and speculation. Bob Petch (1981) and Jeremy Goldberg (1984) suggested a common source for Welwick, the canopied tomb at Bainton and the Percy Tomb in Beverley Minster. Bainton is a most interesting monument but entirely lacks the quality of the Welwick and Percy Tombs, it is also earlier in date. However, the relationship between Welwick and work at Beverley has long been recognised (Poulson 1841, II, p. 510) and research by Nicholas Dawton has indicated that Welwick was carved by one of the members of the team that created the Percy

Tomb. He identified St Catherine in particular as the work of the 'Annunciation Master' (Dawton 1983, p. 127; see also Dawton 1989, Figs 1 & 2 for stone by stone identification of this sculptor's work at Beverley). The Annunciation Master worked at Beverley just on the Percy Tomb, creating a high proportion of the distinctive bas-relief spandrel carving and many of the cusp-mounted flying angels.

It must be acknowledged that the Percy Tomb and Welwick appear quite different. One has a soaring, freestanding, arch and the other is wall mounted with a low segmental arch; one housed a tomb chest with a monumental brass and the other has a bas-relief effigy depicted in an open coffin. The Percy Tomb has a significant secular display of people and heraldry, while Welwick exclusively uses religious imagery. Much of this may reflect the gulf in patronage between a great tomb of the lordly Percy family located in the place of honour in a major collegiate church and the memorial of an ecclesiastical official in a side chapel of a parish church. However, they share low-set recess floors and elaborate rib vaults, both incorporate a myriad of angels in their decorative schemes and there is much to compare in the detail. It is not only the figure of St Catherine that can be compared to the Percy Tomb, the St Margaret of Antioch image can also be related (Fig. 285). Her dragon has two heads and wings with a spiky, cusped outline. It lacks a knobbly backbone but has an unusual armadillo-like body of large overlapping scales. A dragon with the same characteristics can be seen at the feet of St Michael on the south side at Beverley (Fig. 300), also the work of the Annunciation Master, so this man carved both the female saints at Welwick. The large open cloak fastenings of St Katherine and the porch Virgin, with their thin and widely separated cords, resemble more than anything the cloak fastening of the Beverley spandrel lady, again a work of the Annunciation Master.

Fig. 300 Beverley Minster. St Michael slaying the dragon on Percy Tomb.

While the Welwick tomb has exuberance and innovation in large measure, it lacks the architectural integrity of the Beverley designer and this can best be appreciated by comparing the ribbed vaults. At Beverley the pattern is somewhat restrained but very elegant, whereas the Welwick vault, despite being smaller, is more complicated and less successful with some awkward junctions. It looks more angular than elegant, as though a skilful carver has taken charge in the absence of the master designer (Fig. 284). The curvilinear blind tracery at Welwick also finds comparison at Beverley but more with the panels at the back of the reredos than with the Percy Tomb. However, there is commonality between the two tombs in the employment of angels. Dawton (1989) lists sixty-one angels on the Percy Tomb canopy, including three seraphim and the Archangel in the Annunciation scene. Eight are described as 'flying downwards' and two as blessing, one with both hands. There are thirty-three angels surviving on the much smaller Welwick tomb, including those with the effigy and outside, while at least another twelve have probably been lost. This would give a grand total of forty-five, or three-quarters of the number on the much larger Percy Tomb, which has two similarly decorated faces. Perhaps significantly, both flocks of angels include just two with a hand raised in blessing.

Given Welwick's close association with the work at Beverley, it is important to understand that context. Phillip Lindley (2007, pp. 176–80) provides a detailed analysis of the dating evidence for the Beverley reredos and the Percy Tomb, including a description of the interface between them. He concluded that the reredos was probably begun as early as *c.* 1325 and was complete by *c.* 1340. The Percy Tomb followed shortly after, *c.* 1345–50, on the eve of the Black Death. So the likely completion date for the reredos and the construction of the Percy Tomb both fall within the Provostship of William de la Mare.

There are also telling architectural parallels between Beverley and Welwick. The blank tracery of the panels below the shrine platform of the reredos (Fig. 301) has as its 'central motif two mouchettes clasping an onion-shaped quatrefoil' (Pacey 2008, pp. 87–88). This motif, although with a somewhat less onion-shaped quatrefoil, forms the tracery of the chancel side windows (Fig. 302) at Welwick, together with the east window of the south aisle. The simpler two-light windows of the south aisle wall lose the mouchettes but retain the same quatrefoil. A second motif highlighted by Pacey on the Beverley reredos tracery is 'a curve that turns through a right angle', effectively a depressed ogee. This too appears at Welwick, forming the head of the priest's doorway (Fig. 302), which is integral with the sill of a new window and again, on the canopy

Fig. 301 Beverley Minster. Reredos blind tracery.

Fig. 302 Welwick. Priest's door, its head integral with a chancel window.

of the priest's tomb (beneath the diving angels). Pacey attributes the design of the reredos tracery to the 'new man' and goes on also to credit him with the Percy Tomb and the north aisle, including the windows. Many commentators on the architecture and sculpture of Beverley Minster note the hand of a new master apparent in the work of the 1330s and 1340s, including the completion of the reredos and the construction of the Percy Tomb. Pacey (2008) identifies him as William de Malton (see above) and in this he follows many others, including Harvey (1984, p. 193) and Petch (1981), both also attributing the Welwick tomb's design to de Malton. He held the position of Master Mason at Beverley until after 1340 (Pacey 2008, p. 94) but subsequently he disappears. Unfortunately there is a lack of documentary evidence charting his career, the best account being that assembled by Petch based on his observations of masons' marks and sculptural style. However, the close association of the architecture and sculpture at Welwick with broadly contemporary work at Beverley means that the architect responsible for the building and tomb design was almost certainly William de Malton, while the carving of both porch and tomb sculpture involved the Annunciation Master. The Welwick tomb should be viewed as the product of William de la Mare's experience and connections.

The arrival of the Black Death may perhaps have been influential (*5a.v*). The reaction of some to the pestilence was to leave major centres and sit it out in rural retreats. For instance, John Grandisson, the Bishop of Exeter spent the duration at his Chudleigh palace, while back in Exeter it seems that the building work on the cathedral was halted. Perhaps coincidentally, it was at this time that work by masons from the Cathedral seemingly appear in areas far away from the city. The tomb of the bishop's sister-in-law, who died in 1347, at Much Marcle (Herefordshire) was made by one or more men from the Exeter west front team (Gittos 2017b), to be followed by others in the same region. It is conceivable that de la Mare, in making his own tomb at Welwick, funded work and refuge for one or more of the Minster team.

6a.vii Interpretation

Angels are the dominant visual feature, dozens darting and swooping throughout the whole monument. They fly in adoration about the lost figure in the centre of the gable, necks craning to see the principal image (Fig. 303). More attend the effigy and some probably hovered in free space from the outer rim of the vault. They appear to be watching over the dead man to keep his soul safe. The flock is concentrated inside but others can be seen outside the building, performing similar functions. The question is what, iconographically, is signified by the depiction of so many angels at both Welwick and Beverley. The proportion and use of the angels is comparable on both tombs, although the difference in scale means they are much more noticeable at Welwick. The numbers go far beyond the normal escort of two or four, to carry or accompany the soul to heaven. One possibility is a depiction of Paradise or the heavenly host, another is a reference to the funeral services or the Office of

Fig. 303 Welwick. Tomb canopy, adoring angels.

the Dead and a third is a narrative portraying the salvation of the soul. Taking the internal face of the tomb, the focus of the canopy was the lost central image, surrounded by light (perhaps the 'light of light' of the Creed) and by a host of adoring angels. This surely must have been a representation of the Godhead in some guise: perhaps a figure of Christ such as on the Percy Tomb. Petch (1981) had 'little doubt that a figure of Christ in Majesty was intended'. Rays of light surrounding such an image would have enhanced its message and its dominance, corresponding with frequent references in scripture and other religious sources. For instance:

> The people who walked in darkness have seen a great light. A light has risen for the inhabitants of the region of the shadow of death. (Isaiah 9. 2)
> You are the light of the world. (Matthew 5. 14)
> And the light shines in the darkness, and the darkness did not comprehend it. (John 1. 5)
> He was a burning and shining light. So you were willing, at the time, to exult in his light. (John 5. 35)

Considered in this way, the gable seems like a recreation of Paradise, perhaps even a vision from *Revelations*:

> And all the Angels were standing around the throne, with the elders and the four living creatures. And they fell upon their faces in view of the throne, and they worshipped God … (7. 11)

However, two angels, travelling with points of light, follow a different trajectory, diving vertically down with great purpose towards the effigy (Figs 288, 289). These must be angels despatched to collect the soul of the deceased. Nowhere now on the tomb is there a depiction of the soul borne up in a cloth but two of the lost angels hanging above the effigy may have performed this function. Lower down, the angels appear more as guardians, surrounding the body to ward off the unseen demons attempting to snatch his soul, both at the time of his death and on its journey heavenward. Sheingorn (1995) drew attention to the Commendations, prayers recited at the time of death and repeated several times at different stages of the preparation and burial, including the Absolutions of the Dead (and also said at anniversaries). The latter was translated in Barnwell, Cross & Ryecraft (1995, p. 167) as:

> Bring help, O saints of God, speed, angels of the Lord, bearing his soul, offering it up in the sight of the most high. May Christ who called you receive you, and may angels lead you to the bosom of Abraham.

Taken together, the aisle face of the tomb can be read as a salvation narrative, the effigy a realisation of the moment of death, the soul guarded by angels awaiting the arrival of those despatched from on high to bring the soul up to Paradise, depicted as the Deity surrounded by a court of angels. The correlation with the Commendations has been noted above but the correspondence goes further than that. Relevant passages in the Requiem mass (all from Barnwell, Cross & Ryecraft 2005) include:

> And so with angels and archangels, with thrones and dominations and with all the company of the heavenly host we sing a hymn of glory … (pp. 154–55)
> Eternal rest, grant them, O Lord; and let perpetual light shine upon them (p. 148)

The phrases 'lux aeterna' and 'lux perpetua' occur repeatedly through the service. So the internal face can be read on three levels: illustration of the obsequies, salvation narrative and depiction of Paradise.

The meaning of the external face is even more problematic as it has suffered so much but with the internal iconography in mind, it would be unwise to expect it had anything other than a carefully considered message. The use of light in the image canopy raises the question of whether, how and under what circumstances this may have been used effectively. Since the canopy light of both this and the porch Virgin would only be really effective in twilight or at night, it must be possible that one or both played a role in the All Souls rites. The use of exterior light calls to mind the French lanterns of the dead (at least one survives in this country, at Bisley in Gloucestershire), the lamp positions in some churchyard cross bases and also, occasionally, on the outside of the churches themselves. Their use has been little studied but the lit statues at Welwick may belong to the same tradition.

6a.viii Summing up

William de la Mare, Provost of Beverley who died in 1360, was commemorated by an effigy on a low plinth under a rich canopy, amidst the results of his own building scheme, in the south aisle of the remote church of Welwick in Holderness. At some time, possibly in the eighteenth century, part of the tomb canopy both inside and out was broken away, freeing the window behind. This is likely to have been done at the same time the south porch was rebuilt in brick and the priest's door to the chancel was blocked by similar looking bricks. The work was done with complete disregard for the monument, although the stonework has been tidied up, probably to make it weatherproof. Outside, the damage was sufficiently drastic to lose much of the original design. Internally, the central figure (very likely to have been an image of Christ) has been lost and other sculpture damaged, although what remains is in remarkably good condition. The effigy is unusually portrayed as if lying in a shallow coffin with many angels in close attendance. The edges seem to have been designed to support a cover and the front had prickets for candles. The tomb may be unique amongst English monuments in the extent of the scheme continued outside the church. Even more remarkable are the controlled light paths through carefully constructed orifices in the canopy inside and through the gablette externally. In its mutilated state it is very difficult to understand how this was meant to work but inside, shafts of light would have shone from particular parts of the canopy, adding drama to the angels and providing a corona for the central figure. This utilised daylight from the window behind but outside, artificial light sources must have been provided to send shafts of light during darkness through the fully perforated gablettes both on the outside of the tomb and above the Virgin and Child over the porch. Behind the latter there appears to be a stone tray to support such a light, which would have been within the upper level of the medieval porch.

It is clear that this truly innovative memorial and the related porch sculpture were created by part of the team responsible for the Percy Tomb in Beverley Minster. Like Beverley, this tomb incorporates a panoply of angels performing many different functions but it breaks with convention, using a totally original design, narrative iconography, technical complexity and daring execution. At Welwick, we have a visionary tomb commemorating a person who it is possible to name (William de la Mare), which includes extraordinary carving by a man whose work can be seen elsewhere (the 'Annunciation Master') and designed by a known architect (William de Malton). This is indeed a rare combination.

Welwick illustrates many of the main themes of this book, particularly the value of an archaeological approach in discovering how the different parts of the tomb were intended to work and the way it relates to the rest of the building. By demonstrating the monument's integration with the church, it has been possible to dispel the myth of its being brought from elsewhere. The stylistic parallels with Beverley Minster and the Percy Tomb are very strong, providing a crucial link in Welwick's interpretation. The study demonstrates the depth of thought that might be invested in creating an effigial monument and how the historical background can be used to identify those who collaborated in realising such a complex project.

6b Concluding remarks

This observational study has evolved from church visits in the early 1970s into a systematic survey. Its long gestation has had many benefits, amongst them the chance to make repeated visits in differing conditions, each offering fresh observations and thoughts. The new insights have deepened understanding, especially of the more difficult cases, often based on comparisons found elsewhere. A prime example of something not immediately obvious is the recognition that Darrington originally held a lance. This grew from failing to understand how his missing hands could have been at prayer, realising that his right hand held something and then locating evidence of its fixings. This archaeological stand point has led to revolutions in perception, as when careful examination at Nunnington found traces of painted heraldry including gold leaf, transforming the rather dull-looking effigy to a glittering knight with a golden surcoat. Close attention to the tomb structure at West Tanfield revealed that the seemingly coherent monument is nothing of the sort. Created for a single alabaster effigy, the chest was later modified to accommodate a second before its hearse was added. The message is to keep on looking and asking questions of the evidence, not settling for initial impressions.

Awareness of context is also a vital component. One is the building itself, since monuments can be just one component of a larger scheme. This ranges from adjuncts to the tomb itself, such as the Aldbrough great bascinet, to major building schemes as at Goldsborough and Welwick. Whatever the scale, they can be key to understanding the tomb. Another context is the people commemorated, their families and historical circumstances. This type of evidence has made it possible to dispel the myths that, for example, prevented Bainton being recognised as commemorating Sir John de Mauley and Catterick as Sir William Pert. A third is the contemporary scene: what people wore, architectural trends and an awareness of anachronisms. The *c*. 1300 Scarborough knight's unusual cap, straggly hair, bushy moustache and goatee beard can be accounted for by his being recut, at a date betrayed by the seventeenth-century collar. Similarly, the lion masks on the Temple Church knight's sword belt, which are unlike any other carved by his sculptor, can be shown to be due to a nineteenth-century restoration.

Effigial monuments were expensive, only chosen by the few and often commissioned when families were in transition, so it is unsurprising that many were planned with great care. The Bainton and Welwick tombs, built close to relevant altars, are cases in point. The evidence suggests that little was done that lacked meaning and, although much detail has been lost, it is possible to recover something of what the medieval eye would have read with far more understanding. Supported by members of the religious community (Bedale, Thornhill and Sprotbrough), attended by meditating women (Norton, Goldsborough and Womersley) and safeguarded by angels (Birdsall and West Tanfield), they wield swords, shields and even a crosier against the forces of evil. Their souls make their way to Paradise escorted by cohorts of angels (Welwick) to seek rest for eternity on high (York Minster).

In drawing this study to a conclusion it is worth bearing in mind this as a statistically valid sample of English effigies of the period. Almost all of the effigies were made within the study area and it appears that only a few were imported for special reasons, perhaps for prestige or if there was no source of supply at the time. Archbishop de Gray's effigy, like the alabaster Roucliffe figures at Pickering, were the best available at the time and Prince William of Hatfield in York Minster must have been commissioned by the royal family. Most of the effigies are carved from local stone, patrons frequently commissioning whoever was available, rather than calling on an established mason. Consequently, most are individual pieces, unrelated to each other – a pattern also found with grave covers. The few that can be related to each other, betray the work of a single hand or source. Some, like Series E confined to the far north east in the 1340s, found only a restricted, local market, while others supplied a wider clientele but none lasted more than a craftsman's working lifetime. The best, such as Series C, active across the 1330s and into the 1340s, set a high standard as objects of beauty. The A/B sculptor working in the years before and after 1300, was one of the finest of his age. What he achieved is of the first rank, imbued with such knowledge and skill that his carvings warrant a research study in their own right.

Something of this can be appreciated from the front cover illustration showing the Series B effigy at Goldsborough. His finely-wrought face is framed by a coif behaving as real mail should and his shield is detailed with its lining and fittings true to life. On top of his head is a face cloth, stitched to his pillow but lifted back as if at the Resurrection, allowing him to participate in the liturgy before and beside him. The sight lines between the main and side altars run across his strategically placed tomb. Lower down sat someone who was probably his widow reading scripture from a book and over his head is a gablette fashioned using the very latest architectural ideas. Its corbels are tiny crouching men resembling details this gifted carver was producing for York Minster nave. This one image encapsulates the intelligence, observation, innovation and craftsmanship that characterises the best that Yorkshire has to offer.

Medieval effigies were created to perpetuate the memory of those who had died. Perhaps, this book will help some of them achieve their purpose.

Bibliography

Unpublished manuscript sources

Dugdale, W. (1640–41) *Book of Monuments*. British Library Add MS 71474.

Dugdale, W. (*c*. 1667) *Yorkshire Arms*. College of Arms MS RR14/c, compiled *c*. 1667 from earlier notes and sketches, mostly of 1641.

Johnston C 13: Henry Johnston manuscript: Bodleian Library, MS. Top. Yorks. C 13.

Johnston C 14: Henry Johnston manuscript: Bodleian Library, MS. Top. Yorks. C14.

Johnston C 27: Nathaniel Johnston manuscript: Bodleian Library, MS. Top. Yorks. C 27.

Johnston C 31: Nathaniel Johnston manuscript: Bodleian Library, MS. Top. Yorks. C 31.

Torre, J. (1691) *Antiquities Ecclesiastical of the City of York: Also Churches, Parochiall & Conventuall within The Archdeaconry of the West Riding*. York Minster Library, Ms L1/8.

Torre, J. (1692) *Churches Parochiall & Conventuall within the Diocese of York and Archdeaconrys of Cleveland and East Riding*. York Minster Library, Ms L1/9.

Abbreviated references

CASSS III: Lang, J. (ed.) (1991) *Corpus of Anglo-Saxon Stone Sculpture. III: York and Eastern Yorkshire*. London.

CASSS VI: Lang, J. (ed.) (2001) *Corpus of Anglo-Saxon Stone Sculpture. VI: Northern Yorkshire*. London.

CASSS VIII: Coatsworth, E. (ed.) (2008) *Corpus of Anglo-Saxon Stone Sculpture. VIII: Western Yorkshire*. London.

CChR II: Trimmer, R. & Crump, C. (eds) (1906) *Calendar of the Charter Rolls, II, Henry III – Edward I, A.D. 1257–1300*. London.

CChW: Fowler, R. C. (ed.) (1927) *Calendar of Chancery Warrants, A.D. 1244–1326,* I. London.

CCR 1296–1302: Stevenson, W. H. (ed.) (1906) *Calendar of the Close Rolls, Edward I, Vol. IV. A.D. 1296–1302*. London.

CCR 1307–1313: Stevenson, W. H. (ed.) (1892) *Calendar of the Close Rolls, Edward II. A.D. 1307–1313*. London.

CCR 1313–1318: Stevenson, W. H. (ed.) (1893) *Calendar of the Close Rolls, Edward II. A.D. 1313–1318*. London.

CCR 1339–1341: Hinds, A. B. (ed.) (1901) *Calendar of the Close Rolls, Edward III. 1339–1341*. London.

CDS II: Bain, J. (ed.) (1884) *Calendar of Documents Relating to Scotland preserved in Her Majesty's Public Record Office, London: Vol. II, A.D. 1272–1307*. Edinburgh.

Chron. Melsa.: Bond, E. (ed.) (1866–68) *Chronica monasterii de Melsa: a fundatione usque ad annum 1396, auctore Thoma de Burton, abbate. Accedit continuatio ad annum 1406 a monacho quodam ipsius domus*. Rolls Series, three vols. London.

CIM II: Rodney, H. (ed.) (1916) *Calendar of Inquisitions Miscellaneous (Chancery)*, II. London.

CP: Cokayne, G. E. *et al.* (eds) (1910–59) *The Complete Peerage of England Scotland Ireland Great Britain and the United Kingdom extant extinct or dormant*. Thirteen vols. London.

CPR 1272–1281: Black, J. G. (ed.) (1901) *Calendar of the Patent Rolls, Edward I, A.D. 1272–1281*. London.

CPR 1281–1292: Black, J. G., Isaacson, R. F. & Morris, G. J. (eds) (1893) *Calendar of the Patent Rolls, Edward I, A.D. 1281–1292*. London.

CPR 1292–1301: Black, J. (ed.) (1895) *Calendar of the Patent Rolls, Edward I, A.D. 1292–1301*. London.

CPR 1301–1307: Black, J. (ed.) (1898) *Calendar of the Patent Rolls, Edward I, A.D. 1301–1307*. London.

CPR 1307–1313: Handcock, G. (1894) *Calendar of the Patent Rolls, Edward II, A.D. 1307–1313*. London.

CPR 1321–1324: Black, J. (ed.) (1904) *Calendar of the Patent Rolls, Edward II, A.D. 1321–1324*. London.

CPR 1327–1330: Isaacson, R. F., Morris, G. J. & Lawrance, H. E. (eds) (1891) *Calendar of the Patent Rolls, Edward III, A.D. 1327–1330*. London.

CPR 1330–1334: Isaacson, R. F. (ed.) (1893) *Calendar of the Patent Rolls, Edward III, A.D. 1330–1334*. London.

CPR 1334–1338: Isaacson, R. F. (ed.) (1895) *Calendar of the Patent Rolls, Edward III, A.D. 1334–1338*. London.

CPR 1343–1345: Isaacson, R. F. (ed.) (1902) *Calendar of the Patent Rolls, Edward III, A.D. 1343–1345*. London.

CPR 1345–1348: Isaacson, R. F. (ed.) (1903) *Calendar of the Patent Rolls, Edward III, A.D. 1345–1348*. London.

CPR 1385–1389: Morris, G. (ed.) (1900) *Calendar of the Patent Rolls, Richard II, A.D. 1385–1389*. London.

DBA 1: Chesshyre, H., Woodcock, T. *et al.* (eds) (1992) *Dictionary of British Arms: Medieval Ordinary*, 1. London.

DBA 2: Woodcock, T., Grant, J. & Graham, I. (eds) (1996) *Dictionary of British Arms: Medieval Ordinary*, 2. London.

DBA 3: Woodcock, T. & Flower, S. (eds) (2009) *Dictionary of British Arms: Medieval Ordinary*, 3. London.

de la Pryme: Jackson, C. (ed.) (1869) *The Diary of Abraham de la Pryme, The Yorkshire Antiquary*. Surtees Society, 54.

Dodsworth: Clay, J. W. (ed.) (1904) *Yorkshire Church Notes 1619–1631 by Roger Dodsworth*. The Yorkshire Archaeological Society Record Series, 34.

Feudal Aids: Public Record Office (1899–1920) *Inquisitions and assessments relating to feudal aids; with other analogous documents preserved in the Public Record Office. A.D. 1284–1431*. Six vols. London.

Fœdera: Rymer, T. & Sanderson, R. (eds) rev. Clarke, A. & Holbrooke, F. (1816–69) *Fœdera, conventiones, litteræ, et cujuscunque generis acta publica, inter reges Angliæ et alios quosvis Imperatores, Reges, Pontifices, Principes, vel Communitates*. Four vols in 7. London.

FR I: Public Record Office (1911) *Calendar of the Fine Rolls preserved in the Public Record Office: Vol. I, Edward I, A.D. 1272–1307*. London.

FR II: Public Record Office (1912) *Calendar of the Fine Rolls preserved in the Public Record Office: Vol. II, Edward II, A.D. 1307–1319*. London.

FR III: Public Record Office (1912) *Calendar of the Fine Rolls preserved in the Public Record Office: Vol. III, Edward II, A.D. 1319–1327*. London.

FR IV: Public Record Office (1913) *Calendar of the Fine Rolls preserved in the Public Record Office: Vol. IV, Edward III, A.D. 1327–1337*. London.

Glynne 2007: Butler, L. (ed.) (2007) The Yorkshire Church Notes of Sir Stephen Glynne (1825–1874). *The Yorkshire Archaeological Society Record Series*, CLIX.

HKW:I: Allen Brown, R., Colvin, H. M. & Taylor, A. J. (eds) (1963) *The History of the King's Works, Volume I: The Middle Ages*. London.

HKW:II: Allen Brown, R., Colvin, H. M. & Taylor, A. J. (eds) (1963) *The History of the King's Works, Volume II: The Middle Ages*. London.

IPM V: Sharp, J. (ed.) (1908) *Calendar of Inquisitions Post Mortem: Volume V, Edward II*. London.

IPM VI: Sharp, J. (ed.) (1910) *Calendar of Inquisitions Post Mortem: Volume VI, Edward II*. London.

IPM VII: Sharp, J. (ed.) (1909) *Calendar of Inquisitions Post Mortem: Volume VII, Edward III*. London.

IPM VIII: Sharp, J. & Atkinson, E. (eds) (1913) *Calendar of Inquisitions Post Mortem: Volume VIII, Edward III*. London.

IPM XVI: Dawes, M., Devine, M., Jones, H. & Post, M. (eds) (1974) *Calendar of Inquisitions Post Mortem: Volume 16, Richard II*. London.

IPM XVII: Dawes, M., Johnson, H., Condon, M., Cook, C. & Jones, H. (eds) (1988) *Calendar of Inquisitions Post Mortem, Volume 17, Richard II*. London.

IPM XIX: Kirby, J. (ed.) (1992) *Calendar of Inquisitions Post Mortem and other Analogous Documents preserved in the Public Record Office: Vol. XIX 7–14 Henry IV (1405–1413)*. London.

IQD: Crump, C. & Chapman, J. (eds) (1904) *List of Inquisitions ad Quod Damnum*. Two vols. London.

Lanfranc 2002: Knowles, D. (ed.) (2002) rev. Brooke, C. *The Monastic Constitutions of Lanfranc*. Oxford.

Mercurius Rusticus: Ryves, B. *et al.* (1685) *Mercurius Rusticus: or, The Countries Complaint of the Barbarous Outrages Committed by the Sectaries of This Late Flourishing Kingdom*. London.

Monasticon 1661: Dugdale, W. & Dodsworth, R. (eds) (1655–73) *Monasticon Anglicanum*. Three vols. London.

Monasticon 1817–1830: Dugdale, W. & Dodsworth, R. (eds) (1817–30) rev. Caley, J. *et al. Monasticon Anglicanum*. Six vols. London.

O. S. (1987) *The Ordnance Survey Gazetteer of Great Britain*. Southampton.

Pev:D 1985: Pevsner, N. (1985) rev. Williamson, E. *The Buildings of England: County Durham*. Second edition. London.

Pev:ER 1972: Pevsner, N. (1972) *The Buildings of England: Yorkshire: York and the East Riding*. Harmondsworth.

Pev:ER 1995: Pevsner, N. & Neave, D. (1995) *The Buildings of England: Yorkshire: York and the East Riding*. Second edition. London.

Pev:NR 1966: Pevsner, N. (1966) *The Buildings of England: Yorkshire: The North Riding*. Harmondsworth.

Pev:WR 1967: Pevsner, N. (1967) rev. Radcliffe, E. *The Buildings of England: Yorkshire: The West Riding*. Second edition. Harmondsworth.

Pev:WR 2009: Leach, P. & Pevsner, N. (2009) *The Buildings of England: Yorkshire: West Riding: Leeds, Bradford and the North*. Revised edition. New Haven & London.

Purbeck 1994–2003: Gittos, B. & M., Badham, S. & Lankester, P. (1994–2003/4) List of Purbeck Marble Coffin-Shaped Slabs *Church Monuments Society Newsletter*, 16 parts, 10.1–19.2.

Rot. Scot.: Record Commission (1814–19) *Rotuli Scotiae in Turri Londinensi et in Domo Capitulari Westmonasteriensi Asservati*. Two vols. London.

Test. Ebor. I: Raine, J. (ed.) (1836) *Testamenta Eboracensia: or Wills Registered at York: Part I*. Surtees Society, IV.

Test. Ebor. II: Raine, J. (ed.) (1855) *Testamenta Eboracensia: A Selection of Wills from the Registry at York: Part II*. Surtees Society, XXX.

Test. Ebor. IV: Raine, J. (ed.) (1868) *Testamenta Eboracensia: A Selection of Wills from the Registry at York: Vol. IV*. Surtees Society, LIII.

Test. Ebor. V: Raine, J. (ed.) (1884) *Testamenta Eboracensia: A Selection of Wills from the Registry at York: Vol. V*. Surtees Society, LXXIX.

VCH:D:II: Page, W. (ed.) (1907) *The Victoria History of the County of Durham*, II. London.

VCH:D:III: Page, W. (ed.) (1928) *The Victoria History of the County of Durham*, III. London.

VCH:ER:I: Allison, K. J. (ed.) (1969) *A History of the County of York East Riding: I: The City of Kingston Upon Hull*. London.

VCH:ER:II: Allison, K. J. (ed.) (1974) *A History of the County of York East Riding*, II. London.

VCH:ER:III: Allison, K. J. (ed.) (1976) *A History of the County of York East Riding*, III. London.

VCH:ER:V: Allison, K. (ed.) (1984) *A History of the County of York East Riding*, V, *Holderness Southern Part*. London.

VCH:ER:VII: Kent, G. H. R. (ed.) (2002) *A History of the County of York East Riding, VII, Holderness Wapentake, Middle and North Divisions*. London.

VCH:NR:I: Page, W. (ed.) (1914) *The Victoria History of the County of York North Riding*, I. London.

VCH:NR:II: Page, W. (ed.) (1923) *The Victoria History of the County of York North Riding*, II. London.
VCH:Y:III: Page, W. (ed.) (1913) *The Victoria History of the County of York*, III. London.

Published works and online resources

Allen, T. (1828–1831) *A New and Complete History of the County of York*. Six vols. London.
Anon (1867) Antiquarian Discoveries at Guisborough Abbey, *The Building News*, 14, p.719.
Armitage-Smith, S. (ed.) (1911) *John of Gaunt's Register*. Camden Society 3rd Series, XX & XXI.
Arvanigian, M. & Leopold, A. (1998) Illustrative Documents. In D. Rollason & M. Prestwich (eds) *The Battle of Neville's Cross 1346*. Stamford, 132–63.
Aske, R. (1834) Extracts from a Volume of Robert Aske's Collections, Marked with a Cinquefoil, written in the Reign of Henry VIII. *Collectanea Topographica & Genealogica*, I, 168–70.
Aston, M. (1988) *England's Iconoclasts: Volume 1, Laws Against Images*. Oxford.
Atkinson, J. (ed.) (1879) *Cartularium Abbathiae de Whiteby*, II, Surtees Society, 72.
Atkinson, J. (ed.) (1889) *Cartularium Abbathiae de Rievalle*, Surtees Society, 83.
Ayers, T. & Sampson, J. (2000) The Middle Ages. In T. Ayers (ed.) *Salisbury Cathedral: The West Front*. Chichester, 9–82.
Aylmer, G. & Cant, R. (eds) (1977) *A History of York Minster*. Oxford.
Ayloffe, J. (1775) An Account of the Body of King Edward the First as it appeared on opening his Tomb in the Year 1774. *Archaeologia*, III, 376–413.
Ayrton, M. & Moore, H. (1969) *Giovanni Pisano: sculptor*. London.
Badham, S. (1980) A Lost Bronze Effigy of 1279 from York Minster. *The Antiquaries Journal*, LX pt. 1, 59–65.
Badham, S. (1981) A Lost Military Effigy from Leake, Yorkshire. *The Yorkshire Archaeological Journal*, 53, 127–28.
Badham, S. (1989) Monumental Brasses: the Development of the York Workshops in the Fourteenth and Fifteenth Centuries. In C. Wilson (ed.) *Medieval Art and Architecture in the East Riding of Yorkshire*, British Archaeological Association Conference Transactions for the year 1983, IX, 165–85.
Badham, S. (1999) Medieval Minor Effigial Monuments in West & South Wales: An interim survey. *Church Monuments*, XIV, 5–34.
Badham, S. (2008) The de la More effigies at Northmoor (Oxfordshire) and related monuments at Winterbourne (Gloucestershire). *Church Monuments*, XXIII, 14–44.
Badham, S. (2009) Yorkshire's Royal Monument Re-visited. *Church Monuments Society Newsletter*, 25.1, 12–15.
Badham, S. (2010a) A Semi-Effigial Monument to a Lawyer at Wadworth (Yorkshire). *Church Monuments Society Newsletter*, 26.1, 20–22.
Badham, S. (2010b) What Constitutes a 'Workshop' and How Did Workshops Operate? Some Problems and Questions. In S. Badham & S. Oosterwijk (eds) *Monumental Industry*. Donington, 12–36.
Badham, S. (2011) *Medieval Church and Churchyard Monuments*. Oxford.
Badham, S. (2014) Funeral armour, especially helmets and their use in heraldic funerals. Appended to D. Wilson, The Arches Court, Wootton St Lawrence and church monuments. *Church Monuments*, XXIX, 140–45.
Badham, S. (2015a) Medieval Monuments to the de la Pole and Wingfield Families. In P. Bloore & E. Martin (eds) *Wingfield College and its Patrons: Piety and Patronage in Medieval Suffolk*. Woodbridge:135–76.
Badham, S. (2015b) *Seeking Salvation: Commemorating the Dead in the Late-Medieval English Parish*. Donington.
Badham, S. (2016) The rise to popularity of alabaster for memorialisation in England. *Church Monuments*, XXXI, 11–67.
Badham, S. (forthcoming) Lincolnshire Semi-effigials.
Badham, S. & Blacker, G. (2009) *Northern Rock: The Use of Egglestone Marble for Monuments in Medieval England*. BAR British Series 480. Oxford.
Badham, S. & Norris, M. (1999) *Early Incised Slabs and Brasses from the London Marblers*. London.
Badham, S. & Oosterwijk, S. (eds) (2010) *Monumental Industry*. Donington.
Badham, S. & Cockerham, P. (eds) (2012) *'The beste and fayrest of al Lincolnshire': The Church of St Botolph, Boston, Lincolnshire, and its Medieval Monuments*. BAR British Series 554. Oxford.
Badham, S., Gittos, B. & Gittos, M. (1996) The Fourteenth-century Monuments in the Saltmarshe Chapel at Howden, Yorkshire: their History and Context. *The Yorkshire Archaeological Journal*, 68, 113–55.
Baildon, W. (ed.) (1910) *Feet of Fines for the County of York from 1327 to 1347, 1–20 Edward III*. The Yorkshire Archaeological Society Record Series, XLII.
Baines, E. (1822–23) *History, Directory & Gazetteer of the County of York*. Two vols. Leeds.
Baker, J. (1984) *The Order of Serjeants at Law*. Seldon Society Supplementary Series, 5. London.
Baker, J. (2013) English Judges' Robes 1350–2008. In J. Baker, *Collected Papers on English Legal History*. Three vols. Cambridge, 812–31.
Barber, R. (trans.) (1992) *Bestiary: being an English version of the Bodleian Library, Oxford M. S. Bodley 764*. London.
Barker, C. R. (1982) *Churches of the Wolds*. Fife.
Barker, J. (2017) Invention and Commemoration in Fourteenth-Century England: A Monumental 'Family Tree' at the Collegiate Church of St. Martin, Lowthorpe. *Gesta*, 56.1, 105–28.
Barnwell, P., Cross, C. & Rycraft, A. (eds) (2005) *Mass and Parish in late Medieval England: The Use of York*. Reading.
Bartlett, J. (1959) The Expansion and Decline of York in the Later Middle Ages. *The Economic History Review*, New Series, XII.1, 17–33.
Bauch, K. (1976) *Das mittelalterliche Grabbild*. Berlin.
Bayley, T. D. S. (1955) The Bourchier Shield in Halstead Church. *Transactions of the Essex Archaeological Society*, N.S. XXV pt. 1, 80–100.
Beabey, M. & Richardson, T. (1997) Hardened leather armour. *Royal Armouries Yearbook*, 2, 64–71.
Beresford, M. (1952) The Lost Villages of Yorkshire, Part II. *The Yorkshire Archaeological Journal*, XXXVIII, 44–70.

Bergmans, A. & Hans-Collas, I. (2013) Awaiting eternal life: Painted burial cists in the Southern Netherlands. *Church Monuments*, XXVIII, 13–32.

Bertram, J. (2004) *Gough's Sepulchral Monuments, Being a Catalogue of Material Relating to Sepulchral Monuments in the Gough Manuscripts of the Bodleian Library*. Oxford.

Bertram, J. (2012) *Bishops and Burgers, Dukes and Knights: Mediaeval Monuments on the southern and eastern Baltic seaboard*. Privately printed.

Bertram, J. (2015) *Icon and Epigraphy*. Two vols. Privately printed.

Biebrach, R. (2017) *Church Monuments in South Wales, c. 1200–1547*. Woodbridge.

Bilson J. (1909) Proceedings in 1908: St Mary's Church, Welwick. *The Yorkshire Archaeological Journal*, XX, 134–41.

Binski, P. (1980) Chartham, Kent, and the Court. *Transactions of the Monumental Brass Society*, 13.1, 73–79.

Binski, P. (1987) The Stylistic Sequence of London Figure Brasses. In J. Coales (ed.) *The Earliest English Brasses: Patronage, Style and Workshops 1270–1350*. London, 69–132.

Birch, W. de G. (1894) *Catalogue of Seals in the Department of Manuscripts in the British Museum*, III. London.

Bishop, E. (1999) *A Short History of All Saints' Church, Ripley*. Ripley.

Blair, C. (1958) *European Armour circa 1066 to circa 1700*. London.

Blair, C. (1959) Medieval Swords and Spurs in Toledo Cathedral. *Journal of the Arms and Armour Society*, 3.2, 41–52.

Blair, C. (1992) The Date of the Early Alabaster Knight at Hanbury, Staffordshire. *Church Monuments*, VII, 3–18.

Blair, C. (1993) The De Vere Effigy at Hatfield Broad Oak. *Church Monuments*, VIII, 3–11.

Blair, C. (1994) The Wooden Knight at Abergavenny. *Church Monuments*, IX, 33–52.

Blair, C. (1995) Yorkshire Effigies and Ring Scabbard-Attachments. *Church Monuments Society Newsletter*, 11.1, 4–5.

Blair, C. (1996) Again Yorkshire Effigies and Ring Scabbard-Attachments. *Church Monuments Society Newsletter*, 12.1, 16–17.

Blair, C. (2003) The Ingleby Arncliffe Group of Effigies. *Church Monuments Society Newsletter*, 19.1, 5–6; 19.2, (2003/4), 9.

Blair, C., Goodall, J. & Lankester, P. (2000) The Winchester Tombs Reconsidered. *Church Monuments*, XV, 5–30.

Blashill, T. (1900) *Sutton-in-Holderness*. London.

Blore, E. (1826) *The Monumental Remains of Noble and Eminent Persons*. London.

Bloxham, M. H. (1849) *On certain Sepulchral Effigies and Monuments in South Yorkshire*, private publication of a lecture given to the Yorkshire Architectural Society on 25th October, 1849. York.

Bloxham, M. H. (1882) *Companion to the Principles of Gothic Ecclesiastical Architecture*. London.

Bogg, E. (1904) *Lower Wharfedale*. York, Leeds, etc.

Boutell, C. (1847) *Monumental Brasses and Slabs*. London.

Boutell, C. (1854) *Christian Monuments in England and Wales*. London.

Boyne, W. (1855) Fenton Church, in the Wapontake of Barkstone Ash. In W. Bowman, *Reliquiae Antiquae Eboracenses, or Remains of Antiquity, Relating to the County of York*. Leeds, 31–32.

Brault, G. (1997) *Rolls of Arms of Edward I (1272–1307)*. Two vols. Woodbridge.

Britton, J. (1819) *The History and Antiquities of the Metropolitical Church of York*. London.

Brodrick, A. & Darrah, J. (1986) The Fifteenth Century Polychromed Limestone Effigies of William Fitzalan, 9th Earl of Arundel, and his wife, Joan Nevill, in the Fitzalan Chapel, Arundel. *Church Monuments*,1.2, 65–94.

Brown, M. (2008) *Bannockburn: The Scottish War and the British Isles 1307–1323*. Edinburgh.

Brown, S. (2003) *'Our Magnificent Fabrick': York Minster: An Architectural History c. 1220–1500*. Swindon.

Brown, W. (ed.) (1889, 1891) *Cartularium Prioratus de Gyseburne, Ebor. Diœceseos, Ordinis S. Augustini, Fundati A.D. MCXIX*. Two vols. Surtees Society, 86 & 89.

Brown, W. (ed.) (1897) *Yorkshire Lay Subsidy, being a Fifteenth, Collected 30 Edward I*. The Yorkshire Archaeological Society Record Series, XXI.

Brown, W. (ed.) (1902) *Yorkshire Inquisitions Vol. III*. The Yorkshire Archaeological Society Record Series, XXXI.

Brown, W. (ed.) (1913, 1916) *The Register of John le Romeyn, Lord Archbishop of York 1286–1296*. Two vols. Surtees Society, 123 & 128.

Brown, W. (ed.) (1925) *The Register of Thomas of Corbridge, Lord Archbishop of York, 1300–1304: Part I*. Surtees Society, 138.

Browne, J. (1839/47) *The History of the Edifice of the Metropolitan Church of St. Peter, York*. London.

Bruce, J. (1868) An account of recent discoveries at Guisborough Priory. *Archaeological Journal*, 25, 247–49.

Budge, A. (2015) The medieval stone episcopal thrones at Wells and Durham Cathedrals. In C. Tracy (ed.) *Britain's Medieval Episcopal Thrones: History, Archaeology and Conservation*. Oxford, 107–35.

Bulmer, T. (1892) *History, Topography and Directory of East Yorkshire*. Ashton-on-Ribble.

Burton, J. (1758) *Monasticon Eboracense*. York.

Burton, J. (1995) *Kirkham Priory from Foundation to Dissolution*. Borthwick Paper 86. York.

Burton, T. & Raine, J. (1888) *The History and Antiquities of the Parish of Hemingbrough*. York.

Cameron, J. (2011) The Harington Tomb at Cartmel Priory: Making, Legacy and Audience. Unpublished MA thesis, Courtauld Institute of Art.

Camille, M. (1996) *Master of Death: The Lifeless Art of Pierre Remiet, Illuminator*. New Haven & London.

Campbell, J. (1995) *The Ars Moriendi: An examination, translation, and collation of the manuscripts of the shorter Latin version*. Unpublished manuscript, University of Ottawa. Downloadable from: https://ruor.uottawa.ca/handle/10393/10313.

Cannon, J. (2011) Berkeley Patronage and the 14th century Choir. In J. Cannon & B. Williamson (eds) *The Medieval Art, Architecture and History of Bristol Cathedral: An Enigma Explored*. Woodbridge, 148–85.

Capwell, T. (2015) *Armour of the English Knight 1400–1450*. London.

Carrington, D. (2014a) *St. Mary's church Sprotbrough, South Yorkshire: Conservation survey report on two medieval monuments in the Chapel of St. Thomas*. Unpublished report, Skillington Workshop Ltd.

Carrington, D. (2014b) *St. Mary's church, Sprotbrough, South Yorkshire: Report on archaeological finds and observations arising from the conservation of the monument to Philip Copley (d.1577) and his wife Mary (d.1597)*. Unpublished report, Skillington Workshop Ltd.

Cheetham, F. (1984) *English Medieval Alabasters*. Oxford.

Chetwynd-Stapylton, H. (1897) *The Stapeltons of Yorkshire*. London.

Clanchy, M. (2004) Images of Ladies with Prayer Books: What do they Signify? *Studies in Church History*, 38, 106–22.

Clay, J. (ed.) (1900) *Dugdale's Visitation of Yorkshire, with additions*, V. Exeter.

Clifford, H. (1987) *The House of Clifford*. Chichester.

Clifton-Taylor, A. (1972) *The Pattern of English Building*. London.

Coldstream, N. (1994) *The Decorated Style: Architecture and Ornament 1240–1360*. London.

Collier, C. V. (1923) Lowthorpe and its Collegiate Church of St Martin. *The Transactions of the East Riding Antiquarian Society*, XXIV, 28–42.

Collier, C. V. & Lawrance, H. (1928) Ancient Heraldry in the Deanery of Catterick. *The Yorkshire Archaeological Journal*, XXIX, 202–24.

Collin, B. (1955) *The Riddle of a 13th Century Sword-Belt*. East Knoyle.

Collins, F. (ed.) (1896) *Register of the Freemen of the City of York from the city records: Vol. I.: 1272–1558*. Surtees Society, XCVI.

Coppack, G. (1988) *Abbeys: Yorkshire's Monastic Heritage*. York.

Coppack, G. (1993) *Fountains Abbey*. London.

Coppack, G. (2004) *Fountains Abbey: The Cistercians in Northern England*. Stroud.

Coppack, G. & Fergusson, P. (1994) *Rievaulx Abbey*. London.

Coppack, G., Harrison, S. & Hayfield, C. (1995) Kirkham Priory: The Architecture and Archaeology of an Augustinian House. *Journal of the British Archaeological Association*, CXLVIII, 55–136.

Cormack, R. & Vassilaki, M. (eds) (2008) *Byzantium 330–1453*. London.

Coss, P. (1996) Heraldry and Monumental Effigies in the North East. In T. Faulkner (ed.) *Northumbrian Panorama*. London, 3–32.

Coss, P. (1998) *The Lady in Medieval England 1000–1500*. Stroud.

Crossley, F. H. (1921) *English Church Monuments A.D. 1150–1550*. London.

Cross Slabs in Northern England digital database, https://sites.google.com/site/crosslabs/home

Cullum, P. H. & Goldberg, P. J. P. (1993) Charitable Provision in Late Medieval York: 'To the Praise of God and the Use of the Poor'. *Northern History*, 29.1, 24–39.

Cutler, M. (2003) North Yorkshire and the Anglo-Scottish Wars, 1318–27. In R. Butlin (ed.) *Historical Atlas of North Yorkshire*. Otley, 87–89.

Cutts, E. L. (1849) *A Manual for the Study of the Sepulchral Slabs and Crosses of the Middle Ages*. London.

Dalton, J. N. (1917) *The Collegiate Church of Ottery St Mary*. Cambridge.

Daniels, C. (2012) *The Craft of Stonemasonry*. Marlborough.

Davey, N. (1961) *A History of Building Materials*. London.

Davies, R. (ed.) (1859) *The Visitation of the County of Yorke... by William Dugdale*. Surtees Society, 36.

Dawton, N. (1983) The Percy Tomb at Beverley Minster: the Style of the Sculpture. In F. Thompson (ed.) *Studies in Medieval Sculpture*. Society of Antiquaries of London Occasional Paper, (New Series) III. London, 122–50.

Dawton, N. (1989) The Percy Tomb Workshop. In C. Wilson (ed.) *Medieval Art and Architecture in the East Riding of Yorkshire*, British Archaeological Association Conference Transactions for the year 1983, IX.

Dawton, N. (2000) The Medieval Monuments. In R. Horrox (ed.) *Beverley Minster: An Illustrated History*. Beverley, 130–55.

de Sawtry, G. (1837) *The churches of Holderness: Part 1*.

Downing, M. (1995) Military Effigies with Breast Chains. *Church Monuments*, X, 7–19.

Downing, M. (2010) Military Effigies in Eastern England: Evidence of a High-Status Workshop of *c*. 1295–1350. In S. Badham & S. Oosterwijk (eds) *Monumental Industry*. Donington, 66–96.

Downing, M. (2012) *Military Effigies of England & Wales Volume 4: Leicestershire – Norfolk*. Shrewsbury.

Downing, M. (2014) *Military Effigies of England & Wales Volume 7: Warwickshire-Yorkshire East Riding*. Shrewsbury.

Downing, M. (2015) *Military Effigies of England & Wales Volume 8: Yorkshire North Riding-West Riding*. Shrewsbury.

Drake, F. (1736) *Eboracum: or, the History and Antiquities of the City of York*. London.

Duffy, E. (1992) *The Stripping of the Altars*. New Haven & London.

Dyer, A. (2000) Ranking lists of English medieval towns. In D. M. Palliser (ed.) *The Cambridge Urban History of Britain, Vol. 1: 600–1540*. Cambridge, 747–70.

Eastmead, W. (1824) *Historia Rievallensis*. London.

Egan, G. & Pritchard, F. (eds) (1991) *Medieval Finds From Excavations in London: 3: Dress Accessories c. 1150 – c. 1450*. London.

Elizabeth I 1560, *A proclamation against breakinge or defacing of monumentes of antiquitie, beyng set up in churches or other publique places for memory and not for supersticion*. Available online at: http://downloads.it.ox.ac.uk/ota-public/tcp/Texts-HTML/free/A21/A21611.html

Ellis, B. (1995) Spurs and Spur Fittings. In J. Clark (ed.) *Medieval Finds From Excavations in London: 5: The Medieval Horse and its Equipment c. 1150 – c. 1450*. London, 124–56.

Ellis, R. H. (ed.) (1981) *Catalogue of Seals in the Public Record Office: Personal Seals*, II. London.

Emden, A. (1957) *A Biographical Register of the University of Oxford to A.D. 1500*. Three vols. Oxford.

Evans, P. (1995) *Church Fabric in the York Diocese 1613–1899: The records of the Archbishop's faculty jurisdiction*. Borthwick Texts and Calendars 19. York.

Everson, P. & Stocker, D. (2014) The Rector's Gift. Integrating Church Development and Village Landscape at Car Colston (Nottinghamshire) and Elsewhere. *Church Archaeology*, 18, 67–84.

Fallow, T. M. (1900) Note on the finding of a fragment of a monumental effigy of a knight at Ormesby, Yorkshire. *Proceedings of the Society of Antiquaries of London*, 2nd Series, XVIII, 232–33.

Foster, J. (ed.) (1875) Armes taken out of Churches and Howses in Yorkshire Visitacion, A° mdlxxxiv. In *The Visitation of*

Yorkshire, made in the Years 1584/5 by Robert Glover, Somerset Herald. Privately printed, 417–79.

Fowler, C. H. (1877) Stillingfleet Church. *Associated Architectural Societies' Reports & Papers*, XIV.1, 73–80.

Fowler, J. T. (ed.) (1908) *Memorials of the Church of SS. Peter & Wilfrid, Ripon, Vol. IV*. Surtees Society, 115.

Fraser, C. M. (ed.) (1953) *Records of Antony Bek: Bishop and Patriarch 1283–1311*. Surtees Society, 162.

Fraser, C. M. (1957) *A History of Antony Bek*. Oxford.

French, T. (1991) Prince William of Hatfield. *The Friends of York Minster Annual Report*, 62, 45–54.

French, T. & O'Connor, D. (1987) *Corpus vitrearum Medii Aevi. Vol. 3: Great Britain: The medieval stained glass of York Minister, Fascicule 1: The glazing of the West Wall*. London.

Fryer, A. (1924) *Wooden Monumental Effigies in England and Wales*. London.

Furby, J. (1846) *Furby's Hand-Book for Strangers visiting Bridlington-Quay*. Bridlington.

Gale, R. (ed.) (1722) *Registrum Honoris de Richmond*. London.

Gardner, A. (1940) *Alabaster Tombs of the Pre-Reformation Period in England*. Cambridge.

Geddes, J. (1999) *Medieval Decorative Ironwork in England*. London.

Gee, E. (1981) Stone from the Medieval Limestone Quarries of South Yorkshire. In A. Detsicas (ed.) *Collectanea Historica: Essays in Memory of Stuart Rigold*. Maidstone, 247–55.

Gent, T. (1730) *The Antient and Modern History of the Famous City of York*. York.

Gent, T. (1733a) *The Antient and Modern History of the Loyal Town of Rippon*. York.

Gent, T. (1733b) A Journey into Some Parts of Yorkshire. In T. Gent, *The Antient and Modern History of the Loyal Town of Rippon*. York.

Gilchrist, R. & Sloane, B. (2005) *Requiem: The Medieval Monastic Cemetery in Britain*. London.

Gill, M. (1998) Sacred and Secular: The Murals in the Tower Room of St Michael's. In E. Bailey (ed.) *Small is Cosmic: Millennial Issues in Parochial Perspective*. Winterbourne, 30–35.

Gill, T. (1852) *Vallis Eboracensis: comprising the History and Antiquities of Easingwold*. London.

Gimson, G. (1995) Lion hunt: a royal tomb-effigy at Arbroath Abbey. *Proceedings of the Society of Antiquaries of Scotland*, 125, 901–16.

Gittos, B. & M. (1978) An Incised Slab at Burghwallis, Yorks. *Transactions of the Monumental Brass Society*, XII, 319–21.

Gittos, B. & M. (1979a) Etton (Yorkshire). *Bulletin of the International Society for the Study of Church Monuments*, 1, 7–8.

Gittos, B. & M. (1979b) Interesting Discoveries at Eastrington (Yorkshire). *Bulletin of the International Society for the Study of Church Monuments*, 1, 9–11.

Gittos, B. & M. (1980) A Classification of Early Yorkshire Effigies. *Bulletin of the International Society for the Study of Church Monuments*, 3, 53–57.

Gittos, B. & M. (1981) A Military Effigy at Welton, North Humberside. *The Yorkshire Archaeological Journal*, 53, 129–31.

Gittos, B. & M. (1989) A Survey of East Riding Sepulchral Monuments Before 1500. In C. Wilson (ed.) *Medieval Art and Architecture in the East Riding of Yorkshire*, British Archaeological Association Conference Transactions for the year 1983, IX, 91–108.

Gittos, B. & M. (1990) News of Monuments: Etton, Yorkshire, East Riding. *Newsletter of the Church Monuments Society*, 6.1, 7–8.

Gittos, B. & M. (1991a) A Newly Discovered Black Slab. *Newsletter of the Church Monuments Society*, 6.2, 27–29.

Gittos, B. & M. (1991b) News of Monuments: Etton, Yorkshire, East Riding. *Newsletter of the Church Monuments Society*, 6.2, 30.

Gittos, B. & M. (1992) Yorkshire Effigies *c*. 1300 and their Place in English Sculpture. In *Medieval Europe 1992, Art and Symbolism*, Pre-printed papers 7. York, 209–15.

Gittos, B. & M. (1994a) The Goldsborough Effigies. *Church Monuments*, IX, 3–32.

Gittos, B. & M. (1994b) List of Purbeck Marble Coffin-Shaped Slabs in Dorset. *Newsletter of the Church Monuments Society*, 10.1, 6–11.

Gittos, B. & M. (1998) Irish Purbeck: Recently Identified Purbeck Marble Monuments in Ireland. *Church Monuments*, XIII, 5–14.

Gittos, B. & M. (1999) Early Indent from Rievaulx Abbey. *Newsletter of the Church Monuments Society*, 15.1, 8–9.

Gittos, B. & M. (2001) Discussion and Dating. In Funerary Monuments and Devotional Sculpture. In W. Rodwell (ed.) *Wells Cathedral: Excavations and Structural Studies, 1978–93*, 2, English Heritage Archaeological Report 21. London, 495–97.

Gittos, B. & M. (2002a) Motivation and Choice: The Selection of Medieval Secular Effigies. In P. Coss & M. Keen (eds) *Heraldry, Pageantry and Social Display in Medieval England*. Woodbridge, 143–67.

Gittos, B. & M. (2002b) The Ingleby Arncliffe Group of Effigies. *Church Monuments*, XVII, 14–38.

Gittos, B. & M. (2012a) Medieval Ham Hill Stone Monuments in Context. *Journal of the British Archaeological Association*, 165, 89–121.

Gittos, B. & M. (2012b) Gresham Revisited: a fresh look at the medieval monuments of north Wales. *Archaeologia Cambrensis*, 161, 357–88.

Gittos, B. & M. (2013a) The English Medieval Churchyard: What Did it Really Look Like? In M. Penman (ed.) *Monuments and Monumentality across Medieval and Early Modern Europe*. Donington, 31–44.

Gittos, B. & M. (2013b) Acklam's Third Effigy. *Cleveland History: The Bulletin of the Cleveland and Teeside Local History Society*, 103, 15–18.

Gittos, B. & M. (2014a) Patrons of the Fabric: Donor Figures at Sherborne and Closworth. *Chronicle: Journal of the Yeovil Archaeological and Local History Society*, 10.4, 113–19.

Gittos, B. & M. (2014b) *The Monuments of the Athelhampton Chapel, St Mary's Church, Puddletown, Dorset*. Puddletown.

Gittos, B. & M. (2015) Commemoration at Muchelney before the Reformation. *Chronicle: Journal of the Yeovil Archaeological and Local History Society*, 10.5, 148–63.

Gittos, B. & M. (2017a) *Report on the Purbeck Marble Carved Stones (Milton Abbey)*. Unpublished report for Oakford Archaeology.

Gittos, B. & M. (2017b) *The Tomb of Blanche Mortimer, Lady Grandisson: St. Bartholomew's Church, Much Marcle*. Much Marcle.

Gittos, B. & M. (forthcoming) Report on a Newly Discovered Double Effigy at St. Mary's Church, Kilkenny. In C. Ó Drisceoil & P. Kenny (eds) *Archaeological Excavations 2015–16 at St Mary's Church, Kilkenny 12E1314: Final Report*, Kilkenny Archaeology.

Gittos, B. & M. with Butler, L. (1997) The Conservation of the Goldsborough Effigies. *Church Monuments*, XII, 5–13.

Glasscock, R. E. (1976) England *circa* 1334. In H. C. Darby, *A New Historical Geography of England Before 1600*. Cambridge, 136–85.

Goldberg, P. (1984) The Percy Tomb in Beverley Minster. *The Yorkshire Archaeological Journal*, 56, 65–74.

Goldsbrough, A. (1930) *Memorials of the Goldesborough Family*. Privately printed.

Goodman, A. (1992) *John of Gaunt: The Exercise of Princely Power in Fourteenth-Century Europe*. Harlow.

Gough, R. (1786–96) *Sepulchral Monuments in Great Britain*. Two vols in 5. London.

Grassi, J. (1970) Royal Clerks from the Archdiocese of York in the Fourteenth Century. *Northern History*, 5, 12–33.

Green, D. (1998) The Household and Military Retinue of Edward the Black Prince. Two vols. Unpublished PhD thesis, University of Nottingham.

Greenhill, F. A. (1970) The Ripon Lion, *Transactions of the Monumental Brass Society*, X, 461–64.

Greenhill, F. A. (1976) *Incised Effigial Slabs*. Two vols. London.

Greenstreet, J. (ed.) (1886) The Harleian Roll of Arms, *The Genealogist*, NS 3, 37–41, 118–21.

Greenwell, W. (ed.) (1860) *Wills and Inventories from the Registry at Durham, Part II*. Surtees Society, 38.

Griffith-Jones, R. (2010) 'An Enrichment of Cherubims': Christopher Wren's Refurbishment of the Temple Church. In R. Griffith-Jones & D. Park (eds) *The Temple Church in London: History, Architecture, Art*. Woodbridge, 135–73.

Gunton, S. (1686) *The History of the Church of Peterburgh*. London.

Halfpenny, J. (1807) *Fragmenta Vetusta or the Remains of Ancient Buildings in York*. York.

Hall, A. (ed.) (1722) *Nicolai Triveti Annalium Continuatio; ut et Adami Murimuthensis Chronicon, Cum eiusdem Continuatione: quibus accedunt Johannis Bostoni Speculum Coenbitarum, et Edmundi Boltoni Hypercritica*. Oxford.

Hamilton Thompson, A. & Brown, W. (1912) Feliskirk. Church of St. Felix. *The Yorkshire Archaeological Journal*, XXII, 193–205.

Hargrove, E. (1809) *The History of the Castle, Town, and Forest, of Knaresbrough*. Knaresbrough.

Harris, O. (2010) Antiquarian Attitudes: Crossed Legs, Crusaders and the Evolution of an Idea. *The Antiquaries Journal*, 90, 401–40.

Harris, O. (2014) The generations of Adam: the monument of Sir Gawen Carew in Exeter Cathedral. *Church Monuments*, XXIX, 40–71.

Harrison, S. (2010) *Kirkham Priory, North Yorkshire*. London.

Harrison, S. & Heslop, D. (1999) Archaeological Survey at the Augustinian Priory of Gisborough, Cleveland. *The Yorkshire Archaeological Journal*, 71, 89–127.

Hartshorne, A. (1891) The Sword Belts of the Middle Ages. *Archaeological Journal*, 48, 320–40.

Harvey, A. S. (1955) A Priest's Tomb at Beverley Minster. *The Yorkshire Archaeological Journal*, XXXVIII, 504–23.

Harvey, A. S. (1961) Notes on Two Heraldic Tombs. *The Yorkshire Archaeological Journal*, 40, 462–77.

Harvey, J. (1984) *English Mediaeval Architects*. Second edition. Gloucester.

Hasenfratz, R. (ed.) (2000) *Ancrene Wisse*. Kalamazoo. Available online at: http://d.lib.rochester.edu/teams/publication/hasenfratz-ancrene-wisse (accessed 11-8-2018).

Haslam, G. (1987) *Chartham and its Church*. Chartham: Privately printed.

Hasted, E. (1798) *The History and Topographical Survey of the County of Kent*. Second edition, VII. Canterbury.

Hatton, E. (1708) *A New View of London*. Two vols. London.

Hey, D. (1986) *Yorkshire from AD 1000*. London & New York.

Hill, R. (ed.) (1988) *The Register of William Melton Archbishop of York 1317–1340*, III. Canterbury and York Society, LXXVI.

Hodges, C. C. (1893) The Architectural History of Selby Abbey. *The Yorkshire Archaeological Journal*, XII, 344–94.

Hodges, C. C. (1895) The Brus Cenotaph at Guisbrough. *The Yorkshire Archaeological Journal*, XIII, 226–61.

Hollis, T. & Hollis, G. (1840–42) *The Monumental Effigies of Great Britain*. London.

Hope, W. H. St. J. (1900) Watton Priory, Yorkshire. *The Transactions of the East Riding Antiquarian Society*, VIII, 70–107.

Horrox, R. (1983) *The De La Poles of Hull*. East Yorkshire Local History Series, 36. Beverley.

Horrox, R. (ed.) (1994) *The Black Death*. Manchester & New York.

Houlbrooke, S. (2005) A study of the materials and techniques of 13th century tomb of Aveline, Countess of Lancaster, in Westminster. *The Conservator*, 29, 105–16.

Hulbert, A. (1991) Medieval Paintings and Polychromy. In M. Swanton (ed.) *Exeter Cathedral: A Celebration*. Exeter, 91–7.

Hunt, J. (1974) *Irish Medieval Figure Sculpture 1200–1600*. Two vols. Dublin.

Hunter, J. (1828 & 1831) *South Yorkshire: The History and Topography of the Deanery of Doncaster in the Diocese and County of York*. Two vols. London.

Hunter Blair, C. H. (ed.) (1925) *Durham Monuments*. The Newcastle upon Tyne Records Committee, V. Newcastle.

Hunter Blair, C. H. (1929) Mediaeval Effigies in the County of Durham. *Archaeologia Aeliana*, 4th Series, VI, 1–51.

Hurtig, J. (1979) *The Armoured Gisant Before 1400*. New York & London.

I'Anson, W. M. (1917) The Hauxwell Effigies. *The Yorkshire Archaeological Journal*, XXVI, 322–24.

I'Anson, W. M. (1920) Coverham Abbey. *The Yorkshire Archaeological Journal*, XXV, 273–301.

I'Anson, W. M. (1923) Some Yorkshire Effigies. *The Yorkshire Archaeological Journal*, XXVII, 117–39.

I'Anson, W. M. (1926) The Mediaeval Military Effigies of Yorkshire Part I. *The Yorkshire Archaeological Journal*, XXVIII, 345–79.

I'Anson, W. M. (1927) The Mediaeval Military Effigies of Yorkshire Part II. *The Yorkshire Archaeological Journal*, XXIX, 1–67.

Ingamells, R. (1992) *The Household Knights of Edward I*. Two vols. Unpublished PhD thesis, University of Durham.

Jackson, C. (ed.) (1873) *The Autobiography of Mrs. Alice Thornton, of East Newton, co. York*. Surtees Society, 62.

Jackson, E. J. (1855) *The History and Description of St. George's Church at Doncaster, Destroyed by Fire February 28, 1853*. London.

Jefferson, D. (2014) 14th Century Effigies, Church of St. Mary of Sprotbrough: Analyses of the stone used for the effigies and the salts association with their deterioration. In D. Carrington, *St. Mary's church Sprotbrough, South Yorkshire: Conservation survey report on two medieval monuments in the Chapel of St. Thomas*. Unpublished report, Skillington Workshop Ltd. Appendix A.

Jones, B. (ed.) (1963) *Fasti Ecclesiae Anglicanae 1300–1541: Vol. VI, Northern Province (York, Carlisle and Durham)*. London.

Jones, E. (2012) Rites of Enclosure: the English Ordines for the Enclosing of Anchorites, S. XII–S. XVI. *Traditio*, 67, 145–234.

Jowitt, D. (2012) *The Church of St Wilfrid, Langton-on-Swale*. Langton-on-Swale.

Kermode, J. (1998) *Medieval Merchants: York, Beverley and Hull in the Later Middle Ages*. Cambridge.

Kermode, J. (2000) Northern towns. In D. M. Palliser (ed.) *The Cambridge Urban History of Britain, Vol. 1: 600–1540*. Cambridge, 657–79.

Kershaw, I. (1973) The Great Famine and Agrarian Crisis in England 1315–1322. *Past & Present*, 59, 3–50.

King, A. (2012) *Strategic Stone Study: A Building Stone Atlas of County Durham, Tyne & Wear, & Cleveland*. London.

King, J. (1990) The Old Sarum Master: A Twelfth-Century Sculptor in South-West England. *The Wiltshire Archaeological and Natural History Magazine*, 83, 70–95.

Knoop, D. & Jones, G. (1933) *The Medieval Mason*. Manchester.

Knowles, D. (1976) *Bare Ruined Choirs: The Dissolution of the English Monasteries*. Cambridge.

Knowles, D. & Hadcock, R. (1953) *Medieval Religious Houses: England and Wales*. London.

Knowles, R. (1985) A Civilian Effigy in Birkin Church, North Yorkshire. *The Yorkshire Archaeological Journal*, 57, 87–92.

Kowaleski, M. (2000) Port towns: England and Wales 1300–1540. In D. M. Palliser (ed.) *The Cambridge Urban History of Britain, Vol. 1: 600–1540*. Cambridge, 467–94.

Kreytenberg, G. (1994) *Orcagna's Tabernacle in Orsanmichele, Florence*. New York.

Lankester, P. (1987) A Military Effigy in Dorchester Abbey, Oxon. *Oxoniensia*, LII, 145–72.

Lankester, P. (1989) An Effigy with a Bird? at Willoughby, Notts. *Newsletter of the Church Monuments Society*, 4.2, 25.

Lankester, P. (1993) Two Lost Effigial Monuments in Yorkshire and the Evidence of Church Notes. *Church Monuments*, VIII, 25–44.

Lankester, P. (2006) *Medieval Monuments in St Mary's Swine (Yorkshire)*. Unpublished notes accompanying a talk to the Church Monuments Society.

Lankester, P. J. (2010) The Thirteenth-Century Military Effigies in the Temple Church. In R. Griffith-Jones & D. Park (eds) *The Temple Church in London: History, Architecture, Art*. Woodbridge, 93–134.

Lankester, P. J. (2011) Sculpted memorial effigy of a priest. In W. Rodwell & C. Atkins, *St Peter's, Barton-upon-Humber, Lincolnshire: A Parish and its Community*, 1.2. Oxford and Oakville, 640–45.

Lankester, P. J. (forthcoming 2019), 'Blackfriars effigy fragments' in E. Cambridge and A. Williams (eds), *The Friars in Newcastle*.

Lawrance, H. (1946) *Heraldry from Military Monuments before 1350, in England and Wales*. Harleian Society, 98.

Lawton, G. (1840) *Collectio Rerum Ecclesiasticarum de Diœcesi Eboracensi*. Two vols. London.

Leach, A. (ed.) (1903) *Memorials of Beverley Minster: The Chapter Act Book of the Collegiate Church of S. John of Beverley A.D. 1286–1347*, II. Surtees Society, CVIII.

Leland, J. & Toulmin Smith, L. (1964) *The Itinerary of John Leland in or about the Years 1535–1543*. Five vols. Carbondale.

Liddy, C. & Steer, C. (2010) John Lord Lumley and the Creation and Commemoration of Lineage in Early Modern England. *Archaeological Journal*, 167, 197–227.

Lindley, P. (1996) The Black Death and English Art: A Debate and Some Assumptions. In W. Ormrod & P. Lindley (eds) *The Black Death in England*. Stamford, 125–46.

Lindley, P. (2003) The Later Medieval Monuments and Chantry Chapels. In R. K. Morris & R. Shoesmith (eds) *Tewkesbury Abbey: History, Art & Architecture*. Almeley, 161–82.

Lindley, P. (2006a) Two Fourteenth-Century Tomb Monuments at Abergavenny and the Mournful End of the Hastings Earls of Pembroke. In J. Kenyon & D. Williams (eds) *Cardiff: Architecture and Archaeology in the Medieval Diocese of Llandaff*. The British Archaeological Association Conference Transactions, XXIX, 136–60.

Lindley, P. (2006b) New paradigms for the aristocratic funerary monument around 1300: Reconstructing the tomb of John, second Baron Hastings (1287–1325), at Abergavenny Priory, Monmouthshire. *Church Monuments*, XXI, 58–93.

Lindley, P. (2007) *Tomb Destruction and Scholarship: Medieval Monuments in Early Modern England*. Donington.

Lindley, P. (2012) The Artistic Practice, Protracted Publication and Posthumous Completion of Charles Alfred Stothard's *Monumental Effigies of Great Britain*. *The Antiquaries Journal*, 92, 385–426.

Liveing, H. (1906) *Records of Romsey Abbey*. Winchester.

Long, C. (1837) Tournament at Stepney, 2 Edw. II. *Collectanea Topographica et Genealogica*, IV, 61–72.

Longstaffe, W. (1862) *Heraldic Visitation of the Northern Counties in 1530, by Thomas Tonge, Norroy King of Arms*. Surtees Society, 41.

Longstaffe, W. (1892) Norton. *Archaeologia Aeliana*, New Series, XV, 1–13.

Lott, G. K. & Cooper, A. H. (2008) Field guide to the building limestones of the Upper Permian Cadeby formation (Magnesian limestone) of Yorkshire. In P. Doyle *et al.* (eds) *England's Heritage in Stone*. Folkestone, 80–89.

Luxford, J. (2009) Tombs as forensic evidence in medieval England. *Church Monuments*, XXIV, 7–25.

Lysons, S. (1814) Copy of a Roll of Purchases made for the Tournament of Windsor Park, in the sixth year of King Edward the first, preserved in the Record Office at the Tower. *Archaeologia*, 17, 297–310.

MacInnes, I. (2016) *Scotland's Second War of Independence, 1332–1357*. Woodbridge.

Mann, J. (1928) An Appreciation of the Late Mr. I'Anson's Work on Yorkshire Effigies. *The Yorkshire Archaeological Journal*, XXIX, 232–36.

Mapping the Medieval Countryside, http://www.inquisitionspostmortem.ac.uk

Marks, R. (1994) Sir Geoffrey Luttrell and some images of chivalry *c*. 1320–50. *Wiener Jahrbuch für Kunstgeschichte*, 46–47, 344–56.

Marks, R. (2010) 'Entumbid Right Princely': The Beauchamp Chapel at Warwick and the Politics of Interment. In C. M. Barron & C. Burgess (eds) *Memory and Commemoration in Medieval England*. Harlaxton Medieval Studies, XX. Donington, 163–84.

Marks, R. & Williamson, P. (eds) (2003) *Gothic: Art for England 1400–1547*. London.

Markus, M. (1996) 'An Attempt to Discriminate the Styles' – the sculptors of the Harrington Tomb, Cartmel. *Church Monuments*, XI, 5–24.

Martin, M. (ed.) (1909) *The Percy Chartulary*, Surtees Society, CXVII.

McCall, H. B. (1907) *The Early History of Bedale*. London.

McCall, H. B. (1910) *Richmondshire Churches*. London.

McCall, H. B. (1926) Finds at Bedale Church. *The Yorkshire Archaeological Journal*, XXVIII, 448–50.

McClain, A. (2005) *Patronage, Power, and Identity: the Social Use of Local Churches and Commemorative Monuments in Tenth to Twelfth-Century North Yorkshire*. Two vols. Unpublished PhD thesis, University of York.

McDermid, R. T. W. (1980) *The Constitution and the Clergy of Beverley Minster in the Middle Ages*. Unpublished PhD thesis, Durham University.

McDermid, R. T. W. (1990) *Beverley Minster Fasti*. The Yorkshire Archaeological Society Record Series, 149.

McNamee, C. (1997) *The Wars of the Bruces: Scotland, England and Ireland, 1306–1328*. East Linton.

Meara, D. (1990) The Lion and the Dragon. *Monumental Brass Society Bulletin*, 54, 442–44.

Medieval Soldier Database https://research.reading.ac.uk/medievalsoldier.

Mee, A. (1964) rev. Linnell, C. *The King's England: Yorkshire, East Riding with York*. London.

Mee, A. (1969) rev. Beckwith, F. *The King's England: Yorkshire, West Riding*. London.

Mee, A. (1970) rev. Beckwith, F. *The King's England: Yorkshire, North Riding*. London.

Meyrick, S. (1845) Observations on the Monumental Effigy of De Mauley, formerly in the Minster at York. *Archaeologia*, XXXI, 238–48.

Miller, E. (1804) *The History and Antiquities of Doncaster and its Vicinity*. Doncaster.

Miller, E. (1961) Medieval York. In P. Tillott (ed.) *The Victoria History of the County of York: The City of York*. London, 25–116.

Miller, J. (2012) The Building Program of Archbishop Walter de Gray: Architectural Production and Reform in the Archdiocese of York, 1215–1255. Unpublished D. Phil. thesis, Columbia University.

Morris, J. E. (1906) *The Little Guides: The East Riding of Yorkshire*. London.

Morris, J. E. (1911) *The Little Guides: The West Riding of Yorkshire*. London.

Morris, J. E. (1920) *The Little Guides: The North Riding of Yorkshire*. Second edition. London.

Morris, J. E. (1924) *The Little Guides: York*. London.

Morris, J. E. (1931) *The Little Guides: The North Riding of Yorkshire*. Third edition. London.

Morris, R. (2018) *Yorkshire: A Lyrical History of England's Greatest County*. London.

Morris, R. K. (2003) The Gothic Church: Architectural History. In R. K. Morris & R. Shoesmith (eds) *Tewkesbury Abbey: History, Art & Architecture*. Almeley, 109–30.

Nichols, J. (1780) *A Collection of all the Wills, now known to be Extant, of the Kings and Queens of England*. London.

Nicolas, N. H. (ed.) (1829) *Rolls of Arms of the Reigns of Henry III and Edward III*. London.

Nicolas, N. H. (ed.) (1832) *The Controversy between Sir Richard Scrope and Sir Robert Grosvenor in the Court of Chivalry, A.D. MCCCLXXXV – MCCCXC*. Two vols. London.

Norris, M. (1978) *Monumental Brasses: The Craft*. London.

Norton, C. (2007) Richard Scrope and York Minster. In P. Goldberg (ed.) *Richard Scrope: Archbishop, Rebel, Martyr*. Donington, 138–213.

Oakeshott, R. E. (1964) *The Sword in the Age of Chivalry*. London.

Oliver, G. (1829) *The History and Antiquities of the Town and Minster of Beverley in the County of York*. Beverley.

Oosterwijk, S. (1990) Fourteenth Century Sculptures on the Aisle Walls in the Nave of York Minster. *York Historian*, 9, 2–15.

Oosterwijk, S. (1998) Lost, Found and Lost Again? The Continuing Enigma of the Gisborough Priory Effigies. *Journal of the British Archaeological Association*, CLI, 190–202.

Oosterwijk, S. (2000) Chrysoms, shrouds and infants on English tomb monuments: A question of terminology? *Church Monuments*, XV, 44–64.

Oosterwijk, S. (2005) Food for worms – food for thought: The appearance and interpretation of the 'verminous' cadaver in Britain and Europe. *Church Monuments*, XX, 40–80.

Oosterwijk, S. (2010) Deceptive appearances: the presentation of children on medieval tombs. In S. Badham (ed.), *One thousand years of English church monuments: Ecclesiology Today*, 43, 45–60.

Oosterwijk, S. (2016) From Biblical Beast to Faithful Friend: A Short Note on the Iconography of Footrests on Tomb

Monuments. In L. Gelfand (ed.) *Our Dogs, Our Selves: Dogs in Medieval and Early Modern Art, Literature, and Society*. Leiden, 243–60.

Ormrod, W. M. (1997) York and the Crown Under the First Three Edwards. In S. Rees Jones (ed.) *The Government of Medieval York: Essays in commemoration of the 1396 Royal Charter*. York,14–33.

Ormrod, W. M. (2000) Competing Capitals? York and London in the Fourteenth Century. In S. Rees Jones *et al.* (eds) *Courts and Regions in Medieval Europe*. Woodbridge, 75–98.

Ormrod, W. M. (2011) *Edward III*. New Haven & London.

Oxford Dictionary of National Biography. Available online at: http://www.oxforddnb.com

Pacey, A. (2008) The social background and organisation of the late medieval craftsman. In P. S. Barnwell & A. Pacey (eds) *Who built Beverley Minster?* Reading, 81–95.

Palliser, D. M. (2014) *Medieval York 600–1540*. Oxford.

Palmer, R. (1984) *The Whilton Dispute, 1264–1380: A Socio-Legal Study of Dispute Settlement in Medieval England*. Princeton.

Park, D. (2010) Medieval Burials and Monuments. In R. Griffith-Jones & D. Park (eds) *The Temple Church in London: History, Architecture, Art*. Woodbridge, 67–91.

Paxton, F. with Cochelin, I. (eds) (2013) *The Death Ritual at Cluny in the Central Middle Ages*. Turnhout.

Payne, A. (1990) *Medieval Beasts*. London.

Perceval, C. (1863) Two Rolls of Arms of the Reign of King Edward the First; with some Prefatory Remarks by Charles Spencer Perceval, Esq., LL.D., F.S.A. *Archaeologia*, XXXIX, 389–446.

Petch, M. R. (1981) William de Malton Master Mason. *The Yorkshire Archaeological Journal*, 53, 37–44.

Petch, M. R. (1985) *A Guide to St. Andrew's Church and the Parish of Bainton, East Riding of Yorkshire*. Bainton.

Pethick, J. S. (1990) The Humber estuary. In S. Ellis & D. R. Crowther, *Humber Perspectives: A Region through the Ages*. Hull, 54–67.

Pevsner, N. & Wedgwood, A. (1966) *The Buildings of England: Warwickshire*. Harmondsworth.

Phillips, S. (2010) *Edward II*. New Haven & London.

Pickford, S. (2001/2) An Early Unfinished Effigy at St. Nicholas's Church, Grosmont, Monmouthshire. *Church Monuments Society Newsletter*, 17.2, 7–10.

Poulson, G. (1840 & 1841) *History and Antiquities of the Seigniory of Holderness*. Two vols. Hull.

Prestwich, M. (2003) An Everyday Story of Knightly Folk. In M. Prestwich, R. Britnell & R. Frame (eds) *Thirteenth Century England IX*. Woodbridge, 151–62.

Prior, E. & Gardner, A. (1912) *An Account of Medieval Figure-Sculpture in England*. Cambridge.

Raine, J. (ed.) (1835) *Wills and Inventories Illustrative of the History, Manners, Language, Statistics, etc. of the Northern Counties of England, Part I*, Surtees Society, 2.

Ramm, H. G. (1971) The Tombs of Archbishops Walter de Gray (1216–55) and Godfrey de Ludham (1258–65) in York Minster, and their Contents. *Archaeologia*, CIII, 101–47.

Richardson, E. (1843) *The Monumental Effigies of the Temple Church, with an Account of their Restoration in the Year 1842*. London.

Richardson, H. G. (1938) John of Gaunt and the Parliamentary Representation of Lancashire. *Bulletin of the John Rylands Library*, 22.1, 175–222.

Richardson, T. (2016) *The Tower Armoury in the Fourteenth Century*. Leeds.

Richardson, T. (2017) Leather plate armour in medieval Europe. In Q. Mould (ed.) *Leather in Warfare: Attack, Defence and the Unexpected*. Leeds, 48–56.

Richardson, W. (1989) *Some Useful Consumers of Waste: History in two Marshland Parishes: Adlingfleet and Whitgift*. Revised edition, York.

Rijkelijkhuizen, M. & Volken, M. (2017) A poor man's armour? Late-medieval leather armour from excavations in the Netherlands. In Q. Mould (ed.) *Leather in Warfare: Attack, Defence and the Unexpected*. Leeds, 57–77.

Robinson, D. (ed.) (1978) *The Register of William Melton, Archbishop of York, 1317–1340: Volume II*. Canterbury and York Society, LXXI.

Rockwell, P. (1993) *The art of stoneworking: a reference guide*. Cambridge.

Rodwell, W. (ed.) (2001) *Wells Cathedral: Excavations and Structural Studies, 1978–93*, 2. English Heritage Archaeological Report 21. London.

Rodwell, W. & Atkins, C. (2011) *St Peter's, Barton-upon-Humber, Lincolnshire: A Parish and its Community*, 1.2. Oxford and Oakville.

Rogers, N. (1987) English Episcopal Monuments, 1270–1350. In J. Coales (ed.) *The Earliest English Brasses: Patronage, Style and Workshops 1270–1350*. London, 8–68.

Rogers, N. (1996) Brasses in their Art Historical Context. In J. Bertram (ed.) *Monumental Brasses as Art and History*. Stroud, 146–59.

Roper, I. (1931) *The Monumental Effigies of Gloucestershire and Bristol*. Gloucester.

Routh, P. E. (1976) *Medieval Effigial Alabaster Tombs in Yorkshire*. Ipswich.

Routh, P. E. (1982) Henry Johnston and the Missing Lady of Gawthorpe Hall. *The Yorkshire Archaeological Journal*, 54, 99–101.

Routh, P. E. (1987) Henry Johnston. *Church Monuments Society Newsletter*, 2.2, 11–13.

Routh, P. E. (1994) Yorkshire's Royal Monument; Prince William of Hatfield. *Church Monuments*, IX, 53–61.

Ryder, P. (2002) St John's Church, Stanwick, North Yorkshire: The Medieval Cross Slabs. *Church Monuments*, XVII, 5–13.

Saltmarshe, P. (1910) *History of the Township and Family of Saltmarshe*. Privately printed.

Saltmarshe, P. (1914) *History and Chartulary of the Hothams of Scorborough*. Privately printed.

Salzman, L. F. (1952) *Building in England down to 1540: A Documentary History*. Oxford.

Sampson, J. (1998) *Wells Cathedral West Front*. Stroud.

Sauerberg, M. L. (2013) The polychromy of the Coronation Chair: a detailed study. In W. Rodwell, *The Coronation Chair and Stone of Scone*. Oxford, 77–104.

Saul, N. (2001) *Death, Art, and Memory in Medieval England: The Cobham Family and their Monuments, 1300–1500*. Oxford.

Saul, N. (2009) *English Church Monuments in the Middle Ages*. Oxford.

Saul, N. (2017) *Lordship and Faith: The English Gentry and the Parish Church in the Middle Ages*. Oxford.

Scatcherd, N. (1830) *The History of Morley*. Leeds.

Scott, M. (1986) *A Visual History of Costume: The Fourteenth & Fifteenth Centuries*. London.

Sheahan, J. & Whellan, T. (1857) *History and Topography of the City of York; the East Riding of Yorkshire*. Two vols. Beverley.

Sheard, M. (1894) *Records of the Parish of Batley in the County of York*. Worksop.

Sheingorn, P. (1995) "And flights of angels sing thee to thy rest": The Soul's Conveyance to the Afterlife in the Middle Ages. In C. Fisher & K. Scott (eds) *Art Into Life: Collected Papers from the Kresge Art Museum Medieval Symposia*. East Lansing, 155–82.

Siddons, M. (2009) *Heraldic Badges in England and Wales*. Four vols. London & Woodbridge.

Sillence, M. (2005) The two effigies of Archbishop Walter de Gray (d. 1255) at York Minster. *Church Monuments*, XX, 5–30.

Simpkin, D. (2009) The Galloway roll (1300): its content, composition and value to military history. *Historical Research*, 82, 613–34.

Slingsby, F. (ed.) (1956) *Feet of Fines for the County of York From 1272 to 1300*. The Yorkshire Archaeological Society Record Series, CXXI.

Smith, D. & London, V. (eds) (2001) *The Heads of Religious Houses, England and Wales: II: 1216–1377*. Cambridge.

Spencer, A. (2011) A Warlike People? Gentry Enthusiasm for Edward I's Scottish Campaigns, 1296–1307. In A. Bell, A. Curry, A. Chapman, A. King & D. Simpkin (eds) *The Soldier Experience in the Fourteenth Century*. Woodbridge.

Spraggon, J. (2003) *Puritan Iconoclasm during the English Civil War*. Woodbridge.

Stephenson, M. (1926) *A List of Monumental Brasses in the British Isles*. And *Appendix* (1938). London. Ashford.

Stevenson, J. (ed.) (1870) *Documents Illustrative of the History of Scotland*. Two vols. Edinburgh.

Stöber, K. (2007) *Late Medieval Monasteries and their Patrons: England and Wales, c. 1300–1540*. Woodbridge.

Stocker, D. with Everson, P. (1990) Rubbish Recycled: A Study of the Re-Use of Stone in Lincolnshire. In D. Parsons (ed.) *Stone: Quarrying and Building in England AD 43–1525*. Chichester, 83–101.

Stone, L. (1955) *Sculpture in Britain: The Middle Ages*. Harmondsworth.

Stonehouse, W. (1839) *The History and Topography of the Isle of Axholme*. London.

Stones, E. & Simpson, G. (eds) (1978) *Edward I and the Throne of Scotland 1290–1296*. Two vols. Oxford.

Stothard, C. A. (1832) *The Monumental Effigies of Great Britain*. London.

Ternent, L. (1983) *St. Leonard's Church Skerne, Then and Now*. Skerne.

Thompson, T. (1822) Historic Facts Relative to the Sea Port and Market Town of Ravenspurne, in Holderness. In T. Thompson, *Ocellum Promontorium or short Observations on the Ancient State of Holderness*. Hull (1824).

Thursfield, S. (2001) *The Medieval Tailor's Assistant: making common garments 1200–1500*. Bedford.

Tisdall, M. (1998) *God's Beasts: Identify and understand animals in church carvings*. Plymouth.

Titterton, J. E. (2012) *The Grisaille and Heraldic Glass in the Chancel at Norbury, Derbyshire*. Second edition.

Tower, R. (1928) The Family of Septvans. *Archaeologia Cantiana*, 40, 105–30.

Tummers, H. A. (1980) *Early Secular Effigies in England: The Thirteenth Century*. Leiden.

Vale, B. (1987) *The Scropes of Bolton and of Masham, c. 1300 – c.1450: A Study of a Northern Noble Family with a Calendar of the Scrope of Bolton Cartulary*. Two vols. Unpublished D. Phil. thesis, University of York.

Vale, J. & Vale, M. (1992) Knightly Codes and Piety. In N. Saul (ed.) *Age of Chivalry: Art and Society in Late Medieval England*. London, 24–35.

Wagner, A. R. (1950) *A Catalogue of English Medieval Rolls of Arms*. Aspilogia, I. London.

Walbran, J. (1854) On the Excavation now in progress at Fountains Abbey. *Associated Architectural Societies' Reports and Papers*, III, Yorkshire section 54–66.

Walbran, J. (1864) Observations on the History and Structure of the Abbey of the Blessed Mary of Byland. *Associated Architectural Societies' Reports and Papers*., VII.2, 219–34.

Walbran, J. (1875) rev. Raine, J, & Stephenson, W., *A Guide to Ripon, Fountains Abbey, Harrogate ...* Twelfth edition. Ripon.

Walker, J. W. (1926) *An Historical and Architectural Description of The Priory of St. Mary Magdalene of Monk Bretton In the West Riding of the County of Yorkshire*. Yorkshire Archaeological Society. Leeds.

Walter, D. A. (1874) *Ancient Memorial Cross Slabs from the Churches of the City of York and Surrounding District*. York.

Waterer, J. (1981) *Leather and the Warrior*. Northampton.

Weaver, F. (ed.) (1901) *Somerset Medieval Wills (1383–1500)*. Somerset Record Society, XVI.

Wellbeloved, C. (1891) *A Hand-Book to the Antiquities in the Grounds and Museum of the Yorkshire Philosophical Society*. Eighth edition. York.

Westerhof, D. (2008) *Death and the Noble Body in Medieval England*. Woodbridge.

Whitaker, T. D. (1823) *An history of Richmondshire, in the North Riding of the county of York; together with those parts of the Everwicschire of Domesday which form the wapentakes of Lonsdale, Ewecross, and Amunderness, in the counties of York, Lancaster, and Westmoreland*. Two vols. London.

Whitaker, T. D. (1878) rev. Morant, A. W. *The History and Antiquities of the Deanery of Craven in the County of York*. Third edition. Two vols. Manchester & Skipton.

White, G. M. (1997) *An Introduction to St Mary's Church, Etton*. Etton.

Wild, B. (2011) Emblems and enigmas: Revisiting the 'sword' belt of Fernando de la Cerda. *Journal of Medieval History*, 37, 378–96.

Williams, E. (1950) *The Chantries of William Canynges in St Mary Redcliffe, Bristol*. Bristol & Oxford.

Williamson, P. (1995) *Gothic Sculpture 1140–1300*. New Haven & London.

Wilson, B. & Mee, F. (1998) *The Medieval Parish Churches of York: The Pictorial Evidence*. The Archaeology of York Supplementary Series, 1. York.

Wilson, C. (1995) The Medieval Monuments. In P. Collinson, N. Ramsay & M. Sparks (eds) *A History of Canterbury Cathedral*. Oxford, 451–510.

Wood, R. (2001) The Romanesque Memorial at Conisbrough. *Yorkshire Archaeological Journal*, 73, 41–60.

Woodworth, M. (2011) *The Architectural History of Beverley Minster, 721-c. 1370*. Unpublished PhD thesis, Duke University.

Wrottesley, G. (ed.) (1898) *Crécy and Calais, from the Original Records in the Public Record Office*. London.

Young, C. G. (1837) Notices Concerning Religious Houses in Yorkshire, with the Names of their Founders, and of Persons Buried Therein. *Collectanea Topographica et Genealogica*, IV, 73–79 & 128–33.

Young, D. (1978) *A Guide to the Parish Church of St. Patrick, Patrington*. Patrington.

Index

Page numbers in **bold** signify a relevant illustration, usually accompanied by text. Plate numbers are prefixed with Pl. or Pls, as appropriate. Numbers opening with A refer to Appendices and their subsections.

Map Ref.	*Place*	*Riding / County*	*No.*	*Subject*
1	Acaster Malbis	W	1	Military. *c.* 1315–30.
2	Acklam	N	1	Civilian. 1st half 14th C.
			2	Lady (westerly). Late 13th C.
			3	Lady (easterly). *c.* 1400.
3	Adlingfleet	W	1	Lady. *c.* 1320–30. Lincolnshire import.
4	Aldborough	W	1	Civilian, S-E. 1325–50.
5	Aldbrough	E	1	Lady. *c.* 1360–80.
			2	Military. d.1377.
6	Allerton Mauleverer	W	1	Military (smaller). Late 13th C. Wood.
			2	Military (larger). 1340–50. Wood.
7	Alne	N	1	Lady. 1340–50.
8	Amotherby	N	1	Military. 1310–15. Series B.
			2	Lady, S-E. 1300–50.
9	Ampleforth	N	1+2	Civilian + Lady (double effigy). *c.*1390.
10	Appleton-le-Street	N	1	Lady (north side). *c.* 1300–15. Series B.
			2	Lady (south side). 1340–50. Series E.
11	Bainton	E	1	Military. *c.* 1330. Wolds Series.
12	Barnburgh	W	1	Military. 1340–50. Wood.
13	Batley	W	1	Civilian. Late 14th C.
14	Bedale	N	1	Lady. *c.* 1290. Series A.
			2	Ecclesiastic. *c.* 1290– 1300. Series A.
			3	Military (FitzAlan). d. 1306. Series B.
			4	Military ('Sheffield'). 1340–50.
15	Beeford	E	1	Ecclesiastic. *c.* 1340–50. Wolds Series.
16	Beverley (Friary)	E	1	Lady. *c.* 1300–15. Series B.

Map Ref.	*Place*	*Riding / County*	*No.*	*Subject*
17	Beverley (Minister)	E	1	Ecclesiastic. d. 1338.
			2	Civilian. *c.* 1330–50. Wolds Series.
18	Bilton (in Ainsty)	W	1	Lady. *c.*1280–1300.
19	Birdsall	E	1	Lady. *c.* 1330–50. Wolds Series.
20	Birkin	W	1	Civilian. Early 14th C.
21	Bulmer	N	1	Military. Late 13th C.
22	Burton Stather	Lincs	1	Military. *c.* 1340. Series C.
23	Butterwick	E	1	Military. d. 1317. Series B.
24	Cantley	W	1	Ecclesiastic, S-E, fragment. 1st half 14th C.
25	Catterick	N	1	Military. d. 1394–95.
26	Church Fenton	W	1	Lady. *c.* 1330. Series C.
27	Coverham Abbey	N	1	Military (torso). Late 13th C.
			2	Military (larger). *c.* 1290–1300. Series A.
			3	Military (smaller). *c.* 1290–1300. Series A.
28	Crathorne	N	1	Civilian. Early 14th C.
			2	Military. d. 1346. Series E.
29	Danby Wiske	N	1	Lady. *c.* 1340. Series E.
30	Darfield	W	1	Lady (beside 2). *c.* 1400. Midlands alabaster.
			2	Military (beside 1). *c.* 1400. Midlands alabaster.
31	Darrington	W	1	Lady. *c.* 1330. Series C.
			2	Military. *c.* 1330. Series C.
32	Denton (now Bowes Museum)	Dur.	1	Lady, Acc. No.1995.25/ARC. 1st half 14th C.
33	Easby Abbey (ruins)	N	1	Uncertain. S-E. Mid-14th C?
34	Easby Abbey (church)	N	2	?Female, head only. Later 14th C?
35	East Harlsey	N	1	Military. *c.* 1310. Series B.

Map Ref.	*Place*	*Riding / County*	*No.*	*Subject*
36	Eastrington	E	1+2	Military + Lady (double effigy). *c.* 1320–30?
			3	Civilian. 2nd quarter 14th C.
37	Egglestone Abbey (English Heritage)	N	1	Ecclesiastic, EH No. 81027122. 2nd quarter 14th C?
			2	Uncertain, foot support only, Acc. No. 81027101. 1st half 14th C?
38	Escrick	E	1	Military. *c.* 1300. Series B.
39	Etton	E	1	Lady, shoulder only. 14th C?
			2	Uncertain, lower part only. 1st half 14th C?
40	Felixkirk	N	1	Military. 1330–40. Series D.
			2	Lady. d. 1346.
41	Felkirk	W	1	Military. Late 14th C.
42	Filey	E	1	Male, small. 14th C.
43	Forcett	N	1	Ecclesiastic. 1st half 14th C?
44	Foston on the Wolds	E	1	Military. Late 13th C?
45	Fountains Abbey (English Heritage)	W	1	Military, EH No. 88107000. *c.* 1300. Series B.
46	Garton-on-the-Wolds	E	1	Civilian. *c.* 1320–40?
			2	Lady, S-E. 2nd quarter 14th C?
			3	Lady. *c.* 1320–40?
47	Gilling East	N	1	Military, S-E. Mid-14th C?
48	Goldsborough	W	1	Military (under arch). *c.* 1300–05. Series B.
			2	Military (on chest). *c.* 1330–35. Series C.
49	Goodmanham	E	1	Civilian, S-E, fragments. Late 13th / early 14th C?
			2	Lady, S-E, fragments. 1st half 14th C?
50	Goxhill	E	1	Civilian (now Hornsea). 2nd quarter 14th C?
			2	Lady. 1390–1400.
51	Great Langton	N	1	Ecclesiastic. Mid-14th C.
52	Great Mitton	W	1	Ecclesiastic. Later 14th C?
53	Guisborough Priory (English Heritage)	N	1	Military, small fragment. 1st half 14th C?
54	Harpham	E	1	Lady. 1380–90? Lincolnshire import.
55	Hauxwell	N	1	Lady. Late 13th C?
			2	Military. 1st quarter 14th C.
			3	Male. S-E. 1st half 14th C?
56	Hazelwood	W	1	Military (easterly). *c.* 1315. Series B.
			2	Military (westerly). *c.* 1315. Series B.
57	Hedon	E	1	Civilian. Mid-14th C.
58	Hickleton	W	1	Civilian, S-E. *c.* 1340.
59	Hornby	N	1	Lady (churchyard). Late 13th C?
			2	Lady (in chapel). Late 13th C?
			3	Lady (beside 4). Late 13th / early 14th C.
			4	Military (beside 3). Late 13th / early 14th C.
60	Howden	E	1	Lady, half effigy. S-E. 1st half 14th C.
			2	Military (beside 3). 1310–15. Series B.
			3	Lady (beside 2). 1310–15. Series B.
			4	Military (on chest). *c.* 1340.
61	Hull, Holy Trinity	E	1	Civilian (beside 2). *c.* 1390. Alabaster.
			2	Lady (beside 1). *c.* 1390. Alabaster.

Map Ref.	*Place*	*Riding / County*	*No.*	*Subject*
62	Hutton Cranswick	E	1	Ecclesiastic. 1340–50? Wolds series.
63	Hutton Rudby	N	1	Ecclesiastic. Late 13th C.
64	Ilkley	W	1	Military. 1330–40. Series D.
65	Ingleby Arncliffe	N	1	Military (north). 1340–50. Series E.
			2	Military (south). 1340–50. Series E.
66	Ingleby Greenhow	N	1	Ecclesiastic. Early 14th C.
67	Jervaulx Abbey	N	1	Military. *c.* 1280?
68	Kellington	W	1	Civilian? 1st half 14th C.
69	Kildwick	W	1	Military. *c.* 1345. Series C.
70	Kirby Sigston	N	1	Lady. *c.* 1330.
71	Kirby (in Cleveland)	N	1+2	Military + Lady (double effigy). *c.* 1400.
72	Kirkby Fleetham	N	1	Military. *c.*1330.
73	Kirkleatham	N	1	Lady. *c.* 1340–50. Series E.
74	Kirklington	N	1	Lady. *c.* 1370.
			2	Military. *c.* 1370.
75	Leeds	W	1	Military. *c.* 1330–35 Series C.
76	London, Temple Church	Y	1	Military (moved from York). *c.* 1310. Series B.
77	Loversall	W	1	Uncertain, small. S-E. 1st half 14th C.
			2	Civilian. Mid-14th C.
78	Lowthorpe	E	1+2	Civilian + Lady (double effigy). *c.* 1340.
79	Lund	E	1	Ecclesiastic, fragment. 1st half 14th C.
80	Melsonby	N	1	Civilian, S-E. 1st half 14th C.
			2	Lady, S-E. 1st half 14th C.
			3	Military. *c.* 1320–40?

Map Ref.	*Place*	*Riding / County*	*No.*	*Subject*
81	Methley	W	1	Civilian. 1st quarter 14th C?
			2	Ecclesiastic. 2nd quarter 14th C.
82	Middleton on-the-Wolds	E	1	Uncertain. 2nd quarter 13th C.
83	Moor Monkton	W	1	?Male, small. 1st quarter 14th C?
			2	Civilian, S-E, small. 2nd quarter 14th C.
84	Nafferton	E	1	Civilian. 1330–40.
			2	Lady. 1330–40.
			3	Civilian, small. *c.* 1400.
85	Normanby (English Heritage)	N	1	Military, EH No. 88212147, 88212148. 1340–50. Series E.
86	Norton	Dur.	1	Military. *c.* 1305. Series B.
			2	Lady. 1340–50. Series E.
87	Nunkeeling (now Hornsea)	E	1	Lady. Late 13th C.
			2	Military. 1300–30?
88	Nunnington	N	1	Military. d. 1324.
89	Ormesby	N	1	Lady. *c.*1390?
			2	Military. Late 14th C.
90	Patrington	E	1	Lady. 1340–50. Wolds Series.
91	Pickering	N	1	Military. 1340–50.
			2	Military (torso). Late 14th C. Midlands alabaster.
			3	Lady (beside 4). *c.* 1400. Midlands alabaster.
			4	Military (beside 3). *c.* 1400. Midlands alabaster.
92	Pickhill	N	1	Military. 1320s. Lincolnshire import.

Map Ref.	*Place*	*Riding / County*	*No.*	*Subject*
93	Rievaulx Abbey (English Heritage)	N	1	Military, 2 fragments, EH No. 81300201, 81300202. Early 14th C.
			2	Military, 3 fragments, EH No. 81300206, 81300335, 81300319. *c.* 1315–30?
			3	Lady + gablette, EH No. 81300384. Mid-14th C?
			4	Lady, fragment, EH No. 81300233. 14th C?
94	Ripley	W	1	Lady (beside 2). *c.* 1380–90.
			2	Military (beside 1). d. 137 7/7' 8.
95	Ripon	W	1	Lady (beside 2). *c.* 1400.
			2	Military (beside 1). d. 1386 x 1398.
96	Romaldkirk	N	1	Military. 2nd quarter 14th C?
97	Routh	E	1	Military. 1290–1300. Series A.
98	Ryther	W	1	Military. 1330–40. Series C.
			2	Lady. 1330–40. Series C.
99	Scarborough (Museum)	N	1	Military. *c.* 1300, Acc. No. 1938·736. Series A.
100	Selby Abbey	W	1	Lady. *c.* 1315–35?
			2	Military. *c.* 1315–35?
101	Sheriff Hutton	N	1	Military. d. 1344. Series C.
102	Skerne	E	1	Civilian. 1330–40.
			2	Lady, S-E. 1st half 14th C.
103	Slingsby	N	1	Military. 2nd quarter 14th C?
104	South Anston	W	1+2	Civilian + Female child (double effigy). *c.* 1335–50?
105	Spofforth	W	1	Military. 1330–40. Series C.

Map Ref.	*Place*	*Riding / County*	*No.*	*Subject*
106	Sprotbrough	W	1	Lady. 1340–50.
			2	Military. 1340–50.
107	Stainton	N	1	Civilian. 2nd quarter 14th C.
108	Stanwick	N	1	Lady, S-E, small. 1st half 13th C.
			2	Civilian (windowsill, easterly). 14th C.
			3	Civilian (windowsill, westerly). 14th C.
			4	Lady (windowsill). 14th C.
			5	Lady (recess). 14th C.
109	Startforth	N	1	Civilian. 1330–50?
110	Stillingfleet	E	1	Military. 1330–40. Series D.
111	Stonegrave	N	1	Civilian. Early 14th C.
			2+3	Civilian + Lady (double effigy). *c.* 1390.
112	Sutton-on-Hull	E	1	Military. d.1356.
113	Swillington	W	1	Military. Later 14th C. Wood.
114	Swine	E	1	Lady (chancel, eastern pair). c.1370. Midlands alabaster.
			2	Military (chancel, eastern pair). c.1370. Midlands alabaster.
			3	Lady (south aisle, beside 4). *c.* 1390.
			4	Military (south aisle, beside 3). *c.* 1390.
115	Thornhill	W	1	Military. Early 14th C.
116	Thornton Dale	N	1	Lady. *c.* 1330?
117	Thorpe Basset	E	1	Ecclesiastic. 2nd quarter 14th C?
118	Throapham	W	1	Civilian, S-E. 1st half 14th C.
119	Thrybergh	W	1	Ecclesiastic (under tower). *c.* 1300.
			2	Ecclesiastic (corridor). 1st half 14th C.

Map Ref.	Place	Riding / County	No.	Subject
120	Thwing	E	1	Ecclesiastic. Mid-14th C.
121	Treeton	W	1	Military. Late 13th C?
122	Upleatham (old church)	N	1	Bishop / mitred abbot, half length, small. 14th C.
			2	Military (Kirkleatham Museum, Acc. No. 2008.18.1). d. 1346. Series E.
123	Wadworth	W	1+2	Civilian + Lady (double effigy). S-E. 2nd quarter 14th C?
			3	Civilian (legal dress). S-E. Mid-14th C.
			4	Civilian (forester). *c.* 1350–60?
124	Walton	W	1	Military *c.*1370–80.
125	Watton Priory	E	1	Military (fragmentary). Mid 14th C.
126	Weaverthorpe	E	1	Civilian. 1st half 14th C?
127	Welton	E	1	Military. Early 14th C. Purbeck marble import.
128	Welwick	E	1	Ecclesiastic. 1350–60.
129	West Tanfield	N	1	Military (easternmost). d. 1322 Lincolnshire import.
			2	Military (recess). d.1335. Lincolnshire import.
			3	Lady (westernmost). d. *c.* 1360.
			4	Lady (centre). Late 14th C.
			5	Lady (easternmost). Late 14th C.
			6	Military (altar tomb, beside 7). d.1387. Midlands alabaster.
			7	Lady (altar tomb, beside 6). *c.* 1400. Midlands alabaster.
130	Whorlton	N	1	Military. d. 1322. Wood. London import.

Map Ref.	Place	Riding / County	No.	Subject
131	Wilton (in Cleveland)	N	1	Military. 1340–50. Series E.
			2	Lady. 1340–50. Series E.
132	Winestead	E	1	Ecclesiastic. 1340–50. Wolds Series.
133	Winteringham	Lincs	1	Military. 1330–40. Series D.
134	Wistow	W	1	Lady (bas-relief). 1st quarter 14th C
			2	Lady (kneeling), small. 1st quarter 14th C.
135	Womersley	W	1	Military. *c.* 1335–45?
136	Wycliffe	N	1	Civilian. 1st half 14th C?
137	Yarm	N	1+2	Civilian + Lady (double effigy). Late 14th C
138	York (Hob Moor)	Y	1	Military. Early 14th C.
139	York (Minster)	Y	1	Archbishop. d. 1255. Purbeck marble import.
			2	Civilian. *c.* 1370. Alabaster. London work.
140	York (St George Fishergate)	Y	1	Uncertain, small, effaced. Medieval.
141	York (St Olave)	Y	1	Lady, S-E, fragment. 1300–50?
142	York (York Archaeological Trust)	Y	1	Military, Acc. No. 1994·163. Late 13th / early 14th C.
143	York (York Museums Trust)	Y	1	Military (torso), Acc. No. 2013.499. Early 14th C.
			2	Military ('Kildare'), Acc. No. 2010.1218. 1st quarter 14th C.

West Riding
Richmond
Leeds
Sheffield
96
32
86
109
37
136
43
108
137
80
28
33
34
25
29
35
51
55
59
72
70
14
27
67
92
129
74
95
45
4
94
6
48
105
64
69
124
52
56
75
113
81
13
115
41
30
Key
Effigy locations
Larger places
County boundaries pre 1974
Riding boundaries
Numbers index places to the List of Effigies